GW00673410

Frustrated Democracy in Post-Soviet Azerbaijan

Frustrated Democracy in Post-Soviet Azerbaijan

Audrey L. Altstadt

For Ed Dixon,
With best wishes,

Audrey L. Altstadt

27 Feb, 2024

Woodrow Wilson Center Press
Washington, D.C.

Columbia University Press
New York

Woodrow Wilson Center Press
Washington, D.C.
www.wilsoncenter.org

Columbia University Press
Publishers Since 1893
New York Chichester, West Sussex
cup.columbia.edu

Library of Congress Cataloging-in-Publication Data

Names: Altstadt, Audrey L., 1953– author.
Title: Frustrated democracy in post-Soviet Azerbaijan / Audrey L. Altstadt.
Description: Washington, D.C. : Woodrow Wilson Center Press ; New York : Columbia University
    Press, 2017 | Includes bibliographical references and index.
Identifiers: LCCN 2016040500 (print) | LCCN 2016041722 (ebook) | ISBN 9780231704564
    (cloth : acid-free paper) | ISBN 9780231801416 (ebook)
Subjects: LCSH: Azerbaijan—Politics and government—1991– | Post-communism—Azerbaijan—
    History. | Democracy—Azerbaijan—History. | Political corruption—Azerbaijan—History. |
    Authoritarianism—Azerbaijan—History. | Islam and politics—Azerbaijan—History. | Petroleum
    industry and trade—Political aspects—Azerbaijan—History. | Geopolitics—Azerbaijan—History.
Classification: LCC DK697.68 .A48 2017 (print) | LCC DK697.68 (ebook) | DDC 947.54086—dc23
LC record available at https://lccn.loc.gov/2016040500

Woodrow Wilson Center Press and Columbia University Press books are printed on permanent and
durable acid-free paper.
Printed in the United States of America

Cover photo: Riot policemen stand in line in front of opposition members during a rally in Baku,
June 4, 2005. Reuters / David Mdzinarishvili CVI/MAD
Cover design: Naylor Design

Wilson Center

The Wilson Center, chartered by Congress as the official memorial to President Woodrow Wilson, is the nation's key nonpartisan policy forum for tackling global issues through independent research and open dialogue to inform actionable ideas for Congress, the Administration, and the broader policy community.

Conclusions or opinions expressed in Center publications and programs are those of the authors and speakers and do not necessarily reflect the views of the Center staff, fellows, trustees, advisory groups, or any individuals or organizations that provide financial support to the Center.

Please visit us online at www.wilsoncenter.org.

Jane Harman, Director, President, and CEO

Marking the twenty-fifth anniversary of
Azerbaijan's post-Soviet independence, 1991–2016

Dedicated to all those who struggle for a democratic Azerbaijan

Contents

Contents

Maps and Tables

Maps

Tables

Preface

With the reestablishment of independence in 1991, Azerbaijan seemed like a viable, even strong, candidate for developing into a vibrant free market economy with a democratic system of governance. Its oil wealth lay untended, but its people, though poor, enjoyed high levels of literacy and education. They exhibited an entrepreneurial impulse in the sale of goods in local markets and even in the Soviet-era black market which supplied flowers and fruit to Russia. An anticommunist popular front movement had emerged and gained popularity since 1988. Azerbaijan faced a secessionist movement in the Armenian-populated region of Nagorno-Karabagh, which was supported by neighboring Armenia. The collapse of the Soviet Union and Soviet military contributed to the spread of weapons throughout the Caucasus, making the conflict even more lethal. Yet the anticommunist leaders managed to hold a presidential election in 1992 and bring the Popular Front to power. Its leadership lasted one year, but then fell to a coup, followed by the return of a former communist party boss.

As Azerbaijan commemorates the twenty-fifth anniversary of its independence, the Karabagh conflict remains unresolved. Economic development surged to amazing levels, and corruption along with it. The political system became authoritarian under the rule of one family. Opposition groups, even those that had been strong, have been marginalized, co-opted, or crushed, and the civil society that developed in the 1990s and early 2000s has been suppressed. Youth movements, a "next-generation" opposition, came under attack and their leadership quashed. Yet these groups persist, and express their criticisms and their vision for the future on social media.

Many post-Soviet states have sunk into authoritarianism. Despite some similarities, often resulting from shared Soviet legacies, each had a distinctive trajectory. Why did Azerbaijan follow its particular path seemingly toward and then away from democratization? How did the war, the economy, and the choices made by politically active individuals shape this outcome? And what lies ahead for this energy-rich country on the Caspian Sea, which borders Russia, Iran, Turkey, Georgia, and Armenia (with which it remains at war)? What are the implications of Azerbaijan's choices for US interests in this strategically sensitive region? Can the United States have meaningful impact on events there, especially in protecting human rights and fostering democracy, and if so, by what means?

On the twenty-fifth anniversary of the Soviet Union's collapse, the time seemed right for a retrospective that could create a foundation for analysis and forecasting for the coming years. Each chapter examines a key area: geopolitical imperatives, the Karabagh war; electoral politics and the role of political opposition; the socioeconomic impact of oil wealth, foreign investment, and corruption; civil society, dissent, and repression; and the possibilities of a new role for political Islamism. I analyze these factors within Azerbaijan's historical-cultural context, and end with a prognosis for Azerbaijan and considerations for US policy for the coming five to ten years.

Acknowledgments

I am deeply grateful to the many individuals and institutions who, over the past twenty-five years, have made this book possible. I cannot possibly name all those with whom I spoke in that time, nor would they all wish to be named—students, scholars, officials, workers, taxi drivers, newspaper or water sellers, and others. Thanks go to Western specialists, including reporters and scholars who worked or lived in post-Soviet Azerbaijan: Svante Cornell, Thomas de Waal, Nadia Diuk, Fiona Hill, and especially Thomas Goltz. Politically prominent Azerbaijanis who shared their experiences and insights include the late Abulfez (Aliyev) Elchibey, Ramiz Aboutalibov, the late Suleyman Aliyarli, Isa Gambar, Tofiq Gasymov, Iskendar Hamidov, Jamil Hasanli, Ali Kerimli, Jeyhun and Asim Mollazade, Nasib Nasibli, Ambassador (Ret.) Hafiz Pashayev, Sabir Rustemxanli, Dilare Seidzade, Ambassador Elin Suliemanov, the late Bahtiyar Vahabzade, and Leyla Yunus. I wish to thank the many US Foreign Service officers (and several spouses) and other US government officials who allowed me to interview them, including Ambassador (Ret.) Richard Miles, Ambassador (Ret.) Robert Finn, Ambassador (Ret.) Philip Remler, Ambassador (Ret.) Richard and Mrs. Anne Kauzlarich, Ambassador (Ret.) Ross Wilson, Ambassador (Ret.) Reno Harnish, Ambassador (Ret.) Anne Derse, Ambassador (Ret.) Richard and Mrs. Faith Morningstar, Wayne Merry, David J. Kramer, and Jan Kalicki, as well as senior staff adviser Michael Ochs of the Commission on Security and Cooperation in Europe.

During the year of writing of this book, the Woodrow Wilson International Center for Scholars was a wonderfully supportive institution for intellectually stimulating discussion, feedback, and challenges in the work-in-progress seminars and informal exchanges, especially from Matthew Rojansky and William Pomeranz of the Kennan Institute, and Robert Litwak of the International Security Studies program and the scholars' office. Thanks also to my research assistants, Andrew Clinton at the University of Massachusetts Amherst and my Wilson Center research assistants, Ella McElroy and Michael Kohler. I thank most sincerely those who read one or more chapter drafts: Bayram Balci, Robert Cekuta, Cathy Cosman, Robert Finn, Reno Harnish, Richard Kauzlarich, Rajan Menon, Emin Milli, Philip Remler, and Thomas de Waal. Sincere thanks also go to the Woodrow Wilson Center Press and its publishing committee, especially to Joe Brinley and Shannon Granville, and to Anne Routon and Brad Hebel at Columbia University Press. Shortcomings and errors are my own responsibility.

I also wish to thank Julie Candler Hayes, the dean of the College of Humanities and Fine Arts at the University of Massachusetts Amherst, as well as my department colleagues, especially department chair Professor Joye Bowman and professors David Glassberg, Daniel Gordon, and Jennifer Heuer. My deepest debt of gratitude is to my dear friends Bob Fradkin and Goedele Gulikers for their daily support and multilingual good cheer through broken bones and football season during the initial writing of this book, to my amazing daughter Elizabeth, who enthusiastically supported this project and all my work, and to my selfless husband, the Reverend Bruce T. Arbour, who graciously tolerated my long absences and cheered me on during the writing, rewriting, fretting, and soul-searching that accompanied this project: "The Spirit helps us in our weakness."

Notes on Languages and Spelling

In the text, all names and places are spelled to approximate English-language pronunciation or common usage in English; for instance, Jamil, not Cemil. In the case of personal names that are less familiar in English, I have used Azerbaijani Latin alphabet spelling, hence Ilqar and Tofiq rather than Ilgar or Tofik. Place names are given according to accepted English spelling conventions (Baku, not Baki), or follow Azerbaijani and not Russian spelling (Nakhjivan, rather than Nakhichevan).

In the endnotes, Russian is transliterated according to the Library of Congress system. Azerbaijani (from all alphabets) is spelled according to the post-1991 Latin alphabet, which has several characters not found in English, including ə, ı, ö, ü, ç, and ş.

In Azerbaijan, individuals are often known or called by their first names partly because the use of family names became universal only in the Soviet period and some family names are very common (e.g., Aliyev, Huseinov, Mammedov). Therefore, the use of a person's first name in this book follows common Azerbaijani practice and is not necessarily a sign of familiarity or affection. The polite form of address for women is *xanim* (*khanim*) following the first name (e.g., Leyla *xanim*). For men, two variations are in use: from the Soviet period is *muellim*, meaning "teacher," which replaced the prerevolutionary *bey*, a title for a landowner and used in Turkey. Since independence, *bey* has been used (i.e., Yusif Muellim or Yusif Bey), but is often associated with pro-Turkish views.

Acronyms and Abbreviations

ADR	Azerbaijan Democratic Republic (1918–20)
AI	Amnesty International
AMIP	Azerbaijan Milli İstiqlal Partiyası (National Independence Party)
AXCP	Azərbaycan Xalq Cebhesinin Partiyası (Azerbaijan Popular Front Party)
BTC	Baku–Tbilisi–Ceyhan oil export pipeline
CIS	Commonwealth of Independent States
CMB	Caucasus Muslim Board
CoE	Council of Europe
CSCE	Commission for Security and Cooperation in Europe (see also OSCE)
ECHR	European Court of Human Rights
EEU	Eurasian Economic Union

EITI   Extractive Industries Transparency Initiative

ESI   European Security Initiative

EU   European Union

HRW   Human Rights Watch

IMF   International Monetary Fund

NATO   North Atlantic Treaty Organization

NED   National Endowment for Democracy

NGO   nongovernmental organization

NKAR   Nagorno-Karabagh Autonomous Region (Soviet)

ODIHR   Office for Democratic Institutions and Human Rights

OSCE   Organization for Security and Cooperation in Europe

PACE   Parliamentary Assembly of the Council of Europe

RFE/RL   Radio Free Europe / Radio Liberty

SCO   Shanghai Cooperation Organisation

SCWRO   State Committee on Work with Religious Organizations

SOCAR   State Oil Company of the Azerbaijan Republic

SOFAZ   State Oil Fund of Azerbaijan

WTO   World Trade Organization

YAP   Yeni Azerbaijan Partiyası (New Azerbaijan Party)

Frustrated Democracy in Post-Soviet Azerbaijan

Map I.1. Azerbaijan

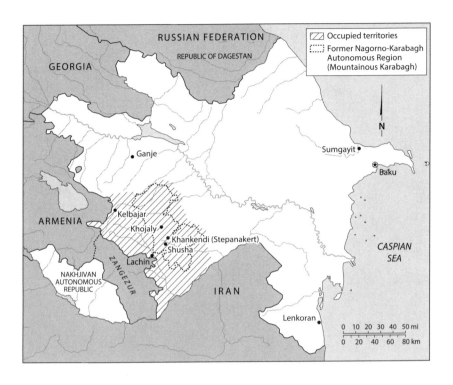

Map I.2. The South Caucasus Region

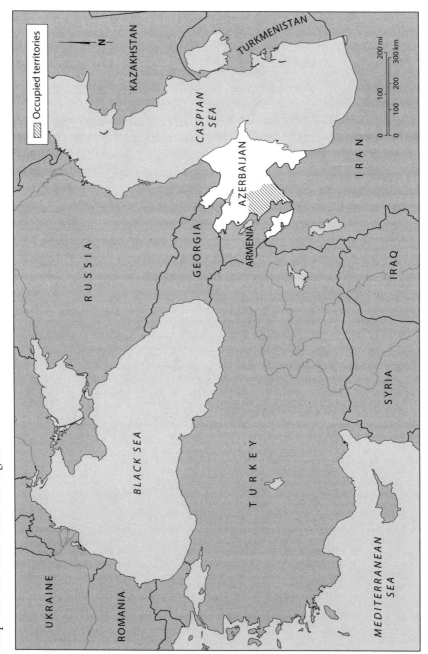

Introduction

In his poem "Hap," the English novelist and poet Thomas Hardy laments his misfortunes. He declares that he could tolerate them if he knew that he was the victim of a vengeful god, against whom he is powerless. But he knows that this is not the case. The tragedies of his life, he concludes, were happenstance. In frustration, he asks, "How arrives it joy lies slain, / And why unblooms the best hope ever sown?" This book similarly begins with Azerbaijan's "best hopes" for independence and democratic society, and explores their "unblooming." In contrast to Hardy's poem, this book is not about chance, but about choice. It examines contextual circumstances—geography, history, culture, institutional constraints—but it focuses on decisions and the people who made them during crucial moments in the trajectory of Azerbaijan's post-Soviet independence.

Azerbaijan's culture, history, and politics are enormously complex and subtle. Analysis is difficult; forecasting perilous. A resource-rich country, Azerbaijan is wedged between Russia and Iran. The region has been ruled by both, sometimes brutally, sometimes loosely. The present-day Republic of Azerbaijan bears the marks of its former overlords in politics, economy, society, and culture. Until the twentieth century, Azerbaijan's models of governance were entirely of despotic rule. Long known for its oil deposits, the county's modern production began outside the Caspian port city of Baku in the 1870s, drawing foreign investors and local wealth. The result was the Westernization of the built environment; the population; and many of its economic, cultural, political, and social components. Its culture was Islamic, mostly Shi'ite with a mix of Iranian and Turkic elements, though the latter

1

aspects came to dominate Azerbaijan by the early twentieth century. A secular, Turkic-speaking Azerbaijani elite led reforms in education and social practices, and also forged the underlying ethnoreligious identity in the late nineteenth and early twentieth centuries, which gradually reoriented the populace away from Iran and toward modernizers in Turkey. This same elite led the republic that emerged from World War I with a Constitution and a parliament. A weak coalition government fell to Bolshevik pressure and the Red Army in 1920. Thus began Azerbaijan's painful life as a Soviet socialist republic.

In the Gorbachev era of the late 1980s, a new generation of intellectuals studied and publicly discussed their forebears of the first republic. The origins of that exploration, initially timid and sporadic, went back to the Brezhnev era of the 1960s and 1970s, when writers and historians began to explore such forbidden topics. These scholars and writers moved from research to politics under the pressure of the armed conflict, as their predecessors had done during World War I.

Apart from the disintegration of the Soviet Union in 1991, the process that most set the stage for post-Soviet political life in Azerbaijan was the war with neighboring Armenia over the territory of Mountainous Karabagh—commonly known with the Russian prefix for "mountainous," Nagorno-Karabagh. The war began in the winter of 1987–88 and galvanized Azerbaijani national consciousness. It is no exaggeration to say that the war itself, the assistance that both Russia and Iran gave to Armenia, and Azerbaijan's own poor showing on the battlefield affected every aspect of life in Azerbaijan. In this context, opposition politics was born. Scholars and the artistic community organized an anticommunist Popular Front, which created mass politics in the Soviet republic in 1988 and introduced an anticommunist, then postcommunist language of discourse. The Popular Front spawned new opposition parties, and was elected to power a mere four years later in the country's first democratic elections in June 1992. Its fall was equally abrupt, before it could celebrate its first anniversary in government. Since then, the democratic opposition parties increasingly have been marginalized in the face of the overwhelming power of the ruling Aliyev family and its inner circle.

With Azerbaijan's independence, oilmen flooded into Baku, outpacing the diplomats. The increasing presence of foreigners was perhaps the most visible indicator to the population that independence was real. The influx of money, mainly to the energy sector and supporting infrastructure, was transformative, and from the mid-1990s to the present it paid for public works and enriched the segment of the population linked to oil and to the foreign community.

It was also used to influence the policies of foreign states and international organizations that dealt with Azerbaijan. Many people were left in poverty. Old skills became obsolete; inflation and currency reforms trivialized Soviet-era pensions and savings. Corruption blossomed and grew in the twenty-first century to astonishing proportions, driving down Azerbaijan's ratings in a number of corruption and democratic governance indices, such as those of Transparency International.

With the growth of central power and constraints on open debate, dissent grew. The regime of Ilham Aliyev (2003–present) did not tolerate criticism or even the free exchange of ideas. Prodemocracy parties and protesters were suppressed with increasing severity, and in 2010 all genuine opposition parties lost representation in the Milli Majlis (National Assembly) in yet another in a series of fixed elections. Dissenters were fined or jailed; investigative journalists were increasingly pressured, beaten, or imprisoned. The fine for unauthorized demonstrations increased tenfold. A new generation of activists was nurtured by established opposition parties but found its own voice through social media and informal organizations. Fearful of youth activism like that found in the color revolutions of the 2000s and the 2011 Arab Spring, the Aliyev regime lured some young women and men into state jobs and meted out harsh repression against the critics of the generation of twenty-somethings. By the end of the summer of 2014, nearly all prominent human rights and civil society activists were in jail, as President Aliyev asserted that Azerbaijan was a democracy and critics of the regime were traitors.

Islam, suppressed under Soviet rule, appealed to many Azerbaijanis who were seeking a new identity in the post-Soviet world. The Soviet-era version of Azerbaijan's history had been discredited, and people had ceased to believe the old regime's claim to have promoted "communist morality." For many, interest in Islam was a matter of historic identity or piety. For others, it was a moral compass or even a political guide. The secular Aliyev regime, which fears Islam for its potential political uses, has claimed to find radical Sunni "Salafi" or "Wahhabi" groups in the country, especially along the Russian border with Dagestan. Believers have been arrested; alleged Islamist groups have been quashed. The Juma mosque in Baku, led by an Iran-trained Shi'ite mullah with human rights credentials, was closed down in 2004, but the mullah was able to start a successful organization with an Internet presence and young followers. Arrests and labels of extremism have kept Islam in the shadows, making its power hard to assess. The emergence of the Islamic State in 2014 has raised the specter of extremism among the Sunni minority in Azerbaijan.

3

Beyond the examination of Azerbaijan's experience, this analysis addresses broader themes that political leaders and diplomats repeatedly have argued. Western, particularly US, policy in Azerbaijan is built on a tripod of energy, security, and democratization. Cooperation in the first two areas has been positive, but the worsening record in the third has become a source of growing tension. Baku has responded to Western criticism by framing its own policies as the product of a stark choice: it must guard its own security, stability, and independence by the means it chooses, or else fall to enemies who can manipulate its "open society." As a Muslim majority society with a secular state, Azerbaijan may be vulnerable to Islamist appeals, especially as the regime has reduced the space for the politically moderate opposition. These are strategic and philosophical, even moral questions that touch on rule by the consent of the governed, the rule of law, and human rights. The US response raises the same concerns with its tripod. These and related issues are implicit in each chapter and are addressed explicitly in the final one, "What's Next"?

This book is possible because of the training I received first as a master's degree student in international relations and then as a doctoral candidate in history at the University of Chicago from 1975 to 1983, when I completed my PhD. At Chicago, I honed the Russian language skills I had developed in high school and as an undergraduate at the University of Illinois (Champaign-Urbana), and began learning modern Turkish and Azerbaijani. As a doctoral student, I first went to Baku in 1980–81, where I developed my language skills to study pre–World War I Azerbaijani culture and politics, navigate the streets and bazaars of Baku, and learn the "ground truth" of Brezhnev-era Azerbaijan. I met colleagues who later became politically active in the Gorbachev era. As an historian, I write about the past, but as a researcher and observer, I live in the present. Through many subsequent research trips to Azerbaijan in 1984 and the post-Soviet decades, I watched the transformation of politics, social and economic life, and the city of Baku itself. I was privileged to watch my peers manage the new conditions and speak more openly to a foreign friend. Finally I was able to meet a younger generation of dynamic Azerbaijanis who knew more of the world but less of the Soviet (or pre-Soviet) past than the previous generation.

The present work is grounded in my many unpublished presentations, briefings, and classes for and with nongovernmental organizations and US government groups since 1990. Drawing on my own experiences and research, I made use of the scholarly work of US, Azerbaijani, and European scholars; and reports from US, European, and Azerbaijani governments, international organizations, nongovernmental organizations, and the press. I have spoken with Azerbaijani activists; local and Western journalists; and diplomats from the United States, Azerbaijan, other countries, and international organizations. I could not include every story, and surely participants in events will challenge some of my choices. I respect their views. In the process of writing each chapter, I explored topics and whole areas that were not on my initial "to do" list, but which I investigated because I wanted to give as full a picture as possible while maintaining a coherent narrative and reasonable length.

This project was completed in 2014–15, thanks to the intellectual and financial support I received as a fellow at the Woodrow Wilson International Center for Scholars in Washington. As we approach the twenty-fifth anniversary of the Soviet collapse, and given the economic and strategic significance of Azerbaijan, the time seemed ripe for a retrospective analysis not only of the road that Azerbaijan has traveled in over two decades but also of the choices and the human agency at work and the meaning of its pathway for Azerbaijan and US interests now and in the years to come.

1

A Starting Point: History and Geopolitics and What They Tell Us

If you have nothing to tell us but that one barbarian succeeds another on the banks of the Oxus, what benefit does the public derive from your history?

—Voltaire, 1769[1]

Voltaire was right, of course. A simple catalog of facts, devoid of explanation and interpretation, is not beneficial or meaningful. It is not even good history. This book strives to be both good history and useful analysis in understanding Azerbaijan from the inside and from a Western policy perspective. The focus of this book is Azerbaijan's post-Soviet path from a troubled but hopeful beginning of democracy-building to the reestablishment of authoritarianism behind a Western façade. Understanding how Azerbaijan's path was shaped—by what events and human agency—and where the country may go in the coming decade is essential to informed policymaking. The following chapters examine selected facets of post-Soviet Azerbaijan's experience to provide a meaningful context and critical foundation to lead a reader to that understanding. To create a frame of reference for the question of Azerbaijan's post-Soviet trajectory, this initial chapter will establish "snapshots" of the country, first as a newly independent state in 1991–92 and then after nearly twenty-five years of independence in 2014–15.

The dissolution of the Soviet Union at the end of 1991 gave reality to the declarations of independence by the individual Soviet Socialist Republics (SSRs) during that year. Western analysts, like the noncommunist factions inside each new state, so fully expected that the former Soviet republics would transition to democracy that programs and publications dedicated to describing the process included the word "transition" in their titles.[2] A body of literature dubbed "transitology" tracked and analyzed the features of various postcommunist states. Though these publications were useful in identifying common challenges to "transition" and instances where political configurations of elites, resources, and public action met and turned at "contestation points," they often suffered from the lack of in-depth knowledge of individual countries and cultures that made a difference in the hoped-for transitions to democracy. They were short on "ground truth."

Most of the literature anticipated the existence of some factors that would facilitate the envisioned transition to democracy: a historical "legacy" that supported democracy, such as elite or societal consensus; some form of civil society; political competition and popular participation; institution-building efforts; and the development of a strong state that is separate from the ruling party. (This last factor stemmed from the consideration that weak states are associated with weak democratization.) These democratization factors relied upon the additional presupposed (and usually unstated) factors of peace, time, and a desire to democratize. By 2010, when democratization had foundered or failed in many postcommunist states, analysts added two more factors to the equation: the participation of the international system and, importantly for Azerbaijan, the role of domestic political leadership in the democratic transition.[3] When looking at the effects of these new factors, analysts most often used the cases of Russia (for instance, the extent to which Russian leader Vladimir Putin quashed Russia's democratic development) and Ukraine, but the example of authoritarian rulers could be applied to Azerbaijan as well. Western democracy-building programs, as external efforts, became more important in this analysis. The conclusions from these new evaluations seemed again to suggest that certain preconditions—namely, peace and prodemocracy leaders—had to exist before a formerly totalitarian state could transition successfully to a democratic one. Post-Soviet Azerbaijan lacked many of these conditions—significantly, peace.

Azerbaijan's particular traits of history and geography made it a poor fit for many of the post-Soviet democratization paradigms because Azerbaijan is on the frontier between Asia and Europe, which therefore bestows on it a unique cultural legacy. For centuries, the area that is now the Republic of Azerbaijan has been part of a wide Turco-Persian Islamic cultural belt, into which Russia intruded early in the nineteenth century. Until the late twentieth century, its political models were almost entirely of despotic rule. Native elites developed a modernization movement decades before the Soviet period , making it unique among the future "Muslim" SSRs.[4] Present-day Azerbaijan is wedged between Iran and Russia, and it shows the effects of having been ruled for centuries by first one state and then the other, sometimes brutally, sometimes loosely. Today, the Republic of Azerbaijan must maintain a balance between these neighbors and others—Armenia, Georgia, and Turkey—even as its politics, society, economy, and culture bear the marks of its former overlords.

Azerbaijan also has an alternative, if short-lived, democratic model with indigenous roots. In the 1870s, the beginning of a modern oil industry in Baku attracted foreigners—Russian entrepreneurs and workers, along with European investors, engineers, architects, and merchants. Foreigners brought the accoutrements of modernization, such as elevators and telephones. Cultural Westernization soon followed. Azerbaijani elites sought Western education for their sons, albeit cautiously at first, in Russia and Europe. By the start of the twentieth century, a second generation of secular reformers was sculpting a modern Islamic-Turkic culture with European elements. These reformers spearheaded education reform for boys and girls, campaigned against polygamy and the veiling of women, and supported a vibrant civil society with a surprisingly outspoken press. The intellectual elites who wrote poetry and opera were also contributors to the urban press, even as they earned a living as schoolteachers. Some of them ran for seats in the Baku City Council and later the Russian State Duma. These men and the few women among them forged a national identity that incorporated a reformed Islamic and ethnic Turkic consciousness. They gained a political education in the few legislative bodies that tsarist Russia created. This modern identity and the commitment to democracy were expressed in the arts and the founding of political parties such as the Müsavat ("Equality") Party, which was founded in 1911 with a mixed Muslim and Turkic program. It became the dominant party in postwar political life.[5]

After the 1917 Bolshevik coup and World War I destroyed the Russian Empire, Azerbaijan's nationally conscious elite formed a parliamentary republic, the Azerbaijan Democratic Republic (ADR), in May 1918. Building on their prewar reform program, the leaders drafted a Constitution that guaranteed electoral rights and civil rights, including freedom of speech, and enfranchised women, the first Muslim society to do so. Their Turkic language supplanted Russian as the official language.[6] Their national anthem, composed by the country's most prominent composer and one of its major poets, blended folk and European themes. The tricolor flag in blue, green, and red represented the coexistence of Turkic national, Islamic, and socialist elements, the hallmark of politics in Baku with its industry and multinational population. The new republic's political parties included an array of Russian, Armenian, and Azerbaijani national parties; socialist and nationalist parties; and Islamic, Jewish, and other smaller parties, including a Russian communist one. Each community had a newspaper, houses of worship, and schools. The ADR's parliamentary system produced a series of coalition governments; the nascent communist movement worked against it. A weak coalition government fell to the combined forces of the Azerbaijani wing of the Bolshevik party and the Red Army in April 1920. Thus began Azerbaijan's painful life as a Soviet Socialist Republic. The elite who had led the ADR fought to defend it. Many were killed, and others fled abroad to continue the war of ideas by publishing newspapers and anti-Bolshevik books, often in Istanbul and Paris. Still others remained in the country to try to retain the cultural and philosophical gains of their prewar movement. Most were purged in the ensuing years; their ideas were distorted, and they were vilified and condemned, to the extent that some of their names were obliterated from the historical record. Studying the prewar reformers and intellectuals and their ideas became "anti-Soviet," and therefore dangerous.

Bolshevik conquest brought despotic rule back to Azerbaijan, but in a modern totalitarian incarnation that penetrated both the form and the content of national identity. The native Turkic language retained official status, though its alphabet was changed twice, from Arabic script to Latin in 1924 and then to Cyrillic in 1940. Each change made the literate population illiterate and cut off new readers from the literature and history of their own past. The substance of culture and the liberal national identity it bore was suppressed in favor of "socialist construction."[7] The authorities pressured schools to expand the teaching of Russian, which was the only language used for the study of technology and science, and required the use of Russian as the lingua franca. After the initial loss of life in the early 1920s, the Soviet regime carried out a nearly continuous purge of intellectuals and artists in the interwar period.

In the Gorbachev era of the later 1980s, patterns of overt dissent became visible. They were attributed to glasnost, the new policy of "openness" and transparency in Soviet government and society, and their appearance was a result of that policy. The origins of this dissent—initially moderate, sporadic, and exclusively in Azerbaijani-language journals and literature—went back to the Brezhnev era in the previous decade, when writers and scholars had begun to examine topics that were forbidden by the Soviet regime. In the 1980s, historians as well as journalists wrote openly and widely about the democratic precedent of Azerbaijan's first republic. Most of the historical pieces were short biographies of people who had been declared "bourgeois nationalists" or other "enemies," and had been purged in the great waves of Stalinist terror in the 1930s or the lesser-known purges of non-Russian leaders in the late 1920s.[8] The ADR and its ideals were articulated as models for the Popular Front when it was formed in 1988–89 and for the other parties that branched off from it, particularly the Yeni ("New") Müsavat Party, named for the original Müsavat Party that had been denounced under Soviet rule.

The Path to the "Second Republic"

The events that set the immediate political stage for the independent post-Soviet Azerbaijan were, unsurprisingly, the disintegration of the Soviet Union at the end of 1991 and the war with neighboring Armenia over the territory of Mountainous Karabagh (Nagorno-Karabagh) from 1987 onward. Within that context, Baku's intellectual elite in the Azerbaijan National Academy of Sciences and Baku State (then Azerbaijan State) University formed the Azerbaijan Popular Front, an organization that gave voice to public anger over the Karabagh issue and many other points of political and social contention. The Popular Front struggled against the communist party, and eventually came to power. The rocky path to post-Soviet independence determined the challenges that the country's first leaders would face.

The struggle over Mountainous Karabagh began in the winter of 1987–88 and galvanized Azerbaijani national consciousness in a way that no other event had done in almost seventy years. Although the impact of this conflict will be discussed in greater detail in the next chapter, it is important to note here that the war itself, the paralysis of both Azerbaijan's Soviet government and the Azerbaijan Communist Party (AzCP), the assistance that Russia and Iran provided to Armenia, and Azerbaijan's poor showing on the battlefield all shaped the country's political life and national consciousness in the years before and after the reestablishment of its independence. When the first Armenian demands to transfer control of the Nagorno-Karabagh Autonomous Region (NKAR) to Soviet Armenia were advanced in 1987–88, Azerbaijanis only gradually became aware of them. Outside academic circles, where scholars were familiar with conflicting historical claims to the land, most people were taken by surprise. They may have been aware that Armenians made up the majority of the population in the NKAR, but they always understood the land itself to be Azerbaijani. When the AzCP and the Supreme Soviet of the Azerbaijan SSR failed to reject the Armenian claims to the land, popular outrage was immediate. This public anger buoyed resistance to Azerbaijan's passive party and state institutions, and eventually spilled out into public demonstrations. The Azerbaijan Popular Front become the organization that voiced the Azerbaijani public's frustration with the weakness of its Soviet leaders, articulated the counternarrative that asserted Azerbaijan's historical claims, and finally led the resistance to both Armenian demands and communist rule in Azerbaijan.

The Popular Front was formed in secret meetings of academicians and literati during 1988–89. Some of its members were already known as dissidents, including the fifty-year-old Abulfez Aliyev, a historian who worked in the Academy of Sciences' archives. He had formerly worked as a translator in Egypt and taught at Baku State University, then was jailed in the mid-1970s for anti-Soviet activity. He emerged as a leading personality in the Popular Front and was dubbed the "messenger" (*elchi*). His family name, a very common one, was later replaced with "Elchibey" (adding the honorific "bey" to the title). At the first congress of the Popular Front in 1989, Elchibey was elected the organization's chairman. Among the other leaders were men and women in their mid-thirties, including Etibar Mamedov, Isa Gambar(ov), Leyla Yunus(ova), and Zardusht Alizade, all of whom later founded political parties.

The first big step toward independence was the November 1988 demonstration in front of the main government building on Lenin Square.[9] Tens of thousands of people, perhaps half a million at times, gathered in the square, which they began to call "Azadlıq Meydani" (Freedom Square) to hear speakers denounce Azerbaijan's government and communist party for its weakness in the face of Armenian demands and more broadly for failing to protect Azerbaijan's environment, monuments, and culture. Thousands camped on the square night and day for over two weeks before attrition and pressure from the police gradually led to their dispersal and the arrest of several leaders on December 3.[10] But public anger had been mobilized and the Popular Front had established itself as an alternative to the existing authorities.

11

The following summer, the Popular Front held its first congress. In its first official program, it called for full civil liberties and human rights for all citizens, equality for national minorities, return of collectivized land (from the early 1930s) to the peasantry, and the end to "barbaric" exploitation of natural resources. Finally, it demanded full "political, economic and cultural sovereignty for Azerbaijan within the USSR."[11] Although the program did not call for secession, its terms effectively called for the dismantling of the Soviet system. Early in the fall of 1989, thanks to pressure exerted through a railway strike, AzCP first secretary Abdurrahman Vezirov was forced to allow the Front to register as a legal organization and agree to a protocol with a host of other demands, including amnesty for the strikers and the end to special military controls in major Azerbaijani cities.[12] The homegrown political movement that had been ridiculed by authorities in August had brought the AzCP leadership to its knees in October.

By late 1989, the reach of the Popular Front had become sufficiently great to frighten authorities in Baku and in Moscow. As its adherents always said, the Front was a movement, not a party. It was beginning to fracture by this time, partly because a few members believed that it was too willing to accommodate the authorities. Those who insisted on independence were dubbed "radicals" by authorities and by some later scholars. Actual radicals formed the factions that carried out violent attacks on Armenians or took over local AzCP offices against the orders of the Baku Popular Front leadership, as was the case earlier in 1989 in the southern Caspian port city of Lenkoran.[13] In December, Moscow ended seventeen months of direct rule over the NKAR, in theory returning it to Azerbaijani rule, but the Armenian SSR seized the moment to declare that it would annex the NKAR and quickly included the region in its 1990 state budget. Disorders broke out throughout Azerbaijan, including some led by rogue chapters of the Popular Front despite the leadership's call to maintain order.[14] The AzCP had no meaningful response and seemed paralyzed. Moscow soon moved against the Popular Front.

On the weekend of January 13–14, 1990, "hooligan elements" tried to evict Armenians from their apartments in Baku. It was more than a few scattered attacks. Thomas de Waal wrote that "murderous anti-Armenian violence overwhelmed Baku." Some Azerbaijanis, including police, were killed, but more than ninety Armenians were murdered and dozens more were wounded. The local forces of the Ministry of Internal Affairs did not intervene, despite Popular Front pleas to do so. Their commander told Kazakh writer Almaz

12

Estekhov, who was then in Baku, that AzCP first secretary Abdurrahman Vezirov had ordered him not to intervene in ethnic conflicts.[15]

Only after the bloodshed ended on January 15 did Evgenii Primakov, a member of Gorbachev's Presidential Council,[16] arrive in Baku to announce that 11,000 Soviet troops were on the way to Azerbaijan "to restore order." A state of emergency was declared in NKAR and along the border between Armenia and Azerbaijan. But in Baku, Ganje, and several other cities, mayors were told to impose curfews. Unnamed sources in Moscow said that the situation in Azerbaijan had "reached the point of attempts at armed overthrow of Soviet power."[17] This was untrue. Protesters had few arms, and authorities knew the situation. A news blackout began that day,[18] although some smaller newspapers (which were illegal in the first place) continued to publish for a day or two. Unarmed civilians put up barricades on roads into Baku. On January 17, demonstrations took place outside AzCP headquarters. On January 18, when Primakov spoke to crowds to say that Soviet troops were coming to Baku to protect the people, he was booed and shouted down—something that would have been unthinkable a few months earlier. Soviet defense minister Dmitry Yazov ordered Soviet troops to open fire if they met resistance on the roads into Baku. The commander of the Baku garrison told Popular Front leaders that if ordered, his troops would "not hesitate" to open fire on the civilian population.[19] Throughout these days of unrest, various Popular Front leaders and those who were working alongside them, including Soviet Muslim leader Sheikh-ul-Islam Allahshukur Pashazade, tried to negotiate with Soviet military leaders to reverse the order for Soviet troops to enter Baku. Their efforts were in vain: on the night of January 19, the power station for Azerbaijan's state radio and television station was blown up—possibly by Soviet special forces—cutting off all national broadcasts to the population. Thereafter, there was no way to announce the imposition of a curfew or a state of emergency, which would be put in place only after the Soviet troops arrived.

On January 20, 1990, just after midnight, the first troops of the Soviet Ministry of Internal Affairs arrived at the barricades on the main road leading into Baku. They opened fire. Here and in other places around Baku that night and the next day, Soviet forces claimed that they were "returning fire," but an independent investigation conducted in Moscow later in the year rebuffed this claim. The Shchit (Shield) Commission, whose report was released in the summer of 1990,[20] rejected the claim that the troops were fired upon, because there was no evidence that those on the barricades had been armed. Elsewhere, there were no signs of bullet holes except where the troops had fired. As Soviet troops advanced, tanks and helicopters continued their assault on Baku, crushing cars and ambulances in their path. In the two-day crackdown, which later would be known as "Black January," over 120 people were killed outright and more later died of their wounds. Many hundreds were wounded, but survived. Sheikh-ul-Islam Pashazade presided over the funerals of 180 people.[21]

Then and later, First Secretary Mikhail Gorbachev made public statements that the military action was necessary to fight "extremists" and "radicals" in Baku. He told the international media that Soviet troops were fighting "Islamic fundamentalists." He had more than enough information to know that this was false. The Azerbaijanis who were wounded or killed, or were merely demonstrating, or were watching behind closed doors, were "extremists" in the same sense as the anticommunist demonstrators that had raised their voices in the Baltic republics and Ukraine. Azerbaijanis on the streets, apart from the leadership related to the Popular Front, were demanding an opportunity for political discourse to debate and discuss possible solutions to the NKAR conflict, but also for other problems that had emerged during the two years of upheaval that preceded the Black January tragedy. But open debate was a threat to the regime. The Soviet state had to control the narrative, and it did. The news blackout had quashed other sources of information, and the rest of the world had no contrary information. Many in the West believed the official Soviet story of "Islamic fundamentalists."

The Soviet regime was in fact defending itself. Soviet Major General Anatoly Kiriliuk of the Ministry of Internal Affairs said later that the Soviet military was sent to Baku "to crush the Azerbaijani drive for greater sovereignty in order to discourage similar movements elsewhere in the USSR."[22] The concrete target of the invasion was the Popular Front, which had given voice to this popular anger, organized it, and mobilized it. Just after midnight, the first wave of Soviet troops surrounded the Popular Front offices and fired upon the building, killing and wounding many of those inside before invading and ransacking it. Files were taken, telephones were removed, and Popular Front members were arrested. Similar events took place elsewhere in the country, from Ganje, the second-largest city, to the western region of Nakhjivan, and Soviet troops were sent there with similar outcomes to that in Baku. Leyla Yunusova called it "Red fascism." Etibar Mamedov escaped to Moscow to give a news conference on the real events of Black January. He was immediately arrested and held incommunicado in Moscow's Lefortovo Prison, infamous as a center of KGB detention and torture of political prisoners.

In the following days, Azerbaijanis were defiant. Despite martial law, they massed for funeral processions of the victims. People burned their party cards in public fires; they denounced Soviet rule, the Soviet military, and Gorbachev. The tragedy of January 1990 was a turning point for the nation. Black January moved most Azerbaijanis from the position of demanding justice and autonomy within a Soviet framework to a new position—rejecting the Soviet Union itself and striving for independence.

The Popular Front soon prepared a new party program, declaring that sovietization of Azerbaijan had been illegal, the result of the Red Army's invasion in 1920. The creation of the NKAR. therefore, was also illegal, and it was to be dissolved, leaving the territory as an integral part of Azerbaijan. The program repeated its earlier support for the guarantee of full civil liberties as well as cultural rights for minorities, the creation of a market economy, and environmental protection, and now added the demand that state and judicial organs be freed from communist party influence. In spite of this anticommunist platform, it did not yet call for independence from the Soviet Union. With this platform, the Popular Front contended in October 1990 elections to the Azerbaijan Supreme Soviet. The elections were marked by restrictions on Popular Front candidates, including jailing of candidates and two murders. US observers noted instances of electoral fraud, including ballot stuffing and voter intimidation. Of 350 seats, 300 went outright to communist party candidates. After runoffs, only thirty deputies came from the Popular Front or the few noncommunist parties that had sprung up. These deputies formed a Democratic Bloc (Dembloc) in the Azerbaijan SSR's legislature.[23]

The AzCP leadership had been changed immediately after Black January, and Baku native Ayaz Mutalibov had been installed as first secretary on January 23. He was Moscow's man, and agreed to reforms only when forced. Slowly, the Popular Front regained its footing, but many members and followers were more strident in their demands for a share of power. In March 1991, the Popular Front could not stop Mutalibov from participating in a unionwide referendum on the proposed New Union Treaty that would renew Azerbaijan's commitment to remain a part of the Soviet Union. But they did force him to prorogue the Supreme Soviet in favor of a new Milli Shura (National Council), a fifty-member body that allowed equal numbers of representatives from the government and the opposition forces that had formed the Dembloc. The Milli Shura sat in continuous session and for all intents and purposes took the place of the now-defunct Supreme Soviet.[24] The Shura freely and publicly discussed politics and passed resolutions, providing the populace with more political education than it had gained at any time since Soviet power was established in 1920. By the summer of 1991, Etibar Mamedov, freed from Lefortovo, broke with the Popular Front to establish the Azerbaijan National Independence Party (Azerbaijan Milli İstiqlal Partiyası; AMIP), whose platform called for independence.[25]

The August 1991 coup against Gorbachev, launched by a group of hard-liners in the Soviet leadership that included Defense Minister Dmitry Yazov, happened while First Secretary Mutalibov was out of the country, in Tehran. Initially, he sided with the conservatives who had carried it out. When the coup failed and Gorbachev reappeared, Mutalibov backpedaled and, under Popular Front pressure, agreed to advocate for a declaration of independence. The declaration was adopted as a constitutional act on October 18, thereafter marked as Azerbaijan's official day of independence. The decision had no enforceable reality, however, until the Soviet Union was officially dissolved by Gorbachev on December 26. Azerbaijan's declaration was ratified by referendum on December 29. Within six months, Azerbaijan would be reconnected to the world, and the Popular Front leader would win the presidency.

The Reborn Republic of Azerbaijan

Despite the obvious challenges—war with neighboring Armenia, thousands of internally displaced persons (IDPs), decades of underinvestment in infrastructure and industry, and a growing illicit economy—the unanticipated Soviet collapse created great hope in the possibility of constructing an independent, prosperous, and democratic Azerbaijan. These hopes were rooted in the memory of the first republic, the potential of the educated elite, international recognition of the new republic, and oil.

With independence, Azerbaijan, especially Baku, faced an influx of foreigners for which neither its people nor its infrastructure was ready. The capital city was run-down and store shelves were often bare. The few decent hotels had housed refugees or functioned as morgues during Black January. The expectations of the arriving Westerners were a mystery to everyone in Azerbaijan, from the border guards who were suddenly forced to manage foreigners in Baku airport to the fruit sellers in the country's bazaars.

The Turks had been the first to recognize Azerbaijan's independence in November 1991, and they were the first to arrive on the scene in the restored republic. Turkish diplomats opened an embassy, and Turkish businessmen followed them, some opening small shops in dilapidated buildings while others made large-scale deals to revamp the long-neglected infrastructure. By the fall of 1992, Turkish companies were replacing the entire telephone system in Baku, a job that seemed to be on schedule despite the brief inconvenience of lost telephone service in one section of the city after another. The result was immediately noticeable. Investments and military training for Azerbaijan's emerging army continued.

For Turkey, the link to Turkic peoples of the Soviet Union had been a sensitive domestic matter which was quickly overcome in 1991–92. In Cold War Turkey, attention to the "outside Turks" in neighboring states, particularly within the Soviet Union, came to be associated with the political right wing, the main faction that continued to pay attention to them. Azerbaijan and Turkey had special places in each other's histories because of their nineteenth-century national identity formation and shared language. At the turn of the twentieth century, reformers in Baku and Istanbul pursued a modernization agenda captured by the slogan "Turkify, Islamize, and Modernize." The underlying impulse was anti-imperial (hence the call to "Turkify" as contrast to being "Ottoman") and to find a modus vivendi between European learning and a reformed Islam.[26] Moreover, this reformist discourse was aided by the mutually intelligible spoken vernacular in both places (as well as Crimean Tatar), nearly a single language with regional variations that were often masked by the Arabic script.[27] In the 1930s, language reform in both Soviet Azerbaijan (where many Russian words were mandated) and the Turkish Republic drew the languages apart. But exposure to their later forms in post-Soviet radio and television broadcasting led most speakers, especially the young, to bridge the gap quickly.

The Turkish embrace was almost overwhelming, despite the longing for this bond to be reestablished. Azerbaijanis' awareness of their first republic led them back to the time when they had had close relations with the Turks. The Turks even sent typewriters to help Azerbaijan return to the Latin alphabet, which both had adopted in the 1920s. But some Turks regarded Azerbaijani as a dialect of their own language, and did not conceal their sense that Azerbaijanis were "mispronouncing" it and using "archaic" words that had long been purged by the Turkish Language Association (Dil Kurumu), the official regulatory institution of the Turkish language. Because the history of Azerbaijan's Turkic language, with its own reforms and history of alphabet change and shifting standardization, was not well documented, the Turkish claims of linguistic superiority could not be rebuffed—and they rankled. Azerbaijanis began to grumble that they had not thrown off one "elder brother," using the old Soviet parlance, for another. Many Turks working in Azerbaijan took the hint and toned down their enthusiasm.

For Iran, the creation of an independent republic in Turkic Azerbaijan was unwelcome. Iran itself has a multinational population, and the Azerbaijani Turks are by far the most numerous minority—perhaps twice as many Azerbaijani Turks lived in Iran as lived in the new republic to the north.[28] For millennia, Iran's history has been characterized by periodic expansion and contraction, often involving external forces on ethnic or religious minorities and the strength of the central government. At times, peoples on the periphery exercised greater autonomy, separated from the ruling regime, or were taken over by a neighbor. The Russian conquest of the Caucasus in the early nineteenth century was one such case when Iran lost substantial fertile and commercial land during a period of dynastic weakness. Iran's cultural Persianization campaign of the twentieth century under the Pahlavi Dynasty denigrated Turkic culture as "nomadic," in contrast to Persian high culture. The Turkic identity was denied, and Turkic speakers in Iranian Azerbaijan were dubbed "Turkicized Iranians." In the 1963 census, only literacy in Persian was counted as literacy.[29] The reign of the ayatollahs since 1979 generally sought to assert Islamic identity over national identity, but the Islamic regime retained many of the shah's policies toward minorities. The hoped-for leveling of nationalities under Shi'ism, which most Azerbaijanis shared with Persians and the Iranian state, could not overcome "Persian chauvinism."[30] Leaders like Grand Ayatollah Mohammad Shariatmadari, who came from Azerbaijan, ultimately were unable to benefit Azerbaijan or its Turkic culture.

In the end, neither Persianization nor the Islamic Revolution erased the Turkic consciousness of Iran's Azerbaijani population. So the emergence of an independent state centered in Baku—a secular Turkic state on Iran's northern border—implied a threat to Iran's own territorial integrity. The use of Azerbaijani as the state language and opportunities for education and publishing in that language made this new state a potential pole of attraction for Iranian Azerbaijanis. Moreover, Azerbaijan was secular, but it was not the atheist society that the Soviet Union had meant to construct. Because Azerbaijani secularism had begun among native elites in Russian-held Azerbaijan in the nineteenth century, it could not be attributed to Soviet rule and in practice it appeared similar to Turkey's secular society. Those secular values and practices were anathema to Iran's Shi'ite hierarchy. For these reasons, as well as post-Soviet conflicts over resource rights under the Caspian Sea, Tehran approached the new republic with caution, delaying recognition but promising future economic assistance.[31] Within a year, Iranian mullahs would be arrested for bringing truckloads of Qurans into Azerbaijan.

Western oil company representatives descended on Baku, often beating out the diplomats (apart from the eager Turks) who were charged with opening embassies in a country that many could not find on a map. Men in Pennzoil caps rode shuttle buses, an oddity in Baku, from one meeting to another. They commented, privately, that they should charge their counterparts for giving them classes in "Economics 101." For the oil companies, the first months were taken up with assessment and exploration. Baku's readily accessible oil, drawn from wells outside the city, had been significantly depleted by waste and fires in the early twentieth century. In World War II, Baku oil became the object of Hitler's Caucasus offensive and was vital to the Soviet war effort. But after the war and reconstruction, investment was reduced again, and other sources of oil, including Grozny in Chechnya, became more important. In the late 1970s and early 1980s, foreign oil companies were working quietly in Baku,[32] but on a small scale only. By the 1990s, the new country's formerly thriving oil sector was left with an outdated and rusted infrastructure. Interest shifted to offshore reserves, but the Soviet Union had not had the technology to exploit them. With legions of Western specialists in Baku, Azerbaijanis had unreasonably high expectations about the time that it would take to explore, extract, and market that untapped oil and start pocketing the cash. Similarly unrealistic were expectations around the politics of oil. By summer, people in and out of government were saying that with US oil companies exploiting Azerbaijan's oil, Azerbaijan's independence was assured because the American government would never let "their" oil be threatened by a Russian takeover. Such thinking was a generally accurate indicator of the effects of seven decades of Soviet propaganda.

At the same time, the war in Mountainous Karabagh continued to escalate. More fighters came from abroad; more weapons came into the region both from foreign sources and former Soviet soldiers who sold their weapons to all buyers.[33] Armed groups were not only in and near the battlefield, but around Baku, as indicated by the occasional sound of distant gunfire.[34] The massacre of nearly 500 Azerbaijanis, including women and children, outside the town of Khojaly on February 25–26, 1992, was the shocking event that led to the downfall of President Ayaz Mutalibov. (See chapter 3 for more on this chain of events.) He was blamed for failing to establish a national army, for he had argued that it was in Azerbaijan's best interests to rely on the forces of the Commonwealth of Independent States—meaning the post-Soviet Russian forces that were still stationed in Azerbaijan. On March 6, Mutalibov was forced to resign, but he handed the presidency to his corrupt sidekick, Yaqub Mamedov. About nine weeks later, Mamedov gave the presidency back to Mutalibov in a noisy session of the resuscitated full Supreme Soviet of Azerbaijan, which had been renamed a "parliament" in the fall of 1991. The trigger was yet another battlefield loss in Karabagh. This time, the major mountaintop city of Shusha, a center of Azerbaijani culture, fell to Armenian forces, as did the Lachin corridor with its road linking the former NKAR to Armenia—which effectively united Mountainous Karabagh and Armenia. These losses were laid at Yaqub Mamedov's doorstep. At a session of the "parliament" on May 14, without a quorum, Mutalibov returned to the acclaim of his supporters. He declared a state of emergency and canceled the forthcoming presidential elections, which had been set for June 7.[35]

The Popular Front refused to accept this turn of events. Abulfez Elchibey and his advisers argued the unconstitutionality of the Mamedov-Mutalibov maneuver. At the same time, the Popular Front's own "watchdog," Iskendar Hamidov, a career police colonel, marched on the parliament building with an armed force. Mutalibov fled the country and later turned up in Moscow, where he continues to reside more than twenty years after his ouster. Under popular pressure, the "parliament," now with a quorum, elected the Popular Front's Isa Gambar to be its speaker and therefore acting president. Gambar reinstated the upcoming presidential elections. This was not, as has been suggested, an attempt "to cloak"[36] Popular Front actions, but rather was an indication of the Front's genuine commitment to establish the most democratic system it could muster under the circumstances. With the June elections, during fighting in Karabagh, the Popular Front would come to power. On June 7, 1992, Abulfez Elchibey was elected president of the Republic of Azerbaijan with about 55 percent of the vote in the first free, multicandidate, and relatively fair elections in Azerbaijan since 1920.

Azerbaijan Today: Two Decades of Independent Statehood

After more than two decades as an independent state, Azerbaijan's top priority is and must be to maintain its independence. No opposition party or group has suggested otherwise. In that sense, the hope has been fulfilled, and a change in government to any parties now on the scene would not affect the commitment to independent statehood. As any textbook on statehood will attest, sovereignty entails territorial integrity. Thus, the lingering conflict over Mountainous Karabagh is an existential threat to Azerbaijan's statehood, in more ways than one. The country's battlefield losses, consolidated in the 1994 cease-fire under President Heydar Aliyev, marked not only the de facto separation of the former NKAR from Azerbaijan but also the Armenian occupation of six adjacent regions of Azerbaijan, totaling about 14 percent of Azerbaijan's territory. Negotiations toward a final resolution have been facilitated by the Minsk Group of the Organization for Security and Cooperation in Europe (OSCE), which was created in 1992 to help manage a peaceful solution to the Mountainous Karabagh conflict, but have been stalled for over two decades. Both the government and opposition parties have used the same rhetoric of the need to retain Mountainous Karabagh within Azerbaijan on the basis of the internationally accepted principle of territorial integrity of states. Willingness to use force to end the stalemate has been suggested more frequently, as Azerbaijan's military budget has increased with the rise of oil revenues in the past decade. The 2015 military budget was nearly $5 billion, and clashes along the line of contact between Azerbaijan and Mountainous Karabagh have spiked.

Within the geopolitical context of the south Caucasus, the Karabagh problem should be considered together with other secessionist movements in the region and the aims of neighboring regional powers, especially Russia. Like the old NKAR, other autonomous regions (ARs) or republics (ASSRs) established for ethnic minorities were products of Soviet policy in the 1920s and 1930s. Officially, these autonomous regions and republics were part of a "nation-building" effort by the Soviet regime, and guaranteed various cultural rights for a republic's minority populations, including native-language education, publishing, and other cultural activities. At the same time, especially in non-Russian Soviet republics, these ARs/ASSRs permitted the Soviet regime to manipulate the national feelings of the minorities against the majority nationality of their republic. Georgia, one of the republics that most consistently resisted Bolshevik conquest and communist rule, had no fewer than three such autonomous entities: the Ajar ASSR and the Abkhaz and South Ossetia ARs. In the post-Soviet era, armed unrest began in at least one of these areas each time Georgia moved closer to the West. The weapons came from Russia, as did air support. The patterns of separatists receiving Russian aid were evident in both Abkhazia (1992–93) and the 2008 invasion of Georgia by Russian forces, ostensibly to protect South Ossetia from Georgian aggression.[37] After 2008, but especially after Russia's annexation of Crimea in March 2014, Vladimir Putin voiced greater support for the separation of both Abkhazia and South Ossetia from Georgia and moved to unite them to Russia. This projection of Russian power was not entirely grasped in Washington during the Russo-Georgian conflict in 2008 until it was repeated in Ukraine in 2014.

Around the time of the Crimean annexation, Putin stepped up efforts to bring the presidents of Azerbaijan and Armenia together to discuss the Mountainous Karabagh stalemate, even as Armenia extended its military agreement with Russia permitting Russian forces the use of Armenian bases until 2044. Russia is positioned to hold the Karabagh conflict in stalemate and shift its weight from one side to the other to get economic or political concessions from the parties. Armenia, for example, joined the Russian-led Eurasian Economic Union in 2014, just after Ukrainian president Viktor Yanukovich was ousted from power for attempting to pursue the same path and pull away from closer ties with the European Union. Azerbaijan maintained neutrality between the Eurasian Economic Union and the EU, but in 2014–15 it increased its oil and gas sales to Russia and cooperated with Russia's deployment of naval forces in the Caspian Sea. Azerbaijan and Armenia petitioned for observer status in the Shanghai Cooperation Organisation (SCO), a Eurasian economic, political, and military organization dominated by Russia and China. It is in Russia's interest to maintain the tension in Karabagh, but giving too much to one side is not, nor is a resumption of the fighting.

Azerbaijan's central government has stressed its need to maintain independence and stability against external and internal threats. This argument, used to justify arrests of domestic critics, has been articulated more often since Russian interference in Ukraine and the seizure of Crimea in March 2014. Azerbaijani analysts have said that Russia is the main threat to independence and resolution in Karabagh, even as Ilham Aliyev visited Moscow and described the two countries' friendship. Also during 2013–14, the Aliyev regime copied Russia's laws banning and restricting the freedom of operation of nongovernmental organizations (NGOs), and employed Russian rhetoric as Baku cracked down on civil society, calling Aliyev's critics "agents" of foreign entities. Since late 2003, when Ilham Aliyev succeeded his father Heydar as president, pressure against critics in the opposition press and human rights activists has increased. During 2013–14, after the Council of Europe (CoE) rejected a 2013 report by its own delegation on political prisoners in Azerbaijan, Ilham himself used that vote in the Parliamentary Assembly of the Council of Europe (PACE) as proof that Azerbaijan "has no political prisoners."[38] The Aliyev regime used the defense of independence and stability argument as justification for a brutal crackdown on dissenters, human rights defenders, NGOs, and journalists. The list of jailed activists, mostly intellectuals of all ages and professions, is a "who's who" of leading human rights defenders, journalists and bloggers, and NGO leaders. The language of regime spokespersons against the opposition is similar to that used in Josef Stalin's purges in 1937: enemies had "sunk deep roots" or "made a nest" in assorted institutions.[39]

Although Azerbaijan's 1995 Constitution specifies separation of powers, the government is centralized in a presidency that effectively dominates other branches of government. The constitutional amendments of 2016 will assure greater presidential power, including the right to dissolve the parliament.[40] Since 1993, none of Azerbaijan's elections has been judged "free and fair" by international observers such as the OSCE's Office for Democratic Institutions and Human Rights (OSCE/ODIHR) and Western embassies, including that of the United States. The legislative body, the Milli Majlis, has been dominated by the ruling New Azerbaijan Party (Yeni Azerbaijan Partiyası, YAP) since its founder, Heydar Aliyev, returned to power in 1993. But until 2010, the major opposition parties—the Azerbaijan Popular Front Party (Azərbaycan Xalq Cebhesinin Partiyası, AXCP) and Yeni Müsavat—were allowed a dozen or more deputies in each tainted election. Since 2010, however, even the minor representation of this opposition has been eliminated. The nominal opposition parties and the "independent" deputies are in fact YAP supporters. The Milli Majlis therefore has become a perfectly compliant instrument of the regime, repeating its official priorities in its official language. In late May 2014, the legislature introduced amendments to the law on citizenship, defining reasons that would justify stripping an individual of her or his Azerbaijani citizenship. Among the new reasons for depriving an individual of citizenship is that "a citizen of the Azerbaijan Republic behaves [in a way that is] damaging to state security."[41] The wording of this provision opens the door to a wide interpretation of behavior that may lead to loss of citizenship—in apparent contradiction to Article 53 of the Azerbaijani Constitution, which prohibits the stripping of citizenship.[42]

The Azerbaijani government's power is enabled by its great wealth from hydrocarbon resources, high-quality light crude oil and natural gas. Oil is its source of fame in the world and supports its independence and security. Postindependence exploration, extraction, and pipeline construction deals brought tens of millions of dollars and thousands of foreign businessmen into Baku in an "oil rush" reminiscent of the nineteenth-century oil boom that first Westernized the capital. The city has again been transformed from its Soviet-era disrepair; by 2014, it was a showcase, with restored historic buildings, glass skyscrapers, upscale shops, and international businesses from Hilton to Maserati. Existing contracts and the promise of future natural gas—oil production has declined from its peak in 2010—link Azerbaijan not merely to its neighbors but to the global economy. Gas will go through a future pipeline across Turkey, the first portion of which runs parallel to the oil-carrying Baku–Tbilisi–Ceyhan (BTC) pipeline that was completed in 2005. European customers hope that gas through TANAP (Trans-Anatolian Natural Gas Pipeline) and TAP (Trans-Adriatic Pipeline) will offset their reliance on Russian gas.

In addition to being a source of great wealth, the oil industry has been a source of trouble for Azerbaijan—economically, socially, and politically. Overseas investors' emphasis on the development of the energy sector drew resources and government attention away from the country's languishing Soviet-era industries and much-needed agricultural modernization projects. Azerbaijan remains vulnerable to the so-called Dutch disease: an imbalance of investment in the energy sector while other industries, including the manufacture and production of consumer goods and agricultural products on which the population relies, are left to languish. Social support programs such as pensions remain low, leading to a wide gap between those who benefit from the energy sector and its supporting industries and services on the one hand and the lingering number of poor on the other.[43]

Moreover, oil money brought the value of corruption to new heights. Corruption makes products and services more expensive, and bottles up money in unproductive endeavors like luxury imports or gambling, rather than supporting industry or infrastructure. It damages the business climate.[44] Even though oil money has flooded into Azerbaijan under the presidency of Ilham Aliyev, he has put only just enough money into politically sensitive work such as IDP relocation and economically necessary improvements such as road and bridge construction to stave off unrest among the majority. Initially, pensions, state salaries, and health care funding grew, but since about 2006 they have not kept pace with the increased costs of living. Corruption in ruling circles is a taboo subject for investigators, but a few investigative reporters have violated that taboo since 2010.[45] These reports indicate stunning levels of theft, fraud, bribery, money laundering, and skimming from state coffers. Transparency International consistently rates Azerbaijan among the world's most corrupt regimes: in 2014, it was placed in a seven-way tie for 126th place (of 174 countries) with Gambia, Honduras, Kazakhstan, Nepal, Pakistan, and Togo.[46]

At the top of the political pyramid sits President Ilham Aliyev. Son of the previous president, Heydar Aliyev, Ilham came into office in 2003 at age forty-one. He inherited his father's advisers, most of whom were Soviet-era politicos who had survived the brief anticommunist period around independence and returned to power when Heydar became president in mid-1993. Ilham had a playboy image. He headed Azerbaijan's National Olympic Committee and was a vice president of the State Oil Company of the Azerbaijan Republic (SOCAR). He had not been groomed for the presidency until late in his father's life. In 2003, he became head of the ruling party YAP when his father fell ill, was then appointed as prime minister and became candidate for president. He was declared the winner of tainted elections (detailed in chapter 3) in the fall of 2003. As president, Ilham not only succeeded his father, who died in December 2003, but created a cult of personality around the deceased "National Leader" to legitimate his own succession. Huge posters around Baku show the son obediently listening as his father seems to advise him from beyond the grave. Reelected in 2008, Ilham retained most of his father's advisers, most significantly the old Soviet "crocodiles"[47] led by Ramiz Mehdiyev, the chief of the president's staff. Before his third term began in 2013, made possible by a change in the Constitution in 2009, Ilham had begun to crack down on civil society to a degree that his father had not. Probably frightened by the color revolutions—especially Georgia's Rose Revolution in 2003 and Ukraine's Orange Revolution in 2004—and the 2011 Arab Spring, he went after bloggers and critics in their twenties and thirties. Laws against NGOs in 2012–14 (see chapters 3 and 5) provided a basis for prosecutions and arrests, even as the Azerbaijani government maintained that it was "a rule of law state." As more and more human rights defenders and journalists went to jail, and reports of torture and deprivation of medical care increased, government spokesmen stressed Azerbaijan's business climate, its strategic partnership with the United States in the war on terror, and its role in European energy security.

The uptick in repression of 2014 has been widely denounced, especially as Azerbaijan chaired the CoE Committee of Ministers from May to November of that year. The European Parliament adopted a resolution in September recognizing the worsening of the human rights situation over the last five years. The United Nations Subcommittee on Human Rights cut short a fall 2014 visit to Azerbaijan because its members were barred from visiting "places of detention" to which they had been promised access. In December, the US State Department called for an end to restrictions on civil society after the arrest of investigative journalist Khadija Ismayilova, a reporter for US-funded Radio Liberty. The United States expressed concern that Azerbaijan was not living up to its international commitments in human rights. The Radio Liberty office in Baku was raided and closed two weeks after her arrest.

The Ismayilova case illustrates the complexity of Azerbaijan's position with regard to its foreign and domestic policy, particularly toward the United States. Although such bodies as the CoE and the United States have framed criticism of tainted elections and human rights violations in terms of fulfilling obligations that Azerbaijan assumed when it joined international institutions (including the CoE), Azerbaijani government spokesmen have long charged that such Western criticism constitutes interference in Azerbaijan's internal affairs. As the crackdown on civil society grew worse in the aftermath of the Russian invasion of Ukraine and seizure of Crimea, the rhetoric from Baku became sharper.[48]

Recently, Azerbaijan government representatives and individuals close to the regime increasingly have said that the West uses a "double standard" in assessing Azerbaijan. The speaker of the Milli Majlis accused the European Parliament of having such a "double standard," and Ramiz Mehdiyev accused critical journalists and NGOs of being "agents" of the United States.[49] More worrying, Mehdiyev and President Aliyev himself have used language similar to that used by Russia in accusing the United States and the EU of fomenting unrest in Ukraine as a means to overthrow the pro-Russian Yanukovich government. In an article released on December 4, 2014, Mehdiyev claimed that the United States was engaging in "colonialism." He also said that employees of the local Radio Liberty station were working for "patrons abroad"—a thinly veiled reference to the United States—and therefore were committing treason. This insinuation is especially ominous, since imprisoned journalists like Khadija Ismayilova would face more severe penalties if they were to be charged with treason rather than with lesser crimes such as libel.

Azerbaijan also seems to be increasing its tilt toward Russia. On a December 2014 visit to Moscow, President Aliyev said that Azerbaijan and Russia plan to enhance their relationship in areas of finance, transportation, and even culture and education. That much was reported in the proregime press in Azerbaijan. The Azerbaijani press did not report Aliyev's charge that "failed policies," apparently those of the United States, were responsible for the rise of extremist groups, including the Islamic State.

Why Should the United States Care about Azerbaijan?

At first glance, Azerbaijan's location as the only state bordering both Russia and Iran suggests its significance in any US geostrategic calculation for both the Middle East and the eastern edges of Europe, as defined by State Department and US military geographic divisions.[50] Azerbaijan can facilitate or obstruct the passage of drugs, weapons, terrorists, human cargo, money or precious minerals and gems, nuclear material, and other commodities or people between Iran and Russia. Its military bases can ease or block US passage to central or south Asia as the northern supply route to coalition forces in Afghanistan. As a hydrocarbon-rich state, it produces oil and natural gas for global markets, though mostly for US allies in Europe and for Israel, and the pipeline system runs through neighboring Georgia and Turkey, skirting long-time US adversaries Russia and Iran.[51]

Azerbaijan's biggest problem, the war in Mountainous Karabagh and occupation of about 14 percent of its territory by Armenian forces, is relevant to US security considerations. Locally, the continued state of war is economically unproductive and drains both countries' economies. Azerbaijan continues to divert its income to weapons, and Armenia supports the impoverished occupied zone. The war is also politically destabilizing because it provides an opening for outside manipulation and enables each government to use the state of war as an excuse to avoid domestic reform and quash internal critics, both of which can enhance popular discontent with the existing regimes. Without a political settlement, all parties run the risk that Azerbaijan will actually use the weapons it has amassed in recent years. Renewed fighting with more lethal and numerous weapons is likely to devastate both countries' populations and land, and could draw in neighboring states like Iran and Turkey, as well as nonstate actors like the Islamic State, leading to a wider regional war in a volatile area.[52]

Azerbaijan's legacy as a secular society (and secular state) with expanding education and use of English, at least among a certain stratum of youth, makes it a potentially suitable partner in this region for US commercial, military, and cultural cooperation. If Azerbaijan were to improve its record on political and electoral democratization, openness of civil society, and human rights, the partnership would appear far more viable. It is, therefore, in US interests to foster such democratization in Azerbaijan and bring it more fully into the Western cultural and political sphere. When US relations with Russia and Iran are strained, Azerbaijan's currency rises in Washington. Conversely, the

Obama administration's 2009 "reset" of relations with Moscow, less than a year after Russia's invasion of Georgia, implied a decline in the importance of the entire south Caucasus region from a US strategic perspective. As the United States improves relations with Iran based on the nuclear agreement of 2015 under President Hassan Rouhani, Azerbaijan seems less important than its larger neighbor. When Iranian oil comes back onto world markets, the quantity may dwarf Azerbaijan's contribution. Given the many advantages of improved relations with Russia and Iran, a realist might argue that it makes sense for the United States to downgrade Azerbaijan in its regional strategic calculus. To say this is shortsighted. Russia has consistent ambitions, and it is not in US interests to see expanded Russian power on the edge of the Middle East, with Azerbaijan's oil and gas resources contributing to Russian control. Good relations, like bad ones, are temporary, and may even be brief. The 2016 resurgence of plans for the Russian-Iranian transit corridor, in which Azerbaijan is a crucial link, should sharpen Washington's attention to Russian power in the Middle East and the implications of relations among Tehran, Baku, Moscow, and Ankara.[53]

Why Should Azerbaijan Incline toward the West?

A more surprising question may well be why Azerbaijan should incline toward the West rather than Russia, especially after the events of 2014–15. For many years, it seemed certain that Azerbaijan's post-Soviet leadership saw itself as a potential model for a secular state with a Muslim population, one that could maintain good relations with the West and interact with numerous international and European institutions. Abulfez Elchibey certainly intended to join the West, and Heydar Aliyev stated his intention to bring Azerbaijan into Europe. In many respects, post-Soviet Azerbaijan looked like Turkey, or at least like Turkey before the advent of conservative President Recep Tayyib Erdoğan. But Western pressure for observance of human rights and democratization of political processes, pressure which always rankled in Baku, was over time openly criticized. Always sensitive to an imagined "double standard," official and quasiofficial voices have recently used the phrase to challenge Western leaders.[54] Saudi Arabia, to take one counterexample, has human rights violations and political prisoners, but the United States treats the kingdom as a close ally. The United States itself is taken to task in every Amnesty International annual report because most US states still have the death penalty. In October 2014, an Azerbaijani in the presidential apparatus wrote a position paper claiming that the United States ought to be and act more grateful toward Azerbaijan for its strategic partnership in the war on terror and energy security.[55] Such gratitude would take the form of US reevaluation of its policies in the region, without which Azerbaijan would incline more toward other international partners, including Russia. In December of that same year, President Ilham Aliyev lauded the possibilities of improved Azerbaijani-Russian relations for trade, tourism, transportation, energy, and even education; he referred to Russia as a "friend country."[56]

Azerbaijan, like any state, is most greatly concerned with maintaining its independence and security, including its territorial integrity. As the only state bordering both Russia and Iran, any Azerbaijani government must seek a balance between the demands of these two powerful neighbors. The 2015–16 discussions on a north-south transit corridor to link Russia and Iran through Azerbaijan reflect more than balancing demands; the project will militate toward political cooperation and bring commercial advantages. In contrast to oil-producing countries that suffer from low oil prices, Europe and the United States have much to offer in terms of markets, financial support, and military and technological systems. But the EU and NATO are far away, and the United States is farther still. The limited Western responses to Russian actions in Georgia in 2008 and the restrained military response to the Russian invasion of Ukraine, including the seizure and annexation of Crimea in 2014, illustrated to Baku that cultivating its Western partnership becomes more risky when its northern neighbor is more aggressive. Indeed, it would be sensible to make friends with Russia—the greatest threat to Azerbaijan's independence. Russia could disrupt Azerbaijan directly or, more likely, indirectly through Muslim extremists in Dagestan or the unresolved war in Mountainous Karabagh. After a cease-fire of more than twenty years, Azerbaijan is armed to the teeth. Its $5 billion defense budget (as of 2015) is larger than Armenia's entire state budget. Baku buys weapon systems from Turkey, Israel, and even Russia, despite Moscow's military cooperation treaty with Yerevan. Russia can use the Karabagh stalemate as leverage against Azerbaijan, because the conflict is not "frozen," but simmering—and a slight increase of heat or pressure can cause it to boil.[57]

Such are the interests of state. But Azerbaijan's elites are also oligarchs with millions, perhaps billions of dollars of private wealth. For them, the West has other advantages beyond military or financial state-to-state aid. Western countries offer legal protection of person and property, and high living standards and privacy for the elites who can afford them. The United Kingdom ranks first among countries in which the world's super-rich will try to gain second citizenship, or primary citizenship for their children.[58] Thus, the interests of elites in cases like that of Azerbaijan must be regarded as separate from the interests of the country and society. In case of revolution, oligarchs want an exit strategy that preserves not only their lives but also their wealth and privilege. These calculations are unspoken, hidden behind the official rhetoric about preservation of statehood and independence.

Using the defense of independence argument, the Aliyev regime has quashed all critics, from investigative journalists to civil society activists and human rights defenders. Yet it uses the rhetoric of human rights and democracy, claiming that it is a democracy with fair elections, separation of powers, and the rule of law. Western criticism angers the regime, but Western silence regarding elections and arrests angers the population and disappoints the prodemocracy forces, weakening the West's image and ability to project soft power. Azerbaijan remains a puzzle, important to the West for energy and security reasons but moving farther from democratic values articulated not only by the Popular Front but also by Heydar Aliyev. How did Azerbaijan's post-Soviet transition come to this point? What were the decisions, the leaders, and the forces that brought the restive but promising Azerbaijan of the early 1990s to its current place of wealth, corruption, and authoritarian rule? If we return to the beginning, we must examine the impact of the open wound: the war in Mountainous Karabagh.

2

The Open Wound: Mountainous Karabagh and National Consciousness

Every shift of a kilometer on the map of the Nagorny-Karabagh war altered people's lives forever.

—Thomas de Waal, *Black Garden* (rev. ed.), 235

The name "Karabagh" is a battle cry, and the conflict there remains an open wound. For Azerbaijan in the late Soviet period, Armenia's challenge to Azerbaijan's possession of this region was the most powerful engine of political change. It drove thousands of ordinary Azerbaijani citizens into public squares, time after time, to demand that local communist party leaders defend their land and their national honor. It triggered the secret and risky anticommunist meetings in the Academy of Sciences that led to the founding of the Popular Front. Passions around Karabagh were so great and so widely shared that the members of the rubber-stamp Supreme Soviet of the Azerbaijan Soviet Socialist Republic risked their careers and personal independence by openly opposing the communist party and denouncing party leaders' inaction in regime newspapers. Leading scholars and writers refused a direct order from the Azerbaijan Communist Party first secretary to write in favor of relinquishing the region to Armenia, and instead published an argument that the land was rightfully a part of Azerbaijan.[1] Without the Karabagh conflict, it is impossible to envision a unified challenge to communist party rule in Azerbaijan in the late 1980s. As the conflict became a war, it focused cultural and intellectual currents and seared a national identity into the Azerbaijani consciousness that had been only partly formed under Soviet-era repressions.

This chapter is not a recapitulation of the struggle, the war, or the complex conflicting claims to Mountainous Karabagh. (In the mid-1990s, I wrote several lengthy articles about the early years of this problem,[2] and other outside specialists, notably Thomas de Waal,[3] have written in-depth, book-length accounts. Armenian and Azerbaijani publicists, scholars, journalists, commentators, bloggers, and others have produced an enormous quantity of material of varying quality.) Rather than go over old ground, this chapter examines the impact of the perceptions and policies around the Karabagh problem on Azerbaijanis, and on Azerbaijan as a country, from the late 1980s until the cease-fire was signed in May 1994. It ends with a brief consideration of significant negotiations that followed.

Mountainous Karabagh—the word *karabagh* literally meaning "black garden"—has been known in the West by the Russian form "Nagorno-Karabagh" from the Soviet-era Nagorno-Karabagh Autonomous Region (*oblast*), which had been created in western Azerbaijan to accommodate the region's concentrated ethnic Armenian population residing there.[4] Even though the autonomous region nominally had been created to protect the rights of the Armenian minority, this Soviet structure allowed the center to maintain leverage over both sides in case of future disputes over such core issues as autonomy.[5] From the NKAR's establishment in the early 1920s, both Azerbaijani and Armenian communist leaders disagreed about its existence as an autonomous region, its status, and its level of autonomy. The disposition of this region was part of a larger territorial settlement concerning three regions—Nakhjivan, Zangezur, and Mountainous Karabagh—claimed by both of the formerly independent neighbors that came under Soviet rule in 1920. Their claims on territory were not "ancient," but were part of the modern national movements in the Caucasus, with their notion of the sacredness of native soil. Wartime population displacement changed some of the concentrations of ethno-national groups from the distributions that had been mapped in the Russian Imperial census of 1897. The presence of Ottoman troops in 1918, the diplomatic relations between the Turkish national (Kemalist) movement and the Bolsheviks, and other international factors affected population movement and political claims to land. In the early 1920s, Nakhjivan became part of Azerbaijan,[6] though it is separated from the main portion of Azerbaijan by Zangezur—which in turn went to Armenia. The Mountainous Karabagh region also went to Azerbaijan and was later defined as the NKAR, with cultural autonomy for the Armenian population. It was administered by a mostly Armenian Communist Party organization.[7]

Armenians reportedly challenged Azerbaijan's possession of the NKAR several times during the Soviet period, but initiatives to make territorial changes were quashed by the central Soviet leadership. In the Gorbachev era, however, Moscow's campaigns for openness (glasnost) and political and economic restructuring (perestroika) seemed to open the door to precisely such revisions of status. In 1986, early in the Gorbachev period, a group of Armenian intellectuals began to circulate a petition calling for the NKAR to be transferred to Armenia, and their demands resonated deeply within the Armenian SSR and among the Armenian portion of the population of the NKAR. In Armenia, scholars wrote historical treatises justifying Armenian claims to the NKAR. Azerbaijani Academy of Sciences scholars responded in kind.[8] The petition movement, the *New York Times* reported in 1988, "inadvertently unleashed" a storm that led to "large-scale civil disobedience, murderous clashes between two ancient peoples."[9] Azerbaijanis living in Armenia fled in "refugee waves, consisting of tens of thousands of people" who arrived in Baku in January 1988. Two more such waves followed. In February, mob attacks on Armenians in the Azerbaijani industrial city of Sumgayit involved the resettled Azerbaijanis who had been forced out of homes in Armenia. Locally stationed Soviet Ministry of Interior troops did not intervene to protect the Armenians or stop the violence until the third day,[10] adding to the emerging belief that the Soviet government was manipulating the conflict to better "divide and rule" the restive populations of its republics or, more subtly, to deflect their anger with Moscow for its failure to settle the dispute. The name "Sumgayit," evoking the dozens of lives lost there, became a touchstone for conflict escalation in Armenian parlance as the words "ethnic cleansing" did for Azerbaijanis.

The Karabagh movement had gained substantial momentum with the support of Armenians in Gorbachev's inner circle, including his economic adviser Abel Aganbegian. It escalated further following former AzCP first secretary Heydar Aliyev's removal from the Soviet Politburo in 1987. Without Aliyev in Moscow, there was no voice at the top to offset the Armenian influence. In November 1987, after Aliyev returned to Azerbaijan, Aganbegian addressed a French-Armenian group in Paris, saying that the NKAR ought to belong to Armenia—a provocative comment that was then reported in the French Communist Party newspaper *L'Humanité*.[11]

Azerbaijanis were taken by surprise by the Karabagh movement in Armenia.[12] The two groups had shared the region for generations and, in the cities and towns, Armenians and Azerbaijanis were often neighbors. One newly displaced group of internally displaced persons (IDPs)[13] from Mountainous Karabagh was certain that their longtime Armenian neighbors could not have been responsible for driving them from their homes. "We ate from the same bowl," said several IDPs from Shusha, interviewed in makeshift refugee camps in 1992.[14] They agreed that if they went back to their homes "tomorrow," they could reconcile with their old Armenian neighbors. They blamed outsiders, agitators from Armenia or from abroad, for the conflict. Their personal views were identical to the foundational view of all post-Soviet Azerbaijani governments—that the war itself was not a secession movement, as the Armenians contend, but an invasion by outside Armenian forces with diaspora support in concert with some Karabagh Armenians. Thus, even the parties' views of the recent origins of the war are at odds.

Because official news about the conflict was limited, Azerbaijanis reacted to the rumors they had heard and to the visible influx of displaced Azerbaijanis. Most people were not initially aware of the substance of complaints from Armenians that Azerbaijan's government had discriminated against the NKAR's cultural autonomy, underfunding areas such as education and health care. When these charges became known, the Azerbaijanis were both puzzled and angry. The popular impression among Azerbaijanis who had visited Shusha or other parts of Mountainous Karabagh was that the Armenian language, to take one example, was not only protected but privileged. Street signs were in Russian and Armenian but not in Azerbaijani, even though the NKAR was part of Azerbaijan. And in material terms, the NKAR seemed to be on the same level as the rest of Azerbaijan. When Azerbaijani scholars finally published a breakdown of official Soviet statistics on such "cultural indicators" as library books and hospital beds per capita, the data showed a mixed picture. The NKAR numbers were slightly better on some indicators (e.g., the number of children enrolled in preschool) than they were for Azerbaijan, but worse than both Azerbaijan and Armenia in other areas. For instance, there were 29 doctors for every 10,000 people in the NKAR, compared with just over 38 per 10,000 in both Armenia and the rest of Azerbaijan.[15] In addition, television broadcasting from Armenia was unavailable in the NKAR—probably because of the region's mountainous terrain.

The main issue was the Armenian charge of "historical injustice" in the placing of Mountainous Karabagh inside Azerbaijan at all. Moreover, in the standardized teaching of history, Armenians felt that their own history was not honored and properly studied. On these matters, the discussions around the petition drive in the late 1980s had provided Armenians with an extensive political education and language of discourse to which there was no parallel in Azerbaijan. The Azerbaijanis began by arguing that the real injustice was the Armenian claim against Azerbaijani land that they had shared with the Armenians. Conflicting historical claims went back not merely to the early 1920s—though the events of that period were hotly contested—or to the period of independence when both the Armenian and Azerbaijani republics had claimed Mountainous Karabagh and other territories. Scholars and writers on both sides looked back to earlier times. The nineteenth century was a well-known time of cultural flowering for the major nationalities of the Caucasus. Ordinary Azerbaijanis might not have realized that the Armenians, too, had shared the land of Mountainous Karabagh and simultaneously nurtured their own cultural awakenings in its cities, specifically Shusha (Shushi, in Armenian) and Khankendi (Stepanakert). But Azerbaijanis could name their "own" poets and composers who came from Mountainous Karabagh, from the woman poet Natavan to the great composer of opera and operetta Uzeir Hadjibeyli.[16] Going back before these more popularly accessible times, scholars argued over medieval, pre-Islamic, and even pre-Christian kingdom borders and population distribution. As scholars disputed early maps and documents and argued points of pre-Islamic Christian history in the south Caucasus, the rest of both populations went to the bottom line: each concluded that Mountainous Karabagh was their own historic patrimony, that the neighboring group was "falsifying" history, and that possessing this land was necessary to right a past historical wrong.

The historical claims are neither fabricated nor trivial. The impact of historical memory, documentable or not, is always constructed, meaning that it is an articulated narrative based on choices about elements to emphasize or exclude. Historical memory or beliefs about the past are more immediate and compelling in the Caucasus than in the United States. Foreign mediators to the dispute, working in the region since the creation of the CSCE (later OSCE) Minsk Group in 1992, had to learn to be aware of the historical sensitivities of the conflict. Both sides have a case to make, and both are quick to vilify those who concede any validity to the other. The use of history as a guide to "just resolution" of the Karabagh conflict has not lessened in more than two decades. It has been amplified and expanded to include toxic rhetoric beyond the issue itself to demonize entire peoples. In 2012, the Institute for

War and Peace Reporting published a study on history textbooks in Armenia and Azerbaijan.[17] The report, coauthored by an Armenian and an Azerbaijani, revealed that recently published textbooks portrayed each country's history in intensely nationalistic terms, selectively highlighting past glories and accusing the neighboring people of evil intentions and acts. The Armenian texts said that the NKAR had wrongly been given to Azerbaijan, and described massacres of Armenians. The Azerbaijani texts described massacres of Azerbaijanis by Armenians who were called "terrorists" and "fascists." Students interviewed for the report faithfully reflected the hatred for the other country written in the books. Even authors and Ministry of Education spokespersons said that the texts were telling the truth, and that using nonaccusatory language in the textbooks would be teaching inaccurate history. This development does not bode well for improved relations or a future settlement.

Mountainous Karabagh and the Azerbaijan Popular Front

Before the Azerbaijan Popular Front was formed, noncommunist opposition groups emerged in the late 1980s around issues of historic and environmental preservation. The focal point of these movements called for the protection of national treasures, including mosques, bridges, inscriptions, cemeteries, and nature preserves. At first, the monuments and natural habitat in Karabagh were merely included in these lists of national treasures, but soon they came to the foreground. In the summer of 1988, news spread that forests in the Topkhana nature preserve[18] in Mountainous Karabagh were to be cut down, purportedly to build an Armenian aluminum factory. This news had unexpected repercussions for Azerbaijani society and for the AzCP authorities. It fed an unauthorized demonstration in November 1988 in front of the government building in Baku on Lenin Square, dubbed Freedom Square, a name made official in 1991. Tens of thousands of ordinary people demonstrated for several days against a range of perceived abuses of Azerbaijani historical and natural resources and, more significantly, against AzCP inaction in the face of Armenian demands for the transfer of the NKAR. In that demonstration, nonparty intellectual and artistic leaders came to prominence. Many of them would later form the Popular Front. Throughout Azerbaijan, popular anger had already been fueled by rumors that Mikhail Gorbachev favored the Armenians and was disposed to support their demand for the territorial change, regardless of provisions in the Soviet Constitution that required the consent of both republics.[19]

The Topkhana issue in particular became an emotional and psychological turning point for Azerbaijan. Whether the proposed building was a factory or a less environmentally harmful structure seems to have been beside the point.[20] The interior journey of many people was articulated by an Azerbaijani college student as he recalled his thoughts and those of his family and friends.[21] Azar Panakhli began with his feeling of resentment about cutting of trees of Azerbaijan for the benefit of "outsiders." He lamented, with drama, the loss of oaks that were said to be 300 years old. He identified the forest as a symbol of

the best, the noblest and the highest level of our culture. . . . It's the birthplace of so many cultural giants—artists, writers, poets, playwrights, musicians, composers, and intellectuals. And so the land has become sacred to us. . . . Outsiders had challenged our authority over our own resources—both physical and cultural.

Panakhli took another step from the idea that Armenians cut "Azerbaijani forests" to a wider view of Azerbaijan's status in the Soviet Union:

When those axes started cutting the trees, the steel blades hacked and brutalized our own souls. . . . And in that pain, a strange phenomenon began to emerge. We started turning inward to examine our own reality. . . . Instead of Topkhana, we started questioning many things. Why, for example, were we being dominated? Why were we being discriminated against? Who was the real enemy? What were the real obstacles to our freedom and independence? . . .

We had grown up believing that we were one nation—the Soviet nation, and one people—primarily Soviet. To be Azerbaijani was to be weaker, somehow inferior, to being Soviet. The truth is, we didn't even know who we were. We had never been taught our own Azeri history except when events paralleled Soviet interests. In literature, our writers were always scrutinized through Soviet lenses. . . . But after Topkhana, we realized there was no such thing as a Soviet people. . . . No one but our own people could understand that Topkhana symbolized more than trees; it was our own identity, our own being.

This narrative is a distillation of the many issues that led Soviet citizens to question and then reject Soviet rule and its ideology. Regime propaganda proclaimed that the Soviet people were building a glorious future. Even after

Stalin's time and into the stagnation of the Brezhnev era, many thought that they were sacrificing "narrow" national interests or the freedom to criticize, but most expected protection and an improved standard of living in return. For the Azerbaijanis, that equation was broken by the Karabagh phenomenon, not only by Armenian demands but also by the inaction of the authorities— the Azerbaijani and Soviet communist parties and the central government in Moscow. Similarly, for the Armenians, the inaction of authorities led to charges that Gorbachev was "pro-Azerbaijani." The conflict may have begun with specific issues, numbers, and examples, but it soon transformed into an emotional, cultural-national typhoon.

The Azerbaijani intellectuals at the November 1988 demonstrations felt and saw this process of disillusionment unfold, and some manipulated it. Many of the prominent speakers in the demonstrations were arrested for short periods, but by the summer of 1989 they were ready to organize themselves: this was the origin of the Popular Front. (See chapter 3 for a more detailed account of the Popular Front and its evolution.) One of the pillars of their organization was the defense of the NKAR and the Azerbaijani historical narrative that underlay it. As intellectuals, and politically powerless ones at that, they had no weapon other than their pens. In the ensuing months and years, opposition groups urged the party and state to defend Azerbaijan's possession of the NKAR and to defend Azerbaijan's historical claims and "national honor" against Armenian accusations and pressure on the ground. But Azerbaijan had no armed force. From the late 1980s through the early 1990s, fighting in and around the NKAR gradually escalated from small-scale groups of mostly local men, without military training and armed only with hunting rifles, to larger units with better weapons smuggled from abroad or acquired from the disintegrating Soviet armed forces that began to sell or abandon their weapons as discipline broke down.

Young Azerbaijanis, an estimated 100,000 of them between 1991 and 1993, volunteered to fight in this environment. They had no training, discipline, or leadership. Many were killed by "friendly fire." Like most peoples from the Central Asian Soviet republics, Azerbaijanis had been placed overwhelmingly in construction battalions (*stroibat*) in the Soviet Army, and therefore they had little real military training. Despite their unpreparedness, they went to fight, moved by a sense of resentment at the exploitation of their natural resources and the suppression of their history. In her study of youth, Nadia Diuk tells the story of a young man who learned only at age sixteen that Azerbaijan had formerly been independent. Like Azar Panakhli, other university students in Baku conflated the Karabagh dispute with Soviet mistreatment of the Azerbaijanis as a nation.[22]

By the time the Popular Front gained power in early June 1992, Mountainous Karabagh had declared independence from post-Soviet Azerbaijan, and much of it was in Armenian hands. The Popular Front government launched a couple of successful offensives and retook northern Karabagh during the summer and fall of 1992, but the tide turned against their poorly trained and ill-equipped forces in 1993. When the cease-fire was finally signed in the Bishkek Protocol of May 1994, Armenian forces controlled all of the land that constituted the former NKAR, as well as five further regions and parts of two others to the south and west of the NKAR.[23] According to official Azerbaijani statements, the proportion of Armenian-occupied Azerbaijani territory is given as 20 percent, but Thomas de Waal has calculated the size of the occupied land as 11,803 square kilometers (4557 square miles) or "13.63 percent of de jure Azerbaijan."[24]

More important than the percentage of Azerbaijan's occupied territory is its strategic and economic significance. The entire area, denuded of the Azerbaijani population, was de facto joined to Armenia by 1994. The fringe of land along the east and north became a wasteland buffer along the Line of Contact. Many outside observers initially saw these areas as potential bargaining chips for Armenia to swap for Mountainous Karabagh itself, but their military use turned them into vital buffer zones. Moreover, the Armenian conception of Artsakh—their name for the region—includes the occupied areas, and thus, for the Armenians, it is part of their historic claim. The swath of land south of the former NKAR along the Iranian border between Nakhjivan and the rest of Azerbaijan was more than doubled, further isolating Nakhjivan and consolidating Armenia's land link to Iran. (Since 1988, the Armenian authorities had blockaded the railroad across Armenian Zangezur into Nakhjivan.) The Azerbaijanis had lost on the battlefield and had been humiliated in the eyes of the world. The Bishkek Protocol established the cease-fire and consolidated this status, giving both sides some relief from the killing and a chance to deal with challenges of economic development. From this breathing space, Azerbaijan benefited greatly.

"Victimhood" Emerges in Azerbaijan

Perhaps it began with the 1992 Khojaly massacre. Perhaps it began earlier with a specific battlefield loss, or with the torrents of refugees. In any case, the cumulative effects of losses of life and land in Karabagh sparked a sense of victimhood among Azerbaijanis. This was new to Azerbaijan. But when President Heydar Aliyev declared in 1998 that March 31 henceforth would be commemorated as Azerbaijan's Genocide Day, he was able to invoke such widely separate events as the March 1918 massacres of Azerbaijanis in Baku under the Baku Commune; the Stalin-era purges of 1937; the Soviet invasion of Baku in 1990 ("Black January"); and the litany from Karabagh, including the overrunning of Shusha, the Khojaly massacre, and the destruction of Kelbajar in 1993. The specter of stranded IDPs languishing in train cars and temporary shelters was always in the public eye. The losses were real, but the construction of victimhood was a strategy. The use of the term "genocide" was intended to demonstrate that Azerbaijanis had suffered deliberate murders that others had failed to acknowledge, and that therefore deserved recognition and perhaps some form of compensation for their losses.

In March 2000, President Aliyev's adviser on ethnic issues announced that the number of Azerbaijanis killed, specifically by Armenians, in the twentieth century was "the astonishing figure" of 2.5 million. This, wrote Tom de Waal, "initiated a duel of the martyred nations."[25] The rhetoric of victimhood was sounded thereafter in the domestic press and sometimes in material for foreigners, especially in Western countries. For years, the Azerbaijani Embassy in Washington has commemorated the Khojaly massacre of February 1992, when nearly 500 Azerbaijanis, from infants to the elderly, were killed one night during escape through a "safe corridor."[26] The tragedy was even advertised broadly in public spaces. In 2012, small ads commemorating the Khojaly massacre were placed on buses in the Washington Metropolitan Area Transit system; in 2015, enormous ads were plastered throughout Metro stations and on the exteriors of city buses. As research on victimhood shows, a group may define its "collective victimhood" narrowly with regard only to specific losses without seeing itself as a victim in general. This is "conflict event victimhood," such as the United States experienced after the bombing of Pearl Harbor in 1941 or the September 11 attacks in 2001. But if the focus is on a longer process of repeated loss and suffering shared by society, and is believed to be inflicted intentionally—such as the Azerbaijani losses and casualties in the Karabagh war—the phenomenon is named "general conflict victimhood."[27]

Despite Azerbaijan's losses to the Bolsheviks in 1920, the suppression of prerevolutionary Azerbaijani culture, and the death and exiling of thousands during the 1920s and 1930s, this rhetoric of victimhood had previously not been used. Victimhood is more common among minority populations, but the Azerbaijanis remained a majority in their republic, though for decades they were outnumbered by Russians in Baku.[28] Perhaps the Soviet regime's positive themes about building a new future and a new "Soviet person" had masked or quashed feelings of victimhood in the past, or perhaps the atomization of Soviet society from fear of retribution for anti-Soviet views prevented people from having the conversations that would have cultivated and expressed a collective sense of victimhood. Now, Karabagh brought it out. The process of self-examination, questioning, and growing resentment described by then-student Azar Panakhli when speaking about Topkhana might have been repeated so many times, after so many losses, that the result was the emergence of "general conflict victimhood" in post-Soviet Azerbaijan. Different writers made use of victimhood in specific ways. Some made use of a "competitive" sense of victimhood, if only by implication, to signal that Armenians who exhibit the widest form of this phenomenon—"historical collective victimhood," based on their memory of long-term repressions—were not the only ones to suffer, and particularly not in Karabagh. The Azerbaijani regime clearly capitalized on the victimhood image, to the extent of launching a major advertising campaign in the US capital that focused on its tragic history.

Svante Cornell argues that the "culture of victimization" is amplified by Azerbaijan's perception of inequitable treatment by Western states. Azerbaijanis have referred to several examples of this inequality. A Western coalition liberated Kuwait after it was invaded by Saddam Hussein's Iraqi forces in August 1990, but the West did nothing to help Karabagh against Armenian invasion and occupation. Serbia's Slobodan Milošević was tried as a war criminal after ethnic cleansing in the Balkans in the early 1990s, but the Armenian leadership has not faced sanctions after ethnic cleansing inside and around the former NKAR. Rather, when the US Congress passed the Freedom Support Act in 1992 to provide aid to post-Soviet states, the bill included Section 907, a sanctions amendment that blamed Azerbaijan for aggression against Armenia and blocked aid to Azerbaijan.[29] This array of examples, compounded by the history of the repressions perpetuated within the first republic, may suggest an unfortunate movement by Azerbaijanis toward "historical collective victimhood." Although any level of victimhood may be used to justify retaliation against the enemy, the more layers of victimhood, the greater the risk that the layers will "feed each other, magnifying and perpetuating the experience of collective victimhood in a vicious cycle."[30]

Moreover, Azerbaijanis suggest that the West favors Armenia as a Christian state, using Section 907 as the first and best example. The amendment blocked the United States from providing government-to-government aid or training to Azerbaijan. But some other examples that Azerbaijanis cite as evidence of a so-called double standard do not sustain the notion that the West automatically will support Christian states against non-Christian states: the defense of Kuwait against Iraq (both Muslim); the prosecution of Slobodan Milošević for his genocidal efforts against the Muslim populations of the former Yugoslavia, among other crimes; longtime US support for both Israel and Saudi Arabia; and frequent tensions with "Christian" Russia. The perceived double standards are not really "double," but rather show the numerous variations in the *application* of standards on the basis of complex factors, including the issues involved, each country's relationship to the United States and its allies, and US domestic issues like ethnic groups and their lobbying efforts on Capitol Hill. Section 907 of the Freedom Support Act was a particular case of energetic lobbying by Armenian Americans, compounded by American lawmakers' lack of familiarity with the non-Russian parts of the Soviet Union, which had suddenly become independent countries.[31] It was a disastrous bit of legislation for many reasons. It launched the Azerbaijani notion of American prejudice against them, even as the United States sent aid to such demonstrably non-democratic post-Soviet states as Uzbekistan and Turkmenistan. It deprived Azerbaijan of useful instruction on writing new laws, setting up election procedures, and initiating judicial and constitutional reforms at a time when the state and society were most willing to make such changes. As a result, the United States lost an important opportunity to support Azerbaijan's development in a way that would have helped Azerbaijani society and the West, while illustrating the strengths of the American system.

The Simmering Cauldron

Outside mediation efforts on Mountainous Karabagh began with the Soviet collapse in 1991, when Russia, Kazakhstan, and Iran attempted to arrange cease-fires or negotiation meetings. When Armenia and Azerbaijan joined the CSCE (which would become the OSCE), that body began efforts at mediation that continued, despite lack of progress, for more than twenty years.[32] Hence, the term "frozen conflict" was applied to Karabagh, but it is surely more accurate to describe it as a simmering cauldron, with issues remaining hot and discussion continuing to be passionate. What factors might "turn up the fire" under this cauldron in order to make it boil and perhaps overflow?

The parties continue to invoke the major principles that they first embraced in 1991. Azerbaijan stressed the territorial integrity of existing states, and Armenia emphasized the right of self-determination of peoples. Even attempts to find an approach to negotiation foundered on the basic disagreements about the timing and status of the process: what would be the timing of the return of Azerbaijani IDPs and the withdrawal of Armenian forces from occupied districts outside the area of the former NKAR? Would Karabagh Armenians, now in de facto control, have a part in the negotiations (which would imply their legitimacy and permanence in power), or would they be represented by Armenia? What would be the eventual status of the region: an independent entity, or part of either Armenia or Azerbaijan? When and among whom would a referendum on final status be held? Over the twenty years of negotiations, at least one of the parties deemed that at least one of these points was so crucial to the larger issues as to be a "nonstarter," and progress was never made.

The OSCE tried to find resolution over and over again, especially through the Minsk Group, the body that was charged with addressing this issue. At the 1996 OSCE Lisbon Summit, three legal principles—territorial integrity, self-determination (described as the "highest degree of self-rule within Azerbaijan"), and the guaranteed security of Karabagh and its population—were proposed as the basis for a peaceful settlement process. These terms faced the challenges noted above, specifically on the final status of Mountainous Karabagh within Azerbaijan.[33] Between 1999 and 2001, negotiations were attempted by holding meetings of presidents Heydar Aliyev and Robert Kocharyan, which took place in Washington, Istanbul, Geneva, Davos, Moscow, Yalta, Paris, and Key West in 2001.[34] The last of these meetings was expected to produce results, but instead produced a crashing disappointment when there was no breakthrough. By 2004, the Minsk Group tried direct bilateral negotiations between the Azerbaijani and Armenian foreign ministers, a structure called the Prague Process. One commentator noted, "In 2004–2006 there was optimism about the window of opportunity to achieve a settlement between the election cycles in both countries (parliamentary elections in 2005 and the presidential elections in 2008 in Armenia and Azerbaijan)." A presidential meeting in Kazan in 2005 led to the Madrid Principles (2007), which strove to outline major steps to a resolution: return of territories surrounding the former NKAR, interim status for "Nagorno-Karabagh" with security guarantees and a corridor link to Armenia, future determination of status "through a legally binding expression of will," the IDP right of return, and international security guarantees including a "peacekeeping operation."[35] Again, disagreements over how to clarify timing issues, such as whether the return of IDPs would precede a referendum ("expression of will"), thwarted full agreement. The parties made no movement toward a resolution.[36]

The blame continued, and continues still. Perhaps predictably, mediators were blamed for failing to find or even impose a resolution. Some analysts noted that disagreement among the cochairs of the Minsk Group—namely the United States, France, and Russia—prevented them from cooperating fully in the peace negotiation efforts.[37] In his 2012 analysis of the conflict, former diplomat Wayne Merry answered such criticism:

> The underlying diplomatic reality is that mediators do not negotiate; mediators mediate. The parties to the conflict could negotiate, but have failed to do so in a serious way while using the Minsk Group as cover. . . . International mediation has enabled authorities in Baku and Yerevan to avoid their core responsibility to inform and educate their respective populations about the compromises required for a peace settlement.[38]

Rather, Merry argued, both sides clung to maximalist demands that could only be achieved by renewed war. And a renewed war would be "a siege" of greater lethality than the previous destructive war that produced 25,000 to 35,000 dead (among combatants, Azerbaijan's losses are estimated at 11,500, compared with 4,000 Armenians, with civilian losses believed to be proportionate), tens of thousands wounded, and more than a million refugees and IDPs on both sides. Moreover, major regional powers Russia, Iran, and Turkey could slide or be pulled into such a renewed war. Despite the frustrations of mediators, therefore, the goal of peaceful resolution is so urgent that the entire region has a stake in it.

Despite the cease-fire and the maintenance of all parties' original political positions, some conditions in Azerbaijan have changed in meaningful ways. Thanks to oil revenues and high oil prices until 2014, Azerbaijan was able to build up a substantial arsenal of sophisticated weapons systems and equipment. Its military budget alone has been estimated for several years as equal to Armenia's entire state budget. The 2014 military budget, despite the drop in oil prices in 2014, was set at $3.4 billion.[39] Officer training by Turkish and US advisers is considered to have raised the proficiency of the Azerbaijani officer corps, though the level of regular fighting forces, including their ability to use sophisticated weapons systems, remains in question. Nonetheless, the military growth and the high prestige of the armed forces among the populace,[40] and demographic factors including a larger population and higher birthrate than Armenia, all suggest a popularly shared sense of power that might tempt some factions into renewed fighting. It is reflected in verbal threats, both overt and implied, from public figures at the highest levels.[41] Some analysts have suggested that Azerbaijan is likely to renew the war. But by these measures, Aliyev's regime had the capability to make that move in late 2012 or 2013, and yet it did not.

Why, if Azerbaijan has the military capability, has the government not started the war? First, it should be admitted that weapons alone do not constitute "capability." Baku may doubt that it has adequate capability for the type of war that this would be—very bloody, and likely to draw other countries and factions into the fight, thereby destabilizing the entire region. The bloody clash of early April 2016, which both sides accused the other of initiating, was curtailed within four days but resulted in dozens of fatalities.[42] The Azerbaijani military showed a new efficiency and gained strategically important high ground, thereby improving Baku's negotiating position without restarting the war.

Another reason why Azerbaijan is not likely to restart the war may be that, capabilities aside, President Ilham Aliyev is primarily a businessman, and war is bad for business. Instability is the greatest danger to commercial interests, from pipeline construction to tourism. The personal wealth of the Aliyev family and their inner circle depends on investments, construction, and globalization (see chapter 4), which the oligarchs are not likely to jeopardize. The nightmare of many observers is that a rogue field commander or domestic rival of the ruling elites will "wake up one day and decide to start shooting."[43]

The political dimension is closely related to the dominance of the oligarchs. To safeguard business interests and income, the Aliyev regime must retain power. It is more convenient to be merely in a nominal state of war, as Azerbaijan has been since 1994, in order to stave off demands for reforms and to focus popular anger and blame on the enemy. As one antiregime émigré has written:

> We have two entrenched autocracies in Baku and Yerevan. . . . But both are clearly undemocratic and corrupt regimes that benefit tremendously from perpetuating the Armenian-Azerbaijani conflict. It allows diverting all the anger and energy of their populations towards each other and away from the despicable theft, plundering, injustice and repressions perpetrated by the ruling elites. Every time any other issue is raised—

economy, corruption, human rights, election fraud, you name it—officials from these two countries conveniently hide behind the same lame excuses: "refugees," "blockade," "occupation," "'threat of war"" . . . .[44]

It is also likely that Russia manipulates the conflict as a means to control the two states. Armenia is a Russian ally, and Azerbaijan has a "friendly" relationship with Russia replete with trade including the sale of oil, gas, and weapons. Nonetheless, Azerbaijani government officials will sometimes note the Russian threat in Karabagh. A balanced tension is in Moscow's interest there, as it is with regard to Georgia's ongoing conflicts in South Ossetia and Abkhazia.

Caucasus specialist Thomas de Waal summarized the situation as of 2013. In the previous decade, he argued, in addition to the military buildup,

the level of aggression in public sentiment has also risen in both countries, particularly among the youth, leading to a polarization so extreme that some in the international community have begun to consider a conflict management process, rather than a peace process, as the only realistic approach. Finally, the lack of domestic political space for constructive dialogue about the issue has resulted in local citizens being unable to extend a hand to the other side without being branded as traitors.[45]

Creative Approaches Meet Hardening Attitudes

Efforts to envision a settlement have been few, but increasing. In a meeting at Harvard University in 2001, Armenian and Azerbaijani scholars met with Minsk Group mediator Carey Cavanaugh for a wide-ranging discussion of the hostilities as well as the analytical blocks to negotiation.[46] Armenian-American scholar Ronald Grigor Suny saw a gap in conceptualizing the problem between academic observers and the majority of people of both nationalities. The latter, he said, were committed to nationalist views, considered national identity to be "primordial," and maintained a rigid idea of sovereignty. In contrast, he presented a possibly fruitful intellectual approach that defined identity as constructed and sovereignty as a possible object of creative restructuring—comments for which he was later denounced in the American-Armenian press.[47]

In 2010, the United Kingdom–based Conciliation Resources formed the Karabagh Contact Group (KCG) "to promote policy-relevant thinking about the Karabagh conflict." The KCG has held low-profile meetings in which participants from both nationalities, as well as outside specialists, have discussed numerous thorny issues, breaking down some of the approaches and arguments to find "entry points" where the parties might begin discussion. The goals have been necessarily modest and progress gradual, but the written products and meetings have been positive.[48]

Resolution of hotly contested issues always requires compromise. The mere whiff of compromise has led to accusations of treachery, disloyalty, and treason. As Suny was denounced by Armenians, so Azerbaijani writer Akram Aylisli was attacked, vilified, threatened, and finally stripped of his title "People's Writer" and the pension that went with it in 2013 after writing a novella about Azerbaijani attacks on Armenians in Sumgayit. But unlike Armenian criticism of Suny, which came from diaspora commentators, the attack on Aylisli came from the government and ruling party of Azerbaijan.[49] Was public opinion against Aylisli? It seems likely that Azerbaijanis would be offended, even infuriated, by his more sympathetic portrayal of the victimized Armenians. But one regime critic argued that in a society without open debate, there is no "civil society," and therefore no "public opinion."

But there are opinion polls. The 2013 Caucasus Barometer showed similar patterns for Armenia and Azerbaijan in their views of the resolution of the Karabagh conflict. In both countries, over half the respondents in all age groups said that they thought that negotiated resolution of the conflict was "very likely" or "rather likely" in the next five years—54 percent in Armenia and 55 percent in Azerbaijan. (A quarter to a third expected fighting in the coming five years.) But more than 80 percent of Azerbaijanis "would never accept" an independent Karabagh, and 96 percent said that they would never accept it as part of Armenia. The mirror image is true for Armenians, among whom 95 percent "would never accept" Karabagh as part of Azerbaijan, with or without autonomy. So when the people said that they believed a negotiated outcome would be "likely," they meant that they imagined the other side would be talked (or forced) into relinquishing the territory.[50] The question that the polls did not ask is how long the respondents would be willing to fight, or to let their children fight, to get this land. This is perhaps the crux of the matter—how many will give up the possession of the graves of their ancestors in order to stop making graves for their children?

3
Azerbaijan's Best and Brightest: The Rise, Decline, and Renewal of the Democratic Opposition

The president you elect in three months will be overthrown in a year. . . . If we fail to create counterbalancing structures, whoever you elect as president will destroy himself or be destroyed . . . because there is no institutional structure to prevent this.

—Abulfez Elchibey, 1992[1]

Abulfez Elchibey, tall and gaunt, stood on the platform beside the long-forbidden tricolor flag of Azerbaijan's first republic. Music swelled in the auditorium. It was the original "National March," composed for the first republic in 1919, banned in the decades of Soviet power, and restored as the official anthem only three weeks earlier.[2] Men and women stood with tears streaming down their faces, and many raised their arms in the clenched-fist salute of their years in anticommunist opposition. The event had been unimaginable a year earlier. This was the presidential inauguration of June 16, 1992, and the Popular Front leader was about to take the oath as president of a new independent Republic of Azerbaijan. As one *New York Times* reporter had declared, no

Soviet-era opposition group had "moved from obscurity to power" quite as fast as the Azerbaijan Popular Front.[3]

The man and the process by which he was elected were equally astonishing for anyone observing the collapse of the Soviet Union. Abulfez Aliyev, better known as Abulfez Elchibey, was a scholar and Soviet-era dissident. Initially trained as an Arabic-Russian translator, he had worked in Egypt in 1963 and 1964. He then taught at Baku State (then Azerbaijan State) University until he was jailed for "nationalism" in 1975. After his release in 1976, he was able to work in the manuscript division of the Academy of Sciences, where he would have no access to students. In 1988–89, he was one of the cofounders of the Popular Front in the academy.

The founders of the Popular Front itself were an impressive collection of men and women, starting with the professors, researchers, and writers at the Azerbaijan Academy of Sciences and Azerbaijan State University. Virtually all were members of the communist party, because membership was essential to any professional career in the Soviet Union. By joining the first discussion circles that voiced concern for environmental protection, historic preservation, and the defense of Mountainous Karabagh, these professionals put themselves at great risk. They could lose not only future promotions, but also their posts, their apartments, and even their individual freedom. Those who wanted to stay safe avoided this risk. Those who formed the Popular Front movement had advanced education and analytical skills that led them to read between the lines of official documents, grasp the implications, and see possible steps to oppose the regime and the party's trajectory. The historians and writers among them had furtively begun to rediscover Azerbaijan's precommunist history, especially the first republic of 1918–20, and they had published their findings in Azerbaijani-language publications in the Brezhnev era. They understood, as the Popular Front's own programs would show, the meaning of political pluralism, rule of law, separation of powers, and free and fair elections. Their course of action required both vision and bravery. These men and women were not ideal types, free of the influence of the old order, but they were, in their time, Azerbaijan's best and brightest.

The presidential election of June 1992 was Azerbaijan's first multicandidate election since the fall of the first republic in 1920. International observers were few in number, but they considered the process as "free and fair" as could be expected in a newly independent former Soviet republic. The observed violations included the head of the family casting votes for the entire family, campaigning near the polling stations, and some poll watchers advocating for specific candidates (although these activities did not seem to favor any particular candidate).[4] Abulfez Elchibey won with about 55 percent of the vote; the next candidate got less than 30 percent.[5] Several people expressed delight at having a choice of candidates.

The 1992 Presidential Election

The path to election day had been rocky and twisted.[6] As the Soviet Union crumbled in 1991, the Supreme Soviet had declared its intention to reestablish Azerbaijan's independence on August 30. Azerbaijan Communist Party first secretary Ayaz Mutalibov declared himself president after a perfunctory, uncontested election in September. The constitutional act that declared Azerbaijan's independence on October 18 established a presidential system with a "parliament" and judiciary each independent from the other and sharing power. The act also included a pledge to defend human rights (article 26), although Article 71 noted that human rights might be "temporarily" frozen.[7] The Azerbaijani declaration of independence was affirmed by popular referendum on December 29, just days after Mikhail Gorbachev declared the dissolution of the Soviet Union. As the new president, Mutalibov had begun to negotiate with the increasingly powerful Popular Front. That negotiation process, and the shooting-down of an Azerbaijani helicopter in Karabagh in November, forced Mutalibov to agree to the creation of a new legislative body to function in place of the Supreme Soviet (renamed "parliament")—which then was put in potentially permanent recess. The new Milli Shura (National Council) had fifty representatives from the prorogued "parliament": twenty-five from the Democratic Bloc, including the Popular Front and regular allies such as Etibar Mamedov's Azerbaijan National Independence Party and Araz Alizade's Social Democratic Party; and twenty-five selected by the Mutalibov government. The ratio implied equality of power between the government and the disunited opposition, which was not quite the case, but it did reflect the loss of influence by Mutalibov and the former communist party leadership. The creation of the Milli Shura put Popular Front leaders many steps closer to power. But those steps were uphill.

When news of the Khojaly massacre on February 26–27, 1992, reached Baku, public fury was expressed in demonstrations outside the Supreme Soviet building.[8] The crowd demanded that Mutalibov resign. On March 3, the Milli Shura called the full "parliament" back into session. The Popular Front hoped that the members would vote to remove Mutalibov and also abolish his presidential apparatus to give the Popular Front a chance to restructure the government. The old communists in the "parliament" hoped to use the session to endorse joining the Russia-led Commonwealth of Independent States (CIS) and remain safely in Russia's orbit. When the full body convened, the members elected a new chair: Yaqub "Dollar" Mamedov, the corrupt head of the medical faculty of Azerbaijan State University. Demonstrators chanting "*Is-ti-fa! Is-ti-fa!*" ("Resign! Resign!") broke through the police barrier that surrounded the building and rushed to the front of the building itself. The furious crowd, mostly women, pounded their fists on the building's floor-to-ceiling plate glass windows in rhythm with their chant, "*Is-ti-fa!*" A foreign observer described the scene: the glass cracked. Then it broke. The women rushed into the lobby of the building, sending the stunned deputies fleeing to the meeting chamber. The leaders of the demonstration then invaded the meeting chamber itself and tried to corner Mutalibov, shouting for his resignation. A shaken Mutalibov resigned.[9] Momentarily, the Popular Front had the upper hand. But as believers in constitutional order and rule of law,[10] the Front's leaders accepted the speaker of parliament, the newly selected "Dollar" Mamedov, as acting president, and set an election to be held within three months. Mamedov duly became acting president, and the election was set for June 7.

The Popular Front leadership considered it more meaningful to elect a new parliament than a new president. The parliament would have the power to draft a new Constitution, breaking the centralized power inherited from the Soviet model. But the sitting "parliament," the old Supreme Soviet with a new name, had no desire to end its own power by such a course of action. In a series of votes under "Dollar" Mamedov, the majority rejected any change in the presidency or the presidential administration (the *apparat*), and demurred on new parliamentary elections. The Popular Front thereby lost its advantage because matters came to a vote; in the vote, they were outnumbered by the old guard.[11]

Mamedov escaped his acting presidency after two months when another bloody disaster befell Karabagh—the fall to Armenian forces of the strategically and culturally important city of Shusha on May 7. Surely, went the common narrative, the city had been sold out. Mamedov and the "parliament" blamed defense minister and Popular Front figure Rahim Gaziyev, a mathematician who had emerged as a military man, a turn of events only possible in the absence of a real army. Previously, Gaziyev had defended Shusha from Armenian forces. Now he stood accused of giving it up. Gaziyev, in turn, blamed "cowards" who had hid in Baku rather than fight in Karabagh. The allegations of treachery at the front allowed the old communists in the parliament to claim that Khojaly had been the result of a similar "sellout" and that the massacre had not been the fault of Ayaz Mutalibov—whose March 6 resignation, therefore, should not have been accepted.

As the deputies discussed this potential about-face on May 14, Mutalibov dramatically returned to the chamber and was restored to the presidency by acclamation, but without a quorum. The action was therefore illegal. In his acceptance speech, Mutalibov proclaimed that democracy had "gotten out of hand."[12] It was necessary to ban political activities and impose martial law. He canceled the presidential election set for June 7, and added that if the country needed a dictator to avert disaster, he was prepared to be that man. He pledged to go to the meeting of former Soviet republics in Tashkent the next day and bring Azerbaijan into the CIS.

The Popular Front and the few foreign diplomats present considered Mutalibov's response to be a coup. Over that tense night and into the next day, the Popular Front leadership planned its response. On the morning of May 15, Abulfez Elchibey addressed crowds that had gathered near Popular Front headquarters and issued an ultimatum—either Mutalibov would vacate the presidential palace by 2 p.m. that day, or "we will throw him out ourselves." The Front's leaders had decided to use violence, or at least the threat of violence, to reject martial law and restore the previous day's political balance, though it was not necessarily in their favor. But the alternative, accepting the illegal restoration of Mutalibov and martial law, would end the chance for an election, thus closing off the Popular Front's opportunity to take power legally. It was a philosophical conundrum, a bold move, and big risk. The balance of armed forces was not clear. The danger of civil war, given that civil war was then raging in neighboring Georgia, was palpable. But the Front leaders knew that they faced one of those rare turning points when the actions they took in the coming hours would affect the fate of their country.

American journalist Thomas Goltz, then living in Baku, witnessed the events.[13] He saw hundreds of armed police with several armored vehicles around the presidential administration building that morning. The men were expecting bloodshed. At the Popular Front headquarters, the 2 p.m. deadline passed, but preparations were continuing; the leaders were wearing body armor. After hours of complex discussion and debate, Elchibey made a final statement about Mutalibov's illegal seizure of power and the need to use force to restore constitutional order. The Popular Front's parking garage doors opened, and an entire armored column rolled out, replete with tanks, armored personnel carriers, soldiers with grenade launchers, and more. This was the work, and could only have been the work, of one man: Iskendar Hamidov, a career police official who had taken on the role of the "attack dog" of the Popular Front.

Compared with the many men who had given themselves the title of "colonel" after building a private army with the accumulated bribes of their Soviet-era jobs, Hamidov had earned his living and his rank. He had the paramilitary training of the regular police and through years of service had achieved the rank of colonel. He commanded the personal loyalty of thousands of willing fighters. He was a traditional man from Kelbajar, a small city in western Azerbaijan. He was more nationalist than liberal, and his personal doctrine was the militant pan-Turkism of the Grey Wolves (Bozkurt) of Turkey. He was a poor fit for the urban intellectuals of the Popular Front, and they were perpetually embarrassed by his words and actions. But as an anticommunist, a man with a short temper and plenty of firepower, Hamidov was a crucial ally. On that day in May 1992, he proved to be instrumental to Popular Front power and the quashing of Mutalibov's coup.

The afternoon of May 15, after a few shots rang out near the presidential administration, it became clear that the main attack was being carried out against the parliament building up the hill. Hamidov's forces seemingly had frightened off many of the defenders in the parliament building. Even though the latter had the advantage of holding the higher ground and firing from inside adjacent buildings, they ran. The armed police down at the presidential administration building saw that they could not face their own uphill assault against superior forces. Without the expected advantage or leadership, they quickly melted away. This apparent countercoup, engineered by Hamidov, had succeeded. Soldiers and civilians literally danced on the steps of the parliament building. Fewer than a dozen had died, and fewer still were injured. Civil war had been avoided, but the danger had not passed. Armed individuals were everywhere, but had no leader and no plan. Mutalibov's whereabouts were unknown for many days until he turned up in Moscow. In the meantime, the Popular Front returned to parliament to resolve the constitutional and legal situation. Iskendar Hamidov was named minister of internal affairs.

Reestablishing legal order was the challenge that the Popular Front leadership was determined to achieve. It was not merely a matter of "cloaking" the events in legality.[14] The individual beliefs of the leaders were embodied in successive Popular Front programs that articulated the Front's commitment to the rule of law. Their legitimacy rested on it. Having used what they considered necessary force against the Mutalibov coup, they would not act like usurpers themselves. Returning to legal provisions and due process was essential for their domestic stature and for Western acceptance of their government. It was not easy to get the parliamentary deputies to convene. Many were reportedly hiding from reprisals and had to be found and virtually dragged to the parliamentary chamber to achieve a quorum, a process that took days. Finally, the required 225 deputies were assembled and, after many shortfall votes caused by abstentions of the old communists, "Dollar" Mamedov's resignation was accepted. After yet more wrangling, including an attempt to nominate former communist leader Heydar Aliyev to the vacated position, Popular Front co-leader Isa Gambar became speaker of parliament and thereby acting president of Azerbaijan. Like Elchibey, Gambar was a scholar in the Academy of Sciences, a soft-spoken and cerebral man in his mid-thirties who was interested in getting down to business without the weight of speeches and rhetoric.

Gambar led the reluctant deputies through urgent tasks. First, they approved a new cabinet. Four key positions—internal affairs, foreign affairs, defense, and the head of the state oil company SOCAR—were filled by Popular Front figures[15] but the rest remained with the "crocodiles," the old Soviet appointees who had held the same posts before. The new leadership had little choice in this matter, because the majority of government posts required more knowledge of Azerbaijan's current government structure, management, budget, and financial matters than the Popular Front and Democratic Bloc possessed. This shortage of loyal cadres would be one of the Popular Front government's great disadvantages. The presidential election was put back on schedule for June 7.[16] Finally, after much rhetorical combat and some foot-dragging, the deputies voted to disband the full "parliament" in favor of the smaller Milli Shura, again giving the Democratic Bloc and the crocodiles equal votes. The hoped-for parliamentary elections were to be held soon. In fact, they would not take place while Elchibey and the Popular Front held power.

The Year of the Popular Front

Abulfez Elchibey was thus elected president on June 7, 1992, after a hard-fought struggle to defeat the hangers-on from the old Soviet system in Azerbaijan. The Popular Front's rise to power was accompanied by anxiety and optimism. The unexpected victory over the old communists had infused Baku with a heady, even giddy sense of possibility. The new leaders had established themselves as proponents of democracy and civil liberties, but also of territorial integrity for the newly independent republic. They meant to stay out of Russia's orbit and fight to regain Karabagh. They were inspired by the example of the first republic, the Azerbaijan Democratic Republic, which had emerged in 1918 out of World War I. They invoked its example and its symbols, down to the flag and the national anthem. The restoration of the first republic's symbols was also a rejection of the overthrow of the ADR by the Bolsheviks and the Red Army in 1920 and of the Stalinist system that had vilified that republic, purged and killed its survivors during the 1920s and 1930s, and blackened the reputations of its images and its leaders. The Popular Front was honoring those long dead. As historians, they wanted to give the country's history back to the people. Their example inspired a population that had grown weary of Soviet repression. Moreover, the Popular Front and other Democratic Bloc parties were led by respected intellectuals. At the same time, those leaders were political neophytes. Few had any administrative experience. Running a state bureaucracy was a huge task, and Azerbaijan's new leaders had to rely on the old bureaucrats who had obtained their jobs under the old system with its familiar expectations. Those higher up in the apparatus, with political jobs, were appointees of the overthrown communists. In the best of circumstances, this bureaucratic configuration and the lingering people who staffed it might have been crippling to a new system—and these were far from the best of circumstances.

The war over Karabagh was raging. Two cease-fire attempts, both brokered by Iran, were followed by Armenian offensives in the spring, the second against Shusha.[17] Internally displaced persons were filling hotels, dilapidated buildings, and even summer camps and train cars, as if they would soon return to their homes in Karabagh. In the summer, arms poured in as the Soviet military divided its weapons among former constituent republics.[18] Azerbaijan launched offensives and retook some territory temporarily. The plight of the civilians of all nationalities was tragic. And war profiteers, looters, and rogue deserters were ubiquitous and immune to love of people or homeland; in one dramatic example, journalist Thomas Goltz came across a rogue fighter who had stored up bodies to conceal their deaths and collect their pay.[19] Ayaz Mutalibov had refused to create an army, and now the new recruits were poorly trained. Mercenaries were well paid, but undisciplined. Units might languish without orders, and deaths from "friendly fire" were common. Patriotism mixed with disillusionment and anger. Recruits continued to deploy as bodies came home for burial.

Azerbaijan's economy had collapsed with the Soviet Union. Economic analysts would later estimate that Azerbaijan lost over 60 percent of its gross domestic product (GDP) in the first year of independence (see chapter 4). Prices rose as the value of currency dropped. The purely nominal jobs that kept people technically employed dried up, and the men spent their days hanging around tea shops, the traditional *chaihana*. Opportunities for large-scale theft of aid supplies and graft enriched a small stratum of bandits. Poachers indiscriminately harvested sturgeon for the caviar, and complex networks were arranged to skim and sell waste oil on spot markets in Europe.[20]

In the summer of 1992, the human tragedies of the country were inscribed on the face of the capital city. Baku seemed as poor as it had been in Soviet times, but it appeared more gritty and run-down after years of war and neglect. The formerly pristine Azerbaijan Intourist hotel for foreigners had had its lobby used as a morgue for the Black January fatalities in 1990 and its guestrooms requisitioned for soldiers and IDPs from Karabagh. The number of people taking evening strolls along the streets and the waterfront boulevard (*bulvar*) had dropped, and gunfire could be heard in the distance.

Despite the grim conditions, but feeling public support, Elchibey's government set about fulfilling its promises. Debate in the media and Milli Shura was open. A National Army was formed, though its training was inadequate, and the few offensives it launched in the summer and fall had only brief successes. The Cyrillic script, imposed by Moscow in 1940, was dropped in favor of the Latin script that had been used in Azerbaijan the 1920s and 1930s.[21] Elchibey stressed the Turkic identity of Azerbaijanis, and cultivated relations with Turkey to an extent that the non-Azerbaijanis felt threatened. The embrace of this Western brother became nearly suffocating and had to be toned down on all sides. His zeal for the Azerbaijanis of Iran, however, managed to alienate Tehran, which feared the separatist implications of Elchibey's appeal to the Turkic speakers who inhabited Iran's border area. Elchibey also moved Azerbaijan away from Russia, gruffly rejecting CIS membership, forcing out Russian troops, and establishing the manat as the national currency to replace the ruble. Elchibey was even poised to sign a production sharing agreement (PSA) with a consortium of foreign oil companies to take advantage, at long last, of Azerbaijan's oil wealth. It was perhaps not a coincidence that both the PSA and withdrawal from the ruble zone were impending when Elichibey's government was overthrown in a Russian-backed coup in June 1993.

Much of the hope that accompanied the election of Elchibey was founded on unrealistic expectations that a democratic government would bring peace and prosperity, and would do so rapidly. Indeed, "democracy" was understood as economic growth—only growth, never decline—rather than a political system that included debate, disagreement, and compromise. From the Soviet vantage point, under which the Azerbaijani people and their forebears had lived for seventy years, disputes and debate signaled chaos—the leaders must not be in charge. Not all those in the Popular Front's orbit understood democracy, and those who did grasp it did not always know how to apply it in the shifting sands of 1992 Azerbaijan. Some were corrupt and used their positions as their communist predecessors had, as a means for personal enrichment. Others were overconfident; some were just naive. Aside from the Popular Front's own lack of sufficient numbers of technocrats and bureaucrats to run the state apparatus, Elchibey and his inner circle—his four selected cabinet ministers, Isa Gambar as speaker of the Milli Shura, Ali Kerimov (Kerimli) as state secretary, and assorted advisers and supporters—were challenged by economic troubles, the war in Karabagh, and the inflated expectations of an anxious populace. Moreover, the (neo-)communist crocodiles lived in fear of being ousted from their jobs as the Popular Front expanded its network. They, and others who merely sought profit, quietly stole natural resources (such as oil and caviar) and worked against the regime, waiting for a change of circumstances. Other post-Soviet cases have shown that the persistence of the old elites impedes potential transition to democracy, and so it would come to pass in Azerbaijan as well.[22] The optimism that was so great on inauguration day was remarkably, but deservedly, short-lived.

During the year of Elchibey's presidency, the stress and blood of war, corruption, poverty, oil money, political factionalism, and foreign pressure came to a head. The visible markers of corruption, including diverting aid for refugees to Baku shops, and even necessary security measures, like Elchibey's bulletproof Mercedes, created an image of elite affluence when the majority remained poor. The antics of Iskendar Hamidov further embarrassed Front leaders. In the fall of 1992, in a fit of anger at reading an insulting article about himself in a newspaper, Hamidov rushed out of his apartment and beat up the journalist who had written the offending article. Responding to the barrage of criticism that followed the assault, Hamidov stated that when he had beaten the journalist, he had done so as an individual and not as minister of internal affairs. Hamidov's behavior was, in an odd way, a sign of change. Rather than use the power of his office to retaliate against the journalist, which had been the norm for seventy years of Soviet rule, he acted as an individual who had been personally offended. Few, however, saw his actions in this way. Hamidov seemed like a liability.

Despite their devotion to legality and institutions, the Popular Front government never held parliamentary elections. With the optimism of Elchibey's victory, the Front might have capitalized on their wave of popular support. Missing this chance was perhaps their crucial error. While the Milli Shura held power, the door remained open for the former communist deputies to call for the return of the full, Soviet-era Supreme Soviet, as they had done in May 1992. Without a new parliament, moreover, work was never begun on a new Constitution, so that Azerbaijan's government and judiciary were working under the patchwork of amendments and laws that had been made to the last Soviet Constitution, which had been adopted in 1977. The war and economic collapse were not sufficient reasons for failing to arrange elections, since presidential elections had just been held under the same circumstances and with greater instability at the top of government. Perhaps the Front was afraid of losing the leverage it had in the Milli Shura once the assorted individual contenders and growing number of parties began to compete for the votes of the politically unsophisticated voters. Waiting only made the situation worse. In the end, the government failed to produce the rapid victories in the economy and the war that people had expected. The failure to hold elections was a particularly damaging omission because it was one that the Elichibey government could have controlled, unlike Iskendar Hamidov's behavior and losses in the escalating war.

The regime came to feel that the catastrophic losses in Karabagh had to be concealed. The control of information reduced government credibility and narrowed the space for public debate, thereby weakening the democracy that the Popular Front leaders had fought so hard to install. Foreign diplomats directly advised government officials, although the Americans were constrained by the infamous Section 907, the sanctions amendment of the Freedom Support Act. This unfortunate amendment singled out Azerbaijan among post-Soviet states and blocked the United States from providing aid to the Azerbaijani government until it ceased its "aggression" in Karabagh.[23] Section 907 remained the greatest sticking point in US diplomats' efforts to help Azerbaijan with democracy-building efforts at a time when Azerbaijan both wanted and needed the help. Its existence would strain US-Azerbaijani relations for years to come.

The Popular Front government was later accused of corruption and of selling out the country, the war, the resources, and themselves. Some individuals in government were corrupt. As for Elchibey's government as a whole, there is more evidence to suggest incompetence—including the inability to stop the theft of weapons and aid—than to prove that they had sold out the fighters or the public trust. Sadly, the deck was so stacked against them and they were so inexperienced, and some were so incompetent or foolish, that the best-intentioned people could probably not have survived. Was Elchibey's fall, then, "inevitable"? Historians do not like this term because it obscures the individual turning points and the human agency that make up particular pathways in history. Invoking "inevitability" shirks the responsibility to analyze and the opportunity to clarify events to the point of identifying the most significant moments. An examination of Elchibey's presidency reveals such moments and decisions that led to his fall from power. The failure to elect a new parliament and write a new Constitution were two such fateful decisions. The most powerful seem to have come from the war.

Karabagh, specifically the war and the losses, was indeed the graveyard of Azerbaijani presidents, from Mutalibov to Elchibey. In February 1993, self-proclaimed "colonel" (and "hero") Surat Huseynov, a former factory manager who had recruited and paid for his own army, pulled his troops off the front line in Karabagh and moved them to his native region of Ganje. The act confirmed the suspicion that the troops were loyal to him personally rather than to the country, and that Azerbaijan's government did not have a monopoly over armed force. Defense Minister Rahim Gaziyev, too, began acting independently, and reportedly tried to take over the broadcasting tower in Baku.[24] Elchibey fired both men in late February, but did not arrest them. Observers who saw Elchibey during this time thought he was often intoxicated, and seemed detached, even immobilized. The greatest disaster of the spring was the fall of Kelbajar on March 31 and April 1, 1993, around which the regime maintained a virtual news blackout. But the slow trickle of information and IDPs, and huge civilian casualties on top of military failures, contributed to the loss of faith in Elchibey and to the belief that the government had "sold" Kelbajar. So when Surat Huseynov launched a mutiny from Ganje in early June, few felt enough loyalty to Elchibey's government to risk their lives to defend it.

Weeks before Surat Huseynov's rebellion, however, Elchibey had lost his best defender: Iskendar Hamidov. In April, when Iskendar was notably traumatized from the fall of his hometown, another incendiary piece about him appeared in the papers. Predictably, he went to the newspaper office to beat up the offending writer. It was predictable behavior, and that is the point.

Iskendar was taunted into one more outrageous act, and Elchibey felt obliged to demand his resignation on April 16. It had the markings of a trap, and they all walked into it. Hamidov was out, and there was no other person who could or would use armed forces as he had to defend Elchibey's government.

When the remnants of the Soviet armed forces left Azerbaijan in May 1993, the commander of the 106th Airborne Division at Ganje had turned the base and its arms over to Surat Huseynov and his 709th Brigade. Surat quickly denounced Elchibey and his closest advisers, supposedly for attacking him and his "heroic troops," and demanded their resignation. On June 4, Elchibey sent a delegation allegedly to negotiate with Surat, but as Thomas Goltz noted in his report of the episode, the group from Baku—which included former defense minister Rahim Gaziyev—seemed to cheer on Surat and his forces rather than advocate for the government they supposedly represented.[25] Huseynov himself appeared to repeat slogans and was unable to articulate cogent answers to any reporters' questions without prompting from members of the "negotiating" team. He was plainly a tool of people who aimed to overthrow Elchibey. The standoff continued. Elchibey was told by several advisers to bring the challenge to an end quickly—deploy loyal troops, and give Surat and his mutineers the ultimatum to surrender. When they refused, as they surely would, Elchibey would have to give the order to open fire. If not, the rebellion would spread. He rejected the advice, allegedly saying that he would not shed the blood of his countrymen.[26] In this sentiment, he was nearly alone. Perhaps he had other considerations. Neighboring Georgia was embroiled in civil war, a fate he did not wish for Azerbaijan. Maybe he did not believe he had loyal troops left. He did not have Iskendar Hamidov when he needed him.

Surat Huseynov and his small "brigade" marched on Baku, moving eastward along the rail line that ran between the Caspian and Black seas. Surat took major towns and the key city of Yevlakh, where the east-west rail line crossed the north-south line. He controlled the railroads in the country a week before he reached Baku. The regime had no defenders and few weapons. The Milli Shura was in turmoil, with rants and blame from deputies who had not darkened its threshold in months, pointing the finger at Elchibey and Isa Gambar, the speaker. Reportedly, it was the Turkish government that persuaded Heydar Aliyev to agree to Elchibey's invitation to return to Baku to stabilize the situation—which Aliyev did, aboard a Turkish jet, on June 12, 1993.

The Return of Heydar Aliyev

Heydar Aliyev, former KGB general and first secretary of the Communist Party of Azerbaijan (1969–82), had left virtual exile in his home region of Nakhjivan to return to the capital.[27] Isa Gambar's resignation from the post of speaker was announced on June 13, and Aliyev was elected in his place. Aliyev then went to Ganje to see Surat Huseynov, and returned on June 15 for a new parliamentary session. After proclaiming his devotion to rule of law, democratic pluralism, human rights and a market economy, Aliyev escorted Elchibey to the waiting presidential limo. By the end of the week, Elchibey had returned to Nakhjivan, his home and Aliyev's.[28] With Elchibey's departure from Baku, another moment of contested power took shape—legally, Heydar Aliyev was only the speaker of the Milli Shura, but his de facto personal authority and the widespread belief in his leadership, especially as Surat's forces approached Baku, loomed larger than titles or law.

Heydar Aliyev was a forceful presence, the most important political figure in Azerbaijan since the fall of Stalin protégé Mir Jafar Baghirov in 1953. Like Baghirov, Aliyev had had a career in the KGB, rising to the rank of general. He became first secretary in 1969 and was promoted to the Soviet Politboro by Yuri Andropov in 1982, where he remained until he was purged by Mikhail Gorbachev in 1987. As AzCP first secretary, Aliyev had subtly supported Azerbaijani arts and history, visiting artists' and composers' unions, paying attention to the trends that affected them. He had an ambiguous record around national culture and identity, as shown by his tolerance of some nationalist literature and art in the 1980s.[29] Nonetheless, he spoke Russian in public and appeared to be a sycophant of long-serving Soviet leader Leonid Brezhnev. When he remade himself as Azerbaijani president in 1993, he spoke only Azerbaijani, and better than many of his Russian-educated colleagues. He controlled the people around him, set up layers of supporters, brought fellow Nakhjivanis into power, combined intimidation with finesse, and displayed infinite adaptability to changing circumstances. He was feared and respected. His strength seemed to be the national salvation in 1993, during a time of chaos. Indeed, the date of his return to Baku was turned into a national holiday called "Salvation Day." He was supremely devoted to his own power. Foreigners who knew him all have their stories of his charm and sharp mind, projection of power, and personal style. Azerbaijanis, too have stories, but they never tell them.

Why had Abulfez Elchibey called Heydar Aliyev to Baku? Was it not obvious that he would never stand in Elchibey's shadow and help restore stability from behind the scenes? Elchibey was reportedly "encouraged" to invite the same man who had put him in jail twenty years earlier to return to Baku as the only person with the clout to restore order. The question is a complex one and is still unresolved decades after the events. The Popular Front leadership was uncertain, fearful, and demoralized. Some did believe that Aliyev would work as Elchibey's partner. Was this good political judgment? In hindsight, no. But in that moment, with a coup in progress and no clear alternatives, the inexperienced Popular Front grasped the only lifeline within reach. There was no one else on the political scene, no one who had successfully held power in Azerbaijan and inspired confidence and fear. Certainly, the Turks supported him and, according to Thomas Goltz, insisted that he was the key to stability. President Suleyman Demirel was Heydar's old friend.[30]

The notion, popular in some circles at the time, that Surat Huseynov's Russian-backed coup was meant to bring Aliyev to power is quite unlikely. More likely, the Russians chose the inarticulate Surat Huseynov as the front man for Ayaz Mutalibov, who was being sheltered in Moscow. Aliyev was already too independent from Moscow and had sought support from Turkey and Iran, not Russia, during his exile in Nakhjivan. Aliyev walked through the door that Surat Huseynov had opened and presented the Russians and everyone else with this fait accompli.

Once in place, Aliyev swiftly took control of matters. On June 18, he announced that Elchibey was missing and that he, as newly elected speaker of the Milli Majlis (the former Milli Shura), was forced to take presidential powers. But it was soon announced that Elchibey was not missing, but had gone to Nakhjivan. Foreign Minister Tofiq Gasymov challenged Aliyev's uncharacteristically crude power grab—a response for which Gasymov later would pay. Gasymov insisted that Elchibey was still president even if he went to Nakhjivan, noting that the president of the United States is still president if he goes to Alaska. Further undermining Aliyev's claim, Robert Finn, the US chargé d'affaires, added that the US president remained president not only in Alaska but also in Paris, and that the United States would continue to regard Elchibey as the legitimate president of Azerbaijan.[31]

Aliyev backed off—but, as Vladimir Lenin said when his initial advances were thwarted, he would simply prepare the ground for the next move. Aliyev's preparation was an energetic, prolonged public campaign to blacken Elchibey's reputation, which was apparently not already bad enough to suit Aliyev. It was in this period that the first accusation was floated that Elchibey was a KGB informer, and even that Aliyev had long been his handler.[32] A motion for Elchibey's impeachment was made, in a bit of knife-twisting, on Elchibey's birthday, June 24. The motion was offered by former Popular Front member Etibar Mamedov, who had broken with the Front in 1991 because he felt that it was not moving decisively toward Azerbaijan's independence from the Soviet Union. Etibar was part of the so-called Yeraz group—Azerbaijanis born in Armenia—that often had been allied with Nakhjivanis.[33] Hoping for a government post, he curried favor with Heydar Aliyev, staking his claim on the assertion that his party (AMIP) was the main opposition party to the Popular Front. He got nothing for his efforts but Aliyev's very public reminder that there was no "main opposition party" until elections showed that there was.[34]

Aliyev's campaign to discredit Elchibey was meant to damn the entire Popular Front government, and especially the former speaker of the Majlis, Isa Gambar. On June 17, during one of many televised sessions of the Majlis (which Aliyev used to embarrass and defame Popular Front leaders), he called on Gambar to report to the Majlis concerning the "Deputies Investigating Commission" that had been formed to investigate the alleged attack by government forces on Surat Huseynov at Ganje on June 4, 1993.[35] The commission's work fit the pro-Surat narrative that portrayed him as a hero and condemned the Elchibey government, the elected and legitimate government of Azerbaijan, as guilty of casualties caused by Surat's coup and of all the losses in Karabagh. As a member of that government, Gambar was under investigation by this committee. No longer speaker, Gambar sat in his deputy's seat facing Aliyev, who now occupied the speaker's chair. Aliyev demanded that Gambar report to the full Majlis, apparently on his own testimony to the commission. Gambar, looking calm and bookish, refused. He had reported to the commission as he was supposed to do, Gambar said, adding that "no one has the right to turn this body into a tribunal." This statement got the deputies' attention—no one refused to answer Heydar Aliyev. Again, Aliyev told Gambar that he was responsible before these deputies and that he must get up and report. Again, Isa refused. A third time, Aliyev insisted, calling him "respected Isa Gambarov," deliberately using the Russian form of his name. The ritual third refusal followed: "I will say for the third and final time, you have no right to turn this body into a tribunal." In his own final speech, Gambar said that Azerbaijan under Aliyev would become a prison. Within days, Gambar was stripped of his parliamentary immunity and jailed for his alleged role in the June 4 events. Strenuous diplomatic efforts led to his release within the month, but Aliyev never forgave this public challenge to his authority.[36]

Gambar's party, Yeni Müsavat, would never stand for elections, nor would Gambar sit in the Milli Majlis while Heydar Aliyev lived.

In rapid-fire succession, Aliyev got rid of the remaining Elchibey appointees, including State Secretary Ali Kerimli (future head of the Popular Front) and Foreign Minister Tofiq Gasymov. (The latter would later end up in a psychiatric ward.) Aliyev then brought Surat Huseynov to the Milli Majlis to have him "elected" prime minister. He also put on Surat's shoulders the Internal Affairs Ministry and Defense Ministry posts, more than a good man could have handled and far above the modest talents of Surat Huseynov. Aliyev's new arrangement was a setup; as Thomas Goltz put it, "Surat had just been given a long and oily rope with which to hang himself."[37]

Then came the referendum on President Elchibey, the national vote of confidence on August 29. Elichbey was overwhelmingly denounced and even cursed by 97.5 percent of the voters, an official and rigged figure that Goltz interpreted as the need not merely to unseat Elchibey but to crush him.[38] The age limit (sixty-five) for running for president was soon abolished, and the campaign to elect Heydar Aliyev as president followed. On October 3, Aliyev became president of Azerbaijan with 98.8 percent of the vote. Mutalibov, in his fixed elections of 1991, had received a paltry 98.0 percent. Heydar's triumph was complete. He was inaugurated on October 10. As he had to outdo Mutalibov in votes, he had to outdo Elchibey in patriotic gestures at his inauguration—not merely displaying the national flag, as Elichbey had done, but dropping to one knee (he was a vigorous seventy-one years old) and kissing it as an orchestra and full chorus performed the national anthem.

Western diplomats had a front seat to the rise and the fall of the Elchibey government. They were not purely observers. Elchibey's government actively sought their advice, especially the diplomats of countries to which they wanted to get closer, including Turkey and the United States. The Turks were first to recognize Azerbaijan's independence in the fall of 1991 and opened their embassy in a suite of rooms in the old Intourist Hotel under their young chargé d'affaires and acting ambassador Mehmet Ali Bayar, then thirty-one years old. With a master's degree in international finance from New York University, Bayar was bilingual and had the skills for this tough, newly established post.[39] The US Embassy was staffed by three veteran Foreign Service officers who among them had two PhDs, over a dozen languages, and fifty years of Foreign Service experience in the Soviet Union and the Middle East.

When Robert Finn opened the US Embassy in March 1992, he took over the suite of hotel rooms that the Turks had been using before they moved into their new building. He opened the embassy, he said, "literally with a box of office supplies, a small American flag, and a tape recording of the *Star-Spangled Banner*."[40] Finn was the US chargé d'affaires until the official ambassador arrived on a date scheduled some months in the future. Finn had a doctorate in Turkish literature from Princeton University, and his dissertation on the history of the Turkish novel had been published before he joined the Foreign Service in the 1970s. When he opened the embassy, placing the flag on his balcony and playing the recording of the US national anthem, he spoke to the crowd assembled below in Turkish, a language sufficiently close to Azerbaijani that his speech needed no translator. It was a sensation. People wept.[41] For seventy years, Azerbaijanis had been told that Russian was the "international language" that they must use to communicate beyond their national community. They expected foreigners to use it. Their own language was treated as second class—their children could study native history, music, or literature in it, but not science or technology. Azerbaijani's closeness to modern Turkish and other Turkic languages was officially denied, and scholars who knew better dared not challenge the regime's claims openly. In 1992, as foreign diplomats came to Azerbaijan, the Europeans indeed spoke Russian. So to Azerbaijanis, an American diplomat speaking "their language" was a signal of respect and knowledge of their culture, not only by Robert Finn but also by the United States of America. Finn's fluency in the language established him as a celebrity and an "insider." This, in turn, implied a thumbing of the nose at Russian claims to the exclusive use of their language in the international arena and, by extension, Russian cultural supremacy.

Finn was joined by Philip Remler as political affairs officer. Remler was moved from Moscow to Baku for the new embassy, and he knew Turkish as well as Russian, Persian, and several other languages. He could attend any meeting or interview without needing a translator or having the Russian or Soviet context explained to him. Finn and Remler were exceptionally smart and politically savvy, and each had a wicked sense of humor that allowed him to weather the oddities and crises of their years of work in Azerbaijan. For a brief period, the two of them constituted the entire complement of embassy officials, aided by a local secretary and some security staff, until the arrival in May 1992 of Ambassador Richard Miles, a former US Marine who spoke Russian and who until recently had been US consul general in Leningrad (newly rechristened to its original name of Saint Petersburg).[42] They were a formidable trio to guide the new US Embassy in a difficult time.

Heydar Aliyev as President

Once in the presidency, Heydar established himself as The Leader. His forceful rhetoric and nonstop denunciation of Abulfez Elchibey and the Popular Front continued in the Milli Majlis and on newspaper and television, where most Azerbaijanis got (and still get) their news. The Popular Front was blamed for corruption, incompetence, inflation, shortages of goods, and losses of territory and lives in Karabagh. Tofiq Gasymov and Iskendar Hamidov were grilled in official televised sessions on their failings. Only after the national referendum on Elchibey was the foreign minister's post finally filled, when Aliyev selected Hasan Hasanov, a career communist ideologue who had been prime minister under Ayaz Mutalibov.

Aliyev could control his government, the Milli Majlis, most of Baku, and all of Nakhjivan, but he could not (yet) control the rest of Azerbaijan or the war. And the battlefield losses continued as Armenian forces took more and more Azerbaijani towns, unleashing a further torrent of displaced people. In the summer of 1993, a short-lived rebellion was quashed in the south.[43] Substantial lands were lost on the west outside the former Nagorno-Karabagh Autonomous Region to Armenian offensives—cities and regions around first Aghdam, then Fizuli, and then the entire swath of land between the former NKAR and the Iranian border. Aliyev had blamed earlier losses on Mutalibov and Elchibey, but the losses on his watch he laid squarely at the doorstep of "traitors" who robbed the government and cared more for their *dachas* (vacation homes) than the country.[44]

As president, Heydar Aliyev kept up an amazing pace. He put down opposition from the weak remnants of the Popular Front government and its supporters as well as an armed rebellion, and still managed to bring to fruition the efforts that Elchibey had not been able to complete—a full transition to a new currency, the manat; joining the CIS without having Russian troops stationed inside Azerbaijan; and sealing the oil deal—"the Deal of the Century," as it was commonly known. Many in opposition groups welcomed his return in the interests of stability, and that he achieved. The difference was not suddenly the loss of a "parliament" or free press and open debate, because the same Milli Majlis continued to meet and the press already had been circumscribed by the Popular Front. In fact, under Heydar Aliyev these freedoms were nominally supported and existed in some measure. In the fall of 1994, while Aliyev was at a session of the United Nations, another coup attempt forced his abrupt return. Surat Huseynov was linked to the coup. In another of Aliyev's public eviscerations of an enemy, the "hero of Karabagh" was stripped of his honors and his posts. Surat and the similarly accused Rahim Gaziyev escaped (or were "allowed" to flee) to Moscow.[45] Aliyev was free to establish a new post-Soviet system with a new Milli Majlis and Constitution. In this instance, and for the future, the measure of democracy to which Aliyev had pledged himself was elections.

The Further Decline of the Political Opposition

Elections for the Milli Majlis (informally called the "parliament") were held in tandem with a referendum on the new Constitution in November 1995. For this and all subsequent parliamentary and presidential elections, the Azerbaijani government invited a monitoring team from the Organization for Security and Cooperation in Europe,[46] which Azerbaijan had joined in January 1992 when the organization was known as the Conference for Security and Cooperation in Europe. Azerbaijan was accepted as an OSCE member after signing a document "accepting all commitments and responsibilities" inherent in OSCE membership, including the democracy-building and human rights aspects enumerated in the Helsinki Final Act of 1975. All OSCE election monitoring was aimed to assess observance of these standards by all parties. In 1995, the OSCE partnered with the UN for election monitoring, but in subsequent elections, OSCE worked with its own Office for Democratic Institutions and Human Rights (ODIHR).

The complexities and depth of OSCE/ODIHR election monitoring require some explanation in order to grasp the significance of the organization's findings. In each case, after a Needs Assessment Mission determines the necessary size and type of monitoring teams, a chairperson and "core" team of one to two dozen international observers arrives in the country about two months before the election date. Long-term observers, a dozen or more experienced individuals, arrive shortly thereafter and begin work so they can understand the milieu in which elections are held. During that time, this Election Observation Mission (EOM) monitoring team sets up offices, hires translators, begins work with local election officials, and monitors the campaign according to an official checklist. The monitors observe and note registration procedures for candidates and publication of voter lists, candidates' speeches, media access, coverage, and related factors, especially comparing the treatment of incumbents to challengers. The team checks on the details of preparation,

[handwritten margin note: core team]

such as printing and distribution of paper ballots and forms for results protocols. In the days before the election, hundreds of short-term monitors arrive and are incorporated into the EOM team.

On election day, these election monitors fan out throughout the country in teams of two and strive to visit twelve to eighteen polling places (precincts), some twice, during the day. A few teams are placed in just one polling place for a full day. Monitors count the voters who come to the polling station and observe whether the election officials in each station observe legally mandated procedures such as checking signatures against registration documents. At the closing of polls, the election observers monitor the counting, tabulation, and transporting of ballots and the protocols with the tally of votes, unused ballots, and invalid ballots from the precincts to the next level (district or territorial) office for aggregate tabulation. The long-term observers and core team remain for a week, sometimes two, after election day to follow the process of reporting results to the public. They observe appeals and complaints to authorities, and whether or how they are resolved. The final OSCE/ODIHR report appears about one month after the election monitors complete their work in a country, and it is required to address both positive and negative features of the election the team observed. In short, the EOM teams observe hundreds of polling stations—a third to half of the total number of polling stations for Azerbaijani elections—and compare the procedures they witness both to domestic law and to international standards accepted by OSCE members. The final reports are detailed and dispassionate. A finding that the elections in question "did not meet international standards for free and fair elections" is a serious, evidence-based conclusion. And this was the OSCE/ODIHR finding for every election observed in Azerbaijan since 1995.

The 1995 parliamentary elections were the first post-Soviet legislative elections and were coupled with ratification of the new Constitution.[47] The Electoral Law adopted by the Milli Majlis on August 12, 1995, established a unicameral legislature with 125 seats, 100 elected on an individual mandate and 25 from party lists, voted nationwide and allocated proportional to the total vote won by each party. The Central Election Commission (CEC) that would oversee elections would have fifteen members: a chair appointed by the president, and the other fourteen chosen by the chair. Half of the CEC would represent "the state and business," 20 percent would represent the candidates, and 30 percent would be reserved for political parties. The ruling New Azerbaijan Party (YAP), chaired by Heydar Aliyev, was sure to dominate the CEC, a body that was meant to be "neutral." President Aliyev nonetheless stressed his personal commitment to free and fair elections.

During the run-up to the elections, the pressure against the major opposition parties looked like a settling of scores. Accusations by the state included the claim that the Popular Front, now the Azerbaijan Popular Front Party (AXCP) led by Ali Kerimli in place of the exiled Elchibey, was "a terrorist organization." Müsavat Party head Isa Gambar was banned from traveling abroad because he could still be indicted for his 1993 official actions against the discredited Surat Huseynov. Several candidates from the Müsavat Party list were arrested—including their number two, Tofiq Gasymov, who had challenged Aliyev's authority in June 1993. He was now accused of treason for allegedly aiding the March 1995 coup attempt led by Surat Huseynov and was sent to a psychiatric hospital, a Brezhnev-era punishment for many dissidents.[48] Journalists, including two from the AXCP, were arrested for "insulting the honor and dignity of the president," a criminal charge. EOM monitors reported that the media were openly biased against opposition candidates.

Disputes emerged over the 50,000 signatures that were needed for a party to secure a place on the ballot for the twenty-five party-list seats. EOM teams noted the lack of stated criteria for judging the validity of signatures, a shortcoming that was never resolved. Election commissions and courts declared thousands of signatures to be forgeries without comparing them to confirmed examples, sometimes even when the person who had signed them testified to their accuracy. Spot checks by EOM teams confirmed tampering and intimidation, in one case by the housing authority, of people who signed lists for the Müsavat Party. The CEC admitted that it had incorrectly disqualified 7,000 signatures for Müsavat when the number should have been only 6,000. Müsavat was excluded from the party-list seats on the grounds that it did not get enough signatures. Similar obstacles applied to individual candidates. The major parties all put forward between seventy-eight and eighty-nine names to run for the 100 single-mandate constituencies, but the proportion judged to have enough "valid" signatures was quite different: Müsavat had only twelve people approved of eighty-three proposed; AXCP got twenty-three of eighty-nine, Etibar Mamedov's AMIP got thirty-three of seventy-eight, and YAP got fifty-seven of eighty-nine.

On election day, EOM designated "many" polling stations as having "good" procedures and "many" as having "serious irregularities," including multiple voting (where people voted more than once, or where the head of a family cast votes for all family members), "widespread interference by representatives of local executive authority including the police," and "highly disorganized counting procedures" at both precinct and district levels.[49] Assessment of vote counting similarly was marked "good" on "some" precincts, but "bad" in "many." Among violations of the law were inflated voter participation rates (one station reportedly went from 20 percent to 90 percent in the two hours between 7 and 9 p.m.), failure to invalidate unused ballots, widespread evidence of ballot stuffing, office lights "accidentally" going out during counting, ballots being moved to a separate room for unobserved counting, and police excluding international and domestic monitors.[50]

Later, the CEC announced the official election results. Only three parties won enough votes (8 percent of total) for a seat: three each for the AXCP and AMIP, and nineteen for YAP. Of the 100 individual mandate seats, 71 were elected; 20 constituencies needed a run-off because no candidate got 50 percent + 1 of the votes; 8 were canceled, some for failing to meet the 50 percent participation requirement; and 3 were annulled for violating the Election Law, although none of these annulled results included anywhere the EOM team had observed violations of electoral procedure. After run-offs and new elections three months later, YAP had a commanding majority in the Milli Majlis, while AXCP and AMIP together had fewer than a dozen deputies and Müsavat was not represented at all. Reportedly 91.9 percent of eligible voters cast ballots on the proposed Constitution, and 86 percent voted to accept it. It remains in force, with amendments, in 2016.

In the end, the OSCE/ODIHR final report concluded that Azerbaijan's 1995 parliamentary elections process "did not correspond to internationally accepted norms" and the irregularities and violations detailed in the report cast "serious doubts as to the fairness of the elections." Among the ten final recommendations to the Azerbaijani government were assuring greater ballot security; care in getting and checking voters' signatures; revision of laws concerning the presence of authorities, including police, in polling stations; and broad civic education for citizens. President Aliyev, though surely disappointed by the language of the final report, conceded that there had been errors but proclaimed that the parliamentary elections were a step toward democracy. Given how much people had to learn, maybe these elections, however flawed, were indeed such a step.

Or maybe they were not. The elections, or more precisely the ways in which they violated new laws and international norms, may have reflected the adaptation of Azerbaijan's Soviet-era system to demands that seemed externally imposed, just as the Soviet requirements had been. It was easy to interpret the OSCE principles as obstacles to evade in order to continue with business as usual. In 1995, Azerbaijani authorities at all levels had adopted and then ignored new laws and principles and reverted to the methods they knew. The return of Heydar Aliyev, the trusted and familiar leader, meant stability. And stability meant reestablishing the old Soviet-era system, including standard operating procedures for elections, dealing with challenges to authority, and talking to foreigners. Rhetoric was for window dressing, for good relations. The monitors were sufficiently savvy to see the efforts to manipulate their presence: "In the eyes of the Government, which had invited international observers, the Mission's role was, above all, to give international credibility to what it considered Azerbaijan's transition to democracy. In the eyes of the opposition, the Mission's role was to help them expose what they considered the Government's undemocratic practices."[51]

By the presidential election of October 1998, Aliyev had complete political control of the country, managing foreign relations and pursuing negotiations with oil companies. The state dominated the media. YAP had control over the Milli Majlis. This election was better in the preparation phase than 1995, but far worse in the implementation of new laws and in the conduct of voting and counting, according to the OSCE/ODIHR.[52]

The opposition parties had little space to articulate their ideas or criticisms of regime policies. Newspapers had not achieved appropriate levels of professionalism, and sometimes were not even available outside the capital. Knowing that they had no chance to win, the major opposition parties—AXCP, Müsavat, and AMIP—planned a boycott of the presidential elections, which was broken when Etibar Mamedov of AMIP announced his candidacy. Boycotting deprived the opposition of even a claim to a public venue to present their views. By the late 1990s, an array of parties existed, mostly small, that articulated similar views around "democracy," independence, and equality. But differences were not always great. AMIP was founded because Etibar Mamedov had felt that the Popular Front under Abulfez Elchibey was too accommodating to the neocommunist leadership under Ayaz Mutalibov. Once Azerbaijan's independence was achieved, there were few programmatic differences between AMIP and the Popular Front. Politics were already driven by personalities and the places of origin of the leaders. As part of the "Yeraz" group of Azerbaijanis, those whose families had come from areas that formerly had been part of Armenia, Etibar's leadership led people to associate "his" party with the Yeraz. As more parties were founded in the coming years, the same identification with leaders and their places of origin dominated the party's identity, regardless of programmatic themes. The operative principle is *yerbaz-lik*, which usually is translated as "regionalism." But the word "regionalism" does not convey the same sense of intense loyalty to one's place of origin, or the origin of one's family, as the term *yerbazlik*. This is not the sense of familiarity that, for example, Chicagoans feel when they find each other in Paris. *Yerbazlik* implies functional loyalty, even obligation to others from your home region. The clue is in the word itself: the suffix *-baz* connotes strong attachment, so "*modabaz*" is someone committed to fashion (*moda*), an extreme "clothes horse." *Yerbazlik* is a sufficiently strong loyalty that it competes with and, taken collectively, may impede a wider national loyalty. This tendency played and continues to play a significant role in Azerbaijani politics.

The opposition parties did not disagree with the regime's key positions—getting advantageous agreements on oil exploitation and export, maintaining balanced foreign relations with neighbors and drawing closer to the West, improving standards of living, and resolving the Karabagh stalemate in a way that led to the return of all land and displaced persons. But the opposition did not trust the regime to pursue these goals honestly for the public good. The public, being inundated by vilification from state-run media, did not have much trust in the opposition. Potential supporters were rarely prepared to face the consequences of supporting the AXCP, Müsavat, or AMIP. Under such circumstances, it might seem that President Aliyev would have no worries in the upcoming campaign. But Etibar Mamedov ran an appealing campaign, and so Aliyev and his minions felt the need to exert themselves according to the old standard operating procedures.

Pre-election laws conformed to OSCE norms in 1998, as in 1995, and the OSCE/ODIHR final report noted that there had been good cooperation from authorities before election day. In the end, Azerbaijani authorities "chose not to provide the Mission with documentation concerning complaints and the tabulation of results." Voting-day abuses were the same, including ballot stuffing and unauthorized persons in polling places, some of whom were "behaving intrusively." Over half the polling stations were considered "good" or "very good"; about 13 percent were rated as "bad" or "very bad." Greater problems were reported during vote counting and tabulation, where the "presence of unauthorized persons" (expressly forbidden by the 1998 election law) was worse than in polling stations and unused ballots were, as before, not invalidated and could be marked during counting. Protocols with vote counts from precinct polling stations came to Territorial Election Commission (TEC) offices as drafts in pencil, in order to be "revised" by the TEC authorities.

Overall, 22 percent of TEC counting was rated as bad or very bad. Neither opposition nor international observers received copies of final protocols or aggregate tables, in violation of OSCE norms. Aliyev's official victory was only 76 percent to Mamedov's 11 percent, although independent assessment put the numbers at 50–60 percent versus 25 percent.[53] The Azerbaijani Supreme Court rejected Mamedov's appeal concerning electoral violations and also rejected his evidence, saying that "the elements of proof already acquired were enough" for a ruling—and it ruled against him. The OSCE/ODIHR final report for the 1998 presidential election made eleven recommendations, again stressing ballot security, antifraud measures including the use of transparent ballot boxes, revision of guidelines on CEC composition to make it a multi-party body, prompt reporting of results by precinct, and separation of administrative work from campaigning by incumbents.

The opposition boycott and various types of vote manipulation prevented anyone from having a realistic idea of public support for the various parties. The 2000 elections for the Milli Majlis would be able to provide such a picture, if they were relatively free and fair. Pre-election laws, as before, looked promising, perhaps because Azerbaijan was trying to get into the Council of Europe (CoE). A "reform" of the CEC composition in May 2000 still ensured YAP dominance, although the opposition parties that had seats in the Milli Majlis, in this case AXCP and AMIP, got one-third of the CEC seats (6 of 18). Another third was taken by the majority party (YAP), and the final third was composed of lawyers nominated by nonparty—overwhelmingly pro-YAP—deputies. In a dispute over one of the nonparty nominees, the opposition members tried to exert their leverage by boycotting the CEC meetings, thereby depriving it of the required two-thirds quorum. If the 1998 boycott had made the opposition parties appear weak, this one made them appear obstructionist.[54] The Majlis simply changed the CEC law, eliminating the opposition's only leverage.[55] The CEC then disqualified eight of the thirteen parties striving to contend for party-list seats. AXCP and AMIP applications were accepted, perhaps to show that they could play the game if they played by the regime's rules. Among those eliminated were, not surprisingly, both Müsavat and the deceptively named Azerbaijan Democratic Party (ADP), which was headed by the made-over neo-communist Rasul Guliyev, who had split from Aliyev's ruling elite in 1996. Like most of Aliyev's inner circle, Guliyev was from Nakhjivan, and reportedly had bankrolled AMIP before getting into politics himself.[56] Weeks before the election, Aliyev "requested" that the CEC reconsider these cases; the eliminated parties were thus allowed to run, but they had little time left to campaign.

Despite improved laws, OSCE/ODIHR monitors judged the 2000 parliamentary elections to be worse than the previous elections, with 24 percent of the polling places observed to be "bad" or "very bad," and the vote count to be "completely flawed and manipulated," with 52 percent of the stations ranked "bad" or "very bad." (See table 3.1 for a comparative OSCE/ODIHR assessment of the state of Azerbaijani polling places, starting in 1995.) Most of the violations were familiar—multiple voting, ballot stuffing, depositing of premarked ballots for YAP candidates, failure to invalidate unused ballots, interference by unauthorized persons. A majority of monitors said that counting procedures were ignored. Some precincts turned in more ballots than they had registered voters. TEC officials were observed changing tallies. Observers were denied access to or were evicted from counting stations and from the rooms where results were being entered into the official computer system. The six opposition members of the CEC voted against the final protocols and refused to sign them. Later results were annulled in about a dozen districts, and new elections were set for January 2001, where many of the same problems surfaced again. In the end, ten opposition deputies won seats in the Milli Majlis. Isa Gambar insisted that the Müsavat candidates had won 50 percent of the votes, a view which, though optimistic, shaped Müsavat's later strategy.[57]

The 2000 parliamentary elections final report expressed frustration with Azerbaijan's electoral process, and ended with over a dozen recommendations, including strongly worded provisions for ending interference by executive authorities and prosecuting those who did interfere; providing comprehensive training; and insisting on principles of impartiality, transparency and accountability. As before, the need to maintain security of ballots was stressed.

Table 3.1. OSCE/ODIHR Assessment of Polling and Counting Stations, 1995–2013

Election Year	1995*	1998	2000	2003	2005	2008	2010	2013
Polling places								
% bad/very bad	N/A	13	24	58	13	n.a.	11	12
Counting stations								
% bad/very bad	N/A	22	52	55	41	23	32	58

*1995 team did not give percentages.

Source: Final reports by OSCE/ODIHR for each indicated year.

With the deterioration of Azerbaijan's electoral process, even after the authorities and the people had received pre-election training, encouragement, and feedback, it was difficult to accept the excuse that Azerbaijan was "a young democracy" and was struggling to take steps toward improvement. In fact, the regime was improving appearances but was taking steps away from democratic elections. The CoE Committee of Ministers was holding off on Azerbaijan's formal admission until after these elections, and the report, of course, was damning. Yet in January 2001, Azerbaijan was accepted into the CoE—along with Armenia, whose most recent elections (the September 1996 presidential elections) had been characterized by similar failings and illegalities according to their own OSCE/ODIHR final report.[58] Deputies in the Parliamentary Assembly of the Council of Europe might genuinely have believed that both states would be brought up to standards by being included in the CoE, a body founded to safeguard human rights. Yet the minority that voted against Azerbaijan's inclusion considered that the country's standards should improve before its admission. For Azerbaijan to be admitted to the CoE immediately on the heels of its worst election since independence, however, allowed the regime and the opposition to infer that elections could continue to violate international norms with impunity. Whatever language the OSCE/ODIHR report might use in its final reports, Azerbaijan would not pay a price for dirty elections.

With the attacks on the United States on September 11, 2001, Heydar Aliyev promptly committed Azerbaijan's full support to the United States. This support translated into landing rights for planes en route to Afghanistan and a small contingent of ground troops there, and later in Iraq. This support for US efforts translated into a major benefit for the Aliyev regime: in January 2002, President George W. Bush waived Section 907, the hated sanctions amendment, and Azerbaijan was elevated to higher levels of security cooperation with Washington. In the face of Azerbaijan's support for the Bush administration's war on terror, tainted elections, opposition parties, and even human rights receded into the background.[59]

Passing the Presidential Baton and Splitting the Opposition

The presidential election of 2003 ended speculation about what would happen after the departure of Heydar Aliyev. After setting up his son Ilham in the YAP leadership, Heydar faded from the scene, and perhaps from this world. He died during treatment for heart disease in the United States at the Cleveland Clinic in Cleveland, on December 12, 2003.[60] Heydar's inner circle certainly guided Ilham toward the presidency. On August 1, he was registered as a candidate for president, and became prime minister three days later. Soon, Ilham had officially replaced his father as YAP's candidate for the presidency. The election was pivotal and the atmosphere full of uncertainty. It was possible that Ilham might be a more liberal and tolerant Aliyev, able to work with the opposition. He had been vice president of the state oil company (SOCAR) since 1994 and had led the country's Olympic committee. His reputation as a playboy and a gambler boded ill. One foreign diplomat commented privately that Ilham had "the attention span of a gnat." If he won, who really would be in control of the state?

Ilham might also be vulnerable to defeat. The opposition parties had forsaken their fruitless strategy of boycotts, but unity eluded them. The leaders of four major parties registered as presidential candidates: Ali Kerimli (AXCP), Etibar Mamedov (AMIP), Rasul Guliyev (ADP), and Isa Gambar (Müsavat)—the last being the opposition figure most despised by Heydar Aliyev. After the four failed to agree on a single candidate, Kerimli backed Mamedov, and Gambar, to the detriment of his own reputation, partnered with corrupt insider Guliyev, agreeing to make him prime minister if Gambar won the presidency. Gambar may have anticipated victory, and needed the visible symbol of a Nakhjivani to attract and reassure the Aliyev allies that they would be secure in a Gambar administration. But they were gambling against the odds. Heydar had left layers of supporters for his son. Moreover, with Gambar and Mamedov both on the ballot, opposition voters were split. Many were dismayed by the disunity and apparent bickering of those contending for power.

Azerbaijan had adopted a new election code in May after lengthy consultations with ODIHR and the CoE's Commission for Democracy through Law, also known as the Venice Commission. Among improvements were the adoption of transparent ballot boxes, and numbering of ballots and results protocols. Police would be present only if called by an election commission chairperson. The law was long, complex, and in places vague or self-contradictory. The OSCE/ODIHR final report on the 2003 presidential elections said that the new safeguards "could have formed the basis for democratic elections [but] authorities did not implement the law in a fair, impartial, or adequate manner." New regulations for appointing the CEC strengthened the ruling party's grip. Opposition representatives were allowed three of fifteen seats, while three went to representatives of parties that had not met the floor for the proportional ballot. The majority party got six seats. The final report also noted that opposition parties had "no confidence" in the CEC or lower-level constituency electoral commissions, whose meetings therefore were highly polarized.[61]

Ruling elites, all of whom were Heydar Aliyev's appointees, worked hard to secure Ilham's victory—which was also, of course, their own. Knowing of Ilham's "image problem," the state-controlled press proclaimed that he had the "right genetic code" to be president, a notion that the opposition openly ridiculed. YAP posters reportedly had privileged positions in public venues, and the electronic media was, as in the past, overtly biased. The EOM reported a "negative and insulting tone" and "a lack of issue-based campaigning." OSCE/ODIHR monitors reported "widespread intimidation" during the campaign, including police and proregime groups initiating violence against peaceful groups of opposition demonstrators and journalists.[62]

The 2003 OSCE/ODIHR team was larger than those for all previous elections.[63] Along with its 11 core staff, it had 20 long-term and 500 short-term monitors so teams were able to view more polling and counting stations. Their final report recorded all the usual violations. The transparent ballot boxes, much touted by the regime, were irrelevant when the polling station officials saw and allowed ballot stuffing. Voter lists were manipulated. Observers were again expelled from many precincts. Counting violations were even worse, with 55 percent of counting stations observed having "significant problems," larger than any previous election. Unauthorized persons were present in more than a third of the counting stations. Some of these unauthorized individuals were directing the counting; others had brought additional ballots, sometimes hundreds of them. Officials sometimes took ballots to a separate room for unobserved counting. At the end of the counting/tallying process, the CEC "inexplicably barred OSCE/ODIHR observers from access to its documents and activities from 17–19 October," the three days before the final election results were announced on October 20. The final report's conclusion was a scathing indictment of the election that brought Ilham Aliyev to power: "The 15 October 2003 presidential election in the Republic of Azerbaijan failed to meet OSCE commitments and other international standards for democratic elections. The overall process reflected a lack of sufficient political commitment to implement a genuine election process." Worse, the "tabulation in secret" of final votes meant that OSCE/ODIHR "could not judge the accuracy or honesty" of the results.[64]

The implications of these comments can hardly be overstated. This language is the most direct assertion of any OSCE/ODIHR report to date of the Azerbaijani authorities' deliberate failure to implement the laws of the country as well as agreed-upon OSCE standards. The regime had received instruction from OSCE and the Venice Commission and had repeatedly assured observers of their intentions to hold clean elections. The "young democracy" excuse rang hollow, but somehow it was—and, over a decade later, still is—repeated in Azerbaijan and by the regime's supporters in the West. Moreover, the admission that the OSCE/ODIHR "could not judge the accuracy" of results threw into doubt Ilham's election and therefore the legitimacy of his presidency.

The impact of the widespread cheating was not lost on the opposition, which claimed that Isa Gambar had actually won the election. According to EOM observers, the crowd that gathered outside Müsavat headquarters that night was peaceful. But the police attacked. That night, the police forcibly entered buildings in Baku that housed the headquarters of the AXCP and AMIP. Police officers were seen beating people after they were arrested and subdued. In the end, four deaths were reported and hundreds had been injured. The Ministry of Internal Affairs reported detaining 400 people throughout the country, but later amended that number to 600. Among those detained were members of election commissions who had refused to sign reporting protocols from their precincts. Officials told EOM observers that all of the detained were released by October 22. But the claim that Gambar had won the election led to what the EOM called "a smear campaign" against him, and the arrest of members of Müsavat and several other opposition parties.[65]

Did Gambar win? There was no way of knowing. The belief that he had won contributed to the polarization of Azerbaijani politics following the 2003 election, although the opposition was marginalized. The regime's oppressive methods, from police violence to rigged vote totals, had all the earmarks of the old communist crocodiles who were fighting for their posts and power without the moderating influence of the savvy Heydar Aliyev. The 2003 presidential election therefore was a watershed in many ways. It consolidated the power of the central government and the weakness of the opposition. Ilham Aliyev succeeded his father with a new high of electoral falsification, and subsequently launched a cult of personality around the deceased but soon-to-be-proclaimed "National Leader." Ilham also inherited all his father's advisers. He made no changes—or perhaps was not able to make changes—for several years. (In his second year, he did create the new National Security Ministry, discussed in greater detail in chapter 4.) Despite economic modernization driven by the development of the oil industry and the construction of an unprecedented, state-of-the-art export pipeline, Azerbaijani politics groaned under the heavy hand of the neo-Soviet politicos.

The Opposition under Ilham Aliyev

Before Ilham could savor his accession to the presidency, one of his father's longtime associates in neighboring Georgia was overthrown in the Rose Revolution. In November 2003, Georgian president Eduard Sheverdnadze was unseated, seemingly at the hands of angry citizens, activist youth, and an American-trained upstart named Mikheil Saakashvili. Within a year, Ukraine's Orange Revolution, another popular uprising sparked by protests against tainted elections, had erupted. Both Georgia and Ukraine had active youth movements, and their involvement in the "color revolutions" was a scenario that Ilham Aliyev and his inner circle feared. Soon, the Azerbaijani regime would target youth activists (see chapter 5).

In the wake of the tainted presidential elections, Müsavat, AXCP, and ADP formed the Azadlıq ("Freedom") bloc. This somewhat incongruous alignment continued the Gambar-Guliyev alliance of 2003. The tactic had failed against Ilham, but with parliamentary elections coming in 2005, incremental gains might be made, and Guliyev had deep pockets to support them. It was a long shot, and in the public eye it seemed to be a compromise of integrity. The bloc's stated intention was to move toward a change of regime with the 2005 parliamentary elections, often referring to the Rose or Orange revolutions and even trying to capitalize on the color theme by using orange banners and T-shirts. Though the bloc intended to achieve regime change legally, their invocation of the color revolutions allowed the Aliyev regime to paint them as radicals. But Azerbaijan was not analogous to either Ukraine or Georgia. The leadership was not as weak; the opposition was not as strong or as united or as trusted by the citizens. At times, noted some observers, Azerbaijan's opposition leaders seemed to be playing to the West more than to Azerbaijani voters. The opposition tried to show the nondemocratic character of the Aliyev regime as a path to power without being destroyed in the attempt. The regime's tactical challenge was how to maintain domestic control while appearing to conform to international standards for emerging democracy.

A youth movement was emerging in Azerbaijan during 2004 and 2005. Eight or nine small groups were established. These groups, especially "youth organizations" of opposition movements such as AXCP and Müsavat, had the same weaknesses as the older generation—they relied too much on the West and its anticipated pressure on the regime. Their programs were unclear, and the main parties did not provide young people with a clear pathway to power. In the summer of 2005, as parties prepared for elections to the Milli Majlis, Yeni Fikir (New Idea), founded as a youth wing of the Popular Front and headed by young activist Ruslan Bashirli, focused on a hunger strike to protest the expulsion of a student from the Pedagogy Institute for participating in political action. These youth organizations wore their orange T-shirts, but chose to fall in line with the main party rather than work independently. Georgia's Kmara, the active youth resistance movement that had played a critical role in toppling Shevardnadze in late 2003, said that it did not partner with Azerbaijani youth organizations because the latter did not yet have a program or strategy.[66] Later in the summer, Bashirli was arrested, tried, and jailed on bogus charges. He was the first example of the Aliyev regime's treatment of the new youth groups: "Strike the head."

The European Union and the United States spent millions for democracy-building in Azerbaijan. In 2004, the EU provided €30 million for "institutional, legal and administrative reform." In 2005, the US Agency for International Development (USAID) spent $3.7 million on democracy-building programs in Azerbaijan, and almost double that amount for other aid including humanitarian assistance; however, much more was spent on Azerbaijan's neighbors, including $10.8 million in Georgia and over $74 million in Armenia. In the summer of 2005, US Ambassador Reno Harnish echoed Secretary of State Madeleine Albright's call to stress the importance of honest elections, which she had made during her visit to Baku that July.[67]

Anticipating the November 2005 elections, PACE and other Western representatives visited Baku to express the urgency of having "free and fair" elections, in contrast to all previous elections. The regime accepted legal reforms but, as the OSCE/ODIHR final report on the 2005 parliamentary elections noted (see below), it did not necessarily carry them out. In August, however, Western pressure diminished. Observers in Azerbaijan noted that representatives of PACE and other Western groups began to say that they were sure the November voting would be free and fair. The change of rhetoric was a signal that foreigners were softening their demands and that the regime, therefore, could get away with a lower standard of fairness and transparency in these elections than had been demanded in May and June. One reason might have been the filling of the Baku–Tbilisi–Ceyhan pipeline with oil, which at the time was priced at over $80 a barrel. Or perhaps Azerbaijan's cooperation with the United States in the war on terror took priority over democratic elections that might, given the upheaval of the color revolutions in other post-Soviet states, further destabilize the region.

By election time, the wide range of opposition parties, some of which were actually progovernment, splintered the non-YAP vote. There were two main opposition blocs. The first was Azadlıq, encompassing five large and many small parties and nongovernmental organizations, plus sixteen "minor" parties and blocs officially contending against YAP.[68] The second major bloc was YeS, short for Yeni Siyaset (New Politics). YeS was formed in April 2005 and presented itself as a "third force" for those disenchanted with both the government and the existing opposition parties.[69] Its founder was Eldar Namazov, a former aide to Heydar Aliyev who had become a critic of the regime. Namazov cooperated with four other prominent figures, including Etibar Mamedov (who had resigned from AMIP) and Lala Shovket Taghiyeva of the Azerbaijan Liberal Party. Numerous NGOs and other parties, including AMIP, joined YeS. Lala Shovket Taghiyeva, however, soon broke away from YeS and cooperated, through her party, with the Azadlıq bloc.

Some new parties contended on their own as moderate or "loyal opposition" parties, suggesting that Müsavat and AXCP were "radical," as the regime increasingly claimed. These new groups, however, were established by people of the same generation and were often former members of the Popular Front. The right-center Azərbaycan Demokratik İslahatlar Partiyası (Party of Democratic Reforms) advocated for business interests and cooperation with YAP in the Milli Majlis. Its founder, Asim Mollazade, once a member of Abulfez Elchibey's inner circle, said that people were "tired of mass politics,"[70] an observation that Isa Gambar had made a decade earlier. But Mollazade acted on that conviction by avoiding rallies, advocating in smaller venues for greater privatization and quicker transition to a market economy. He was first elected to the Milli Majlis in 2005 and also was appointed by the Aliyev government to Azerbaijan's delegation to PACE. Although some parties represented clearly defined interests or segments of society, the proliferation of parties and the shifting alliances appeared chaotic and personality-driven, and thus further weakened the public image of the opposition forces.

In the 2005 parliamentary elections, the OSCE/ODIHR core team of eighteen staff members plus thirty long-term monitors noted technical improvements in balloting, such as inking the fingers of voters to prevent double voting.[71] The party list seats had been abolished, making all 125 seats representative of single-mandate constituencies. As in previous elections, the pre-election campaigning was marked by clear repression of opposition groups and biased media operations that continued to give a large majority of coverage to the president and YAP candidates. Police used roadblocks to prevent citizens from attending Azadlıq rallies, and in some cases used "disproportionate and unprovoked violence" against peaceful pro-opposition demonstrators and even *presumed* Azadlıq supporters.

Of the 2,063 registered candidates, half were self-nominated or "independent" (among whom were 332 YAP members). Local voters knew who was aligned with each party, so labels were not important. About a quarter of the candidates dropped out on the eve of elections, some reportedly under pressure or at the request of Constituent Election Commissions (ConECs). Among "opposition" candidates were old communists like Ayaz Mutalibov, who had been living in Moscow since 1992, and Rasul Guliyev, who had been living in the West. Mutalibov, as the nominal head of the Civil Unity Party, still advocated close ties with Russia. Guliyev presented himself as a democrat, and had even published a book on the history of democracy (starting with Adam and Eve), but he could not conceal his revulsion at being criticized.[72] He tried to fly to Baku to campaign, but armed forces at the airport prevented him from landing. The attempt provided an excuse for Ilham Aliyev to purge two ministers from his own cabinet on allegations of conspiracy: the prominent Yeraz leader Ali Insanov, minister of health, and Ferhad Aliyev (no relation to the president's family), minister of economic development.

On voting day, over 600 observers under OSCE/ODIHR auspices visited more than 2600 of the country's 5,053 polling stations. The voter participation rate was officially 42.2 percent (the 50-percent-plus-1 requirement for valid elections had been dropped with the new election law in 1998). Only 13 percent of voting places were rated as "negative," both for the usual reasons of fraud or intimidation and now for the new violation of failing to ink voters' fingers or check to see whether a voter's finger already had been inked. Monitors saw interference in polling stations by representatives of the local executive authority as well as intimidation of voters. But, as in the past, the real problems were with counting at the end of the day. In these cases, 41 percent of counting and tallying stations were assessed as bad or very bad. Violations included tampering with the reporting protocols, intimidation of observers, and the presence of unauthorized persons interfering with the vote count. Further up the line, at the constituency administration level, 34 percent of the tabulating ConECs were assessed as bad or very bad. EOM monitors observed no actions against those who had violated regulations, but noted some instances of retaliation against those who pointed out the violations. In the end, four of the fifteen members of the CEC, all from the opposition, refused to sign the final protocol, although two of them agreed to sign later.

On and after election day, over a thousand election-related complaints were filed, far more than previously had been filed, but according to the OSCE report the CEC did not address most of them. Contrary to the law, the CEC did not consider complaints as a body, but assigned each to one member whose conclusions were accepted by the body without detail or evidence. Complainants were not informed when their cases were being considered. Appeals courts "in most cases" rejected complaints as groundless without the judge considering the merits of the cases, in violation of Azerbaijani law. EOM observers noted that the process "fell short of international norms." Allegedly because of extreme irregularities, the CEC invalidated the results of 625 Precinct Election Commissions (12.2 percent). Repeat elections were set for May, and five officials were sacked.

Official results affirmed YAP domination with 61 of 125 seats; the leading opposition parties Müsavat and AXCP won five seats and one seat, respectively, but ADP got none. "Independent" candidates, many of whom supported the regime, got forty-three seats. According to exit polling group Mitofsky International, the ruling party YAP should have gone down to fifty-six seats and the Azadlıq bloc should have gone up to twelve.[73] Results in ten districts were annulled, leading to new elections in May 2006. Although the invalidation of election results may seem like a response to irregularities, the investigation of the results in those specific districts suggests another story.[74] The precincts where results were annulled and officials sacked included at least five in which Azadlıq candidates, including AXCP head Ali Kerimli, had won. In fact, the regime was not punishing officials who had failed to uphold standards, but rather those who had failed to block the opposition. AXCP, ADP, and other parties boycotted the repeat elections, expecting continued falsification. Azerbaijani officials refused to meet with PACE rapporteurs who advocated sanctions for the failures of the 2005 parliamentary elections.[75]

Again, Azerbaijan's elections had failed to meet international standards. Again, the opposition made plenty of errors and failed to forge a united platform. Real opposition parties were successfully marginalized by illegal practices. Early in the pre-election analysis, Western observers such as OSCE, PACE, and the United States had insisted that clean elections were crucial to setting Azerbaijan on the path to democracy. That rhetoric had raised the stakes. What would these Westerners do now that OSCE/ODIHR had judged the 2005 elections to be no better than the ones that had come before? Apart from the final report, and related debate and resolutions in PACE, Azerbaijan was not penalized for its electoral failings. A US Embassy statement even said that it welcomed working with the new parliament.[76]

During 2005, the Baku–Tbilisi–Ceyhan pipeline was completed and would soon be filled with oil priced at over $80 a barrel. Even individuals within international bodies whose raison d'être was human rights or democratization, such as the CoE, sometimes had business interests in Azerbaijan, or for political or ideological reasons were prepared to excuse the failings of this "young democracy."[77] Such diversity of opinion was mapped by the European Stability Initiative (ESI), when CoE deputies sometimes argued against monitoring or even commenting on Azerbaijan's elections. Some of the deputies believed that international oversight reflected a lingering colonial sense of superiority over this new state; others reflected the impact of Azerbaijani lobbying and gifts. Another aspect of the story is compartmentalization, or the "stovepipe" effect within larger organizations, especially governments. The "stovepipe" isolates topics from each other, so the government section or agency that monitors human rights is separate from the one that promotes commerce. Only a policy-level decision can bring these separate priorities into harmony. Until such coordination is effected, a nation's abysmal human rights and democracy record is not likely to affect the pursuit of trade and commerce.

The 2008 Presidential Election

By the time of the 2008 presidential election, Ilham Aliyev had consolidated his position as president, or perhaps his father's advisers had shored it up on his behalf and their own. The Baku–Tbilisi–Ceyhan pipeline was two years into full operation. Summertime oil prices that year were near $145 a barrel, and money was flowing into the country at an unprecedented rate. The oligarchs were growing richer, not directly from oil income but from unregulated construction of buildings, roads, and communications, all financed indirectly by oil revenues. Collapsed buildings and poor-quality roads that rapidly required reconstruction revealed the dangers of this construction free-for-all. Opposition deputies in the Majlis were ignored or silenced when they complained, opposition newspapers were fined or closed, opposition journalists and editors were threatened or arrested. The number of political cases was reflected in a PACE resolution of May 2008 that "took note" of the release of 173 prisoners, including at least 12 journalists and 23 human rights defenders, in presidential decrees of December 2007 and March 2008.[78] (See chapter 4 for more information on corruption, and chapter 5 on repression of the media.) The new wealth of the oligarchs allowed their families to build mansions, buy real estate abroad, and send their children to foreign schools. They had more at stake in the continuity of the regime than they had had five years earlier.

Azerbaijan had escaped a color revolution in part by muzzling the opposition. As oil money flowed into the country, the political climate had become more restrictive. Human Rights Watch noted, "The Baku municipal authorities have implemented a blanket ban on all opposition demonstrations in the city center since early 2006. The authorities have broken up unsanctioned ones—often with violence—and have arrested and imprisoned peaceful protesters, organizers, and participants."[79] Quashing youth activism was another part of the strategy. Arrests, threats, and other pressure against youth activists were complemented with perpetual offers of foreign education and jobs for those who avoided politics or chose to work for YAP or the state. The regime was competing for the new generation's best and brightest. "Don't go to jail," one pro-YAP Milli Majlis politician told young people. "Go to Europe."[80]

The ruling hierarchy now included experienced people who knew how to improve the forms, if not the substance, of the electoral process. Long-suggested but mostly superficial reforms, in areas such as training of election-day workers, were adopted to meet OSCE and Venice Commission requirements.[81] Azerbaijani officials highlighted their efforts to improve and cooperate with international norms. But none of the changes affected YAP's monopoly on power in the elections commissions or the use of laws or police to restrict access to rallies or media. Party members and officials at all levels knew the regime's standard operating procedures, and would turn out the vote and ensure victory. In short, the regime had a lid on society and was prepared to run a successful campaign for their man.

In the run-up to the presidential election, Ilham Aliyev made the usual claims to democracy, as if the assertion alone made the process democratic. The PACE Monitoring Committee prepared a draft resolution in May calling for Azerbaijan to provide conditions that would support democratic elections. The draft resolution read, in part (emphasis added):

On 15 October 2008, Azerbaijan will be holding its second presidential elections since its accession to the Council of Europe. Considering that

all ballots held since accession have generally failed to meet basic democratic standards, the Parliamentary Assembly considers the forthcoming ballot to be *crucial for Azerbaijan's democratic credibility*. Azerbaijan
cannot afford to fall short again in meeting Council of Europe commitments and standards for democratic elections. . . . Restrictions on
the freedom of expression, the harassment and intimidation of opposition journalists through defamation court proceedings, imprisonment,
physical attacks and threats, and limitations of the right to freedom of
assembly and association are matters of great concern *which the Assembly
considers inadmissible in a Council of Europe member state*.[82]

As in 2005, this key Western organization indicated here that free and fair
elections were "crucial" and continued failure was "inadmissible." In preparation for the elections, the Aliyev regime had invited the Venice Commission to
provide training and advice during July, August, and September.[83]

In August, the short Russo-Georgia war over South Ossetia sent shock
waves through the region. Russia's use of force in Georgia beyond South
Ossetia showed that when Russia flexed its muscle in its "near abroad," the
West, which had courted Georgia and welcomed the Rose Revolution, was
not prepared to make a military response. Strategically, this Russian foray into
Georgia increased the importance of stability in Azerbaijan; in the presence of
an aggressive Russia, stability seemed to mean continued rule by Ilham Aliyev.
That line of thinking was short-sighted, since a new, more democratic government would be similarly pro-Western and, if it remained popular, ultimately
would be more stable. But near-term stability was considered paramount. The
European Parliament noted Azerbaijan's "astonishing importance for regional
stability."[84] If the toppling of an Azerbaijani ruling elite friendly to Russia,
even because of elections, would provoke Russian intervention, then perhaps
Western states should take a softer tone.

The October elections proceeded with Russian troops in Georgia, oil at $84
a barrel, YAP dominating the mechanism of the election, and an opposition
boycott. The OSCE/ODIHR acknowledged that technical progress had been
made, including CEC-led training of election workers, although that training
missed some of the most crucial aspects of checking and transmitting the vote
count on election day. In many respects, the "election process failed to meet
some OSCE commitments." The elections commissions at all levels were still
dominated by YAP, whose work still reflected "confluence with official structures." The campaign was marked by "lack of robust competition . . . [and]

political debate." The media environment had "deteriorated in recent years," and the authorities restricted campaign rallies even though the law permitted them to be held. The boycott by the major opposition parties "limit[ed] the scope of credible choice." It also deprived the opposition of a voice in the campaign—always the cost if you want to demonstrate that you are being excluded, and end up excluding yourself. A new factor in 2008 was a radical shrinking of the campaigning period from sixty days to twenty-eight, which not only put challengers at a disadvantage but also allowed authorities to deny opposition requests for rallies as not being within the legal campaign period. The OSCE/ODIHR final report noted that "hierarchical networks" of people in the workplace or school—most of whom were linked to YAP—were instrumental in securing people's votes.

A younger set of critical voices was emerging in monitoring organizations, primary among which was the Election Monitoring Center. Established in 2001 as a domestic monitoring NGO, it was "de-registered at the request of authorities" in May 2008, six months before the election.[85] The center's leadership, headed by Anar Mamedli, reorganized to form the Election Monitoring and Democracy Studies Center (EMDSC), and sought registration so it could monitor the fall election. Its requests for legal registration were ignored, rather than denied.[86] For the 2008 election and all subsequent elections, its monitors registered as individuals.

As in all previous elections, the international monitors in 2008 observed ballot stuffing, multiple voting, failure to use or check for finger inking, and interference by "unauthorized persons" during voting. Over 102,000 voters were allowed to register on election day, despite the pre-publication of voter lists and the fact that 224,000 voters had been added shortly before the day of the election. The pattern had been repeated so many times that it seems unlikely that the problem was confusion. Rather, it is in the interests of those seeking to manipulate results to maintain uncertainty about registration.[87] Again, vote counting was far more flawed than the voting process itself, with 23 percent of the stations being rated as bad or very bad. In 33 to 40 percent of the ConECs, observers saw incompletely filled-out protocols. Tabulation was bad or very bad in 21 percent of observed places, with violations including manipulation of the totals and failure to enter totals into the electronic system. Ilham Aliyev officially received over 88 percent of the votes, and none of the six candidates, who each got less than 3 percent, complained of irregularities. The ODIHR team, forced to compromise with pro-Aliyev members of PACE, softened the language to note approvingly the lack of violence in the aftermath of the election and avoided writing a conclusion that would cast doubt on the result.[88]

As soon as Ilham was (re)elected in 2008, for his second and legally final five-year term, the Milli Majlis, which his party dominated, moved to abolish term limitations so he could run for a third term in 2013, and again thereafter. Deputies voted 100 to 7 to put the change in the Constitution to a popular vote in March 2009. Radio Liberty quoted Majlis deputy and YAP executive secretary Ali Ahmedov's remarks to the assembly that this constitutional change would not harm democracy: "If the president is elected once, twice, or three times, it's not a democracy issue, but a legislative issue."[89] The Venice Commission expressed concern at the speed with which this amendment was formulated and adopted, and characterized it as a "serious setback on Azerbaijan's road to consolidated democracy."[90] Opposition parties and NGOs objected to no avail.

The Last Nail: The 2010 Parliamentary Elections

The Milli Majlis election of November 7, 2010, was the final nail in the coffin of the established opposition parties of Azerbaijan. With this utterly flawed exercise, the AXCP and Müsavat were completely deprived of representation. They and their publications continued to function, but with a lower profile, as their offices were forced to the outskirts of Baku and their publications lost funding or editors. Twenty years since the emergence of the Popular Front, its young firebrands were now in their fifties and looking like the "older generation" with few successes to their credit.[91] At the same time, the younger generation, who had been in their teens when the Soviet Union collapsed and were now in their thirties, began to express criticism of and opposition to the regime's corruption and control of the media. They did not often form political parties, but worked as journalists, bloggers, activists in groups or movements, or as election monitors. They used the new technology of their generation and began to create a separate network on social media. They increasingly paid the price for opposition in harassment or threats, sometimes in arrests, beatings, jail terms, or murder.

The context of the 2010 elections, noted ODIHR long-term observers, was characterized by "deterioration of the freedom of expression, including pressure on and detention of journalists" and domination of the "public and political life" by YAP and therefore "marginalization of political alternatives." The media lacked "independent and objective reporting," and freedom of expression had shrunk in the face of violence, detention, defamation lawsuits, and other forms of pressure. Two young Internet bloggers who had been arrested in the summer of 2009 for "hooliganism" after making a satirical video on a corruption scandal about imported donkeys were still in jail. (See chapter 5 for more information on the arrest and detention of the "donkey bloggers.") Citizens lacked confidence in the election process, and monitors heard credible reports of intimidation and threats against those who supported opposition candidates.[92]

The ODIHR team for Azerbaijan's 2010 parliamentary election had a core of 16 staff members, with 22 long-term observers and more than 400 short-term observers. The OSCE/ODIHR final report concluded that the conduct of elections did not "constitute meaningful progress in the democratic development of the country." Among the major reasons listed for this finding were continued YAP domination of the CEC and other election commissions, and the failures of the CEC and the Court of Appeals to "provide legal reasoning" for their decisions on complaints of irregularities, merely ruling in favor of the state despite a two-day conference in July with the Venice Commission on precisely this topic.[93] The official election period had been reduced from seventy-five days to sixty, an echo of reduction for the 2008 presidential campaign, and campaigning was limited to twenty-three days. Candidate applications were tipped in favor of YAP, all of whose candidates were registered, compared with fewer than half of other bloc or parties—for instance, the Müsavat-AXCP bloc proposed eighty-eight candidates, of whom only thirty-eight were allowed to register. Rejections were, as before, based on a ruling that signatures were not valid without comparing them to other samples.

Turnout was officially reported at 49.56 percent. The OSCE/ODIHR assessed voting "negatively" in 11 percent of polling stations and in 32 percent of counting ConECs. Observed polling-place errors included the usual flaws: ballot stuffing into the transparent ballot boxes, failure to ink voters' fingers or to check for ink (or, in 7 percent of polling stations, allowing people with inked fingers to vote again). The EOM monitors observed open intimidation of voters, unauthorized persons in polling stations (79 locations), and poll workers obstructing or evicting international monitors (114 polling stations). In the counting process, poll workers again failed to invalidate unused ballots or to separate spoiled ballots; protocols in forty-two stations were submitted in pencil for "correction" by the ConEC; ballots were more numerous than the signatures of voters, and even more ballots than there were registered voters in several precincts. Uninvited police were present in 31 percent of counting stations observed. In some cases, PEC workers delivered boxes of unmarked ballots during the counting.

These practices reflect Azerbaijani officials' deliberate choice to permit irregularities rather than unfamiliarity with process or ignorance of proper procedure. The OSCE/ODIHR final report for the 2010 elections concluded there was a "strong indication" that the results had been manipulated beforehand. Among more than 120 postelection complaints, reviews "lacked due process and transparency;" 60 went to the Appeals Court, and all were dismissed without investigating the claims or summoning witnesses. In the end, YAP candidates got 69 of 125 seats for a clear majority, and the "independents," mostly pro-YAP candidates, got 46 seats, leaving only 10 seats open to genuine but minor opposition parties.[94]

The exclusion of the major opposition parties from the Milli Majlis signaled a new and ultimately unwise tactic. Heydar Aliyev had always allowed some space for the opposition in the Majlis and in the public sphere, because no opposition threatened him and their functioning allowed him to present himself to the West as a democrat. His son Ilham, however, was and is weaker as a political figure and as a personality. It is not clear whether he controlled his advisers or whether they controlled him; what is clear is that they cannot tolerate criticism. Rather than put up with hostile speeches from a few opposition deputies, they excluded the opposing voices in favor of pliant supporters in the guise of "nonparty" or "independent" candidates. In this way, the regime could appear to satisfy CoE criticism about opposition parties while further shrinking the space for political participation or criticism of the regime. Anticipating criticism of the 2010 elections, the two "donkey bloggers" who had been arrested in 2009 were released from prison within days after the election, after serving seventeen months of their two-year sentences for "hooliganism." It was a sop to public and international opinion after the regime's complete exclusion of real opposition in the Milli Majlis. But it was not the sign of a thaw in any sense. Intolerance of criticism and of critical voices grew stronger. Collisions would become more powerful.

New Opposition and Old: The 2013 Presidential Election

After the 2010 elections, the new youth movements and civil society groups, bloggers, and journalists increased in numbers and activity despite the serious penalties for their actions. The regime tried to suppress those youth who would not take the safer and easier road to YAP or to well-paid government or nonpolitical jobs in the private sector. (The trend is described in greater detail in chapter 5, though it is noted here as the beginning of a new generation of opposition activists and potential leaders.) Some of the activism by the under-forties took the form of organizations such as Real Alternative, or REAL, which had been formed in 2008. REAL leader Ilgar Mammadov was a lawyer who was active in Resource Watch Institute, a civil society partner for the Extractive Industries Transparency Initiative's efforts to establish transparency in Azerbaijan's oil and gas sector. As a public intellectual and activist, Ilgar presented a political and financial threat to the Aliyev regime. He also understood and represented Western views and arguments. The tools of protest had changed—appeal to the European Court of Human Rights (ECHR), for instance, had become more common. Ilgar Mammadov was arrested in early 2013 for inciting violence when he visited the scene of a disturbance in Ismayilli. He was subsequently convicted and sentenced to a five-year jail term, but appealed his sentence to the ECHR.

The regime responded to the younger generation's use of social media by extending criminal defamation to the Internet. Together with threats and attacks on journalists, ODIHR long-term observers characterized the 2013 media environment as "unbalanced."[95] CoE human rights commissioner Nils Muižnieks wrote in 2012 that he was "seriously concerned at the apparent intensification of the practice, highlighted by his predecessor in 2010 and 2011, of unjustified or selective criminal prosecution of journalists and others who express critical opinions."[96] At the same time, Aliyev's inner circle maintained its carrot-and-stick approach to criticism. During the spring of 2013, presidential chief of staff Ramiz Mehdiyev presented further legislative restrictions on NGOs as an effort to "maintain stability" in the face of alleged interference in Azerbaijan's internal affairs by foreign forces. YAP legislator Samad Seyidov, who represented Azerbaijan in the CoE, toured the United States to pitch Azerbaijan as a "stable partner" for the United States, lodged between Iran and Russia.[97]

In preparing for the 2013 presidential elections, the major opposition parties managed to form a single bloc and maintain unity throughout the campaign and election, fielding one candidate to confront Ilham Aliyev. Azerbaijan's major opposition parties AXCP, Müsavat, REAL, and others formed the Demokratik Qüvvələrin Milli Şurası (National Council [Milli Shura] of Democratic Forces) and agreed to choose a single candidate.

Rather than confront their old conundrum of agreeing on one of the leaders of the major parties, they forged a consensus by selecting an outsider, the Oscar-winning film director Rustam Ibrahimbekov. At age seventy-four, Ibrahimbekov had long worked and lived in Russia and had no political experience. Milli Shura members suggested that he was chosen as a moral authority untainted by Azerbaijani politics. To the outsider, the opposition's choice of this celebrity suggested either a lack of political acumen or a recognition that the election would be fixed and a celebrity candidate would at least ensure publicity for their cause. The CEC ultimately rejected Ibrahimbekov's application on the basis of new requirements for presidential candidates: according to the revised rules, presidential nominees must have lived in Azerbaijan for the previous ten years, hold a college degree, and never have been convicted of a serious crime. Ibrahimbekov not only lived outside Azerbaijan but held dual Russian-Azerbaijani citizenship, which Russian authorities refused to rescind. (Observers considered this refusal to be Russian president Vladimir Putin's favor to Aliyev.)

A summertime survey of 1,000 Azerbaijani adults in Baku and four other cities revealed support for some notion of "democracy" and the opposition, and also showed that many equated democracy with stability and financial security.[98] Over 57 percent of respondents said that democracy was either "low" or nonexistent in Azerbaijan; in another question, 38 percent said that the Azerbaijani government was a pseudo-democracy. Confusion about the meaning of democracy, reflecting the lack of post-Soviet political education, was evident. Asked about the source of sovereignty, only 43 percent were aware of the basic democratic ideal, stated in the Azerbaijani Constitution, that sovereignty resides in the people. Nearly as many believed that sovereignty resides in the president (37 percent) or in another part of government. Most associated democracy with freedom of speech (53 percent), but only 28 percent associated it with the rule of law, a more elusive concept. Only 17 percent equated democracy with "free and fair elections." As with other such polls, a large number (32 percent) said that stability and high wages are more important than free elections. Only 35 percent regarded the "Western model including Turkey" as the one to emulate; 13 percent thought that "Arab countries" would be a suitable model, and a similar number chose the defunct Soviet Union. When asked generally about voting for an opposition candidate, about 61 percent said that they would do so, versus 31 percent that would vote for a government candidate. Asked their specific choice for president, over half named one of three opposition leaders: 29 percent of the respondents would, if possible, vote for Isa Gambar and 7 percent for Ali Kerimli, neither of whom was a candidate, and almost 17 percent chose the official Milli Shura candidate Rustam Ibrahimbekov. Since 26 percent planned to vote for Ilham Aliyev, in a fair election, those results would lead to a runoff between him and Gambar.

After the CEC rejected Ibrahimbekov as a candidate, the Müsavat briefly considered a separate move to put forward Gambar. But the Milli Shura agreed on a new candidate, historian Jamil Hasanli, a Popular Front member and former Milli Majlis deputy. At the age of sixty-one, Hasanli was part of the Gambar generation, but had not been one of the perpetual candidates of the opposition partly because he had not given up his academic career for politics. He taught in the state university and published hefty books on Azerbaijani history. He is considered, first and foremost, a serious and respected academician and, second, a political figure. Hasanli used his oratorical and research skills in his campaign. Referring to the Aliyev regime as "the criminal government of Azerbaijan," he used official documents and investigative reports to reveal official corruption, and filed complaints with both the CEC and the courts about the conduct of the election campaign and election-day voting and counting irregularities.

The 2013 campaign included, for the first time, blatant attacks on the children of political figures. Turkel Kerimli, Ali Kerimli's son, was arrested and sentenced to twenty-five days in jail for allegedly destroying an opponent's campaign posters while working for Jamil Hasanli's election campaign. The sixteen-year-old son of Oqtay Gulaliyev, Hasanli's spokesperson, was stabbed and beaten, putting him in the hospital. These attacks on family members, formerly rare in Azerbaijan, appeared as a new operating procedure for the regime and would escalate. Even Hasanli's daughter, a mother of two small children and not involved in politics, would later be the target of prosecution after a phony car accident.

The OSCE/ODIHR monitors judged that the 2013 campaign's shortcomings were similar to those of past elections, but enhanced by "credible reports" of intimidation of candidates and voters as well as by laws passed in 2012–13 that limited public meetings and sharply increased fines for noncompliance. New guidelines for candidates, including the requirement to have a college degree, were "at odds" with international standards. The media was "unbalanced" and free debate was "obstructed," as reflected by the example of opposition candidates' six minutes on television in moderated "debates" among all candidates.[99] Jamil Hasanli protested the format of the debates and petitioned to use his time in a format of his own choosing, but his request was denied. In the second debate, on September 19, Hafiz Hajiyev of the progovernment Modern Müsavat Party began shouting during Hasanli's presentation, throwing a plastic bottle at him and preventing him from being heard, though not before Hasanli referred to "the criminal government of Azerbaijan" that "throws drugs into the pockets of our children" as an excuse to arrest young activists. Although the moderator had Hajiyev removed from the studio, he did not give Hasanli additional time to make up for that lost in the fracas.[100]

The OSCE/ODIHR final report for the 2013 presidential election detailed the failures to adopt long-suggested changes in law and practice, regretted the continued "lack of substantive debate," and listed the flaws of the election day itself. It concluded that enumerated problems, including the fact that 58 percent of counting stations had been rated as bad or very bad, "underscored the serious nature of the shortcomings that need to be addressed in order for Azerbaijan to fully meet its OSCE commitments for genuine and democratic elections," to say nothing of casting doubt on the legitimacy of the outcome of the election.[101] This final report included a link to the Venice Commission's report based on consultations requested by Azerbaijan during the summer. The Venice Commission report commented on Azerbaijani laws on criminal defamation and the long-standing recommendation to decriminalize both defamation and insult to the president. The commission asserted that more than a decade after Azerbaijan's accession to the CoE, freedom of expression "remains considerably problematic."[102] As such meetings (and their resulting reports) have taken place at least once each year since 2010, Azerbaijani authorities' responses to criticism in 2014–15 as a "crusade" against them by the country's enemies in the West is at best disingenuous.[103]

It soon became clear that the government of Azerbaijan had worked at least as hard to influence reporting on the election as it had worked on the election itself. The authorities had recruited teams of international monitors who had commercial interests in Azerbaijan or were recipients of gifts from lobbyists or state-owned entities such as SOCAR. They wrote reports attesting to the "democratic" nature of elections, or excusing its "shortcomings" as part of being a "young democracy" in a "tough neighborhood."[104] Among monitoring groups, ODIHR alone fielded long-term observers, visited hundreds of polling precincts and dozens of counting stations, and remained in the country weeks after the election to follow up on complaints. Only their report included team observations of violations during balloting, falsified counts and protocols, and the lack of judicial reasons on the cursorily treated legal complaints.

Domestic monitors remained a thorn in the regime's flesh, especially Anar Mamedli's EMDSC, which declared the elections "neither free nor fair." The EMDSC problem was easily solved; after the elections, it was investigated for functioning illegally and its offices were raided. Mamedli himself was arrested in December 2013 for illegal entrepreneurship because he had received funding for EMDSC, which had repeatedly been denied registration. Human Rights Watch concluded that his arrest was a result of his monitoring team's verdict on the presidential election.[105] In 2014, Mamedli was sentenced to five years in prison for tax evasion, illegal entrepreneurship, and abuse of power. As with Ilgar Mammadov, these criminal sentences will bar Mamedli from running for president as long as the 2013 guidelines remain in place.

OSCE/ODIHR stood alone as a critic of Azerbaijani elections. The Aliyev regime promptly downgraded the Baku OSCE office to a projects office. Despite the cooperative stance of the new OSCE ambassador, Alex Shahtakhtinski, a French citizen of Azerbaijani origin, that office was closed in mid-2015.[106] Yet even though the local OSCE office had been shut down, Azerbaijani authorities issued the usual invitation to the OSCE/ODIHR to monitor the upcoming Milli Majlis elections, set for November 1, 2015. The pre-election Needs Assessment Mission arrived in August as usual and proposed a monitoring team of 30 long-term and 350 short-term monitors, similar to the structure of the teams for previous elections. In September, Azerbaijani authorities said that the OSCE/ODIHR teams were twice the size of what the government considered necessary, and announced that the government would permit only half the proposed number of monitors. Refusing to work within those constraints, the OSCE/ODIHR for the first time refused to monitor Azerbaijan elections.[107] The elections took place with the usual results, a large YAP majority and few changes in seats. The outcome had been predicted a month earlier by Milli Shura head Jamil Hasanli.[108]

It is hard to say whether the major opposition parties, represented by the Popular Front and Yeni Müsavat, ever had a viable chance of returning to power after Abulfez Elchibey was overthrown in 1993. Elchibey's main partners were disbursed, jailed, or continuously and publicly vilified, as was Elchibey. Many never returned to politics; a few headed opposition parties. But disunity and personal competition plagued them. Their programs took a back seat to the criticism of the regime, so voters could not know what these other parties had to offer. Most Western diplomats who served in Azerbaijan during the past twenty-five years of post-Soviet governence said that the opposition was always too divided, too personalized to fight for power. The harshest comment, perhaps unfair, was that the opposition was marginal "and these were marginal men."

At the same time, Heydar Aliyev, his inner circle, and his son and successor Ilham never ceased to blacken the reputation of the opposition and use every tool against them in public debate and elections. Even a more adept opposition probably would still have been frozen out of power. By 2000, the regime had adjusted to life on the world stage. Old methods persisted, like the older generation, but younger men and women in government and in opposition learned the methods of international politics, business, law, and information management—the use of English and the language of "democracy," sound bites of social media, a slick look for their websites and themselves, and (in the case of government) the use of professional lobbyists. They used all these tools in the struggle for power in Azerbaijan and to shape Azerbaijan's image and exert influence in the West. And these tools cost money, so having oil-based income was a vital component of these efforts.

4

Oil Lifts All Boats? Social and Economic Repercussions and the Rise of Corruption

Corruption remains a major problem in Azerbaijan affecting all levels of society and threatening the economic, social and political development of the country.

—Resolution of the Parliamentary Assembly
of the Council of Europe, 2007

The wrecking ball was poised over an apartment building in central Baku as the last sobbing residents were forced into the street. Cell phone videos captured police roughly hustling out old women and men, mothers with babies, and small children. They had been warned. Residents had complained that they were not being offered enough money to find new homes in the city. Many had no place to go, so they had stayed in their apartments with all their belongings. Appeals were not possible. The wrecking crews and police arrived. Everyone had to get out. It was time to build the Crystal Hall for the 2012 Eurovision Song Competition.

The razing of old apartment buildings to make way for new construction, among them the proposed Eurovision venue, was a recurring scene and emblematic of many aspects of the impact that oil money had had on

Azerbaijan: the gap between rich and poor, the glitz that money could buy, the personal profits of the oligarchs—including the president's family. This chapter is not about the oil and gas industry or oil money per se, but about their impact on Azerbaijani society.[1]

The income gap and corruption were not new to Azerbaijan. Soviet-era bureaucracy in Azerbaijan was considered corrupt, with bribery and nepotism being essential to functioning in the Soviet framework.[2] Communist party leaders in the final decades of Soviet power surrounded themselves with relatives and school chums as a form of protection in a cutthroat system. Bureaucrats expected *bakshish*, or "tips," to complete their paperwork. Plumbers and repairmen had to be paid extra just to do their jobs; one dentist required extra payments to insert false teeth in elderly jaws, before he left a toothless patient and went on vacation. Even the marriage bureau was not above accepting "gifts" to move a couple's wedding date.[3] But the relative poverty of the Soviet system put a cap on the levels that monetary corruption could reach, and the egalitarian official ideology encouraged people to hide their wealth. One might have to answer to higher authorities if corruption among officials became too visible or inconvenient. Officials could charge their rivals with corruption, because such charges were nearly always true.

With the flood of oil money in the post-Soviet era, especially once the Baku–Tbilisi–Ceyhan pipeline brought oil to world markets in 2006, the money available became almost unimaginable. The highest authorities were fully in the game. On-paper institutional checks were meaningless, because the law enforcement and the judiciary were complicit. It was neither poverty nor wealth, but the rapid enrichment of the few before the eyes of the many and the ubiquitous corruption, that were and remain potentially destabilizing to Azerbaijani society. Today, many of Azerbaijan's poor are better off than they had been in the 1990s, and there are better roads and utilities for most of the country. Unemployment is lower and household incomes are higher, though grinding poverty remains in pockets even in Baku within sight of the Crystal Hall. At the other extreme, millionaire (and billionaire) oligarchs maintain foreign bank accounts, own luxury condos—even entire buildings— in Dubai or London, and buy sports cars, private jets, diamonds, construction companies, plastic surgery, and high-priced Western education for their children. Because public officials are banned by law from owning private companies, their children own large corporations, some created after opaque privatization of public resources. Nepotism and favoritism dominate public projects. To counteract criticism, Azerbaijan has poured millions into lobbying efforts in the United States and European Union, some of which crossed the line into unethical territory or illegality.[4]

The Transparency International Corruption Perceptions Index (CPI), an annual ranking of countries by their perceived levels of corruption, repeatedly has ranked Azerbaijan among the world's extremely corrupt states. In 2007, the first year reflecting full-year income from the BTC pipeline, Azerbaijan's raw CPI score was 2.1 (of a possible 10), putting it in twelve-way tie (with Belarus, three Central Asian states, and six African states) for 150th out of 180 countries. Despite the country's anticorruption laws, Azerbaijan's score dropped, then rose within a narrow range over several years. By 2011, its score was 2.4 and it was ranked 143rd of 183 countries. In 2014, a new methodology established percentiles for easier comparison over time, and Azerbaijan was placed in the ninth percentile in a five-way tie (with countries such as Honduras and Pakistan) for 126th of 175 countries. It was now worse than Belarus, but better than Russia.[5] Similarly, Freedom House's Nations in Transit ratings, which examine democratic markers in twenty-nine former communist countries, reflected a deterioration of seven markers of democratic practice and civil society life. Azerbaijan's 2015 NIT rankings deepened its "not free" status, with the corruption score sliding from 6.25 in the early 2000s to 6.75 out a possible worst score of 7.[6]

In such an environment, political life cannot be divorced from endemic corruption, especially when ruling circles are mired in it. When the government can buy cooperation and compliance, pay for votes and flattery, provide jobs and apartments for their supporters, and control information, there is no need to generate consensus on policies or be accountable to the people.[7] Forms of democratic government may exist, but not function. Moreover, a corrupt government is lacking in moral authority and legitimacy. Because it cannot tolerate criticism, it is always vulnerable to open investigation and debate. Thus, a highly corrupt centralized government cannot permit independence in other branches of government, nor can it allow the free functioning of opposition groups or independent media.

A Brief History of Baku Oil

Oil was the great hope for Azerbaijan's future—the resource that would make it Switzerland, and not Swaziland. Exploited successfully in the late nineteenth century, Baku's "oil rush" turned it into a modern city with a telephone system, a stock exchange, a casino, and beautiful multistory residential and commercial buildings.[8] Oil made Baku the object of Bolshevik desire, leading to the Red Army's invasion of the independent republic in April 1920. The same need for oil drew Hitler to the Caucasus with his fully mechanized *Wehrmacht*—a war *machine*, after all, that required oil to function. In postwar decades, investment fell off and the onshore oil reserves were depleted.[9] Soviet technology could not extract the offshore resources, so starting in the 1970s Westerners and their technology were brought to Baku, though their work remained small scale until the fall of the Soviet Union.[10]

In 1991, newly independent Azerbaijan was poor. The republic had received inadequate infrastructure investment from Soviet planning authorities. The state planning agency Gosplan had kept Azerbaijan as a raw material supplier of oil, steel, and caviar for export or use in other republics, rather than building manufacturing potential. Part of the greater openness under glasnost in Azerbaijan was economic analysis by native scholars that revealed this pattern. Steel from Azerbaijan went to Georgia, where cars were made to be sold back to Azerbaijan. Economic historian Mahmud Ismayilov called this trade structure a form of colonialism.[11] With the disintegration of the Soviet Union, the damage to the old Soviet ruble's currency value and the loss of the built-in trade network hurt all post-Soviet states. Azerbaijan lost almost 60 percent of its pre-independence gross domestic product.[12] Independence brought the hope and expectation of using oil to entice Western businessmen. In this, Azerbaijanis had foresight, but forging the initial deals took time and skills for which Soviet education had not prepared them.

Oil company representatives beat many of the diplomats to Baku in the winter of 1991–92, but the war with Armenia was raging, the government was unstable, and the Azerbaijanis had no training or experience to prepare for making business deals. During his year as president, Abulfez Elchibey attempted to forge a deal for extraction and marketing of oil. He was overthrown just as he was about to accomplish that deal and other important changes, including Azerbaijan's leaving the ruble zone. Heydar Aliyev, in 1994, closed the "Deal of the Century," a production-sharing agreement that created the Azerbaijan International Operating Company (AIOC) and gave Azerbaijan's state oil company SOCAR signing bonuses and a generous cut of profits.[13] The "Deal of the Century" was a public relations coup for Heydar Aliyev—for whom it may well have been the deal of the century—but probably not for the rest of the world. BP (then known as British Petroleum) came to dominate the oil scene, heading the AIOC with almost 36 percent of the shares. Next came SOCAR and Chevron, with just under 12 percent each, and several others with smaller shares.[14] SOCAR would get greater percentages of future deals.

Measured in US dollars, oil revenues grew from $450 million in 1998 to $2.5 billion in 2004, a fivefold increase.[15] Not surprisingly, official data show that 1995 was the first year of an upward trend in Azerbaijan's state income. It was also the year of the first World Bank assistance project to Azerbaijan, meant to expand capacity and train Azerbaijanis in SOCAR and government in numerous business and financial aspects of the oil industry.[16] This first World Bank project, with the International Development Association (IDA), offered extensive technical and financial aid. It ended around 2000 and was declared "satisfactory" in a 2001 report on its outcomes. In fact, the entire project was deeply flawed. The low oil prices of the late 1990s, between $18 and $20 a barrel, reportedly cooled investor interest, but by the mid-2000s the price and interest in investment would soar. But getting oil out from under the Caspian Sea, whose division was disputed by the five littoral powers, was only part of the story.

The vision for a pipeline from the landlocked Caspian Sea to global markets seemed more a pipedream than a plan when initially proposed by Turkish president Suleyman Demirel in 1992. In the early planning stages, oil prices were so low that the investment hardly seemed worth the cost. Complicating such a project was Azerbaijan's state of war with Armenia, the jealousy of Russia (whose pipeline system had a monopoly on Azerbaijan's exports), and US sanctions against any dealings with Iran, an obvious partner. Turkey, moreover, did not want more oil tankers passing through the crowded, narrow, and ecologically sensitive Bosporus Strait at Istanbul, so the terminus of the pipeline could not be on the Black Sea. The proposed pipeline would run from Baku to the Turkish Mediterranean port of Ceyhan through Georgia, skirting Armenia and avoiding Russian and Iranian pipeline systems. It would be 1,768 kilometers (1,099 miles) in length and laid through mountainous terrain in a seismically active zone. It continued to be regarded as a "political pipeline"—a term of derision, suggesting that it would never be built. Geopolitical considerations trumped the costs for many partners, especially Azerbaijan and Turkey. The Baku–Tbilisi–Ceyhan Company was formed in 2002, and construction on the BTC pipeline began in April 2003. The BTC was completed in 2005 at a cost of almost $4 billion. Pumping of oil began from Baku on May 10 of that year—Heydar Aliyev's birth anniversary, which was being celebrated as Flower Day, a national holiday[17] overseen by Heydar's son, President Ilham Aliyev.

By 2005, the price of oil was near $40 a barrel and heading upward. The BTC was filled by the spring of 2006. US president George W. Bush was "an oilman in the White House,"[18] and people in the industry as well as in Baku saw green lights ahead. Production increased rapidly and export followed. The 2007 output was nearly double that of 2005,[19] and its value was more than double, from $3.7 billion to $7.8 billion.[20] The oil went out; the money poured in.

"Poverty Amid the Cell Phones": The Dutch Disease and the Visible Income Gap

"It's a pity about the Soviet Union—*heyif Soviyet Ittifagi*," said the petite lady in the kiosk. "Yes," she insisted, and repeated her expression of regret, "I say '*heyif*.'" After nearly a decade of independence, she lamented the disappearance of the hated Soviet Union and the hated communist system. She was a teacher, trained in a pedagogical institute, and had taught elementary school for thirty years. In her mid-fifties, she had retired, like most Soviet teachers, to get their pensions, one of several monetary contributions to her multigenerational household. And she prepared, like most Azerbaijani grandmothers, to care for her extended family—babysit, cook, clean, and shop. Instead, with her Soviet pension worth nothing and others in her family poorly paid or unemployed, she worked eleven hours each day in a newspaper kiosk—a box about nine feet high, seven feet wide, and four feet deep—in downtown Baku, selling magazines, newspapers, and cigarettes to people who rarely greeted her or even looked into her face. To get to the kiosk from her distant apartment, she took several buses for a ninety-minute commute each way. The oil wealth, the new shops, the fancy cars for foreign businessmen—these were not signs of post-Soviet prosperity; they were things she could not hope to get. They meant less than nothing to her. They were signs of the downward slope of her hard life.

She was not alone. Walking through the streets in Baku in the 1990s and early 2000s, pedestrians passed village women wrapped in colorful shawls, crouched on street corners selling apples out of buckets. Young men in expensive suits, talking on cell phones, passed them without looking. No one bought the apples. Old men with deeply lined faces, bedecked with medals from the Great Patriotic War, held out their hands for tips for "guarding" parked cars on perfectly safe streets. The specter of the poor, people half a step from begging and, indeed, beggars themselves, haunting the streets of increasingly beautiful

Baku were a terrible sign that the tide of oil and oil revenues was not raising all boats.[21] By 2012, the poor were gone—not employed or enriched, but swept off the streets of the beautified capital.

Even before the completion of the BTC, goods in shops had become more expensive. The few clerks were young, skinny girls in heavy makeup and stiletto heels. Soon, one could find consumer goods from Gucci and Benetton, but not affordable working-person's shoes from the old shoe factory, now overgrown with weeds on the outskirts of the city. Foreign investment went to the energy sector and its infrastructure. Domestic investment, too, had remained lopsided. Factories or schools that could have created jobs and provided retraining for those outside the energy sector were underfunded and sometimes ignored. Pensions were nudged up once in a while. Inflation averaged 8 percent but sometimes spiked to near 20 percent.

Poverty statistics, mostly originating with the government of Azerbaijan, confirm the anecdotal picture of severe poverty throughout the 1990s (about 62 percent were below the poverty line in 1995–96) and the early 2000s.[22] The situation was worse in the west (including Nakhjivan) and among internally displaced persons and refugees than in Baku. With World Bank and International Monetary Fund (IMF) initiatives, Azerbaijan prepared its Poverty Reduction Strategy Paper in 2001 and developed its State Program on Poverty Reduction and Economic Development for 2003–5, followed by its second plan for 2006–15, to take advantage of incoming oil revenues with the BTC and rising oil prices.[23]

How effective were the plans for poverty reduction? Spending to reduce poverty increased from 1997 to 2004, and data show that poverty did decrease in that timeframe. But as IMF data demonstrate, the rise in social safety net spending was not nearly as much as the increase of oil revenues. Oil revenues grew fivefold before the BTC was built, from $450 million in 1998 to $2.25 billion in 2003. In those years, total state expenditures only doubled, from nearly 3 billion manat to just under 6 billion (then the equivalent of an increase from $600,000 to $1.3 million). Azerbaijan spent 18 to 19 percent of its growing total budget on "social security" from 1997 to 2004, peaking at 23 percent in 1998. It spent less than half that level on "health" (7 percent declining to 4 percent during those years) and even less on housing (3 percent).[24] In 2002, a group of angry citizens broke through a security perimeter to give President Heydar Aliyev letters complaining of inadequate gas supply and electricity outside Baku, unemployment, and low incomes. Increasingly, younger men were migrating to Russia for work. The president got the message. He sacked the mayors of several towns and replaced them with younger, "reform-minded" men. The next year, Ilham succeeded his ailing father and made rural infrastructure and services a priority. He visited openings of new power plants, schools, and other developments.[25]

Official statistics show a steady reduction in the poverty rate from 47 percent to 8 percent between 2002 and 2011, coinciding with the upsurge in oil revenue.[26] Visible poverty, especially outside Baku, cast doubt on these figures. Second, safety net spending did not keep pace. By 2014, the World Bank noted that spending on social assistance had increased until 2009 and declined thereafter, reaching only 6 percent of the population in 2013. Moreover, Azerbaijan was spending less on social assistance than most countries of Europe *and* Central Asia.[27] Ordinary people *felt* that they were not gaining economically. A 2004 survey showed that over 80 percent of those surveyed did not see a significant change in "family well-being" in the previous five years; about 30 percent each said that there had been "no change" or only "slight improvement" in their households, and about 25 percent said that their circumstances were "slightly worse."[28] Another 10 percent assessed their situation as "significantly worse," and only 5 percent said that it was "significantly better."

The BTC Pipeline: Oil Money Lifts Some Boats Higher Than Others

Money from production sharing agreements raised state income starting in the 1990s, but the completion of the BTC in 2005 and first sale of oil in 2006 caused incomes to spike. The ensuing construction boom was apparent to all observers. As long as oil prices remained high, until 2014 (despite a falloff in production after 2010), the regime had not merely tens but hundreds of millions of dollars at its disposal. GDP and government expenditures, already on an upward trend, moved up sharply.[29]

Much spending was devoted to infrastructure, estimated at $120 billion between 1995 and 2012.[30] The investment in the oil sector and the income generated by it appeared to produce lopsided development, evoking fears of the sector investment imbalance known as the Dutch disease. The regime denied that any such imbalance was happening. People involved with the oil sector and industries linked to it became wealthy and engaged in conspicuous consumption. It was in these years that the regime and ruling party squeezed the democratic opposition out of its offices, media, and public spaces so that the room for lawful and peaceful criticism was circumscribed. Official rhetoric and statistics showed aggregate growth, implying a better life for all. In all these areas, a breakdown of data provides a more textured picture of the impact of oil revenue.

Does Azerbaijan suffer from the Dutch disease? Various economists and international institutes have addressed this question. One particularly useful article covers the period from 2000 to 2007, encompassing the years before, during, and after the construction and full operation of the BTC.[31] In his analysis using official data, Fakhri Hasanov demonstrates that Azerbaijan exhibits many symptoms of the Dutch disease—dramatic expansion of the oil sector; shrinking of the "non-oil tradable" sector (a range of commodities from shoes to housewares and food to pianos); and growth of the "nontradable" sector of construction, communications, and services that is "pulled" by oil sector development. The oil sector increased from 32 percent of Azerbaijan's GDP in 2000 to 62 percent in 2007, and drove up government spending. Oil exports accounted for 80 to 90 percent of all exports on the eve of the BTC pipeline's completion and rose above 90 percent starting in 2006.[32] At the same time, the share of non-oil commodities dropped from 52 percent of total exports in 2004 to only 5 percent in 2008. Few jobs seem to have been created in the non-oil tradable sector, but thanks to new construction, employment in the nontradable sector grew in absolute numbers and as a percentage of total employment. Wages, too, grew in this sector, producing smooth upward curves in charts showing *aggregate* income (adjusted for inflation) increasing from 44 manat per month in 2000 to 93 in 2004 to 185 in 2007. The non-oil tradable sector, however, showed much lower rates of wage growth. Using disaggregated data, Hasanov concluded that the higher wages and growth "in the whole economy would be related to the 'spending effect,' created mainly by government expenditures"[33] and not by economic diversity. Hasanov, like others, recommended that greater government attention be paid to the non-oil tradable sector, including agriculture.

The independent Caucasus Barometer, in contrast to much of Azerbaijan's official data, seeks to measure wages, jobs, and expectations at the household level.[34] Surveys for 2008 to 2013 asked for specific information about jobs and income, and also about self-classification and expectations.[35] This sample included 40 to 50 percent rural residents and youth aged 18 to 35. The picture painted by the survey responses is less rosy than the official figures would have it; from 2008 to 2013, when oil prices remained high, about half the sample surveyed said they had had to borrow money to buy food at least once in the previous twelve months. An even larger number said that they had not had enough money to buy food at least once in the past twelve months (63 percent in 2011, during a spike in food prices, down to 56 percent in 2013).

Other figures reflected the global recession of 2008–9 and the degree of actual or perceived recovery. The number of people who perceived their overall economic condition as "poor" went from 18 percent to 34 percent of the sample from 2008 to 2009. But that self-ranking as "poor" lingered until 2013, when the number that rated their household in that category fell to 31 percent. Those who considered their economic situation "good" had the opposite pattern, dropping from 28 in 2008 to 10 percent in 2009, and recovering very slowly to only 15 percent by 2013. The middle held steady around 50 percent for the entire period.[36]

In contrast to the general labels of "poor" or "good," reports on actual household expenditures and income over these six years showed that as the number of poor declined, the number of rich increased. About 30 percent were in the middle, but this was not necessarily a middle class in the Western sense. The number of people in the lower categories, those who spent less than $250 per month, steadily declined from 2008 to 2013, confirming a reduction in poverty. The number in the higher categories, spending $400 and more, grew slowly but steadily. The higher spending could reflect inflation, which was estimated to average 8 percent annually. But incomes had the same pattern—the number in the lowest income categories shrank and the number in the more affluent levels grew. Finally, the amount of money people believed that they needed for a "normal" life surged upward starting in 2009, perhaps because of fear of income loss and the need for some buffer. Indeed, from 2009 to 2013, 40 percent of the survey respondents were "uncertain" about their likely economic condition in the coming five years. In 2008, only 17 percent of the respondents felt that they needed $1,200 per month household income, but thereafter this number jumped and mostly[37] held steady from 46 to 66 percent.

The economic profile painted in this survey is not dire, but neither is it a hopeful example of the "trickle down" of oil wealth. Coupled with data showing that government spending has been driving the growth in wages and the expansion of the large nontradable sector of the economy, the downturn in oil prices experienced from 2014 through 2016 will continue to have serious negative consequences for Azerbaijan's economy, as dramatized by the currency devaluation of February 2015 and the floating exchange system adopted in December of that year. The longer-term picture for society is grim if government spending does not diversify, non-oil sectors are not developed, and oil prices continue to remain low. Ironically, foreign investment from Europe, including the Netherlands, has begun to offset the Dutch disease focus on energy.[38] In 2014–15, Italy increased investment in Azerbaijan, which helped to replace Russian investment that also had suffered because of low oil prices.[39]

Azerbaijanis have found at least one significant safety valve: working abroad. Increasing rates of migration to Russia and elsewhere for work indicate that domestic poverty reduction and job creation programs were not reaching their intended constituencies. Data on migration and remittances are incomplete but suggestive.[40] The majority of Azerbaijanis who emigrate for work go to Russia, and most tend not to register when they are performing temporary work. Analysts believe that the official number of work permits issued represents only about 57 percent of the population of Azerbaijanis working in Russia.[41]

Table 4.1. Work Permits of Azerbaijanis in Russia and Money Transferred from Russia to Azerbaijan, 2006–11

Year	Work Permits of Azerbaijanis in Russia	Money Transferred from Russia to Azerbaijan (US$ million)
2006	28,319	378
2007	57,562	653
2008	76,283	887
2009	60,664	661
2010	40,349	794
2011	N/A	1049

Sources: Compiled from Bara et al., *Regional Migration Report*; and Iontsev and Ivakhnyuk, *Role of International Migration.*

The amount of remittances these workers have sent back to Azerbaijan is perhaps more significant. Data on official money transfers from the Russian Central Bank for 2006–11 (see table 4.1) show a pattern similar to work permits for the first four years, but thereafter remittances continued to grow even though the number of work permits dropped.[42] The pattern probably represents a decline in worker registration. A related study claimed that only 65 percent of the remittances were sent by official bank transfers, and the rest were brought or mailed by individuals. The creator of this study, Building Migration Partnerships, estimated the 2007 remittance total from Russia to Azerbaijan as $1.5 billion,[43] much higher than the amount suggested by the data in table 4.1.[44] The money sent as remittances is used for basic needs, such as food, housing, and for paying routine bills, but not for investment.

Repercussions: Bribes, Embezzlement, Morality

The cost of living in Azerbaijan includes paying bribes. From 2008 to 2013, the number of people reporting in the Caucasus Barometer surveys that they or someone in their household had paid a bribe for a service went from one-third of the respondents to one-quarter—a lower figure, but still a large proportion.[45] According to the Transparency International Global Corruption Barometer for Azerbaijan in 2010–11, 52 percent of respondents said that corruption had become worse in the previous three years, and 47 percent had paid bribes, including to the police, regarded as the most corrupt institution in Azerbaijan. The judiciary was not far behind.[46] Common incidents of small-scale corruption include traffic police stopping motorists, who then pay petty bribes to avoid an official fine.

One recent reform affects only low-level institutional corruption, but its effects have been highly visible. In 2011, Azerbaijan joined the Open Government Partnership, an intergovernmental organization promoting transparency and civil society involvement in monitoring state finances. As part of its membership, the government adopted the National Action Plan for 2012–2015 and set up a State Agency for Public Service and Social Innovations, supervising the Azerbaijani Service and Assessment Network (ASAN). As part of ASAN, nine ministries and agencies offer numerous services, some online, including issuing residence permits and birth certificates.[47] The speed and simplicity of this process, and elimination of bribes for these transactions, have won enthusiastic praise from citizens. The state also created a nominally independent anticorruption department of the state prosecutor's office.[48] These recent measures may be the reason that polls from 2013 showed that 68 percent of those asked said that government anticorruption measures are effective.[49]

Real estate is another place for a wide range of bribery and kickbacks. Details of one case—similar to the example in the opening of this chapter of old buildings being razed to make way for new construction—surfaced in February 2010.[50] Residents of apartments on Fizuli Street in downtown Baku were being forced from their homes to make way for a park project. They were offered compensation of 1,250 AZN (then about $1,525) per square meter, an amount well below market price. An advocate with the Azerbaijani NGO Bureau of Human Rights and Respect for the Law explained that when residents complained to the presidential administration, they were told that the state had allocated 4,000 AZN ($4,880) per square meter for compensation. Moreover, hundreds of apartments were involved. Thus less than one-third of the money allotted for the residents was being offered to them. For each square meter of housing, 2,750 AZN was being stolen. Since "hundreds" of square meters were involved, local officials were sharing a "take" of more than 275,000 AZN ($335,000). The rights advocates believed that this skimmed-off compensation money went into the pockets of the local authorities. Residents who complained were told to take the 1,250 AZN without further complaint, or they would be forcibly ejected from their homes without any compensation.[51] This reply indicates that local officials were confident that residents would get no satisfaction from official complaints to higher authorities or the courts. Such confidence means that higher officials have limited power over their underlings, or are colluding with them in a well-established system—known in Russian history as *kormlenie*, or "feeding"—to ensure that local officials receive an adequate income at the expense of the local population.

This story is not unique. It suggests that criminal graft is occurring locally, at the lower and middle levels of bureaucracy, and that the amounts are significant—in the Fizuli Street example, about two-thirds of the residents' allocation was being stolen. Citizens and observers say that corruption of all types is a daunting problem.[52] The Parliamentary Assembly of the Council of Europe, which Azerbaijan joined in January 2001, considered Azerbaijani corruption to be so serious a problem that it adopted this resolution in 2007:

> Corruption remains a major problem in Azerbaijan affecting all levels of society and threatening the economic, social and political development of the country. The Assembly urges the Azerbaijani authorities to implement the recommendations made by the Group of States against Corruption (GRECO). . . . The Assembly welcomes the fact that the Azerbaijani authorities are preparing a national strategy for increasing transparency and combating corruption, in co-operation with their international partners.[53]

In fact, the regime continued to prepare and advertise strategies, plans, and vision statements, but it has acted on none of them. In 2009, two years after this CoE resolution, a Bloomberg reporter wrote about popular discontent with corruption, income inequality, and the potential for Islamic extremism, partly generated by economic decline: "In 2006, [Azerbaijan]'s GDP rose by 30.5 percent, in 2007, by 23.3 percent, according to the IMF. At that time Azerbaijan was the world's fastest growing economy. The country remains financially stable, its budget is balanced, and unemployment does not exceed several percent."[54] The problem of conspicuous consumption was clear. This anonymous reporter described a familiar scene:

> Baku flaunts its oil money . . . in the good road from the new air-port, the skyscrapers springing up in the center, the lavish dachas by the seaside, villas belonging to government officials surrounded by several-meter-high fences with black Hummers parked in front.[55]

The government claimed that the 2008–9 financial crisis had missed Azerbaijan. People believed this claim, "until oil prices dramatically fell and Baku's construction sites came to a standstill."[56] Wages were delayed; inflation remained a problem.

This reporter interviewed working-class Azerbaijanis, finding that many "have lost their belief in a better future. Common people often stress that they no longer believe that they will share the profits from oil and gas sales. They do not trust the government, perceiving its members as 'parasites' who care only for their own interest." The reporter concluded, "Azerbaijani society has been passive for years and has represented no threat for the regime. But signs of change are there for those who look." Hikmet Hajizade, a local analyst, said, "Unrest among young people is on the rise: they discuss, set up their organizations, opposition websites, and blogs." Indeed, Hajizade's own son was one of these young dissidents, arrested the same year this story was published (see chapter 5). Some of those interviewed inclined toward Islam as a moral compass. One said, "Only Islam can save Azerbaijan from the influence of the rotten West." Ultimately, "Among the major threats to Azerbaijan's internal stability are massive corruption, nepotism, and the dependence of the economy on energy resources. No country struggling with such problems can be considered securely stable."[57]

Anticorruption Measures and "the Rotten West"

Despite such criticism of "the rotten West," the institutions that strive to address such problems as corruption and lopsided economic development are in the West. These organizations include Transparency International, the Organization for Economic Cooperation and Development (OECD), the Natural Resource Governance Institute, the Extractive Industries Transparency Initiative (EITI), and others like the World Bank Group. In the 1990s and 2000s, Azerbaijan joined many such organizations in an attempt to show that its leadership had pro-Western, pro-reform inclinations, even when they meant merely to "tick the boxes" rather than engage in the process of change. As it turned out, some people in those international organizations, as well as civil society activists in Azerbaijan and the West, expected Baku to take its commitments seriously. The result was some reform and much conflict.

In the 1990s, Azerbaijan was fixated on oil, so Baku first reached out to Western banks and other financial institutions.[58] The newly independent but crippled government joined the World Bank Group in phases: in 1992, Azerbaijan joined the International Bank for Reconstruction and Development (IBRD) and the Multilateral Guarantee Agency (MIGA), thereby securing access to lending and insurance mechanisms that would enable foreign direct investment, an essential factor for expanding the oil industry. In 1995, Azerbaijan joined the IDA, which provides development grants and lends at concessionary rates. The IDA drafted a limited Country Assistance Strategy for Azerbaijan in 1995, and a full assistance strategy was "discussed in 1996, but apparently never approved.[59] According to a 2000 Country Assistance Evaluation from the World Bank, first among the goals of that full strategy was "establishing a policy and institution framework conducive to efficient and equitable private sector-led sustainable growth."[60] This goal apparently turned out to be unappealing to the ruling elites.

Azerbaijan applied to join the World Trade Organization (WTO) in June 1997. A working party on its application was immediately created, but meetings were infrequent, compliance was delayed, and even a draft working report took years to produce. As of 2015, the WTO website notes that "multilateral work is proceeding on the basis of a Draft Working Party Report, since December 2013."[61] Like other Western institutions, the WTO requires a level of disclosure of financial and commercial processes that Azerbaijan appears unwilling to adopt.

More fruitful was Azerbaijan's membership in the EITI, an international organization established to provide citizens of resource-rich countries with information on their government's earnings from the sale of natural resources.[62] Its underlying concept is that "natural resources . . . belong to a country's people." EITI was established in 2002, and Azerbaijan was one of its early participants, with Azerbaijani civil society groups partnering with the government. Azerbaijan was one of the first states to be judged compliant with EITI standards in 2009, and Baku's participation in the EITI was hailed by the international community as an important move toward transparency in the oil industry. Of fourteen foreign oil and gas companies operating in the country, however, only BP has made its sales statistics partially available publicly, as had SOCAR, the state oil company.[63] A 2013 report by Global Witness, a natural resources transparency advocacy nonprofit, argued that EITI regulations were, before 2013 changes, sufficiently limited that a country could be judged "compliant" despite lack of transparency in many areas. (This report will be discussed in greater detail later in the chapter.)

In 2005, Azerbaijan adopted its own anticorruption law,[64] and it ratified the UN Convention Against Corruption.[65] Despite the terms of the former—specifically, Article 5, which requires that public officials disclose their personal wealth, value of bank accounts, and property—most officials have not made such disclosures. Azerbaijan's track record appears to be a long run of signing agreements, joining organizations (such as the OSCE and Council of Europe discussed in chapter 3 and the Natural Resource Governance Institute, another resource transparency NGO), or passing laws, but failing to implement their terms.[66] Western partners, individuals, and sometimes entire institutions have turned a blind eye to Azerbaijan's failings or excused inaction, low-level compliance, or violations because Azerbaijan is "in a tough neighborhood."[67] Several such cases involve human rights and are examined in chapter 5, and some cases concerning high-level corruption will be explored later in this chapter.

Despite corruption and tainted elections, Western countries continue to do business with Azerbaijan because of the oil and developing gas export sector, to say nothing of its strategic location. The 2009 Bloomberg article noted the fallout from the West's decisions, in that "disillusionment with the West is a new phenomenon in Azerbaijan, and it is getting stronger. Many Azerbaijanis perceive the West as a cynical player that calls for democratization but values Azerbaijani oil more. The West is also commonly perceived as supporting [Ilham] Aliyev's authoritarian regime."[68] Indeed, more than a decade after completion of the BTC pipeline and two decades after post-

Soviet independence, corruption penetrates every level of Azerbaijani society, business, and government. A small number of investigative reporters have provided ample evidence of it.

Corruption at the Top (Where the Big Money Is)

The Energy Sector

At the end of 2012, Ilham Aliyev was named "person of the year" by the Organized Crime and Corruption Reporting Project (OCCRP). This corruption and crime monitoring NGO drew on Transparency International ratings that called Azerbaijan one of the most corrupt countries in the world and "cited the failure of Azerbaijani oil and gas companies to provide corporate disclosure; . . . the widespread bribery of public officials, customs officers and police officers, as well as kickbacks paid to politicians." [69] But OCCRP attributed its 2012 choice to "extensive reports and 'well-documented evidence' that 'the Aliyev family has been systematically grabbing shares of the most profitable businesses' in Azerbaijan for many years." The OCCRP report recapped the Aliyev family's "secret ownership stakes in banks, construction firms, gold mines, and telecommunications firms."[70]

Many of the reports about the Aliyevs emerged from investigative projects by OCCRP affiliate Khadija Ismayilova, a journalist with Radio Free Europe/Radio Liberty's (RFE/RL) Azerbaijani Service.[71] Two years later, after writing more exposés that touched on the family, Ismayilova was in jail, allegedly for inciting a colleague to attempt suicide but actually for her revelations about the financial dealings of Azerbaijan's first family. The problem of high-level corruption in Azerbaijan brings together not only the crime, greed, and privilege of the ruling oligarchs, but also the use of the country's institutions and legislative and legal systems to protect the ruling elites; the siphoning of resources that could be used for public benefit; and the quashing of the media that revealed the theft.

High levels of corruption are by no means exclusive to the oil/gas economy, but the enormous oil income without transparency makes it a good place to start. Transparency International's division on oil and gas industries observed:

Too often, wealth stays in the hands of politicians and industry insiders. Revenues don't get published. Payments made to governments to exploit resources remain secret. Bribery and embezzlement go unchecked. . . . [Opacity] allows corrupt leaders to hide stolen funds unnoticed. Inadequate financial statements make it easy to disguise corrupt deals, and impossible for any of us to monitor them.[72]

Azerbaijan's energy earnings and management are repeatedly criticized as opaque. The state oil company, SOCAR, is one component of this complex issue and will be discussed in greater detail. Perhaps more significant in terms of managing the resource income of Azerbaijan is SOFAZ, the State Oil Fund of Azerbaijan. SOFAZ was founded in December 1999 to manage oil incomes for the benefit of major infrastructure and other public works projects and to invest for the future of Azerbaijan.[73] Its director is a presidential appointee who reports directly to the president, not to the National Assembly, as is the case for its ostensible model, the Norwegian Oil Fund. Funds are also transferred from SOFAZ to the state budget to make up deficits, which has reportedly become its main use (see table 4.2).

Table 4.2. Income from Exports and SOFAZ Assets, 1999–2014

Year	Income to SOFAZ (US$ billion)	SOFAZ Assets (US$ billion)
1999	–	0.30
2002	–	0.45
2006	1.1	–
2007	2.16	–
2008	14.0	13.0
2009	–	17.8
2014	–	30.0

Source: Ciarreta and Nasirov, "Analysis of Azerbaijan Oil and Gas Sector."

SOFAZ's total assets in 1999 were about $300 million, and had reached $450 million in 2002 when it was subjected to an audit by Ernst and Young.[74] Oil profits are distributed among stakeholders, with the state's share going to SOFAZ.[75] In 2006, the first full year of BTC operation, SOFAZ received $1.1 billion from oil and gas sales; in 2007, revenue nearly doubled. In 2008 it skyrocketed to almost $14 billion. With $4.56 billion in transfers out of SOFAZ, its assets reached $13.5 billion, and only went up thereafter.[76]

International Business Times reported in June 2012 that SOFAZ had "a treasure chest of $30 billion, a figure that is expected to grow to $34 billion by the end of 2012 and soar to $50 billion over next five years."[77] Of course, both the 2014–15 drop in oil prices and the devaluation of the manat undermine such forecasts. One year-end report for 2015 noted that almost 91 percent of SOFAZ transfers went to support the state budget.[78]

The picture of oil income is distorted by incomplete reporting and weak oversight of revenue flow. Despite the monitoring of production and income from natural resources through the National Budget Group, an umbrella watchdog organization, oil revenue distribution did not become more transparent. Resource-related income had partly disappeared from the state budget by 2013.[79] Economist Qubad Ibadoglu estimated that more than $12 billion had been "hidden" from the export-import accounts from 2010 to 2012, a major reason that Azerbaijan did not complete its application to join the WTO.[80] Finally, it is Azerbaijan's president who orders transfers from SOFAZ to other accounts; the Milli Majlis (National Assembly) may also approve transfers, but it does not appear to do so without presidential authorization.[81] Therefore, YAP control over the Milli Majlis is imperative to the president's exclusive control over the billions in SOFAZ.

SOCAR was a major source of income for the state and for the ruling elites. Trouble was evident even in the 1990s in connection with opaque privatization of state enterprises. As in Russia and other post-Soviet states, state enterprises were sold off to citizens by the issuing of vouchers (potential shares). But because those who received the vouchers often did not understand the implications of selling their few shares, they often sold them to banks or former state enterprise managers, who thus accumulated enough shares to gain control of huge enterprises—SOCAR being foremost among them—and become wealthy.[82] The first World Bank project with IDA, described above as a capacity-building and training program for the Azerbaijani oil industry, was first evaluated in 2001. That report did not directly address privatization, but excused the government's failure to reform corrupt or outdated practices by saying that production sharing agreements for oil revenue were being signed so quickly that they outpaced both the IDA's instructions and its efforts to reform the industry. Moreover, the speed at which agreements were concluded seemed to render "unnecessary" the petroleum laws that the World Bank had envisioned as part of the loan package: "The Government decided early in the project's implementation not to develop petroleum legislation under this project, in part because the legal framework for petroleum was evolving in a somewhat different direction."[83] A later evaluation of the same project, presented by a new team in 2006, rated the performance of both the Azerbaijani government and the World Bank as "unsatisfactory" because of the "limited capacity" of both to cope with "policy conditions." This 2006 report was described in an outside analysis conducted in 2008 by the Government Accountability Project, a protection and advocacy NGO. The 2008 analysis decoded the 2006 report's language to mean that "the government of President [Heydar] Aliyev was not committed to regulation and proved unwilling to allocate resources necessary to implement it."[84] SOCAR not only continued as the state oil company and "major stream of income," as the 2008 report put it, but developed sophisticated means to funnel public revenues from the oil sales into private hands.[85]

SOCAR and some of its agreements and contracts came under scrutiny by Global Witness, a UK-registered nonprofit NGO that works for greater transparency in the use of natural resources around the world.[86] Its 2013 report *Azerbaijan Anonymous*, mainly the work of Azerbaijani investigative journalist Khadija Ismayilova, mapped an intricate web of contractual relationships of SOCAR with privately owned companies that were linked to one man: Anar Aliyev.[87] The report's main concern was not the fact that private companies had contracts with SOCAR, but rather that the role that these companies played often seemed "to lack a business purpose"—and yet yielded a large return on investments. Anar Aliyev, about whom little was known[88] except his age (thirty-five) and his origin (Nakhjivan, home of the ruling family and many oligarchs), "held stakes in 48 different joint ventures, production sharing agreements, alliances or other business partnerships with SOCAR." In one case, a company he owned made a profit of $118 million in a SOCAR subsidiary on an investment of $5 million, a rate of return over 3200 percent.[89]

The network of private companies linked to SOCAR seems to have begun in 2006, the first full year of BTC operations when increasing oil revenues were anticipated.[90] The story reads like a mystery novel. The state-owned SOCAR created an oil trading subsidiary with the stated rationale of removing "middlemen" and increasing its own profits. But the path to this oil-trading subsidiary was indirect. First, SOCAR created Supra Holding, Ltd., registered in Malta. SOCAR owned only half of the company's shares; the other half was divided equally between Heritage General Trading (registered in the United Arab Emirates) and Renfrel Holding (registered in the British Virgin Islands). Malta, the United Arab Emirates, and the British Virgin Islands are among the many countries in the world that permit secret ownership of registered companies.[91] Heritage General Trading was owned by Anar Aliyev, and Renfrel Holding was owned by Valery Golovushkin, a former vice president of the Russian company Lukoil. Supra Holding then became the 100 percent owner of SOCAR's oil-trading subsidiary, called SOCAR Trading, SA (registered in Switzerland). Anar Aliyev was one of its directors and Golovushkin was its chief executive officer. Thus, stressed Global Witness, "half the money [that SOCAR Trading] was earning," over $33 million in 2011 alone, "was going into private hands."

SOCAR's rationale for partnering with these little-known companies ostensibly involved their "experience" and financing. Global Witness was unable to find evidence of experience on the part of Heritage. The unquestionably experienced Golovushkin was also chief executive officer of SOCAR Trading and therefore was a salaried SOCAR employee, making the reason for this more expensive partnership unclear. As for capital, the two private partners together provided only a comparatively small amount, $6.25 million ($5 million from Heritage and $1.25 million from Renfrel), in a year in which Azerbaijan produced over $7 billion worth of oil and SOFAZ received, after SOCAR and AIOC recovered their own costs, over $2 billion from oil sales. In 2012, SOCAR bought out the shares of the two private companies for $133 million, paying Anar Aliyev's Heritage General Trading $103 million on its $5 million investment and Renfrel Holding $30 million on its $1.5 million.[92]

After buying out its private partners, SOCAR would have been the sole handler of its oil trading operation. But SOCAR repeated the pattern, creating another company between itself and Supra (the parent company of SOCAR Trading). The new company, SOCAR International DMCC—also registered in the United Arab Emirates—was, again, half privately owned. Its sole function, based on the financial statements of both entities, was selling SOCAR oil to the now fully SOCAR-owned SOCAR Trading, SA. The money involved was not trivial: $1.68 billion in 2011 and $5.77 billion in 2012. "This appears to be a very strange business arrangement," according to the Global Witness report, which raised a pertinent question:

Why is SOCAR Trading SA not buying its oil directly from its ultimate owner, SOCAR, as before, but from SOCAR International DMCC, 50% of which is currently owned by hidden individuals? . . . The people of Azerbaijan therefore do not know who stands to profit from the 50% stake in SOCAR International DMCC.[93]

One audience for the Global Witness report is EITI, which has a mission to ensure that citizens know who is benefiting from the natural resource wealth of their countries. EITI had ruled Azerbaijan to be compliant with its transparency guidelines in 2009, and the country was not due for another review until 2015, when it would have to comply with the new rules established in 2013. The Global Witness report concluded that the previous EITI rules had been limited enough that Azerbaijan could engage in nontransparent deals, and even repress its civil society partners, and still meet existing EITI requirements. Thus, Global Witness supported the 2013 revision of EITI rules, which demand the disclosure of far more information, including actual owners of companies doing business with state-owned enterprises and disaggregated data on a project-by-project basis.[94] Publicly, Azerbaijani authorities lauded the new EITI rules, but changed nothing in practice.[95] On the contrary, in the face of outside pressure regarding the management of its natural resources and the laws and institutions governing them, Azerbaijan has responded by increasing secrecy. Though laws permitting the nondisclosure of company owners are common, Azerbaijan's law permitting secret owners was passed only in June 2012.[96] Azerbaijan thus has been moving away from transparency in law as well as in practice despite its membership in EITI, just at a time when EITI was discussing tightening its rules.

Part of the EITI membership entails partnering with civil society in each resource-rich country. Governments, companies, and civil society institutions are expected to act as stakeholders of the resources and partners who engage in discussion on their management. One of the Azerbaijani government's civil society partners was the Revenue Watch Institute. In February 2013, just three months before EITI adopted its tougher new regulations, Revenue Watch board member Ilgar Mammadov was arrested for "inciting riots." Mammedov, a lawyer, was the leader of an opposition group called Real Alternative. He was planning to run as a candidate for president in the fall 2013 elections, but according to Azerbaijan's amended electoral laws of 2013, his criminal conviction would bar him from candidacy permanently. Amnesty International regarded Mammedov's arrest as "politically motivated," and as of the writing of this book he remains in jail. (See chapter 5 for more details on his arrest and incarceration.) Mammedov's arrest was part of a larger pattern of arrests of civil society activists and journalists, striking at the root of EITI's basic premise of civil society partnership. As a result of the crackdown on civil society, EITI conducted an early review and downgraded Azerbaijan to "candidate" status in April 2015.[97]

Holdings within Holdings

Outside the immediate sphere of extractive industries in big-money areas like construction and transportation are more documented cases of opaque, questionable dealings and outright illegality. The most damning and embarrassing revelations in this regard came, again, from the pen of investigative journalist Khadija Ismayilova. She dug into the privatization and ownership of large companies, especially those in natural resources and other lucrative areas, and found the investments and holdings of the presidential family and families of other top officials. Her findings appeared as a series of articles that appeared in both Azerbaijani and English[98] from 2010 until her arrest in December 2014.

One of the earliest pieces in this series was the story of Silk Way Holding, a company that took over a wide range of companies linked to Azerbaijan Airlines (AZAL), the state-owned airline. [99] These companies, all part of the Silk Way Holding Group (also called SW Group on its website), included services such as meal catering (Sky Catering), ground transportation (Airport Gate), aviation technical support (Silk Way Technics), and duty-free shops (DutyFree.az). Silk Way Holding itself is reported to be "controlled by" the president's family.[100]

One component of Silk Way Holding is Bank Silk Way, formerly part of AZAL. At the end of 2008, the bank, after its privatization in January 2008, had three owners: Silk Way Airlines, a private cargo airline company registered outside Azerbaijan, and two Azerbaijani citizens—Zarifa Hamzayeva, the wife of AZAL president Jahangir Askarov, and Arzu Aliyeva, daughter of President Ilham Aliyev. To buy into the bank, each woman paid 6.4 million manat (about $7.8 million) and each then increased her shares with an additional 4.5 million manat ($5.7 million) to reach 35 percent ownership each. Investigators wondered first about the money: how did the twenty-one-year-old daughter of the president have the capital to buy into this company? President Aliyev's annual salary is $230,000, although his previous salary at SOCAR is not known.[101] Neither he nor his wife Mehriban, a member of the Milli Majlis and therefore also a public officeholder, has reported their net worth despite legal requirements that all public officials do so.

Investigation of the acquisition of Bank Silk Way raised the larger question about the lack of transparency in the privatization process of AZAL, a state-owned company like SOCAR. In connection with this case, Ismayilova consulted Anar Khanbeyli, a financial expert with Azerbaijan's nonstate Turan news agency. Khanbeyli said:

Normally, the state's share should be privatized through the State Committee on Privatizing State Property. And the privatization of the state's share in the bank was supposed to be conducted by the same committee. They're supposed to make an announcement, accept bids, announce conditions for participating in the tender, and then announce a winner. None of these procedures was followed. The spokesperson for the Privatization Committee said he had no information on who privatized AZAL.[102]

After privatization, Silk Way Holding became the sole contractor for several AZAL projects, including the construction of three airports: Ganje in the west, Lenkoran in the south, and Zaqatala in the north. The total value of the projects was $150 million. The AZAL website notes that the Ganje airport was completed in 2006 and Lenkoran and Zaqatala were completed in 2008.[103]

Less than one year later, another investigative article appeared, exploring cell phone companies, a fast-growing area in Azerbaijan given the poor state of the old landline telephone network, the many foreigners doing business in the country, and growing tourism. In June 2011, Khadija Ismayilova wrote about the cell phone company Azerfon, which was founded in 2006. The Communications Ministry spokesman said that Azerfon was owned by a German and a British company, but it was actually owned jointly by state-owned telecommunications company Aztelekom and four private companies. Three of the four private companies are registered in Panama; each of these companies holds 24 percent of Azerfon, and Ilham Aliyev's daughters Leyla and Arzu are listed as the president and treasurer of all three. Azerfon somehow got an exclusive 3G license to provide cell phone data services, while the applications of its larger competitor, Azercell, were repeatedly denied.[104] Several years later, Ismayilova documented a still more complex set of links among cell phone companies in Azerbaijan and Europe, showing that the Aliyev daughters, in addition to their control of Azerfon, had acquired a substantial interest in Azercell, Azerbaijan's largest cell phone provider:

> Through a trail of owners and offshore registrations, the two daughters of President Ilham Aliyev appear to be connected to Azerbaijan's largest mobile phone business, Azercell. Records indicate they are linked to two of the three largest providers, which means the government is potentially controlling nearly three-quarters of the mobile market. This raises serious questions about Internet surveillance and communications

security within Azerbaijan and may help to explain complaints about costly service.[105]

The surveillance matter was not simply paranoia. Rashid Hajili, head of the Azerbaijan-based Media Rights Institute, explained that "the Internet is heavily monitored by the Azerbaijani government, which has a history of blocking websites that criticize it, . . . [and] the Ministry of Communication requires all communication companies to provide equipment and special facilities to the Ministry of National Security for surveillance." Hajili was forced to close the Media Rights Institute on August 15, 2014.[106]

Mining is another national resource that provides opportunities for profitable investment, and the first family is involved there, too. The Azerbaijani government awarded rights to exploit gold and silver mines in western Azerbaijan to a privately owned company in partnership with the Azerbaijani government in an arrangement that resembles the SOCAR deals with the Anar Aliyev companies. The private company in the gold mine deal is called Azerbaijan International Mineral Resources Operating Company, Ltd. (AIMROC) and controls a 70 percent stake in the mines; the government controls the other 30 percent.[107] AIMROC was formed by presidential decree in 2006; in 2007, it was awarded thirty-year leases on the mineral rights to the multi-billion-dollar gold fields. The awards were made over the objections of some members of the Milli Majlis, before the opposition was entirely excluded from it in 2010. No government spokesmen would discuss how this company won the leases. There was no public tender.

AIMROC itself is a joint venture of four companies that reportedly were created for this deal but have no mining experience. One of those four is a UK-registered company called Globex, and Globex in turn is owned by three companies, all registered in Panama, the "senior managers" of which are Leyla and Arzu Aliyeva and a longtime Aliyev family friend, Olivier Mestelan, a Swiss businessman who was also involved in the mobile phone deals. The other partners in AIMROC appear related to Globex by a series of interlocking directorships. One poignant aspect of this story emerged from an interview with an impoverished IDP family living in a mud house near the mine. The family members said they were hoping to get a job at the mine. During the interview, they revealed that AIMROC had recently blocked one of only two streams that supplies their village with fresh water. The head of the family said that they were sure that the president does not know about the water problem or about their poverty and their need for jobs.

As Baku was preparing to host the glamorous Eurovision song contest in June 2012, Khadija Ismayilova published another investigative piece that revealed a relationship between the first family and the subcontractor for the construction of the Eurovision performance venue, the Crystal Hall. Although the contractor for this 32,000-seat, $134 million, glass-and-steel, state-of-the-art multivenue hall was Germany's Alpine Bau Deutschland AG, equipment at the construction site was marked Azenco. "Rolf Herr, a representative of Alpine Bau in Azerbaijan, described Azenco as a subcontractor." Neither Herr not the company office would give information on how subcontractors were chosen. Ismayilova's investigation showed that, like AIMROC, Azenco was owned through

> a series of front companies that masks the real owners. The official newspaper of the Agency for Privatization of State Property in Azerbaijan announced in 2010 that Baku-based Interenerji MMC acquired 97.5 percent of the shares of Azenco. According to privatization records from March 2010, ADOR MMC, another Baku-based company, controls 70 percent of the ownership of [formerly state-owned] Interenerji. Company registration documents list ADOR's legal address [as the home of the president's family].[108]

This time, however, presidential spokesperson Azer Gasimov, who had confirmed in the Silk Way case that Arzu Aliyeva was the purchaser named in the Bank Silk Way documents, did not return Ismayilova's calls regarding this story. Azenco, moreover, has been the recipient of many other state-funded contracts, including contracts for military construction: "State Procurement Agency records show that in 2010 alone the company was awarded contracts worth $79 million. The company also recently gained control of Sumqayit Technology Park, a former state-funded enterprise started by Azerenerji, the government-owned energy producer."[109]

Azer Mehtiyev, director of the independent research organization the Center for Assistance to Economic Initiatives, suggested that "Azenco looks like a clear example of a scheme to 'misappropriate' some of the country's oil wealth." Mehtiyev's description of the Azenco situation also was applicable to the other cases that Ismayilova had investigated:

> With the big oil money flowing into the budget, a parallel process of monopolization of spheres of economy, redivision of state property...

[made] way for the misappropriation of revenues. . . . Big infrastructure projects financed by oil revenues are mainly distributed to companies which belong to high-ranking officials. The government keeps the information about owners of the companies secret. The state contracts are assigned to companies established in offshore zones with unknown owners making public control over the process impossible.

Despite the 2004 law on disclosure of assets of public officials, the Aliyev family and other top officials in government had never made such disclosures.

Oligarchs outside the presidential family were investigated before and after the stories on the Aliyev daughters' corporate interests appeared in the press. Earlier stories had revealed suspicious business deals by both Minister of Transportation Ziya Mammedov and Minister of Emergency Situations Kemaleddin Heydarov. As with the Aliyev family, the children of the ministers owned and may have run the private companies, and the main businesses were related to their father's ministry—Mammedov's son's company imports buses and taxis, and Heydarov's sons' companies oversee, among other things, security inspections on new construction.

ZQAN industries, an RFE/RL report noted in December 2009, was one of the best-known companies in Azerbaijan. Its head is Anar Mammedov, son of Ziya Mammedov, the minister of transportation. The main question raised in the RFE/RL article was whether some form of corruption, such as nepotism, had been involved in the process by which ZQAN Holding built a new international bus station in Baku. Namiq Hasanov, the head of the press section for the Ministry of Transportation, responded to questions about the process of choosing ZQAN's proposal:

> As head of the press section I don't distinguish among companies. ZQAN is one company and its plans were very advantageous. That plan was accepted and the partnership occurred. What is shameful in that? Any person may have a son who has a company. It is natural that this company would participate. There is nothing surprising here.[110]

Economist Zohrab Ismayil, however, thought that there were "many surprising things" in this process. When the Ministry of Transportation gives an order for a project and it is granted to a company owned by the minister's son, he said, that is "head-to-toe corruption."[111] Rena Safaraliyeva, the head of Transparency Azerbaijan (the Azerbaijani affiliate of Transparency

International), noted that there are "gaps" in Azerbaijani law on nepotism, specifically in regard to public officials' relationships with relatives working in private companies. But such relationships as the one that ZQAN has with the Ministry of Transportation falls under wider conflict of interest provisions, said the director of the Constitution Research Fund. Within a few years of the first report on the Ministry of Transportation and ZQAN, the corporate structure and the links between the ministry and the minister's family businesses became more complex.[112] Ziya's son Anar and Ziya's brother Elton have a business partnership with a family that founded Baghlan Holding in 2007 (registered in the United Arab Emirates). Baghlan, which has extensive projects with the Ministry of Transportation, imported 1,000 London taxis to upgrade intracity transportation in Baku. Soon after the new cabs arrived, restrictions were placed on all other cabs on where they could wait and how they had to pay registration fees—only at the bank owned by Baghlan. Meanwhile, Anar was working on behalf of his country's image—creating the Azerbaijan-American Alliance in Washington. (This organization will be discussed in more detail later in the chapter.)

An unsigned February 2010 Radio Liberty story, titled "Sons of K. Heydarov in Business," was the first clear description of rumored shady dealings of Kemaleddin Heydarov and his sons.[113] The information on the Heydarov family businesses had been carefully guarded, but the website of their company United Enterprises International, also called UEI Holding, provided information. The company was formed in 2008, by which time Kemaleddin had been moved from the Customs Administration to the newly created Ministry of Emergency Situations. This ministry's broadly described purpose was to be in charge of all possible materials and processes that might lead to or result from an "emergency." It has the right to inspect and declare structures unsafe for any reason at any time during construction and to levy a "security tax" per square meter of new construction. It oversees grain supply, the country's fire service, and its own paramilitary force. Although the work is presented as a branch of state security, interviews with Azerbaijanis reveal that many regard it as a cash cow for the minister.[114] Observers had thought that Heydarov's political influence appeared out of proportion to his official posts, even though he had risen quickly in the Azerbaijan Communist Party, and they attributed his clout to his Nakhjivan origins and his father's longtime friendship with Heydar Aliyev.

Kemaleddin Heydarov's corruption and wealth were rumored, but no documentary evidence had been produced. Since the law barring state officials from owning commercial enterprises was passed in 2004, Heydarov would not have been able to found or own UEI. His sons Tale and Nijat are both graduates of the London School of Economics and reside in the United Kingdom. Tale heads The European Azerbaijan Society, which boosts Azerbaijan's image in the United Kingdom, providing free trips and kilos of caviar to members of parliament. The Heydarov sons were chair and vice chair of UEI's board of directors, each owning £5,000 (then about 6,400 manat) worth of stock. UEI Holding has offices in the United Kingdom, Germany, and Azerbaijan, but the RL story focused on the companies that the Heydarovs then owned in Azerbaijan.

The first of the Heydarovs' Azerbaijani companies was Caspian Sea Caviar. This particular company was noteworthy because from 1995 to February 2006, Kemaleddin Heydarov had been director of Azerbaijan's Customs Administration, which oversaw the export of, among other goods, caviar. But caviar exporting was among the most lucrative of Azerbaijan's products. As with privatization of other state-owned companies, the question of the process of privatization and the origin of the initial capital to acquire the caviar export operation remain unanswered. In 2011, the Caspian Sea Caviar online store was advertising 1.8 kilograms of caviar for €13,770.

Another UEI subsidiary is Gilan Holding. In the summer of 2015, the Gilan website revealed the company's scope of operations, including construction, tourism, and "industries" that mostly include agricultural products.[115] UEI brands such as Gilan, Gabala, and Qafqaz are among the most widely sold in Azerbaijan, from juice (the Jala brand) to nuts; as well as canning, plastics, and other industries. UEI companies also are involved in tourism, with ten or more tourist hotels and facilities and construction, asphalt, bricks, and ceramics firms similarly bearing the names of Gilan and Gabala. As might be expected, Gilan Holding has its own bank, AFBank, one of the few banks apparently not owned by the Aliyev or Pashayev (the family of Ilham Aliyev's wife, Mehriban) families. Most appealing of all these many subsidiaries and partners is Inspection Development Monitoring (IDM), an enterprise that apparently prepares builders in Azerbaijan for inspections conducted by the Ministry of Emergency Situations headed by the Heydarov brothers' father, Kemaleddin.

IDM's own website identifies its "main services within the construction sector," which include "monitoring of ongoing construction projects, on-site safety control . . . process control" and "inspection of completed construction projects." It assures potential customers, "We manage development projects to international quality standards and are committed to efficiency, transparency and integrity."[116]

Coming to a Head: The Crackdown of 2014

The year 2014 in Azerbaijan became known in international human rights and democratization circles as "the Crackdown" because of the sudden upsurge in the detentions, arrests, and convictions of prominent journalists, internationally known human rights defenders, and civil society activists (see chapter 5). It was also the year that details about high-level corruption in Azerbaijan were publicized internationally, drawing the attention of governments and international organizations.

In an exposé of May 2014, Khadija Ismayilova revealed "what you didn't know" about the major Azerbaijani conglomerate Pasha Holding—and none of it was very flattering.[117] Pasha Holding and its many subsidiaries, including Pasha Bank, Pasha Insurance, Pasha Life, and Pasha Construction, are the property of the powerful Pashayev family, of which Azerbaijan's first lady Mehriban Aliyeva (neé Pashayeva) is a member. Her father Arif is an academician and headed the country's Aviation Academy, from which position he acquired the Pasha Holding empire until his retirement in 2013. At that time, Arif Pashayev turned over control of the companies to his two granddaughters, Leyla and Arzu Aliyeva, daughters of President Ilham Aliyev.[118] This arrangement was no surprise to the reading public, but the details of some of the holding company's projects that formerly had been hidden were brought to light.

Pasha Holding's subsidiary Pasha Hotels and Resorts built the Four Seasons Hotel in downtown Baku, a major construction project that involved destroying, without public discussion, part of the historic wall of the Inner City. This wall had been built in the sixteenth century under Iran's Shah Abbas, part of the Safavid Dynasty that emerged from Iranian Azerbaijan and is considered part of modern Azerbaijan's history. Moreover, during the construction of the hotel, workers found an underground tunnel running beneath the wall, as old as or even older than the wall itself. Such a discovery would have brought construction to a grinding halt had it happened in a city like Rome, where historic preservation is a key political and cultural priority. But in Baku, where the Ministry of Culture is also the Ministry of Tourism, and the construction company involved in the unexpected excavation is owned by the president's children, the tunnel was filled in and paved over.[119]

An even larger project of Pasha Hotels and Resorts was the Pik Palace on Shahdag Mountain in northern Azerbaijan, an enormous skiing and winter sports complex whose total cost was in the billions of dollars. The project involved sale of public land, but as economist Rovshan Agayev explained in a 2014 interview, the land sale and project construction processes were not transparent, so there is no way of knowing the terms or costs. According to Agayev, more than $1 billion in public money was spent on the project.[120] The rationale for the high degree of spending was provided by an Austria-based consulting firm for the project, which noted that the Ministry of Culture and Tourism had decided to support the use of the Shahdag Mountain area as a tourism destination.[121] The land on which the complex was built had been owned by approximately four thousand local villagers. Several locals said that they had been offered low compensation for their land, while others said that they had been forced to agree to the low amounts, and some had never received anything. One villager said that he was offered 2,400 manat for his three hectares of land, or about $1,800 for 7.4 acres on the mountain. He refused the low offer, but was "forced," he said, to accept it. He did not know who was making the offer, whether it was a company, the Ministry of Culture and Tourism, or someone else. When Khadija Ismayilova contacted the ministry, its spokesperson refused to reply to her inquiries, and operators at Pasha Holding repeatedly said that people who could have answered her questions were not available.

Financing for both the Four Seasons Hotel and the Pik Palace described above involved Pasha Bank, formerly owned by Arif Pashayev (10 percent), the Aliyev daughters' company ADOR MMC (30 percent), and Pasha Holding (60 percent). ADOR had been part owner of Azenco Construction, the firm that had built the Crystal Hall and another high-profile site in Baku, the huge National Flag Square. In mid-2013, Pasha Bank was restructured, with each Aliyev daughter's share at 45 percent. This information had to be obtained from the Georgian branch of Pasha Bank, because Georgian law requires that corporations reveal actual, not only legal, persons as owners. The evidence suggests that the Pashayev-Aliyev combined clan made money from these construction and development ventures, and others described above, from varied sources, primarily from their ownership of separate but interlocking companies and with subsidies from state coffers in the guise of support for development of tourism.

In December 2014, four days after Khadija Ismayilova was arrested, the last of her completed research articles on corruption was published by RFE/

RL. This article focused on the companies owned by presidential adviser Ali Hasanov, and mapped the links between the various businesses owned and run by Hasanov's wife, Sona Veliyeva, and his son, Shamhal Hasanli.[122] Sona Veliyeva is the editor of *Kaspi* newspaper, which takes the name of Azerbaijan's influential reformist newspaper of the late nineteenth and early twentieth century. She is currently a member of the National Television and Radio Council (NTRC), and other media and education groups. Their son Shamhal is founder, cofounder, director, or otherwise guiding light of assorted television and radio companies, including the popular, formerly state-run Araz Radio and Kaspi Global, a company that makes television series such as soap operas. Ali Hasanov, another regime official from Nakhjivan, is about the same age as Ilham Aliyev and studied in Moscow at the same time. Hasanov worked in the ideology department of the ruling party YAP before moving directly into state service as assistant and then head (since 1996) of the social-political section of the presidential administration. This section oversees, among other areas, print publishing and other media.[123] The allocation of state funds for making television series and movies that will show Azerbaijan's culture and character is not a practice that is unique to Azerbaijan. Yet the abundance of state contracts that go to one particular operation, Hasanov's son's Kaspi MMC television company, seems to suggest nepotism and indirect control over a purportedly independent media outlet, and it sends a signal, as one of Ismayilova's sources noted, that this media company is the "only one place entrusted with this [national] image."[124]

In a 2010 radio license approval decision, the NTRC—of which Sona Veliyeva is a member—granted a license to Golden Prince MMC, a company coowned by Azer Veliyev, an Iranian citizen who is related to Sona Veliyeva. This decision was problematic for at least two reasons. The previous year, BBC broadcasting had been banned from Azerbaijan's local frequencies on the grounds that the BBC was a foreign-owned company. By contrast, the fact that Golden Prince is half-owned by an Iranian citizen does not seem to have affected its licensure. Moreover, Sona Veliyeva's familial relationship with Azer Veliyev should have raised red flags with any approval committee. Azerbaijani activist Rasul Jafarov, who also was bidding on a radio license in the 2010 competition, claimed that his bid had lost because of nepotism, and he filed a complaint against the NTRC that reportedly went to the European Court of Human Rights.[125] Furthermore, Azer Veliyev also was appointed to head the International Press Center, which runs the only remaining press club in Azerbaijan—another indirect means of influencing the media. The other major press venue, the Baku Press Club, came under fire when Ali Hasanov reportedly threatened it with closure when it rejected his demand to refuse permission for a Chechen human rights group to meet on its premises. The electricity was cut the same day. The Baku Press Club subsequently closed.[126]

Spin: Is the Glass Half Full?

It is not as if the international business community or Western legislators are unaware of the many questionable and corrupt business dealings taking place in Azerbaijan. In addition to reports by anticorruption groups, the American, British, and European press have published many articles on most of these issues.[127] Apparently, business and government oversight bodies do not always connect the dots; they may even entertain a certain cognitive dissonance. Azerbaijan's business partners and admirers abroad seem to be able to live with sharply contradictory realities since Azerbaijan is ranked as a fairly good business partner, thanks to reforms in selected areas. During 2013–14, Azerbaijan's World Bank Doing Business ranking improved from 88th to 80th out of 189 countries. With a new methodology, Azerbaijan's ranking improved again in 2015 to 63rd place, below its neighbors Georgia and Armenia (partly because of Azerbaijan's difficulties in getting credit and permits, and the high costs involved in exporting) but higher than Ukraine and all Central Asian states except Kazakhstan.[128] The most significant of these reforms involves a simplified process for paying taxes online.

At the same time, other reports concede that corruption is a huge impediment to business. In July 2014, a coalition of organizations that support EITI denounced the "continuous pressures and restrictions" that forced the coalition and a majority of its members to suspend their activities in Azerbaijan.[129] Another anticorruption report of October 2014 showed poor progress toward business reforms in Azerbaijan, despite the creation of a National Anti-Corruption Plan for 2012–15. The report identified extortion, bribery, and favoritism as factors that "distort the country's business environment and reduce opportunities for fair market competition. A weak judiciary and insufficient enforcement and implementation of regulations lead to government officials acting with impunity."[130]

Western lawmakers are aware of the corruption, though more so in Europe where there is more Azerbaijani business and political activity than in the

United States. The Parliamentary Assembly of the Council of Europe was the target of Azerbaijani lobbying, which in turn came under scrutiny by such groups as the European Stability Initiative, whose 2012 exposé *Caviar Diplomacy* documented the extent of influence-peddling by Azerbaijan in the Council of Europe. In the United States, knowledge about Azerbaijan has long been confined to offices like the Department of State and the Department of Commerce. Sometimes, these officials "don't care" about human rights or democracy; they care about energy or military cooperation.[131] But the circle of knowledge and influence has been widening since the completion of the BTC pipeline, and more dramatically since 2011 with the upsurge in both official and unofficial lobbying. Washington politicians are being educated about Azerbaijan, yet much of their information is coming from the Azerbaijani government and its official lobbyists. The most-courted politicians are those with energy interests, but many legislators without particular commitments in the Caucasus are invited to banquets, concerts, conferences, or even junkets to Azerbaijan. From these experiences, they come away with a conviction that Azerbaijan is a good partner for energy, military cooperation, and support for Israel, all of which is true. When confronted with the evidence of faked elections, human rights violations, or jailed journalists, however, US politicians who have been influenced by Azerbaijan repeat the Azerbaijani regime's line that the country is a "young democracy" in a "tough neighborhood" struggling to democratize, as reflected by the international agreements it has signed.[132] Some US lawmakers note that the United States, too, has flaws, but it has been building democracy for over two hundred years.[133] By contrast, the human rights and democratization community challenges this one-sided notion. These groups reply with a litany of arrests and prolonged detention, torture, and suppression of media and public demonstrations. But because these groups refrain from acknowledging Azerbaijan's strategic importance, they are ignored by the pro-Aliyev crowd and attacked by the Azerbaijan government and its embassy in Washington as "anti-Azerbaijani" and worse.

Lobbying takes the form of friendship associations in some cases and "hired guns"—that is, paid lobbyists—in others. In 2011, Anar Mammedov, son of Minister of Transportation Ziya Mammedov and head of ZQAN Holdings Baku, established the Azerbaijan-America Alliance (AAA),[134] a group that self-identifies as "a non-partisan, non-profit organization which seeks to develop closer Azeri-American bonds,"[135] and was described by PR News as "a leading non-profit group promoting broad cultural and political relationships between the people of Azerbaijan and the people of America."[136] Anar presents himself as a patriot, wrote one journalist, but it is hard to erase the memory of his earlier escapades, including "once allegedly paying a restaurant in the Gabala region of Azerbaijan $1 million to slaughter and grill a bear for him." Former US congressman Dan Burton (R-IN), a longtime member of the House Foreign Affairs Committee, became the president of the AAA.[137]

The AAA has courted elected officials and partnered with other groups, specifically associations like the Turquoise Council of Americans and Eurasians (TCAE), which has been linked to US-based Turkish religious figure Fethullah Gulen (Gülen).[138] The TCAE—with funding, it turned out, from SOCAR—hosted a lavish conference in Baku in May 2013 to "acquaint" US lawmakers with Azerbaijan. The foreign funding of the trip triggered an investigation by the House Ethics Committee, which demanded that the representatives return the gifts—which only one of them had claimed, as House ethics rules require representatives to do. The representatives were cleared of wrongdoing in the summer of 2015.[139] One, and only one, US journalist covered the conference on his first visit to Azerbaijan:

> No doubt this was among the biggest concentrations of American political star power ever seen in the Caucasus—317 delegates from 42 states, including 11 sitting members of Congress and 75 state representatives, not to mention the former governors of New Mexico and Oklahoma as well as three ex–Obama White House insiders.[140]

The Americans at the conference, and many others who have become acquainted with Azerbaijan in this way, repeat the Baku line. It is a secular Muslim country with friendly ties to Israel and an unhindered Jewish community. It has been a good strategic partner to the United States since 2001 on Iraq and Afghanistan, allowing transit of troops and supplies to and from the conflicts. It is an important partner in energy security with potential to offset lost oil and gas from Russia to Europe. And these things are true, as is the rapid development of Baku itself and the reduction in poverty. But, as foreign policy neophytes with little knowledge of democratization or human rights efforts, they do not ask questions about the costs of the luxury, the political prisoners, the displaced populace, the unfree media, the opaque privatization and budget, or the lavish spending of which they were clearly beneficiaries. Many of the Americans seem to have been seduced by the hospitality, the glitz, and the gifts of their hosts. They parrot Azerbaijan's claim to be a "new democracy" without noting the long record of electoral failings, the regime's repression of the opposition, or documented corruption. In an apparent show of bipartisan agreement, congressmen Ted Poe (R-TX) and Gregory Meeks (D-NY) went so far as to claim that Azerbaijan was a "free and shining light of democracy" and even "what democracy is all about."[141] Poe and Meeks serve on the House Foreign Affairs Committee and its Europe, Eurasia, and Emerging Threats Subcommittee that deals with Azerbaijan. That subcommittee's former chair was Dan Burton, who became AAA chair in 2013—a fact Burton that did not disclose in January 2015 when he wrote an article for the *Washington Times* titled "Why Azerbaijan Is Important to America and the Free World," stating that the country's religious tolerance, freedom, and democracy make it "a model in the Caucasus."[142]

Paid lobbyists are paid very well. In 2012, the Azerbaijani Embassy in Washington employed the DCI Group for $20,000 per month to write and place favorable op-eds in the media. The firm also briefed supposedly independent witnesses for congressional testimony. The DCI Group was on "a quest to dominate the entire intellectual environment in which officials make policy decisions."[143] By 2013, Azerbaijan's bill for lobbying in the United States was $2.3 million. In 2015, the embassy increased the monthly retainer of the Podesta Group, its main Washington lobbying firm, from $50,000 to $75,000. According to a 2015 *Foreign Policy* account, Podesta was "not above crossing ethical lines" in calling congressional offices to persuade staffers to skip meetings by US-based or international human rights groups. The firm even sent its own staffer to pose as a graduate student to attend a human rights group's strategy session for an upcoming congressional briefing on Azerbaijan's political prisoners, an action that may have enabled Podesta to pass along information to the Azerbaijani government.[144]

Are the results worth the money? It is hard to say. But members of Congress who have attended the events, and who have talked to lobbyists and the "independent" witnesses they brief, do claim that Azerbaijan is not merely a "good energy partner," which it is, but that it shares the same democratic values as the United States, which it does not. The state-controlled media in Azerbaijan has been able to use these significant statements from US representatives to show its own population that the regime and its policies have widespread support in the United States. For some years, these tactics have been effective, but with each tainted election, each arrest of a human rights defender, and each revelation of corrupt business practices, such endorsements help the Aliyev regime less and hurt the United States' reputation more.

The 2015 European Games

The European Games of June 2015 had much in common with the Eurovision song contest of 2012, including new construction, expensive preparation, and public hype. President Aliyev and Azerbaijan's ruling circles wanted to be sure that one thing that the games would *not* have in common with Eurovision was the presence of protest movements. In 2012, the regime had been stung by the opposition's protests during Eurovision, especially the younger generation embodied by Rasul Jafarov, the initiator of the "Sing for Democracy" countermovement. Critical journalists were jailed in the months preceding the games, and just before the games began, Jafarov was arrested and was sentenced to six and a half years in jail. In mid-May, the Aliyev regime issued a set of guidelines—"official bans" and "official recommendations"—for Baku during the period of the games, June 12 to 28. Officially banned were parking in reserved areas, driving pickup trucks in Baku, driving on streets marked only for European Games, and selling alcohol near the venues. The population received official "suggestions," likely to be treated as official bans by most people and by police, to avoid having weddings or setting up wedding processions or funeral tents (in an effort to keep crowds from clogging the streets); avoid driving old cars in Baku or using any private car as a taxi; and avoid hanging laundry on the street side of buildings. Comments from people on the street showed the public's reaction: "Tell people 'don't get married,' and 'don't die.' How can you do that?"

The price of beauty was, in one case, life itself. Big money went to beautification of older buildings, including the installation of polyurethane facades. The improper installation of one set of such facades led to a fatal fire in May 2015. With the rapid speed of construction, building disasters were not unprecedented. In 2007, a multistory high-rise under construction in Baku collapsed, killing several workers, and a similar incident killed three workers in 2010. Suspect construction has become widespread in Baku, to the point where speculative real estate ventures in central Baku, including new high-rise buildings, largely remained vacant because locals wanted apartments in sturdier, safer older buildings. The May 2015 building fire, however, had different repercussions. It was fast-moving, and observers caught the images on smart phones and spread them on social media. The deaths of fifteen people, including two children, and the hospitalization of more than sixty others sparked popular fury. The cause of the fire was improperly installed polyurethane panels, placed more than a foot from the concrete building wall, that had created a column of oxygen and facilitated the rapid movement of the fire. In the aftermath of the blaze, authorities ordered the panels removed from the other buildings where they had been put in place—the mayor of Baku said that there were just over 100 such panels, but Turan news agency put the number closer to 800. Panicked residents, fearful of another fire disaster, began to peel the panels off the walls with hammers or bare hands. Global Construction, the company that had installed the panels, was blamed rather than the Ministry of Emergency Situations, whose inspectors were supposed to prevent such disasters. In fact, early investigation showed that the ministry had responded to residents' previous questions about the material by saying that the panels had been tested and determined to be safe.[145] Global Construction itself was not new to controversy; even after the fire, it remained under investigation in 2015 for having received "suspicious loans" of over $540 million in 2011 from the International Bank of Azerbaijan (IBA).[146]

The cost of hosting the European Games themselves was enormous. Officials admitted to spending just over one billion manat on the games, including new construction, free transportation, and athlete housing. Others have put the figure at ten times that sum, with the opening ceremony alone costing $95 million.[147] Minister of Youth and Sports Azad Rahimov gave the total as €960 million. Considering the 34 percent devaluation of the manat in February 2015, there was "even some saving," Rahimov said.[148] The expenses were no loss to the oligarchs. The new construction involved Aliyev family-owned subcontractors with consultation by the Heydarov-owned consultants and Ministry of Emergency Situations inspections. The free flights for athletes used airport and ground services owned by the Aliyev family and transportation owned by the Aliyev and Ziya Mammedov families. Some hotel rooms for the games were surely in hotels owned by Pashayev or Heydarov families. The European Games thus represented a circulation of money from the state budget to enterprises owned by the families of the president and his inner circle. At the end of 2015, with revenue losses and a weakened manat, construction in Baku continued—President Aliyev inspected new streets, and the SOFAZ budget included millions for construction projects.[149] Though many projects are necessary, the lack of transparency in contracts continues to raise the specter of private gain through public works.

In the face of such complex contracts, credit and debt issues, falling oil prices, the devaluation of the manat, and a worsening public image, the regime apparently needed cash to pay the bills. Approximately a month before the European Games, reports began to emerge that authorities were squeezing people who had the cash to "contribute" to the games, targeting possible sources of revenue from the rich to state employees. First came the shakedown of the oligarchs.

"Oligarch Hunt": The Authorities Shake Down Businessmen

In mid-May, a month before the European Games, dozens of prominent and wealthy businessmen, mostly chief executive officers (CEOs) of their companies, were arrested or brought for questioning to either the Ministry of Internal Affairs or the Ministry of National Security. The use of two different ministries for these interrogations gave rise to suspicions of an intraelite struggle. Once in custody, the CEOs were accused of illegally profiting from the 34 percent currency devaluation that had taken place that February by manipulating currency exchanges and loans, all linked to the IBA, the country's largest bank (50.2 percent state-owned). A few months earlier, in March, IBA chairman Jahangir Hajiyev had been removed from his position for "health reasons."[150] All the companies owned by the first half-dozen businessmen arrested shortly before the games had substantial loans from the IBA that had not been repaid. The exchange of large sums of manat for dollars or euros during the devaluation had drained the bank's foreign currency reserves. (In 2011, a similar scandal centered on the IBA had involved the bank's granting loans to a friend of the bank president, even though the borrower in question previously had failed to repay earlier loans). Other such bad debts to the IBA were recapped in connection with the arrests of May 2015.[151] At one point, official sources publicly posted the names of seventy businessmen who were under investigation.

One of the first to go down was Nizami Piriyev, cofounder and head of the vast PNN Group, and with him were heads of four other large companies.[152] Piriyev was held at the Ministry of Internal Affairs in the Division Against Organized Crime.[153] News sources did not mention whether he had been put on trial, but reported that he was sentenced to four months in prison for swindling. Piriyev was released after two weeks when he repaid some undisclosed portion of his debt to the IBA, and he explained that he was resuming his position as head of the Methanol Plant, one of the largest components of the PNN Group.[154] The quick release of Piriyev, who in effect bought his way out of prison by repaying his debt, enforced suspicions that the government needed money to pay for the European Games. Businessmen with outstanding debt were good targets for a shakedown, as the drop in oil prices had cut into the state's revenue stream. Nonetheless, the targeted CEOs and their personal histories suggested that something more was going on behind the scenes.

Around the same time that Nizami Piriyev was arrested and jailed, Reshad Mammedov, head of the large and influential Azimport, was taken into custody at the Ministry of National Security. Mammedov had been the head of the State Flag Square Complex Administration, a state property, but had been removed on May 4 by an order signed by President Aliyev.[155] Mammedov's company, Azimport, was founded in 2004; according to its own website, it is a "collection of companies" (this phrase is in English although the site is Azerbaijani) and is in the construction and design business. One of its most highly touted projects was the State Flag Square Complex—the subcontractor for which was Azenco Construction, owned by the Aliyev family—in 2007.[156] The Flag Square was a large concrete "park" with the tallest flagpole in the world (at the time of its construction), built to display an enormous Azerbaijani flag. It is used occasionally for ceremonial purposes but otherwise is closed to the public. Critics regarded this park as a completely useless project, an excuse to spend public money in the name of patriotism as a public works project (qualifying for SOFAZ funding) and to develop waterfront property by employing companies owned by the president's family. In previous years, Azimport had been associated with illegal seizure of land and razing of buildings in the Bayil region near the site of the future State Flag Square Complex, as well as expropriation of private property near other construction sites. The Bayil case was especially dangerous because trees that stabilized the hillside soil were removed contrary to orders by state ecology authorities and even the Ministry of Emergency Situations.[157] The fact that these revelations appeared in February 2015 on the Haqqin.az site, which presents itself as an independent source but often supports proregime views, shows that Mammedov had been in trouble months before his arrest.

The meaning of these arrests and others was not immediately clear. At one level this was an obvious shakedown of businessmen with money and a history of suspect if not criminal behavior. But Nizami Piriyev was held at the Ministry of Internal Affairs, allowed to pay off some of his debt, and released within two weeks. Reshad Mammedov went to the Ministry of National Security and remained in pretrial detention. The involvement of two different security ministries raises questions of factional rivalry among oligarchs in the government under the guise of an "anticorruption" campaign. Ramil Usubov heads the Ministry of Internal Affairs, where most of the businessmen were interrogated. He is part of the old guard—of the same cohort as

Ramiz Mehdiyev, the head of the presidential staff—and is a Heydar Aliyev appointee. In contrast, the minister of state security, Eldar Mahmudov, was one of Ilham Aliyev's few appointees and had held this post since 2004, just after Ilham's accession to power. In mid-October 2015, Aliyev removed Mahmudov from his post without explanation. Within days, Mahmudov's relative Beytullah Huseynov, CEO of Baku Telephone Communications, was removed from his post and detained. Seven senior national security officers from the ministry were arrested on charges of "abuse of power, arbitrary and illegal inspection of businesses, extortion, bribery, and entering into business share by means of blackmail." Mahmudov's removal is believed to be related to his own political ambitions as well as corruption and incompetence.[158] In December 2015, Ilham Aliyev replaced the Ministry of National Security with a new security service, which leaves Internal Affairs as the primary ministry to oversee domestic security.

As a postscript to this internal drama, on June 29, 2015, Moody's downgraded Azerbaijan's banking system from stable to negative.[159] The report forecast only 1 percent growth in 2015 and an increase in "problem loans." On July 15, Ilham Aliyev quietly signed a decree for the "improvement and privatization" of the IBA,[160] a step that the IMF had urged in 2012.[161]

And the Small Change

Oligarchs were not the only source of compensatory funding for the European Games. "Contributions" were systematically squeezed from bureaucrats, customs officials, and even private citizens such as doctors. The customs officials probably had the most to contribute, in view of the quantity of unregistered imports—$1.6 billion from Russia, Turkey, and Georgia alone in 2015.[162] The demands on doctors touched ordinary citizens. A few doctors said off the record that they had to come up with "contributions" to support the European Games, a cost they apparently passed along to their patients. Some patients claimed that they had been deprived of medications and treatments, even for serious diseases, though treatments were to resume in July—that is, after the Games ended. State workers reportedly had been receiving under-the-table bonuses to supplement their official salaries, but learned that these payments would stop for the duration of the Games. These losses, however critical for those affected, were perhaps small change compared with the money that might be disgorged from Baku's oligarchs. Officials denied all the accusations.[163]

The suspected costs, repeated in the independent media, inflamed popular anger, but the full story was kept from public view. The management of the games' publicity was so tight that even the story of a local bus hitting two Austrian swimmers was followed quickly by assurances that the women's injuries were "not life threatening." A local police officer filmed the incident and sent it to a friend to post on social media—and the officer was fired. The immediate prosecution reflects the level of surveillance of cell phones as well as the concern over the image of Azerbaijan during this critical time for its public relations.[164]

Switzerland or Swaziland?

Oil revenues developed Azerbaijan and allowed the country to reduce poverty, renew its infrastructure, and develop a high international profile that paved the way for tourism as well as defense spending, parliamentarians' junkets and international conferences, caviar diplomacy, and Western education. Did oil make Azerbaijan more like Switzerland than Swaziland? Visitors who go to Azerbaijan on SOCAR-funded junkets, travel the eight-lane highway to the Four Seasons Hotel in Baku's city center, and then take a luxury van to the Pik Palace Resort might well think they are in Switzerland. But if they were to go outside the bubble, they would see the shabbily dressed people of Shahdag Mountain, whose land and homes were seized to build the resort. If they took a walk past the walls that line the airport highway, they would see ramshackle houses and sickly children in tatters, the country's real poverty. They would get a glimpse of the price that many Azerbaijanis pay for the luxury of the few.

Unlike Switzerland, Azerbaijan has largely opaque finances, an obedient judiciary, an unfree press, political prisoners, poor and ailing IDPs, and an autocratic ruling cabal of one family and a circle of oligarchs who use the state's resources for personal gain. One shorthand way to compare the numbers might be through the Transparency International CPI rankings for 2014. Not surprisingly, Switzerland ranks high; its raw score of 86 (of a perfect transparency score of 100) puts it in fifth place. Swaziland, a poor country, has a CPI score of 43 and ranks in 69th place. Azerbaijan is like neither. In 2014, its CPI score was 29, placing it 126th (the 9th percentile) of 175 countries in the world. Thus, in perceived corruption, Azerbaijan is nearly as many places behind Swaziland as Swaziland is behind Switzerland.

5

Jail for the "Donkey Bloggers": Crushing Youth Activism, Human Rights, and a Free Media

[Journalists, bloggers, and human rights defenders] are often harassed with unjustified or selective criminal prosecution on charges that defy credibility. . . . It is high time that Azerbaijan complies with its obligations and restores a climate in which dissent can be expressed without fear of repression.

—Nils Muižnieks, Council of Europe commissioner for human rights[1]

The Video

News of the scandal broke in the spring of 2009. Azerbaijan's Ministry of Agriculture had imported two donkeys from Germany for breeding at a cost of €42,000 each. The opposition press had a field day. In a country with a vast agricultural hinterland, the notion of importing donkeys was on the face of it ridiculous, and the cost was obscene. The scandal touched on wider issues of public trust, government oversight (or the lack of it), and corruption.

Opposition groups asked questions: How did this deal happen? Who had made a personal profit from it? Why would the government spend such a large amount of money to import two donkeys when state salaries and pensions remained low? Azerbaijan's corruption rankings on the Freedom House index and the Transparency International Corruption Perceptions Index continued to decline. Local officials might demand bribes for expediting paperwork, but high-level corruption was mostly hidden from public view or embedded in complex business deals that most people would not understand. So when two German donkeys were imported at a price that was many times the average salary in the country, people openly talked about dirty deals and kickbacks. The fact that the scandal involved donkeys called for ridicule.

In July, two young men, both active in opposition circles as political bloggers, made a satirical video about one of these "top-quality" donkeys—portrayed by one of them in a donkey costume—giving a mock press conference explaining why he was worth €42,000. He speaks three languages and plays the violin, which he demonstrates. Asked the old Soviet-era question, "Where is it better?," the donkey says that in Azerbaijan, donkey-like behavior is highly respected, and that conditions are very good for donkeys and for "donkeyness" in general.[2] The short video, just over five minutes long, went viral on YouTube, and earned Adnan Hajizade (then age twenty-six) and Emin Milli (age twenty-nine) the epithet of "the donkey bloggers."

A few days later, the two bloggers were sitting in a cafe in Baku when they were attacked and beaten by men in jogging suits, the common "uniform" of undercover police. When they went, bleeding and stunned, to the police station to report the assault, they were inexplicably charged with hooliganism under Article 221 of the criminal code, which carries up to a five-year jail sentence. They did not receive medical treatment. On August 25, a second charge under Article 127 of the criminal code was brought of "intentional physical violence," which carries a maximum sentence of two years in prison. Their arrest sparked strongly worded protests from the US and British ambassadors and several human rights organizations, including Reporters without Borders and the UN Human Rights Committee. At its session on July 31, the latter organization accused the Azerbaijani government of systematically using charges of hooliganism and defamation to suppress free expression. The trial of the donkey bloggers began on September 4, 2009, and ended with a sentence of two years for Hajizade and two and a half years for Milli.

The case of the donkey bloggers was symptomatic of the Aliyev regime's growing fear of youth activism. Hajizade and Milli were members of active youth organizations, Ol' ("Be") and the Alumni Network, an association of young adults who had received higher education in Western countries. Hajizade, a cofounder of Ol', explained that the organization's name was an exhortation to youth "to *be* democratic and to *be* tolerant."[3] All such groups sent a chill up the collective spine of the authorities because of the role that youth organizations had played in Georgia's Rose Revolution in November 2003—which had taken place right after Ilham Aliyev became president in the fixed elections of October 2003—and Ukraine's Orange Revolution in November 2004. The civic organizations of twenty- and thirty-year-olds in Georgia (Kmara) and Ukraine (Pora) were linked to each other and to Otpor!, the youth protest organization that had been active in the overthrow of Serbia's Slobodan Milošević in October 2000. All three revolutions had forced out authoritarian leaders. Although outside analysts have debated the real impact of the youth organizations in the color revolutions,[4] it seems that Aliyev's administration was concerned about potential similarities, because it began its campaign against politically active youth in Azerbaijan in the summer of 2005.

Earlier Repressions

As a protest against the expulsion of a student from the Azerbaijan Pedagogical Institute in Baku for his political activism in the spring of 2005, students in the capital organized a hunger strike to demand his reinstatement. The hunger strike was a low-profile event (probably a reflection of the organizers' inexperience with publicity) that dragged out over a week in an empty room in a remote corridor of the building where the Azerbaijan Popular Front Party and its newspaper *Azadlıq* had their offices. In the end, it was successful. The student was reinstated. One of the media coordinators for the hunger strikers was Ruslan Bashirli, a leader of the youth organization Yeni Fikir (New Idea), which had been founded in 2004 and was affiliated with the Popular Front. The sympathy and success of the hunger strike might have been the trigger that showed that organized youth were serious about demanding changes to society.[5]

Shortly after the hunger strike, on August 3, 2005, Bashirli was arrested after returning from a trip to Georgia. He was said to be in touch with young men from Kmara. Indeed, other Azerbaijani youth organizations were founded in 2005 with inspiration or assistance from Kmara.[6] The actual charges against

Bashirli were sinister and likely to turn public opinion against him: conspiring with Armenian intelligence to overthrow the Azerbaijani government and engaging in illegal business activities. Bashirli said that he had met with prodemocracy groups in Tbilisi, not secret agents. Public opinion overwhelmingly accepted the government's story, according to an opinion poll by a Baku research group that may have been under government influence. Of those polled, 63 percent condemned Bashirli's alleged treachery, and 43 percent blamed him for the plot. But 18.5 percent blamed the leader of the Popular Front (AXCP), Ali Kerimli, and another 13 percent thought that "the opposition parties" collectively were to blame. Only 10 percent thought the government was culpable in the affair.[7]

Arrested soon after Bashirli and tried with him on the same charges were two deputy leaders of Yeni Fikir, Said Nuriyev (later "Nuri," arrested September 12) and Ramin Taghiyev (arrested September 14). Nuriyev had just returned from a conference in Poland. Taghiyev was accused of "molding opinion about the falsity of elections among the population."[8] The World Organization Against Torture (Organisation Mondiale Contre la Torture; OMCT) and Amnesty International reported that the men were tortured in custody and denied medical treatment.[9] Because of the allegations of a plot to overthrow the government, the trial, which took place in the spring of 2006, was closed to outside observers, including monitors from the Organization for Security and Cooperation in Europe and other international groups. The prosecution wove an intricate accusation involving the three defendants, foreign governments, and nongovernment organizations who allegedly instructed Yeni Fikir members on subversive political tactics. Among those specifically accused during the trial were Norwegian ambassador Steiner Gil, who was famous (or infamous) for his defense of human rights in Azerbaijan; former US presidential advisor Zbigniew Brzezinski; and the Washington-based National Democratic Institute (NDI) chaired by former US secretary of state Madeleine Albright. Nelson C. Ledsky, NDI's regional director for Eurasia, rejected the accusation and stated that NDI had "no involvement" with Bashirli.[10] The defendants released their lawyers and took a posture of "nonparticipation" in their own trial.[11]

On July 12, 2006—the same day that the Baku–Tbilisi–Ceyhan oil pipeline opened—Bashirli, Taghiyev, and Nuriyev were all convicted of "actions aimed at the violent overthrow of the Azerbaijani government" under Article 278 of the Azerbaijani Criminal Code, in what Amnesty International characterized as "an unfair trial":

No evidence was brought at the trial suggesting that the three accused intended to engage in violence, for example through the purchase of weapons. The court only heard testimony from prosecution witnesses, and in contravention of Azerbaijani law, no jury was appointed as required in cases of crimes punishable by life imprisonment. After the defendants refused lawyers in order to conduct their own defense, the court appointed lawyers to represent them. These lawyers were allegedly not familiar with the materials of the case, to the extent of reportedly not knowing their clients' names.[12]

The case of Bashirli and his fellow youth activists was part of a pattern of arrests of reportedly 100 opposition activists in the summer and fall of 2005, during the runup to the November 2005 Milli Majlis elections.[13] Many activists and journalists were under forty years of age, and although they were not part of youth organizations they nonetheless were considered part of the same "threat."

At the same time, a shakeup took place at the top of government. Minister of Health Ali Insanov and others were sacked and brought to trial on charges of corruption and planning to overthrow the government. The accused allegedly had stockpiled weapons and made plans for a coup. It was more likely a move by Ilham Aliyev and his backers to rid themselves of political opponents.[14] In a setting where process is opaque and news is restricted, conspiracy theories abound. The public often believed the charges of a planned coup, some with fear, others with hope. Those removed were not the "power" ministers, but rather heads of ministries of health, telecommunications, and education.[15] With this rhetoric and arrests of ministers of his own cabinet, Aliyev was able to maintain a climate of crisis, justifying arrests and repressions to protect the country.

Among the most egregious violations of Azerbaijan's laws and constitutional provisions on freedom of speech has been the suppression of opposition journalists. Many have been threatened, beaten, or arrested. A few have been killed. On March 2, 2005, investigative journalist and editor Elmar Huseynov was murdered in the entrance of his apartment building. The thirty-seven-year-old editor had worked for several Russian-language newspapers in Baku, and in 1995 had founded the weekly magazine *Monitor*. It and other publications he edited had been shut down and Huseynov had been threatened many times because of his criticism of President Ilham Aliyev and his predecessor and father, Heydar Aliyev. Huseynov had received death threats prior to his murder. At the time of the murder, President Aliyev condemned the murder, saying that it was an attempt by anti-Azerbaijani elements to destabilize the country before elections, which were not to be held for six months. Local police refused to admit the testimony of Elmar's wife, who had seen a man run from the doorway. The investigation quickly petered out, and the crime was classified as "terrorism"—and thus as a security matter that could be kept secret. Azerbaijani authorities named a group of Georgians as suspects, none of whom was ever extradited from Georgia because of lack of evidence. No one has ever been tried for the murder. On the second anniversary of the murder, Huseynov's former colleague and fellow journalist Eynulla Fatullayev published his own investigation of the murder and concluded "that the murder had been ordered by high-ranking officials in Baku and carried out by a criminal group."[16] Fatullayev, editor-in-chief of *Real'nyi Azerbaidzhan*, had been a target of repression and threats before publishing this conclusion and came in for much harsher treatment thereafter.

The human rights abuses of 2006 were described in the Council of Europe Resolution 1545 (2007) on compliance with terms of democratization and human rights that Azerbaijan had accepted with its accession to the CoE in 2001 and its ratification of the European Convention on Human Rights in 2002. The resolution addressed issues of law as well as human rights, stating that the Parliamentary Assembly of the Council of Europe "*reiterates* that the Criminal Code of Azerbaijan should be amended in line with recommendations made by Council of Europe experts in December 2005 as regards in particular its compatibility with the European Convention on Human Rights."[17] The resolution noted the specific case of the Yeni Fikir defendants, and expressed "hopes that the Supreme Court will fully examine the reported violations of fair trial in the procedure before the lower courts as well as the allegations of ill-treatment during police custody made by Mr. Bashirli."[18] When Bashirli was finally released six years later, in 2012, he renounced politics.[19] Other activists later believed that he had been "turned" and now supported the regime. Concerning human rights, the resolution indicated that PACE had raised the same problems in the past: "concerning freedom of expression and of the media, the Assembly recalls the serious concerns it expressed in its Resolution 1505 (2006) about violent incidents directed against journalists. Regrettably, instead of improving, *the general environment for the independent media in Azerbaijan has since deteriorated*" (emphasis added).[20] Although President Aliyev had announced a moratorium on defamation prosecution in March 2005, "the number of civil and criminal defamation proceedings brought against opposition journalists and newspapers by public officials has recently increased."[21]

What followed in the PACE resolution was a list of cases of individuals and media outlets that had been pressured by the regime, as well as threats to journalists that had not been investigated by authorities. Individuals who had been threatened included Eynulla Fatullayev, who had received death threats; and well-known poet and satirical journalist Sakit Zahidov, who was "convicted to a three-year prison sentence . . . based on no credible evidence." The Popular Front's organ *Azadlıq* had been evicted from its offices in November 2006, and "on the same day the most watched independent television channel in Azerbaijan, ANS, was silenced following a decision taken by the National Television and Radio Council not to extend its license on the basis of alleged violations of the relevant legislation; the channel was allowed to recommence broadcasting three weeks later pending the decision on the offer of a new tender."[22] (Among the members of the NTRC was Sona Veliyeva, wife of presidential aide Ali Hasanov, whose media connections were described in greater detail in chapter 4.) The critical PACE report was accepted by a large majority of the assembly, voting 99-1-4, including most of the delegation from Azerbaijan. The delegation leader, Samed Seyidov, commented that he could vote for the report's adoption because even though it was critical of the regime, its criticism was "objective."[23]

When Western diplomats raised the matter of political reform, Azerbaijani officials already, in 2006, had their official line in place. They were "committed to political reform" but democratization was "a slow process." Presidential Chief of Staff Ramiz Mehdiyev reportedly affirmed President Aliyev's commitment to democracy and integration with the West, but said it was part of "gradual, evolutionary change." Mehdiyev, who had worked in the communist party with Heydar Aliyev in the 1970s, was perhaps the originator of the fully developed argument about Azerbaijan's "tough neighborhood." He painted the prodemocracy opposition as "radical," and suggested that it was receiving financial support from abroad. Mehdiyev attributed to Heydar Aliyev a steady "step-by-step" approach to reform because the single most important factor for democratic and economic development was stability. Indeed, government actions soon showed that "maintaining stability" was the excuse for continuing pressure against the media and human rights defenders.[24] If the regime was following Heydar Aliyev's "step-by-step" approach, then with regard to human rights and democratization, it was in the form of the Leninist "one step forward, two steps back."

At the end of 2006, major media outlets were under crippling pressure. As mentioned in the 2007 PACE resolution, on November 24 the Azerbaijani government suspended broadcasts by the independent television and radio station ANS. Within hours of ANS's suspension, the courts ordered the eviction of the AXCP, its newspaper *Azadlıq*, and the independent Turan News Agency from their offices in central Baku, an action that "raised concerns of freedom of speech in Azerbaijan." In this instance, international organizations and Western embassies "strongly condemned" the actions.[25] Their strong language would grow milder over the years. The regime moved against the opposition newspaper *Hurriyyet* soon thereafter.[26] ANS was restored in 2007, but ceased to function as an opposition media outlet.

The media situation continued to deteriorate, and much of 2007 was taken up with the civil and criminal trials of journalist and editor Eynulla Fatullayev. Fatullayev previously had been a target of repression for his own critical publications: "In July 2004, he was severely beaten on a street in Baku. . . . In August 2006, the interior minister, Rasul Usubov, brought three defamation claims against Fatullayev, and one month later a court convicted him, with a two-year suspended sentence and a fine of more than US$10,000." In 2006, Fatullayev's father had been kidnapped and threatened with death if Eynullah did not cease publishing his newspaper. Fatullayev had ceased publishing at the time, but resumed after his father's release. The kidnappers were never apprehended.[27] Most likely, Fatullayev's 2007 arrest was punishment for his stubborn investigation into the 2005 murder of Elmar Huseynov, but he was arrested and charged with civil and then criminal defamation in connection with another article he had written in 2005, just after Huseynov's assassination.

Fatullayev's inflammatory 2005 article in *Real'nyi Azerbaidzhan* had explored the 1992 massacres at Khojaly and the related war in Mountainous Karabagh. He was convicted of defaming survivors of the massacre and "the Azerbaijani army," although no real army existed in early 1992. On the heels of the conviction in April, another case was brought against him. The second was a criminal case stemming from a 2007 article he had written called "The Aliyevs Go to War," which speculated on the risks to Azerbaijan of its military cooperation with the United States as tensions with Iran increased. Because the article listed government facilities that were at risk of being bombed in a US-Iranian war, the government charged Fatullayev under Article 241.1 of the criminal code, "terrorism or the threat of terrorism." He was convicted of these and other charges, including inciting ethnic hatred, and sentenced to a total of ten years in prison. In September 2007, Fatullayev appealed to the European Court of Human Rights under the terms of the Convention for the Protection of Human Rights and Fundamental Freedoms, to which

Azerbaijan is a signatory. The final decision of the court and its opinions would have wide-ranging implications for the Azerbaijani government's conduct in cases of media freedom and legal matters, including the presumption of innocence of an accused person, but this decision would not be handed down until the spring of 2010. (The ECHR decision is discussed later in this chapter.)

With so many journalists and human rights defenders behind bars, it was not surprising that in the spring of 2008, in the runup to October's presidential elections, the PACE Monitoring Committee felt the need to issue a warning about clean elections and the observance of human rights. The committee used strong language:

> On 15 October 2008, Azerbaijan will be holding its second presidential elections since its accession to the Council of Europe. Considering that all ballots held since accession have generally failed to meet basic democratic standards, the Parliamentary Assembly considers the forthcoming ballot to be *crucial for Azerbaijan's democratic credibility.* . . . Restrictions on the freedom of expression, the harassment and intimidation of opposition journalists through defamation court proceedings, imprisonment, physical attacks and threats, and limitations of the right to freedom of assembly and association are matters of great concern which the Assembly *considers inadmissible* in a Council of Europe member state.[28]

The draft resolution "condemned" the government's actions in targeting the opposition *Azadlıq* newspaper and its staff and reporters.[29] Even the resolution's acknowledgment that the government had released jailed journalists and political prisoners hinted at a large but unknown number behind bars. The resolution "took note" of the release of 173 prisoners, including at least 12 journalists and 23 human rights defenders, by two presidential decrees of December 2007 and March 2008. Two other journalists were released from prison thereafter. However, PACE "strongly regretted" that "none of the prisoners referred to in Resolution 1545 (2007) has been released and that the three journalists associated with the most vocal opposition newspapers—Ganimat Zahidov, [his brother] Sakit Zahidov, and Eynulla Fatullayev—remain in prison."[30]

Ilham Aliyev himself repeated the arguments that his ministers had been making for years—democracy would undermine Azerbaijan's independent statehood and secularism. In July 2008, he told a Western diplomat that the

147

main beneficiaries of greater democracy in Azerbaijan would be Russia and Iran: "Russia uses Azerbaijan's democratic development to promote its own interests," Aliyev said. "We didn't become a Russian satellite or an Islamic state." Quashing the media was also a defensive measure, Aliyev claimed, because Dagestan and Iran were buying "agents" in the press and even in parliament. When asked about violence against journalists, Aliyev commented that "some of these beatings never happened." Referring to the June 7, 2008, incident in which Institute for Reporters' Freedom and Safety director Emin Huseynov allegedly was beaten by police, Aliyev said that the "journalist was detained, not beaten."[31]

At that time, it became clear that the Azerbaijani government had influenced some deputies of the CoE to argue against PACE oversight. According to ESI's *Caviar Diplomacy* report, the PACE Monitoring Team preparing for the upcoming presidential elections had already shifted in favor of progovernment deputies. A hint of this change came in Khadija Ismayilova's July 2008 interview of Terry Davis, CoE secretary-general and a member of the British House of Commons:

> [Ismayilova asked] Davis, "Do you think Azerbaijan has more media freedom now than when it joined the Council of Europe in 2001?" This, he replied, was "impossible to assess." When Ismayilova pointed out that Baku had not implemented a series of recommendations by the Council of Europe's Venice Commission, Davis replied: "Recommendations are recommendations. People are entitled not to accept recommendations."[32]

The August 2008 Russo-Georgian War showed the limits of Western reach and willingness to intervene, even with a Russian invasion of a state in the Caucasus. How much less likely was it that the European Union or the United States would respond to human rights violations by the victims' own government? Among the lessons that Azerbaijan's leadership may have taken from the Russo-Georgia war were that the West was far away in many senses, and that Russia made a reasonable partner. Ignoring Russia was too costly; emulating it was nearly cost-free.

In October, Ilham Aliyev ran for reelection without meaningful opposition as major parties boycotted the lopsided campaigning climate and anticipated a fixed election. Indeed, the president was "reelected" for his second and, according to constitutional provisions, final term. Immediately, the YAP-dominated Milli Majlis moved to abolish term limitations (see chapter 3). The change in the Constitution was accepted by popular vote in March 2009. The Venice Commission considered this decision a "set back" on Azerbaijan's road to democracy consolidation.[33]

In December, foreign broadcasters—including the BBC, Voice of America, and Radio Free Europe / Radio Liberty—were banned from using domestic broadcast frequencies inside Azerbaijan, effectively removing them from the scene. The move against the foreign radios came on December 30, in the middle of the holidays, and was set to take effect on January 1, 2009. In this climate of greater regime control, the "donkey blogger" incident took place, and Adnan Hajizade and Emin Milli were sentenced to prison for a satirical video that named no individual or ministry. Having been stung perhaps by past criticism from the CoE and the ECHR about Azerbaijan's criminal defamation laws, a situation was set up so that Hajizade and Milli could be charged with "hooliganism" and sent to prison.

Among serious sentences for some dissidents, one seemingly minor incident in August 2009 revealed the regime's state of mind and the extent of its surveillance over the population, especially young people.[34] Rovshan Nasirli, a young Azerbaijani, was summoned to the National Security Ministry on August 12, 2009, for having voted—on his cell phone—for the Armenian song in the 2009 Eurovision music competition of the previous spring. Nasirli had voted for the song as a protest because that one performance was blocked by Azerbaijan's television broadcasters. The security officers told him that voting for Armenia was a matter of national security and reflected his lack of ethnic pride. They forced him to explain himself in a written statement, then released him. Other young people who voted for Armenia in Eurovision were similarly questioned, warned, and released.[35] Human rights activist Avaz Hasanov said that the incident suggested that Azerbaijan had become a "police state."[36]

Yet the watchdogs seem to have been thrown a bone from Baku. PACE discussions became surprisingly contentious. Strongly worded critical reports on Azerbaijan's failings were being criticized by some deputies in the same language that the Aliyev regime used—the country needed more time to develop democracy, Azerbaijan was being unfairly criticized, assistance and nurturing were needed rather than criticism or sanctions. Andres Herkel, head of the monitoring team, and his work were criticized as unfair. The team that oversaw the October 2008 presidential elections included members who were openly proregime.[37] On October 16, the day after the elections, a joint PACE–OSCE–Office for Democratic Institutions and Human Rights statement noted "considerable progress, [although the election] did not meet all of the country's international commitments."[38] In the next two years, according to ESI, PACE deputies who criticized election shortcomings were sidelined, and those who were sympathetic to "postcolonial" states that were building democratic institutions were put on the monitoring team for Azerbaijan. In short, the years 2008–10 saw a shift in PACE's monitoring of Azerbaijan's elections and compliance with human rights and civil society provisions when a faction supporting the Aliyev government gained a more secure hold within PACE.[39]

A Worsening Climate

Starting in 2010, the pace of arrests quickened, and charges against regime critics, human rights defenders, journalists and political activists, and even their families became more severe. To find the causes of this crackdown, it is necessary to look at the interplay of domestic and foreign events from the regime's point of view. Fear of being overthrown hovered over Ilham Aliyev after the color revolutions. The founding of Yeni Fikir in 2004 with its links to Georgia's Kmara was followed by the founding of other youth organizations, including Dalga and Ol', in 2006, even as trials of Yeni Fikir leaders took place. Although the long-established opposition parties may have seemed marginalized even before 2010, these youth organizations represented an untamed force that was outside the hierarchy of the older opposition parties[40] and of YAP and the regime. The triumph of BTC construction in 2005 and revenues from its first oil in 2006 gave the regime the means to get all the luxury anyone might imagine and to suppress opposition. Oil revenues also gave—or the regime thought that they would give—immunity from Western pressure, since the West seemed mesmerized by the flow of oil. The ruling elites, soon to be oligarchs, wanted to protect the profits. And who threatened their profits? Those who threatened their hold on power.

The threat to power in a repressive society comes from investigative journalists who reveal abuses of power and wealth, and from watchdog groups that see and report dirty elections, sycophant judges, and the suppression of critics. By 2010, the ranks of Azerbaijan's media professionals, activists, and political organizers were filled more and more with men and women of the younger generation. The regime had to target them all. The government's need to defend itself against foreign critics appeared later in part because the ruling circles did not expect oil buyers in the West to complain about human rights or vote fraud. At first, the regime used excuses about its tenuous status as a young democracy, coupled with reminders of Western failings from racial tensions and wider unrest. However, these claims were not enough to silence its critics. The Aliyev regime had to persuade CoE deputies to defend it, and plied the deputies with caviar and other gifts.[41] To establish a broader offensive and hone a better image, Baku added professional lobbyists and a few former members of parliaments and the US Congress to testify to the democratic leanings of the Azerbaijani government. This was the origin of the "caviar diplomacy" that whitewashed Azerbaijani elites' reputations and state policy.

The human rights community felt the impact. Most organizations, from Human Rights Watch to Reporters Without Borders, criticized the politically motivated arrests, bogus charges, torture, and disproportionate punishments. But groups with leverage, including PACE, did not take action beyond the critical reports and public statements. Representatives of Western governments, even aside from the split among legislators between supporters and critics of the regime, had to struggle to manage a balance between energy security and antiterrorism measures on the one hand and the defense of human rights and democracy-building on the other. The West often coupled assurance of continued partnership with expressions of "concerns" and "hopes" for greater democratization and individual freedom.

Domestic policy was even more multifaceted and nuanced. By 2010, the young firebrands of 1990 were middle-aged and their parties had been both physically and politically marginalized by the regime. The generation born at the end of the Soviet period or during independence were now coming of age within a new global political context and new technology. As they moved into political adulthood, they sought education, jobs, and (in some cases) opportunities for political participation. The regime cleverly mobilized an array of proverbial carrots and sticks. Potential carrots included education abroad ("Don't go to jail, go to Europe," said one pro-YAP member of the Milli Majlis) followed by jobs in government or government-friendly businesses. Young people then could be attracted to nominally nonpolitical work that would put them in de facto alignment with the regime. The regime's sticks became thicker and harder—harassment, interrogation, beatings, loss of jobs, arrest, criminal charges, and imprisonment. At the same time, protests increased, especially in new media, and revelations about high-level corruption made heroes of investigative journalists. The ruling circles tried to excuse their repressions by claiming that they had to maintain state security and independence against threatening neighbors or international terrorists. Many young adults followed the carrots, some hoping to work for change from the inside. But some refused, and risked the government's sticks to oppose the increasingly authoritarian rule of Ilham Aliyev's government.

Aliyev was clearly afraid—and subsequent events seem to have reinforced the fear—of being unseated by revolution. His regime conflated its own survival with the survival of the state. Aliyev also feared and loathed the prospect of being ridiculed, a revulsion that is embedded in both Azerbaijani and Soviet culture.[42] As journalists probed more deeply into the finances of his family members and those of the men in his inner circle, and the country's youth became more politically engaged, Ilham—or his lieutenants—turned increasingly to violence.

The regime, powered by oil revenues and fear of a color revolution, forged ahead with new efforts to stifle dissent. In February 2010, the Milli Majlis passed a new law restricting the rights of media representatives to record or film public figures. Jacqueline Carpenter, democratization program director at the Baku office of OSCE, told an NGO roundtable that the amendments were "problematic" within the context of Azerbaijan's OSCE commitments to freedom of expression and the media's right to collect and disseminate information. She suggested that the amendments "spring from a 'deep misunderstanding of the role of journalists to work for the public interest,'" and expected other restrictions as "the government consolidates power." The Majlis defended the restrictions, claiming that they were essential to national security.[43]

Within two months of the passage of the new media restrictions, the ECHR released its decision on the case of Eynulla Fatullayev, the persistent journalist who had been convicted in 2007. The ECHR explored the many layers of two complex cases against Fatullayev in its judgment of April 2010.[44] Its ruling instructed the Azerbaijani government on the role of free media in a democracy, and thereby constituted an embarrassment to the Aliyev regime. Among particulars of the government's charges and the application of law to the sensitive questions of the Karabagh war and 1992 Khojaly massacre, the court stated:

> The freedom of expression is applicable not only to "information" or "ideas" that are favorably received or regarded as inoffensive or as a matter of indifference, but also to those that offend, shock or disturb the State or any sector of the population. Such are the demands of pluralism, tolerance and broadmindedness without which there is no "democratic society." (paragraph 86)

Moving to a wider view, the court laid down principles about the media:

> Another factor of particular importance for the Court's determination
> of the present case is the vital role of "public watchdog" which the press
> performs in a democratic society. . . . Although it must not overstep cer-
> tain bounds . . . , its duty is nevertheless to impart—in a manner consis-
> tent with its obligations and responsibilities—information and ideas on
> political issues and on other matters of general interest. (paragraph 88)

The court concluded:

> In view of the above, the Court finds that the interference with the
> applicant's exercise of his right to freedom of expression cannot be con-
> sidered "necessary in a democratic society." (paragraphs 104–5)

The court therefore found "a violation of Article 10" of the Convention on
Human Rights and Freedom in the first criminal case and came to the same
conclusion with regard to the second. In the second criminal case, concerning
charges of terrorism, threat of terrorism, and inciting ethnic hatred stemming
from the 2007 *Real'nyi Azerbaidzhan* article "The Aliyevs Go to War," the
court again stated a principle with wide applicability for Azerbaijan's treatment of the media:

> In a democratic system the actions or omissions of the government
> must be subject to the close scrutiny not only of the legislative and
> judicial authorities but also of public opinion. Moreover, the domi-
> nant position which the government occupies makes it necessary for it
> [the government] to display restraint in resorting to criminal proceed-
> ings. (paragraph 116)

In conclusion:

> [123 . . .] The Court cannot but conclude that the domestic courts'
> finding that the applicant threatened the State with terrorist acts was
> nothing but arbitrary. . . . Neither did the applicant voice any approval
> of any such possible attacks, or argue in favor of them . . . the only
> means by which the applicant could be said to have "exerted influence"
> on the State authorities in the present case was by exercising his freedom

of expression, in compliance with the bounds set by Article 10, and voicing his disagreement with the authorities' political decisions, as part of a public debate which should take place freely in any democratic society.

124. In view of the above, the Court finds that the domestic courts arbitrarily applied the criminal provisions on terrorism in the present case. Such arbitrary interference with the freedom of expression, which is one of the fundamental freedoms serving as the foundation of a democratic society, should not take place in a state governed by the rule of law. (paragraphs 123–24)

In this situation, the court also found that Article 10 had been violated.

Despite the requirement that the government of Azerbaijan conform to the court's judgment, as stated in the Convention on Human Rights and Freedom, the authorities in Baku did not free Fatullayev. Though some of the charges against him were dropped, he continued to be held for added drug possession charges—for drugs found in his clothing while he was in prison.[45] He was released in May 2011, and in July he established a pseudo-opposition website, Haqqin.az, registered with the Ministry of Justice. Its language is more subtle than openly proregime media, but its word choice (calling Heydar Aliyev "Our National Leader") and its publishing of congratulations on National Press Day from Ilham Aliyev's aunt make its loyalties clear.[46]

The year 2010 was a turning point year in Azerbaijani journalism when Khadija Ismayilova began her investigative work on high-level corruption, leading to revelations of hidden stock holdings and wealth in the hands of the presidential family. She collaborated in a *Washington Post* story published in March that revealed that $44 million worth of property had been purchased in early 2009 in the name of Ilham Aliyev's eleven-year-old son Heydar. [47] Sometimes alone, sometimes with a coauthor, Ismayilova researched and published stories on mysterious businesses and high-level corruption and found herself immersed in the finances of the presidential family.[48] Perhaps the earliest of these cases was an investigation of Silk Way Holding, the holding company that had taken over all operations of the state airline AZAL as well as services in Heydar Aliyev International Airport. A principal owner of Silk Way Holding's Silk Way Bank was found to be Arzu Aliyeva, the president's twenty-one-year-old daughter.[49] This analytical report raised questions about the source of the millions of dollars necessary to buy into the Silk Way Bank, the ability of Silk Way Holdings to buy up other services in the airport, and the even larger process of privatization of the state's share of AZAL.

Discovering and writing this story constituted a risk for these journalists in the increasingly authoritarian setting. Such work put Ismayilova on the map in Azerbaijan and internationally. The depth of investigation and the coverage of the president's own family were unprecedented. With this story, and others like it, Azerbaijani journalism took a leap beyond reporting on ballot stuffing in elections or police brutality at public demonstrations.

The ruling family was, of course, embarrassed and infuriated. Revelations about the family's private holdings let a glimmer of light into the vast corruption that put tens of millions of dollars in the family's coffers and, as became apparent, those of other oligarchs. Repression of parties and journalists might be explained as necessary to stability, but a $44 million condo in Dubai was only about personal luxury. The decision to purchase such a condo in the name of an eleven-year-old boy suggested that there were more financial dealings that had been hidden from public eyes. Subsequent stories about family ownership of cell phone companies, gold mines, and construction companies (see chapter 4) revealed what some of those deals were.

To divert attention or to throw a sop to the most reluctant critics, the regime began to "give back" a little in exchange for some of its major gains. The textbook case involved the 2010 Milli Majlis election, in which the genuine opposition parties were completely deprived of representation and proregime deputies were elected as "nonparty" independent candidates or members of nominally opposition parties. Within two weeks of the 2010 elections, the donkey bloggers were released from prison, after serving seventeen months of their sentences. It was a small "giveback" after the regime's complete exclusion of opposition in the Milli Majlis, but it was not the sign of a thaw in any sense. Both bloggers were blackballed and could not find work. On the surface, the bloggers' release gave reluctant critics of the regime an opportunity to welcome the "progress" represented by the freeing of two young men arrested in "politically motivated cases," while hundreds more languished in jail.[50]

With the Milli Majlis entirely dominated by YAP, journalists silenced in jail, and foreign critics seemingly stuck in a feedback loop, Azerbaijan's ruling circles could envision themselves enjoying greater influence in the West and a freer hand at home. Then came the Arab Spring of 2011. Always afraid of a color revolution, the Aliyev cohort now watched young men and women across the Middle East use social media to rally and organize opposition to entrenched, corrupt regimes. Could the regime fail to see the parallels? If these uprisings came from youth and social media, then the government would have to treat them more brutally. In February 2011, Azerbaijani youth founded a new organization called NIDA, with the stated goals of "freedom and justice," specifically the defense of provisions of the Azerbaijani Constitution that guarantee human rights and democratization.[51] NIDA members have spoken of themselves a "civic movement," not a political party, employing nonviolent methods such as sit-ins, flash mobs, and protest art. Despite the modest character of their actions and goals, the timing of NIDA's creation, as revolutions were erupting across the Arab world, was unfortunate. The regime promptly called NIDA members extremists and implied that they were a threat to national security.

The more manageable threat remained the nonrevolutionary but organized and well-known NGOs. In February 2011, the Milli Majlis promulgated another law to restrict NGOs. President Aliyev promptly signed it, and within a month the Cabinet of Ministers shut down several NGOs without giving them time to comply with the new regulations. Fifteen NGOs inside and outside Azerbaijan sent a petition to PACE to request a Venice Commission ruling on both the 2009 and 2011 amendments to the NGO laws.[52] Before the end of the year, the commission ruled that "the 2009 amendments to the Azerbaijani NGO Law and the 2011 decree setting new requirements for foreign NGOs overturn the efforts to meet international standards," calling "registration of foreign NGOs among the most problematic aspects."[53] Referring specifically to the 2011 decree of the Council of Ministers, the commission highlighted the decree's language that NGOs "must respect the national-moral values . . . and the organizations must not be involved in political or religious propaganda. . . . The regulations do not define 'national moral values,' 'political or religious propaganda,' or what involvement in such propaganda would constitute."[54] Nonetheless, like earlier restrictions, the laws limiting NGO operations remained in force.

Eurovision Comes to Baku

The glitziest story of 2011 was the Azerbaijani victory in the Eurovision song contest in mid-May. Eurovision is the most-watched nonsporting event in Europe. The country whose entry wins is entitled to host the competition the following year. Although the contest is expensive to produce and logistically challenging, Eurovision is an immense opportunity for a country to get international publicity, bringing into the host city hundreds of European performers and thousands of tourists. The Aliyev regime began to prepare for the 2012 contest in August 2011 with the start of the construction of the Crystal Hall, a $134 million project, on Baku's shoreline. As reported by Khadija Ismayilova, the company contracted for the work was Germany's Alpine Bau Deutschland AG. Some of the equipment at the construction site was stamped with the company name Azenco, owned by the Aliyevs, so that, Ismayilova wrote, "the first family is personally profiting from the massive construction project through its hidden ownership in the Azenco construction company."[55]

Old apartment buildings full of working-class residents stood in the way of the new construction. Local and foreign reporters wrote about the ensuing evictions: "The government of Azerbaijan has forcibly evicted homeowners and demolished their homes for urban development projects in Baku, where the arena for the 2012 Eurovision song contest is being built."[56] The UN followed with a video of women protesters organizing against forced evictions from their homes. The protesters created a Woman's Parliament and worked with Transparency Azerbaijan's head Rena Safaraliyeva. One victim of demolition was a building with a women's crisis center and the office of activist Leyla Yunus's Institute for Democracy and Peace.[57]

In order to shine the Eurovision spotlight on the regime's poor human rights record, the head of a local prodemocracy NGO organized a countermovement to Eurovision, called "Sing for Democracy."[58] Rasul Jafarov, then age twenty-nine, chairman and CEO of the Baku-based Human Rights Club, said "Eurovision must be yet another tool to promote Azerbaijan's European integration, first of all through the improvement of the situation with human rights." The Human Rights Club, an NGO that received funding from the US-based National Endowment for Democracy, spearheaded this effort with other young activists, starting the same time as construction of the Crystal Hall in August. They reached out to international news media, diplomats, and human rights defenders. Their three-minute YouTube video showed dramatic scenes of police violence against residents of buildings under the wrecking ball and peaceful demonstrators of all ages.[59] In the end, they got the attention they sought—and the predictable backlash from authorities.

Both the construction and public relations efforts of the regime and the protests of Sing for Democracy picked up momentum in 2012. Against the backdrop of the official "Light Your Fire" logo for Eurovision, Human Rights Watch and the *Guardian* carried stories of the human rights abuses and blocking of media freedom and free speech in Baku during the weeks before Eurovision opened on May 26. Hugh Williamson's detailed coverage for Human Rights Watch described six journalists in jail at that time on trumped-up charges and others who were attacked and beaten: "One of the most recent victims was Idrak Abbasov, a respected reporter [who] . . . was filming forced evictions and house demolitions by the country's state oil company when the firm's security officials, along with police, viciously beat him unconscious, leaving him hospitalized. Investigations into this and other cases are half-hearted at best."[60]

The day before Eurovision opened, a BBC report noted that police broke up a protest outside the Azerbaijani television station that would broadcast Eurovision where demonstrators were chanting "Freedom for Political Prisoners." The police detained more than thirty people. In a low-profile protest, "around 100 activists simply walked around Baku—to avoid being arrested, they carried no placards, they did not chant slogans. But they wore T-shirts bearing the words 'Sing for Democracy.'"[61] The Swedish singer Loreen, who later won the competition, met with local human rights activists, much to the chagrin of the authorities. In the post-Eurovision "giveback," Aliyev signed a pardon to release sixty-six prisoners, nine of whom were considered political prisoners, after their arrest in opposition rallies of April 2011. The men had been sentenced to two to three years in prison. The most prominent of the released prisoners was the deputy head of the Müsavat Party, Arif Hajili.[62]

In the end, Sing for Democracy enjoyed the success of notoriety: "The campaign organized numerous events, reports, and press conferences [in] which Azerbaijani journalists, human rights defenders and watchdog groups were able to highlight the government's repression on an international level."[63] Some performers did not want to be bothered by these issues, and many people never saw the protest campaign. The hundred people walking around Baku in their T-shirts were a small number in a city of millions swollen by thousands of visitors.

But the regime's main takeaway from Eurovision was not the small scale of a hundred people among millions, but the embarrassment of negative international reporting. From that viewpoint, the actions of the youth, such as the Sing for Democracy crowd, were threatening. The authorities continued to target the youth activists, especially their leaders. Similarly in the authorities' crosshairs were the groups that report on human rights, political prisoners, and continuing arrests—foreign and local human rights groups and journalists.

During the Eurovision hoopla, a smear campaign was launched against investigative reporter Khadija Ismayilova. In early March 2012, Khadija received photos of herself, taken covertly in her apartment, of "a personal nature and a note saying, 'Whore, behave. Or you will be defamed.'" She took a camera crew to her apartment to photograph a network of wiring for cameras she had found inside the walls.[64] The Baku office of Radio Liberty, Azadlıq Radiosu, where she worked, said that such blackmail efforts "have no place in a civil society."[65] She had been the local station manager from 2008 to 2010, and then had resumed work as an investigative reporter. She was concurrently the regional coordinator for the Caucasus branch of the Organized Crime and Corruption Reporting Project. Her case reveals not only the pressure on an investigate journalist who revealed corruption at the top of government but of the judiciary's failure to respond to citizens' complaints.[66] Her situation was included in the March 20, 2012, Report on Media Freedom to the OSCE by Dunja Mijatović, the OSCE representative on freedom of the media.[67] Khadija decided to reject the threat with a statement on her Facebook page despite the personal cost. She would not "behave," but fight for freedom of expression. Soon the intimate pictures of Khadija appeared on the Internet. Weeks later, on the eve of Eurovision, she published a story on the Aliyev family's acquisition of gold mines in western Azerbaijan.[68]

In September, NIDA cofounder Zaur Gurbanli was arrested.[69] Other NIDA activists were arrested soon afterward. Around the same time, Nigar Yaqublu, a young activist of the Müsavat Party's youth wing and a daughter of the deputy chair of the party, was arrested in connection with a car accident in which party member Aydin Ayalov lost his life. Nigar was kept in pretrial detention. Her father, Tofiq Yaqublu, believed that this action against his daughter was meant to create pressure on him and his family for his political activism. Tofiq himself would later be arrested for inciting unrest in Ismayilli in January 2013.[70] In December 2012, Nigar was sentenced to two and a half years in penal colony, though her lawyers said that the prosecution had failed to prove her guilt.[71] She was freed two months later.[72] By then, however, her father was in prison.

Efforts to describe the situation of Azerbaijan's political prisoners faced an uphill fight in the CoE. The special rapporteur on political prisoners, Christoph Straesser, struggled repeatedly to have his report on Azerbaijan discussed in PACE. As Straesser had been denied a visa to Azerbaijan since the beginning of his appointment as special rapporteur in 2009, Azerbaijani government deputies and lobbyists argued that he would not be capable of producing an accurate report. Moreover, the Azerbaijanis claimed there was no definition of "political prisoner," so the work could not be valid. In early October 2012, PACE debated the definition of political prisoner. The debate drew an unusually large number of energetic Azerbaijani lobbyists, who sought to discourage deputies from voting for the definition. In the end, the measure passed by a narrow margin.[73] But the lobbyists were more successful when Straesser's report itself was discussed in PACE in January 2013 and voted down, 125 to 79. Human rights observers considered this vote to be a decisive sign to Azerbaijani authorities that they had a free hand to continue to jail regime critics,[74] and even to deny there were any political prisoners in Azerbaijan, as Aliyev did at a press conference at NATO.[75] The Aliyev regime seemed to be in a strong position for the 2013 presidential election.

As PACE rejected the political prisoner report, demonstrations in Azerbaijan led the regime to take more prisoners. Demonstrations in Baku against noncombat deaths of army recruits were met with police violence, in which dozens were arrested and fined. Further unrest emerged over rent increases in Baku. Yet it was the riot in the town of Ismayilli in January 2013 that had the widest repercussions. As word of the protest against the local governor spread, opposition political leaders and journalists went to Ismayilli to get the full story. The disorder in Ismayilli soon died down,[76] but events there provided an opportunity to arrest two prominent political figures on charges of "instigating public unrest," even though the unrest had begun and mostly ended before they arrived.[77] The key detainees were Ilgar Mammadov, head of the opposition organization Republican Alternative (REAL), and Tofiq Yaqublu, deputy head of the Müsavat Party.[78] As mentioned earlier, Yaqublu's daughter Nigar had just been sentenced to a penal colony in connection with a car accident the previous fall. Yaqublu, a journalist, had gone to Ismayilli to cover events there for his newspaper.

Mammadov, a lawyer who had decided to become a candidate for president in the fall 2013 elections, was the bigger fish of the two. REAL's leadership and most of its members were young, age forty and under. During the early months of his incarceration, Mammadov's followers in REAL collected the required 40,000 signatures for his presidential candidacy. But the Central Election Commission, dominated by the ruling YAP, had declared so many signatures to be forgeries that Mammadov was never registered as a candidate. He was later sentenced to seven years in prison. He appealed to the ECHR. Tofiq Yaqublu, despite having displayed his press pass in Ismayilli, was arrested with Mammedov on January 24, and on February 4 he was charged with organizing the riots. Yaqublu's daughter was released just as he was taken into custody. He was convicted and sentenced very quickly, on March 17, to five years.[79] He and Ilgar Mammadov remained in jail at the end of 2015. During 2015, Mammedov refused to be X-rayed after repeated threats of harm by prison officials. In mid-August, he was placed in solitary confinement.[80] After reported mistreatment on at least two occasions, he was reportedly severely beaten in October.[81] Although Mammedov and Yaqublu were on a proposed list of prisoners to be released for the new year in January 2016, they were not on the list of the 110 released. Yaqublu was subsequently released in March.

During late 2012 and early 2013, the Aliyev regime increasingly used financial weapons against its critics. The Ismayilli demonstrators of January 2013 were assessed fines "ranging from $380 and $760. The average salary in Azerbaijan is about $400 per month. The new law, passed in November [2012], increased fines up to thirtyfold, with a maximum penalty of $3,800."[82] Fines against NGOs that violated the increasingly detailed and demanding laws were also raised. The February 2013 amendment to NGO law introduced "big fines on NGOs which fail to register grants with the authorities within a certain period. NGO officers would have to pay between 1,500 AZN (1,428 euros in 2012) and 2,500 AZN and the NGOs themselves between 5,000 AZN and 7,000 AZN. The fines are to be greater if NGOs accept donations without grant agreements."[83]

Because of these fines and restrictive legislation, Human Rights Watch noted a "dramatic decline" of NGOs in the previous three years.[84] Official data recorded more than 2,900 NGOs registered with the state,[85] though many of these were actually government-organized (so-called GONGOs), and as many as a thousand remained unregistered in the fall of 2013.[86] Some major NGOs—including the Institute for Peace and Democracy, headed by Leyla Yunus; the Election Monitoring and Democracy Training Center, led by Anar Mamedli; and Rasul Jafarov's Human Rights Club—had tried unsuccessfully to register for years.[87]

Opposition journalists and bloggers put together a video contrasting the regime's public face with the repression of media and human rights behind it. A twelve-minute video clip, called "Amazing Azerbaijan," was posted on YouTube in January 2013. The host was Khadija Ismayilova, who began the widely viewed clip by repeating questions that others had asked her: "Baku is so beautiful and people look so happy, why do you complain?" She answered this with her own question: "Did you ever see the wall along the road from the airport to the city? We call it the 'wall of happiness,'" she said, and behind it is the ordinary life and misery of the people of Azerbaijan. The clip highlighted the preparation for Eurovision, recapping the demolition of apartment blocks as unwilling residents were dragged out by police, and her own reports about the president's family benefiting from the new construction. Donkey bloggers Adnan Hajizade and Emin Milli discussed their 2009 video that had landed them in jail. Adnan said: "If I knew that I would be arrested, I would do so much more. . . . I would be much more outspoken. So after you get arrested, you actually know you got arrested for some real things, not for some silly video."[88] But for the increasingly authoritarian regime, all criticism and all satire constituted real enough things to provoke arrests, beatings, and jail terms.

As a presidential election year, 2013 was somewhat unusual. It was the first time that Ilham Aliyev would be reelected after the rescission of term limits. One outside observer dubbed it a "crossing of the Rubicon" because other authoritarian rulers had found ways to skirt the term limits of their national law (in Vladimir Putin's case, for instance, by taking another post for one term) rather than go directly into a third term. The campaign itself also had unique features. The main opposition parties remained united throughout the campaign. Rather than try to agree on one of their leaders, they eventually chose a distinguished historian and longtime opposition activist, Jamil Hasanli. He had little time to campaign, but he made the most of it.

Nine candidates ran for president—nominally opposition candidates, eight of whom devoted their time to flattering the incumbent, who said he would not campaign. The one outlier among the contenders was, of course, Jamil Hasanli, a truth teller who minced no words and said what others avoided saying. In one televised debate, which was the only approved way for candidates to use their legally allowed media time, Hasanli was able to speak only briefly on regime corruption before being interrupted by a screaming rant from another candidate who threw a plastic bottle at him. Hasanli revealed the lie under so many staged arrests of political activists on phony drug charges: "What kind of government throws drugs into the pockets of its young people?" The effort to disrupt Hasanli's presentation backfired, since independent camera crews mobbed him as he left the television station, giving him ample opportunity to repeat, uninterrupted, the criticism of the ruling elite and of the president himself.

Predictably, Ilham Aliyev was awarded another lopsided victory, though domestic monitors, as in 2003, found so much fraud that they claimed that Jamil Hasanli had actually won. The unusual feature was the array of international monitors, most recruited by the Azerbaijani government and prepared to claim that all was well. The Russian monitors even did so in advance of the elections. Most distressing to Western democratization organizations were reports from the PACE and European Parliament delegations, who had been heavily lobbied by the Aliyev regime. PACE and European Parliament monitors, who were there only for the days around the voting itself, concluded, amid some mildly worded criticism, that "we have observed a free, fair and transparent electoral process; . . . we did not witness any evidence of intimidation against voters, in or close to polling stations; . . . We also believe that the opposition has had—although reduced—a window of opportunity for this election which must be developed for the future."[89] Western democratization activists were dumbfounded.

Naturally, the Azerbaijani authorities expressed outrage at the one international monitoring report that suggested that the elections still had not met international standards of freedom, fairness, and transparency. That report was written by OSCE/ODIHR, with its hundreds of long- and short-term observers who visited about half of all polling stations in the country (see chapter 3). Although it did not contain a statement that the election was invalid, it used very strong language in characterizing the flaws that it had observed, including "credible reports of candidate and voter intimidation" and "bad or very bad" counting procedures in 58 percent of the observed polling places. Postelection appeals were routinely dismissed by Azerbaijani courts, and the four they did hear were decided in favor of the YAP-controlled Central Election Commission.[90] The OSCE, already suggested as a culprit in the color revolutions of Georgia and Ukraine, was accused of bias. Aliyev insisted that the OSCE office in Azerbaijan be reduced to a mere "projects office," and OSCE was forced to comply.[91]

Among domestic monitoring NGOs that criticized the elections was the Election Monitoring and Democracy Studies Center, headed by Anar Mamedli. In its final report, OSCE/ODIHR noted the pressure that had been brought to bear against the EMDSC; because it was not granted legal status, it had to accredit observers individually, as it had done in previous elections. "Following election day, the General Prosecutor's Office conducted a search of their premises and informed the EMDSC director [Anar Mamedli] that he was not permitted to travel abroad [to the European Union's Eastern Partnership Vilnius summit] due to criminal investigations against his organization." In December, Mamedli was arrested on charges of illegal entrepreneurship. He was later sentenced to five years in jail. In the aftermath of the elections, several journalists were arrested, one on drug charges (Rashad Ramazanov, who was sentenced to nine years). And the Popular Front's newspaper *Azadlıq*, one of the major opposition dailies, was shut down.[92]

"The Crackdown" of 2014

The events of late 2013 constituted the beginning of the repressions of 2014, the pace and extent of which were so serious that observers called it simply "The Crackdown." The EuroMaidan movement in Ukraine had just begun, seeming to shadow Ilham Aliyev's reelection just as the Rose Revolution had followed the 2003 election. Azerbaijan's leadership saw parallels for Baku. Stung by criticisms of the recent presidential elections, recalling the embarrassment around Eurovision in 2012, and looking forward to the first European Games in 2015, Aliyev and the ruling elite had no intention of leaving their critics at large. The regime was already imposing tighter control on NGOs with the laws of 2012–13 described above, as well as the arrests of journalists and human rights defenders; and manipulation of electoral law, elections, and the judiciary. Further restrictions on NGO financing followed. Human rights and political groups were decapitated by the arrests of their leaders, as REAL and EMDSC had been in 2013. AXCP came under further attack with arrests of *Azadlıq* journalists, and in March, just two weeks after Ukrainian protesters drove President Victor Yanukovich from power, a mysterious explosion in Baku demolished the building that housed the Popular Front headquarters. The official cause, announced on the scene without investigation, was a gas explosion from a faulty propane tank in a basement barbershop. The barber said that he had no such tank.[93]

Political trials continued. In May, six NIDA activists who had been arrested the previous spring were sentenced to six to eight years in prison.[94] They and a few others began a hunger strike. Amnesty International considered them all to be prisoners of conscience. The head of the OSCE projects office, Alex Shahtakhtinski, a French citizen of Azerbaijani and Nakhjivani origin, explained the sentences to a foreign visitor by saying that the young men were "extremists." One of the activists told his lawyer that he retracted a confession made "under duress, [and] Ministry of National Security officials punched him and beat him with clubs. As a result he could not walk for four days and lost hearing in his left ear."[95] After sentencing, in an apparent deal with the authorities, one NIDA activist wrote a petition for pardon on May 19, in which he renounced NIDA and asked that his name be removed from lists of political prisoners. In October, four activists were pardoned in a group of eighty prisoners. Although prosecutors had insisted that they had not been arrested for political reasons, the men pardoned were all required to sign statements renouncing political activity and pledging support for the present government. Two were filmed, in a staged event, bringing flowers to the grave of Heydar Aliyev.[96] Anar Mamedli of EMDSC was convicted of illegal entrepreneurship, tax evasion, and abuse of authority, and was sentenced to five and a half years in prison. In August 2014, PACE awarded Mamedli its prestigious Václav Havel Human Rights Prize.[97] After many calls for his release, he was freed in March 2016.

The ECHR issued a judgment in the case of REAL chairperson Ilgar Mammadov, concerning his 2013 arrest and conviction in connection with the unrest in Ismayilli. In its ruling of May 22, the court found that Azerbaijan, in its police and court proceedings against Mammadov, had committed five violations of the Convention for the Protection of Human Rights and Fundamental Freedoms, which Azerbaijan had accepted when it joined the CoE. The judgment concluded (paragraph 143) that "the actual purpose of the impugned measures was to silence or punish the applicant for criticizing the Government and attempting to disseminate what he believed was the true information that the Government were trying to hide."[98] The court ordered his immediate release.[99] As of August 2016, however, he remains in prison. As before, the Azerbaijani government ignored the court's judgments against it, even as they took—and were allowed to take— the chairmanship of the CoE's Committee of Ministers, the West's premier guardian of human rights, in May 2014.

In the summer, with Azerbaijan chairing the CoE Committee of Ministers, the pace of arrests, prosecutions, and repressions quickened. NGO finances were targeted, then individual heads of democracy and human rights watchdog organizations, then journalists, and even the daughter of the only real 2013 opposition candidate for president.

The concept of an NGO was alien in the Soviet system, where *nongovernmental* meant *antigovernmental*. The thinking survives in many post-Soviet states, especially where Soviet-era officials remain in power. In Azerbaijan in the twenty-first century, the room for NGOs has shrunk compared with the 1990s, possibly because of a sense of insecurity that the country's leadership did not feel under Heydar Aliyev. Azerbaijan had established a Council of State to Support NGOs in 2007, in keeping with official emphasis on cooperation between the state and NGOS, as well as GONGOs.[100] Early in 2014, President Aliyev signed a law on public participation, providing for the creation of Public Councils whose job mimicked one NGO function, the initiation of public consultations.[101] A major regime argument against NGOs is that they, together with foreign sponsors and donors, work to interfere in

Azerbaijan's internal affairs. Registration of NGOs was blocked even when they followed regulations. The International Center for Non-Profit Law noted that Azerbaijan had lost at least five cases before the ECHR, which ruled "denials of registration to violate the freedom of association." But laws passed in 2014 created new obstacles, including registration requirements on individual grant recipients that formerly were applied only to organizations.[102] A Venice Commission report found that 2013 and 2014 amendments to the NGO law had failed to address previously identified obstacles to registration and activity of NGOs, and had "raised barriers." Regulations were called "cumbersome"; fines for errors in application were excessive. Registering departments appeared to have wide discretion for registering NGOs, and often delayed the process. Amendments to the Law on Grants, also adopted in 2014, effectively eliminated foreign donors from making grants to NGOs in Azerbaijan.[103] Those who received grants, sometimes as individuals rather than as NGOs, were open to prosecution for tax or other financial violations.

Despite international pressure, or perhaps because of it, in November 2014 President Aliyev signed into law an amendment to subject NGOs' receipt of foreign grants to approval from "executive organs."[104] Fuad Aleskerov, an official for law enforcement oversight in the presidential administration, cited this and previous measures as necessary for transparency and security. He claimed that some foreign grants supported NGOs that were trying to destabilize Azerbaijan.[105] In year-end budget discussions, Alaskerov stated that the 2015 budget had sufficient funds for Azerbaijan's NGOs, so they would not need to obtain money from foreign grants. He said that Azerbaijan has money for international efforts, such as the fight against the Ebola virus, that are not, he added pointedly, aimed at interference in the internal affairs of other states.[106]

Acting on the 2013–14 amendments to the NGO law, the government froze the bank accounts of international NGOs operating in Azerbaijan, including the International Research and Exchanges Board (IREX), Oxfam, the National Endowment for Democracy, and the National Democratic Institute. These organizations were forced to reduce or eliminate their activities in the country. IREX closed its offices after bank accounts were frozen and teams from the prosecutors' offices intruded into the office and seized computers and other equipment.[107] Similarly, a group of NGOs in a coalition to support the Extractive Industries Transparency Initiative, of which Azerbaijan was an early participant in 2003, had its accounts frozen. Mirvari Gahramanli, an anticorruption and transparency activist and head of the Oil Workers Rights' Protection Organization, an EITI NGO network member, was blocked from accessing both her personal and the organization's bank accounts. She had successfully registered a foreign grant in 2013, but in 2014 she was unable to access the funds. Gubad Ibadoglu, an economist and member of the EITI board in Azerbaijan, described the pressure on NGOs. He said that the government's goal was not to enhance transparency and accountability, but "to weaken independent NGOs funded by foreign donors.[108] His office was unable to pay rent or continue its projects. The bank accounts of the Democratic Institutions and Human Rights Public Union were frozen, as was the personal bank account of its director, Elchin Abdullayev. The Ministry of Justice rejected the group's application to register a foreign grant.[109] The Baku office of Transparency International met with the same treatment in August.[110]

Heads of NGOs came under fire, even when the NGO was nonpolitical. Hasan Huseynli, head of the Intelligent Citizen education NGO in the city of Ganje, was arrested for allegedly stabbing a man who Huseynli said had attacked him. The incident took place on March 30. The investigation and trial reportedly were marked by serious irregularities. Huseynli was sentenced to six years in jail. Khalid Baghirov, a lawyer from the REAL movement and defender of Ilgar Mammadov, said that the case bore "uncanny similarities" to others brought against human rights and political activists. He gave the example of Müsavat Party figure Yadigar Sadiqov, who was convicted of assault in January 2014, though he says that the alleged victim had been the one to attack him.[111] Subsequently, opposition journalist Seymur Hazi, a former Yeni Fikir activist, also was arrested in September for "assaulting" someone who reportedly had attacked him.[112]

In April, Azerbaijani journalist Rauf Mirqadirov, who had been living in Turkey, was seized by Turkish authorities and deported to Baku. He was arrested on arrival and charged with treason on the basis of his role in track-two ("citizen") diplomacy, working with an Armenian journalist over the stalemate in Mountainous Karabagh. Mirqadirov worked for the Baku-based Russian-language newspaper *Zerkalo*. He had been an outspoken critic of Vladimir Putin as well as of the Azerbaijani and Turkish governments. His arrest was unusual for two reasons. First, he had extended his visa to remain in Turkey, but authorities there said that it had expired. Second, his extradition involved the Turkish judicial system, not only Azerbaijani authorities. As in other political cases, his pretrial detention in Baku was extended repeatedly. After twenty months, he stood trial for treason in late 2015. He was sentenced to six years (although the maximum sentence is life imprisonment) by the Court of Grave Crimes in a closed trial, a sentence that was reduced to five years by the Court of Appeals. In March 2016, he was "conditionally" released.[113] He initially had been arrested on the heels of a visit by Turkish president Receb Tayyib Erdoğan to Ilham Aliyev, leading observers and Mirqadirov's lawyer to suggest that a deal had been made between the two increasingly authoritarian presidents.[114] Because of Mirqadirov's criticism of Putin, this case also had implications for Aliyev's relations with Moscow, which were friendly, even as Russian forces seized Crimea and occupied eastern Ukraine. The charge of treason against Mirqadirov was, said commentators, a de facto ban on even small track-two diplomatic efforts in Karabagh, and thus it opened a campaign against other Azerbaijanis who engaged with Armenian counterparts—including the most prominent and active among them, Leyla and Arif Yunus.[115]

A new assault against human rights defenders came in the spring and summer. Some of the regime's zeal may have been related to the EuroMaidan movement in Ukraine after the ouster of Yanukovich. Leyla Yunus, head of the Institute for Peace and Democracy, and her husband, historian Arif Yunus, were removed from an outbound international flight on April 28 and taken to the prosecutor's office for questioning. They were released the next day, but their passports were confiscated. Leyla, a Chevalier of the (French) Order of the Legion of Honor, was subsequently arrested on July 30, 2014, and charged with treason (in connection with her track-two diplomacy efforts) as well as fraud, tax evasion, and forgery in connection with her Institute. Arif was charged with treason and fraud; at first, he was placed under house arrest because of his poor health, but then was incarcerated on August 5. The couple's international prominence for peace activism made their arrest particularly shocking to prodemocracy groups in the West. Leyla, a diabetic, was reportedly denied appropriate food, medicine, and medical care. She reported being beaten by cellmates and a guard in prison, but prison administrators rejected the claims without investigating.[116] She was later deprived of several of her team of lawyers when they were declared by authorities to be witnesses in the case against her.[117]

Leyla had been working with Rasul Jafarov, head of the Human Rights Club and organizer of Sing for Democracy in 2012, to compile a unified list of political prisoners. Their working group produced a list of about a hundred prisoners, replete with details of each case. Jafarov was arrested on August 2. Both he and Leyla were now added to the list.[118] Several days later, Intiqam Aliyev, a human rights attorney who had argued several cases before the ECHR, was arrested, accused of illegal business practices and tax evasion. The US State Department and various Western groups called for their release, but all remained in prison. Emin Huseynov, head of the Institute for Reporters' Freedom and Safety, was warned of his impending arrest. He had previously been arrested and severely beaten. In August, he disappeared. His supporters and family said that he "went into hiding."[119]

In August 2014, *The List: Political Prisoners in Azerbaijan* was made available by the ESI.[120] The ninety-eight-page report grouped prisoners by category and provided information on each individual, the charges against them, their location, and the sentences they had received. The largest category, about half, was religious activists, mostly Muslims. (See chapter 6 for more details on government activity against Muslim activists.) The charges against the prisoners all are criminal charges, including a litany of the same charges over and over: planning and carrying out violence, hooliganism, fraud and tax evasion, treason, and weapon and/or drug possession, the latter especially common among youth activists. These charges bolster the regime's contention that these are criminals, not political prisoners.

Arrests continued as European and US criticism became sharper. Moreover, in addition to the general accusations from Baku about "outsiders" interfering, some of the repressions took a decidedly anti-American tone at the time that US Ambassador Richard Morningstar was completing his term and leaving the embassy at the end of July. For the rest of 2014 and early 2015, there was no US ambassador in Baku.

Said Nuri (formerly Nuriyev of Yeni Fikir) had immigrated to the United States in 2006 and become a citizen in 2012. Although he had visited Azerbaijan four times after obtaining US citizenship, during a visit to his family in September 2014 he was prevented from boarding his return flight from Baku International Airport. The procurator's office stated that the government "does not recognize" his US citizenship.[121] He was held for several weeks, then was released and allowed to return to the United States.

Gunel Hasanli, daughter of the 2013 presidential candidate and Milli Shura chairperson Jamil Hasanli, was the object of a staged accident on September 19. An elderly woman fell in front of Gunel's car outside the Hasanli family's apartment building. The woman later said that she was unhurt, but ten days after the event, Gunel was summoned to the police and formally charged with failing to report an accident. Her father stated publicly that the charges were retaliation for criticisms he had made during the presidential campaign one year earlier.[122] At her subsequent trial in the winter, Gunel, who was a mother of two small children and had no record of political activism, was judged guilty and sentenced to one to one and a half years in a penal colony. This was the same pattern as with Tofiq Yaqublu's daughter, except that in Gunel's case, there was really no accident, no one was hurt, the alleged victim insisted that she had not been hurt, and the activist's daughter was not involved in politics. As one former Western diplomat commented, "It's a new low."

Meanwhile, the CoE and UN bodies were turning more attention to the human rights violations in Azerbaijan as Baku was denouncing their "interference." Human Rights Watch noted in August that the freezing of bank accounts was a method used against groups involved in an anticorruption initiative, and it observed that the pressure had been escalating since the 2013 presidential election.[123] Like other watchdog organizations, Human Rights Watch noted the number of these abuses that took place while Azerbaijan chaired the CoE Committee of Ministers:

> Over the last two-and-a-half years Azerbaijan has brought or threatened unfounded criminal charges against at least 50 independent and opposition political activists, journalists, bloggers, and human rights defenders. Most of them remain behind bars. In the months since Azerbaijan assumed the chairmanship of the Council of Europe [Committee of Ministers] the government has dramatically escalated its attack on activists, with authorities arresting at least eleven people and convicting at least nine others on politically motivated charges, sentencing them to various prison terms following flawed trials.[124]

CoE human rights commissioner Nils Muižnieks expressed "serious concern" about freedom of assembly and the harassment and arrest of journalists in Azerbaijan. In August, Muižnieks visited Anar Mammadli and Leyla Yunus in prison. He urged the Azerbaijani authorities to stop reprisals against human rights defenders.[125] He called the wave of arrests "totally unacceptable," and said that the pattern "flies in the face of the human rights obligations undertaken by Azerbaijan" when it joined the forty-seven-nation European human rights body.[126]

The European Parliament adopted a resolution in September 2014 recognizing the worsening of the human rights situation over the past five years. The UN Subcommittee on Human Rights cut short a visit to Azerbaijan because it was barred from visiting "places of detention" to which it had been promised access.[127] The US State Department changed its tone from gently reminding Azerbaijan of its international obligations in June to calling for an end to restrictions on civil society in August,[128] when the US representative to the OSCE released a statement identifying individuals arrested on politically motivated charges and calling on the government of Azerbaijan to release its political prisoners.[129]

Muižnieks, after his visit in October 2014 to Azerbaijan, wrote that "Azerbaijan will go down in history as the country that carried out an unprecedented crackdown on human rights defenders during its chairmanship [of the CoE Committee of Ministers]. All of my partners in Azerbaijan are in jail."[130] By December, the number of political prisoners was over a hundred—more than Russia and Belarus combined. Journalists were under increasing pressure, and there had been an increase in the number of disbarments of lawyers who had defended regime critics.[131] In early December 2014, State Department spokesperson Jan Psaki said that "the government of Azerbaijan is not living up to its international human rights commitments and obligations. We urge the government to respect the universal rights of its citizens and allow them to freely express their views. They will be best able to ensure their future stability and prosperity by allowing a more open society." [132]

The day after Psaki's statement, Ramiz Mehdiyev published a long article claiming that the United States was trying to overthrow the Aliyev government using NGOs and American-funded, "disloyal" Azerbaijanis. Two days later, on December 5, investigative journalist Khadija Ismayilova was arrested. Her most recent in-depth article on high-level corruption had explored the connection of President Aliyev's daughters and the mobile phone carrier Azercell.[133] Apart from these investigative pieces, Khadija hosted a daily interview and call-in show, *After Work*, on Azadlıq Radiosu, the local office of the US-funded Radio Liberty. In the broadcasts, she covered a wide array of topics, many controversial, but it was her guests and callers, not Khadija herself, who voiced the criticism of regime policies and rarely of regime figures.

After Khadija's arrest, US secretary of state John Kerry spoke by phone to President Aliyev. A State Department spokesperson reported, "We are alarmed by the Government of Azerbaijan's crackdown on civil society. The Secretary raised our concerns in his December 21st phone call with President Aliyev."[134] A week after that conversation, on December 26, the Azerbaijani authorities raided and closed the office of Radio Liberty, which had operated in Azerbaijan since the 1990s. Equipment was seized, and staff were taken for questioning on multiple occasions without legal representation. Broadcasting resumed from Prague, but the staff remained under threat, including foreign travel bans. The day after the assistant secretary of state for European and Eurasian affairs, Victoria Nuland, visited Baku in February 2015 and announced a joint commission on human rights, the pretrial detention of Arif Yunus was extended by five months. The pretrial detention of his wife Leyla Yunus, as well as investigative journalist Khadija Ismayilova, already had been extended by several months each. Nuland was vilified in a Russian publication as "an agent for US-supported regime change in the former Soviet sphere, and her visit anywhere in that space should be seen as the bad omen that it is."[135] The Russian charge that the United States had engineered all the color revolutions was repeated increasingly in Baku. In view of the close proximity of each of these Azerbaijani actions to a call or visit by a US official, it seemed that the Azerbaijanis were thumbing their collective nose at US expressions of "concern" about Azerbaijan's civil society.

Reflecting on the patterns of 2014, analyst Giorgi Gogia noted three things in Azerbaijan that had "never happened before":

> First, the government arrested the towering figures of the NGO movements. Second, since last January, it hasn't registered a single foreign grant. . . . Third, the government went after and froze the bank accounts of over 50 NGOs and their leaders, including [Emin Huseynov]. Very suddenly, from a very bad human rights record, it turned into a closed-country human rights record.[136]

The Trials of 2015

The pattern of threats, arrests, intimidation, pretrial detention, vilification, and convictions continued into 2015 with extensions of pretrial detentions of Leyla and Arif Yunus; Intiqam Aliyev; Rasul Jafarov; journalists Rauf Mirqadirov, Seymur Hazi, Parviz Hashimli, and Khadija Ismayilova; and the conviction of Gunel Hasanli. Journalist Emin Huseynov had been in hiding in the Swiss Embassy since August. He was allowed to leave it and Azerbaijan on the eve of the European Games, set for June.

Legal restrictions that could be used against investigative journalists continued to tighten: in March, the prison term for divulging "state secrets" was lengthened. The Milli Majlis amended Article 284 of the criminal code to impose a strict but ill-defined "liability for disclosure of state secrets." The crime, formerly punishable by two to five years, would now be punishable by three to six years. If "grave consequences" resulted, the punishment would be increased to three to seven years. And for "illegally obtaining information constituting a state secret, items containing state secrets by force or threat of force or other coercion, fraud, robbery, *or by technical means*, with no signs of high treason or espionage, will be punished with a prison sentence of 2 to 5 years."[137] The law seemed to target investigative journalists. By being put on the books at this time, before Khadija Ismayilova went to trial, the longer sentences would be available to use in her case.

Khadija was a special target, certainly for her reporting on corruption that led to the hidden finances of the first family and other oligarchs. One week after these amendments to the criminal code were adopted, she was deprived of one of her team of lawyers, Yalcin Imanov.[138] Then, Khadija's accuser Tural Mustafayev retracted his claims that Khadija had pressured him to attempt suicide, saying that he had been tortured into making the claims against her.[139] Even though her accuser had recanted, she was not released, because by then other criminal charges had been filed against her, virtually identical to those used against human rights defenders and NGOs—engaging in illegal business, tax evasion, and abuse of power. She remained defiant, writing from prison: "If we can continue to reject the thinking that is imposed on us and believe that human dignity is not for sale, then we are the winners, and they, our jailers both inside and outside prison, are the losers." In April 2015, in recognition of her unique contribution to investigative reporting in Azerbaijan and her bravery in continuing her work in the face of regime-sponsored blackmail, Khadija Ismayilova was awarded the prestigious PEN/Barbara Goldsmith Freedom to Write Award.[140]

The trials of human rights defenders and others who had been arrested in 2014 began in January 2015:

- In January, journalist Seymur Hazi, who was attacked at a bus stop and then arrested for hooliganism, was sentenced to five years in prison.
- In April, Rasul Jafarov, the organizer of Sing for Democracy, was sentenced to 6.3 years in prison, a sentence that was upheld on appeal in August.
- In April, human rights lawyer Intiqam Aliyev, whose health concerns were ignored, was sentenced to seven and a half years in prison, another sentence that was upheld on appeal.
- In May, EMDSC head Anar Mamedli, who had been arrested in December 2013 after denouncing the presidential election of that fall, was sentenced to five and a half years in prison. In September 2014, Mamedli had been awarded the CoE's Václav Havel Award for Human Rights.[141]

The most high-profile defendants were tried in the summer, the height of vacation season across Europe and North America. In late July and August 2015, after a year in pretrial detention, Leyla and Arif were tried on the economic charges they faced, separate from the charge of treason. The trial lasted only a few days in a tiny room that could not accommodate the press or more than few international observers. Motions to delay because of Arif's poor health were denied, though he was repeatedly given injections in the court room to keep him conscious during the trial. They were found guilty on all counts. Leyla was sentenced to eight and a half years and Arif to seven years, which they and others called "a death sentence" that they could not survive. Western sources denounced the proceedings and called for the couple's release.[142] Authorities said they would later be tried on the treason charge, which carries a life sentence.

Khadija Ismayilova went on trial at the same time. At the session of August 14, she petitioned that Judge Ramella Allahverdiyeva not preside. The public prosecutor rejected her petition as "unreasonable." She asked that the court secretary be dismissed because he had not taken accurate notes in the trial protocols. The judge rejected this petition, too. Finally, one of Khadija's colleagues from Radio Liberty petitioned to testify at the hearing, but this was denied "due to lack of legal ground[s]."[143] Khadija's trial took place in August 2015, with brief sessions and long delays. No witness testified against her, but all her motions were denied by the judge. Like the Yunuses, she was kept in a soundproof glass enclosure during the trial, but was allowed at the end to respond to the verdict. In what was called a "blistering attack," she ridiculed the lack of proof against herself: "She called the trial a 'poor quality scam' and said, 'I am more successful in this business of finding proof than is the notorious prosecutor's staff.'" On September 1, she was convicted of criminal libel, tax evasion, embezzlement, illegal entrepreneurship, and abuse of power, and was sentenced to seven and a half years. The OSCE representative on freedom of the media, Dunja Mijatovic, like many international media rights representatives, called on the Azerbaijani government to "stop targeting journalists."[144]

Repressions continued. In August, unknown thugs beat journalist Rasim Aliyev so severely that he died in the hospital after two days. His attackers were allegedly relatives or friends of a soccer player whom Aliyev had criticized on his Facebook page.[145] But the media community believed that unhindered police beatings of reporters established a precedent for attacks on journalists. President Aliyev expressed concern that this matter constituted a "threat" to what he called Azerbaijan's "freedom of speech." By the end of 2015, no arrests had been made on this case and the investigation, like so many others, had been quietly dropped.

The attack on families of regime critics has also continued with the sacking of the father of NIDA activist Mamed Azizov, as Mamed himself was put in solitary confinement.[146] At the end of 2015, the brother-in-law of Emin Milli was arrested, and Emin has been threatened for his work on Meydan TV, an independent online news outlet based in Europe. Twenty-three members of Emin Milli's family members signed a letter to Ilham Aliyev, denouncing him.[147]

On November 12, within two weeks after the tainted elections to the Milli Majlis, Arif Yunus was released from prison on health grounds, but the charges against him remain. PACE president Anne Brasseur welcomed his release and called for the release of other political prisoners, especially those in poor health:[148]

> That said, the concerns raised by the legal proceedings against Arif Yunus and other human rights defenders and journalists have not been resolved. I appeal, once more, to the authorities of Azerbaijan to act in accordance with the standards of the European Convention on Human Rights and their commitments and obligations to the Council of Europe.

Brasseur alluded to the June 23 PACE Resolution 2062 (2015) on the functioning of democratic institutions in Azerbaijan.[149]

Leyla Yunus was released to house arrest on December 9, but none of the charges against her was dropped. Like her husband, she was released from prison on health grounds. Leyla, who turned sixty later in the month, suffers from hepatitis C and diabetes. She appeared frail when she left prison, walking slowly with a cane and leaning on Arif, as recorded in a journalist's video.[150] Arif's health improved after release, but Leyla reportedly needs surgery. Both were barred from leaving the country for medical care.[151] In the spring of 2016, the couple was first denied and then permitted to go to Europe for treatment, where they remained as of mid-2016.[152]

By the end of the year, criticism from international organizations, including PACE; the OSCE's refusal to monitor the November elections under the restrictions that Aliyev had tried to impose; and the downgrades in 2015 ratings from Freedom House and other human rights and prodemocracy groups apparently reached critical mass in Washington. Representative Chris

Smith (R-NJ), chairman of the US Helsinki Commission, drafted a congressional resolution called the Azerbaijan Democracy Act. The act condemned Azerbaijan's human rights record and, in an echo of the Magnitsky Act against similar human rights violations in Russia several years earlier, called for the denial of visas to senior Azerbaijani officials.[153] As Smith said:

> It is unacceptable that senior members of the Azerbaijani government are free to visit the United States while courageous women and men like investigative journalist Khadija Ismayilova, attorney Intigam Aliyev, opposition politician Ilgar Mammadov, and activist Anar Mammadli are locked away in prisons with inadequate access to legal or even medical assistance. . . . If they can pay the price for standing up for human rights, the least we can do is to stand with them.

Officials in Baku promptly replied with shrill rhetoric on US "double standards," and charged that the Armenian-American lobby was "buying" members of Congress. The Aliyev's government's only real weapon in this exchange was the political prisoners themselves. Hope for the customary holiday pardon was dashed when the list was made public on December 28. Though the list was unusually long, with 210 names, not one of the people released was a political prisoner or prisoner of conscience.[154] On the same day, journalist Rauf Mirqadirov was sentenced to six years in prison for espionage in connection with his track-two diplomacy.[155]

A War of Ideas

Part of Azerbaijan's onslaught on democratic ideals in 2014–15 entailed increasing criticism of Western "interference" as a reply to outside condemnation of human rights violations. At times, the United States was specifically the target. The peak of anti-US rhetoric from an Azerbaijani official was a lengthy and tendentious article of December 3, 2014, by chief of the presidential staff Ramiz Mehdiyev.[156] The document repeated accusations that Mehdiyev and other regime spokespersons had made earlier in the year, rejecting criticism by Western governments and international organizations on the crackdown on Azerbaijan's human rights defenders, journalists, and NGOs.[157] Mehdiyev argued that the NGOs in Azerbaijan represent "foreign interests" trying to destabilize Azerbaijan. He went so far as to accuse the

West, and the United States specifically, of attempting to subvert Azerbaijan using Azerbaijani citizens and NGOs as a "fifth column." He named Khadija Ismayilova as an example—and two days later, she was arrested. He criticized EU president Martin Schultz and US president Barack Obama, accusing them of trying to overthrow the Aliyev regime in the guise of building democracy using NGOs.[158] A few weeks later, the Azerbaijani government raided and closed the Baku office of Radio Liberty.

Mehdiyev's tirade is an example of the misuse of terms like democracy, subversion, interference, "fifth column," and "anti-Azerbaijani." Official Azerbaijani rhetoric asserts that Azerbaijan is a democracy and that NGOs are subversive political actors. Efforts to assert values like human rights are conflated with interference in Azerbaijan's domestic affairs. Azerbaijanis who believe in these rights, as well as in clean elections and free speech, are, in this vision, a "fifth column" who can only be favoring a foreign takeover of their own country. Open criticism, whether of policies or individual actions, is not considered a tool for political discourse, but is a sign of disloyalty and perhaps treasonous intent. Disagreement with the regime becomes not only impossible, but criminal. The debate essential to civil society and popular rule—that is, democracy—is quashed. Further, by equating the Aliyev government with Azerbaijan itself, the regime employs the term "anti-Azerbaijani" to denounce those who criticize the ruling elites and their policies. Pro-Azerbaijani therefore means pro-Aliyev—even in Western circles, where it is used to describe the Aliyev regime's lobbying efforts. The Aliyev regime asserts thereby that it *is* the state, and embodies both the state and popular interests. Separating the regime from the state (and the people) conceptually is therefore a crucial step in discussing policy and moving toward democracy. With regime control over the media, the populace remains, for the most part, as politically naive as they were under communist rule. The confusion of political terms and ideas is a clever weapon by which the regime prevents the majority from gaining political education or having the tools to fight a political fight.

In May 2014, a group of Azerbaijani civil society activists and journalists wrote an open letter to CoE secretary-general Thorbjørn Jagland that revealed this manipulation of words by the proregime Milli Majlis:

The members of the National Assembly, Milli Majlis, have called for legal persecution and harassment of the non-governmental organizations engaged in criticism of official Baku. . . . Following Transparency Azerbaijan's criticism of Azerbaijan's Parliament, the MPs called for the "boycott" of this NGO and "investigation" into its activity . . . they publicly branded civil activists "anti-nationalist force"[and "traitors to the nation" for exposing human rights problems.[159]

The same accusations against civil society activists as traitors were repeated in the Majlis's November budget discussion. In contrast, at the end of the month, President Aliyev's Twitter feed not only proclaimed: "Our system is a model of the European political system," but also: "All fundamental freedoms . . . are provided in Azerbaijan."[160]

Gerald Knaus, director of the European Stability Initiative, has rightly identified the Aliyev regime's claims to democracy as a version of Orwellian Newspeak. In George Orwell's dystopian novel *1984*, the center of torture is named the Ministry of Love, and the office for propaganda and altering history is the Ministry of Truth. More to the point are conceptual terms like *blackwhite* (simultaneously maintaining that opposite ideas are true) and *thoughtcrime* (thinking outside Newspeak formulae). In a January 2014 interview with Emin Milli, now head of Meydan TV in Germany, Knaus denounced the misuse and redefinition of words whose meanings Westerners all know, or knew in the past, such as democracy and freedom. In recent years, said Knaus, authoritarian regimes, among which he included Azerbaijan, have engaged in the hijacking of words and in subtle manipulation:

> Recognizing the power of this vision [of democratic society, autocrats] have tried to take it for themselves. They want to destroy the notion that we know what democracy is. . . . It's not that people believe Azerbaijan is a democracy today, but they stop realizing where the differences are, they stop envisaging a different future. And this is a very powerful instrument.[161]

The redefinition of terms, Knaus said, is a war of words, which is in essence a war of concepts and values. This process undermines points of reference that define core shared ideals, without which democracy can be undermined, not only in recently totalitarian states like former Soviet republics but also in the West. Knaus insisted that democracy could be defended precisely because such a war of ideas can and must be fought with debates and transparency. Political prisoners therefore must not be called "normal" prisoners; when elections are stolen, they must not be labeled as free and fair. Western citizens who elect the CoE, or parliamentary representatives who become election monitors, must question those representatives about their judgments when they condone nondemocratic practices under the rubric of some "special form of democracy."[162]

Nor are the Aliyev regime's defenders in the war of ideas and words confined to Europe. Americans, including former elected officials, have become part of a lobbying effort on behalf of "Azerbaijani interests" as defined by the Aliyev regime, especially concerning commerce, investment, and security. In the defense of commerce, they marginalize and ignore human rights. Since 2010, Azerbaijan has spent over $2.5 million annually on lobbying in Washington.[163] But efforts to improve relations in the present climate necessarily bring American supporters of the Aliyev government into the war of words and ideas. In January 2015, on the heels of the Mehdiyev diatribe against the United States, the Aliyev government's closing of Radio Liberty in Baku, and with a hundred political prisoners in Azerbaijani jails, former US congressman Dan Burton wrote this astonishing praise of Azerbaijan in the *Washington Times*:

> As America and Azerbaijan continue to face common challenges to our *increasingly common values and goals*, US officials should congratulate them for their *total commitment to religious tolerance, freedom and democracy*. America and the rest of the free world need more friends like Azerbaijan.[164]

6

Allah-u Akbar: Islam in Azerbaijan—
Piety, Politics, and the Future

Where does politics begin and religion end?
Where is that line? I don't know; you tell me.

—Haji Ilgar Ibrahimoglu, Baku, 2005

In the "human rights versus state security" debate, no problem is thornier than
the question of political Islam. The core question is this: must human rights,
including religious freedom, be sacrificed for security?[1] This view has proponents. In the era of al-Qaeda, the Taliban, and the Islamic State (also known as
ISIL or ISIS), extremist interpretations of Islam have demonstrably threatened
the security and the existence of governments and states, to say nothing of
cultural monuments and individuals. Those states that allow free communication run the risk that extremists will use that freedom for propagandizing
and recruitment. The control-versus-freedom debates have been repeated in
democratic countries, including the United States, even before the September
11 attacks. European and US views differ on the degree of acceptable restrictions in the face of a potential threat to security. International consensus and
law are on the side of states and regimes defending themselves from attack
and attempts at violent overthrow. The question of security versus human

180

rights arises when a state's defense against actual violence is juxtaposed with restrictions on the free exercise of speech, assembly, and religion, all of which may be critical of a regime without threatening to overthrow it. Between the extremes is the case of Islam as a major world religion; a nonviolent political program; a language of criticism; or a basis for identity, morality, and personal piety. Political activity of an individual Muslim or group of Muslims therefore may be nonpolitical or it may represent advocacy that would be protected as a human right. The difficulty emerges in trying to determine when such speech or activity represents the thin end of a wedge that may lead to instability, violence, or revolution. The case is yet more complex in a state where the ruling regime blocks open discourse, arrests its critics, and engages in large-scale corruption and manipulation of political and judicial institutions. By thus depriving the population of legal means to express discontent, the regime itself is driving society toward radicalism. When the deprivation of the rights to speak, assemble, and associate enhances the danger to the state's security, then the protection of human rights and democratization also becomes a matter of state security.

Islam and Modernization Movements in Azerbaijani History

Islam in Azerbaijan is a complex matter, even before taking into account its potential political role. The Russian Empire took the Caucasus from Iran early in the nineteenth century. The population at the time was mostly Shi'ite Muslim, like the rest of Iran was, since Shi'ism had been adopted as the state religion in the beginning of the sixteenth century under the Safavid Dynasty. The entire South Caucasus had been a frontier zone where the Iranian world met the Turkic, and with the adoption of Shi'ism it became a region where Shi'a Islam met Sunni Islam. Throughout Islamic history, the two sects often had been in conflict, and here they amplified their political rivalry. In the eighteenth century, Iran's Nader Shah worked for sectarian reconciliation, according to historian Altay Goyushov.[2] Iran's rival, the Ottoman Empire, was not only a Sunni power; its ruler, the sultan, had long been proclaimed caliph of the faithful. Thus, there were political implications to sectarian identity and loyalties. In the 1830s, after the Russian conquest, a local census in the Caucasus region showed that the Sunni and Shi'ite populations were about equal. Russian pressure on the North Caucasus and the forces of Shaykh Shamil, who led the resistance to Russian occupation, forced thousands to emigrate from the North Caucasus to the Ottoman Empire. By the 1860s, the Shi'ite population was about double that of the Sunni.[3]

A cultural-enlightenment movement of the second half of the nineteenth century, initiated in the Russian Empire by Turkic-speaking elites, stressed a Turkic ethnolinguistic identity over the sectarian. Azerbaijani modernists cooperated with counterparts among the Crimean and Volga Tatars, who had established the Jadid ("new") movement for modernization of Islam and society, as well as reformers among the Ottoman Turks.[4] These three groups were Sunni Muslims, and therefore a sectarian enemy from a traditional Shi'ite viewpoint.[5] But all shared the modernization agenda and later cooperated in the politics of the Russian Empire such as the State Duma and Muslim Congresses that met from 1905 to the middle of World War I.[6] Not all the faithful accepted the reconciling posture any more than they accepted modernization; rural areas remained conservative and mostly illiterate, and the urban modernist elites struggled against the conservatives perhaps more at times than against the Russian state.[7] In the Russian Empire, the term "Muslim" had social and legal implications, because non-Christians had only restricted access to higher education or local office holding. For the prorefom Azerbaijanis and Tatars, the term was a cultural as well as confessional marker. They considered themselves modern Muslims in terms of faith, but aimed to wrest control of education from poorly trained mullahs in order to spread secular learning in schools for boys and girls where science was to be reconciled with faith. Integral to their vision were social reforms, including a raised marriage age, a ban on polygamy, and criticism of veiling. Early in the twentieth century, Baku had a girls' school with female teachers; it was so popular that parents called for second one. Wives of wealthy Azerbaijanis publicly worked in charitable and public health efforts. Azerbaijan's influential Müsavat Party, founded in 1912, identified as "Islamic," but its program supported the reforms of the modernizers, which suggests that the term was more cultural and legal than purely confessional.[8] Parallel to this cultural enlightenment, in connection with the language of publication and instruction, an ethnolinguistic self-definition as "Turks" was forming. Although Russian officials called Azerbaijan's Turkic speakers "Muslims" or (incorrectly) "Tatars," the Turkic speakers of Azerbaijan various called themselves "Azerbaijani Turks," "Caucasus Turks," or just "Turks."[9]

The height of this reform movement's power was the first Azerbaijan Democratic Republic, which existed from 1918 to 1920. Constitutional order, multiparty elections, and a universal franchise, including women, distinguished this first republic of a Muslim society. In the multinational setting of Baku, Russians, mostly workers, were the largest community (35 percent).[10] Armenians (19 percent) had grown considerably since the 1903 city census and exercised substantial economic power. Jews were welcome, and many Jews who had fled pogroms in Russia and Ukraine flooded into Baku in this period. These factors, on top of the intellectual and philosophical disposition of the elites, dwarfed the sectarian divisions within the Azerbaijani Muslim community in Baku.

Azerbaijan and Islam under Soviet Power

The Soviet era began in 1920 with the invasion by the Red Army and the overthrow of the republic. Bolshevik power ushered in a complex mix of policies, but in religious terms, the first years were marked by brutal violence against all religions, their clergy, believers, and structures.[11] To avoid inflaming interethnic enmity, Armenian and Russian communists led the attack against their respective Orthodox churches, and Muslim communists attacked mosques and mullahs. Religious leaders of all faiths were exiled or killed. In the mid-1920s, the Soviet Communist Party established in Azerbaijan a branch of the League of the Militant Godless, the party's antireligious organization, which continued the attack on religious practice and instruction. The most intense period of antireligious pressure, which often was combined with the vilification and criminalization of nationalism, ended with World War II, as the Soviet regime needed all available tools, including religious and national loyalties, to mobilize its citizens.

In the postwar decades, antireligious pressures ebbed and flowed, but Islam, like other religions whose centers were outside Soviet borders,[12] was perpetually vilified as a significant danger. At the same time, the Soviet regime created an "official Islam," sanctioned and controlled by the state and the communist party. The advanced madrassa in Bukhara, Mir-i Arab, offered instruction to students from both Sunni and Shi'ite backgrounds. Its seven-year program did not even touch upon religious subjects until the fourth or fifth year, so students who left before that time received a good liberal education but little religious training.[13] The mullahs produced by this system generally were regarded by the Soviet Muslim population with suspicion as possible KGB informants. They were the only mullahs available for burials, weddings, or circumcisions, and were well paid for these essential life-passage ceremonies. Paradoxically, the career of a state-sponsored mullah was a path to affluence, with good state salaries and cars. Despite its internal weaknesses, this official structure and its cadre of "clerics" allowed the Soviet Union to present a "Muslim face" to the Islamic world. A few graduates of the Mir-i Arab Madrassa (or the Islamic University in Tashkent, Uzbekistan) even went to Cairo's Al-Azhar University for advanced study—an effort that was part of Soviet foreign policy in the Islamic world. In contrast, Moscow pursued more cautious relations with Tehran, then a US ally.[14] This was official Islam.

By contrast, "unofficial" Islam—including folk "mullahs," healers, cults of saints, and shrines, as well as the spiritual practices of Sufism—was outlawed but very popular, especially in rural areas. By the Gorbachev era, pressures on Orthodox religions (especially the Russian Orthodox Church) were minimal, but Islam—especially in Shi'ite Azerbaijan in the aftermath of the Islamic Revolution in Iran—was elevated to the status of imminent threat.

The impact of Ayatollah Ruhollah Khomeini and the 1979 Iranian Revolution on Azerbaijan is worth extended consideration.[15] It is likely that in religious villages, especially those near the southern border and outside Baku where Shi'ism was strong and shrines were objects of pilgrimage, local believers supported and welcomed Iran's reign of the ayatollahs. In view of the obvious corruption of the shah's regime, Islam offered a model of morality, and Khomeini's charisma was powerful. But in Baku, where a large Iranian consulate loomed across from the city administration building, the images that it posted of masses of Iranians chanting "*Allah-u Akbar*" was a matter of curiosity but not an attractive model. The secular life of Baku had been established for almost a century. Even communist restrictions sat lightly in the stagnation of the Brezhnev era. Although "respectable" behavior did require body coverage and personal space among Azerbaijanis of different sexes, society was a long way from segregation of sexes or veiling, the thought of which made style-conscious women (and not a few men) shudder. In multinational Baku, the Azerbaijanis felt cultural pressure from the Russians, who had outnumbered them since the early twentieth century and treated them as a lower order of cultural being.[16] The urban and the educated Azerbaijanis did not see Islam as an answer to that problem. On the contrary, many had adopted the Russian language and Russian habits rather than emphasize their native language and way of life. Others embraced the Azerbaijani language and traditions, including Islam in some form, as low-profile resistance. In 1980, young artists said, with a grin, that they would sometimes paint crescent moons into their paintings just because "it makes the Russians nervous." But there was one attractive feature in the Islamic Revolution for Baku's intellectuals. They drew a parallel between the corruption and despotism of the shah's regime and that of Soviet rule. The Iranians, despite the power of the shah and his secret service (SAVAK), had overthrown a powerful dictator who had the backing and the weapons of a superpower. If the Iranians could get rid of their foreign overlord, might not the Azerbaijanis someday be rid of theirs?

In the decade between the Islamic Revolution of 1979 and the Soviet collapse of 1991, two other components affected Islam in the Soviet Union, including Azerbaijan. One was the 1979 Soviet census, which reflected a population explosion among Muslim peoples. The other was the Soviet invasion of Afghanistan at the very end of the same year. Although the latter affected Central Asia more immediately and directly, the shock of Soviet (mostly Russian) troops fighting in a neighboring Muslim country seems to have struck a sensitive chord for other traditionally or culturally (though not necessarily observant) Muslim peoples in the Soviet Union. Soon, the repercussions of the arrivals of sealed coffins and traumatized veterans, some from Azerbaijan and neighboring Dagestan, took a psychological toll as well. Though less traumatic, the 1979 census had powerful implications.[17] In Azerbaijan, the census revealed substantial growth in the Azerbaijani population and a drop in both the Russian and Armenian populations from about 10 percent of the republic's population to just under 8 percent. No data on individual cities were published, which Azerbaijanis took to mean that they had regained their majority in Baku for the first time since the city census of 1903. Like other Muslim groups, their birth rates were far higher than those of the Russians. They sensed their growing demographic power.

It is not clear that Islam as a faith gained more adherents in Azerbaijan in the late Soviet period. After seven decades of Soviet rule, with pressure against Islam and the ban on teaching religion, the level of religious knowledge among most people was very low. Traditional practices and pre-Islamic holidays like Novruz (the vernal equinox or "new year") were confused with Muslim practices and holidays. Visits to shrines, seeking blessings from holy healers, and other practices reflecting bits of Sufism, Shamanism, and other unorthodox practices were common, especially in rural areas. If people learned to pray, they learned from a grandparent in secret.[18] By the late 1970s and certainly the 1980s, many such practices—even polygamy among rural communist party bosses—came out in the open, and were studied by sociologists and other researchers in the Soviet Union. The events of 1979 seem to have fostered conditions favorable to greater cultural and religious identity. Opinion polls showed that the majority of traditionally Muslims peoples believed in God (versus only 20 percent among Russians).[19] The designation of "Muslim" as a national or cultural marker became more common to distinguish Azerbaijanis or nominal/traditional Muslims from Russians or other Christians. The term was also used to indicate a person of good morals: "He is not a bad person; he is a Muslim." In the same vein, the line between Sunni and Shi'a was unclear to late Soviet-era youth. Young people might identify with the sect of their parents or grandparents, but not feel especially attached to that identity themselves—they lived in an almost "post-Islamic" consciousness.[20]

National minorities within Azerbaijan, the two largest being the Talysh in the south and the Lezghi in the north, seem to have been affected more by national than religious consciousness. The Lezghi and others in the north are mostly Sunni; the Talysh in the south are Shi'ite and have a language that is close to Persian. In the Soviet period, the Talysh talked privately of their separate identity and language, but officially they were nearly assimilated into the Azerbaijani majority. Resentment did linger below the surface—on the Talysh side for the assimilation, part of Soviet policy from the 1930s, and on the Azerbaijani side because the Talysh were perceived as having proliferated in the Baku police organs in the 1970s. Anyone from the south, the Lenkoran or Astara region, was presumed to be Talysh. Recent survey data suggest that both groups have sufficiently embraced "civic nationalism," as a result of mixed-nationality social networks and a supranational view of Islam, that their separate identities are not presently a threat to Azerbaijan's integrity as a state.[21] The large Armenian and Russian minorities, both Orthodox Christian, were mostly living in compact areas, mainly in Baku (and Armenians also in Mountainous Karabagh), but as peoples with majorities in neighboring republics and with considerable networks, economic opportunities, and representation in the communist party, their situation was not fragile like that of the Muslim minorities or the Jewish Tats in northern Azerbaijan.

Foreign Religious Influence after Independence

Post-Soviet opportunities for religious freedom were greeted by many, perhaps a majority of Azerbaijanis, as the chance to eat the long-forbidden fruit. Many Azerbaijanis sought knowledge of Islam out of curiosity as well as piety, a search for a spiritual component of identity, or a moral compass. Had it not been for the Iranian Revolution, perhaps few outsiders would have construed Azerbaijan's embracing of Islam as a political threat. From Baku's viewpoint, the rush of foreign Muslim clerics and activists—from neighboring Iran and Turkey or more distant Saudi Arabia—was both a religious and a political matter.[22]

Iran: Twelve years after its Islamic Revolution, Iran's mullahs and Qurans came over the long and porous border with newly independent Azerbaijan. Their main areas of activity were in places that were known to be more religious—near the Iranian border and villages on the Apsheron Peninsula near Baku—Mashtaga and Nardaran. Former first secretary–turned-president Ayaz Mutalibov drew much of his political support from these villages and from the Iranian-funded organizations that were born there, most significantly the Islamic Party of Azerbaijan in 1991. The chaos of the first year of independence made it impossible to control the border or the countryside, so the mullahs did not have to be "particularly covert."[23] Under Mutalibov, the Iranians were free to do their work among the population. But the Turcophile Elchibey government, in power from June 1992 to June 1993, was unreceptive to Shi'ite proselytizing and to Iran. Its officials turned back Iranians when they were able to do so.[24] Heydar Aliyev, president from 1993 to 2003, took a cautious approach at first and then blocked Iranian activities by the mid-1990s, the time when the government revoked the registration of the Islamic Party of Azerbaijan. Reportedly, Iranian Hezbollah affiliates were working in Azerbaijan in internally displaced persons camps and villages, and were believed to have been responsible for the murder of academician Ziya Buniatov in 1997. After that time, the Aliyev regime cracked down on religious groups that were linked to Iran.[25]

Simultaneously, Iran's approach became more subtle, training Azerbaijani religious students in Iranian madrassas. Iranians successfully maintained networks in rural areas, but educating the new leaders was more important.[26] By the mid-2000s, 200 to 250 Azerbaijanis were studying in Iran.[27] Judging from the position of Iran-trained Shi'ite leaders in Azerbaijan in the 2010s, this policy can be considered a success. One of their most prominent products of this Iranian training is Haji Ilgar Ibrahimoglu (Allahverdiyev), leader of Baku's Juma congregation at the historic Juma Mosque.

By the mid-2000s, analysts began to perceive Iranian Islamic influence as a potential threat:

In the so-called "Islamist belt" of the country's southern districts, Iranian preachers have been active. In villages near Baku one can see portraits of Khomeini and Islamic quotes in the windows of houses and on walls. The rallies staged by the Union of Azerbaijani Forces in 2002 became one of the biggest protest actions by the opposition, with many Islamists carrying green banners of Islam and shouting *"Allahu Akbar"* [while] participating. A couple of years ago, few could take the threat of fundamentalism in Azerbaijan seriously. However, the threat of Islamic fundamentalism now seems imminent.[28]

Iranian-Azerbaijan relations are complicated by Azerbaijan's good relationship with Israel, a major enemy of Iran.[29] Azerbaijan supplies Israel with as much as 40 percent of its oil and buys advanced weapons systems from it.[30] The foundation for these friendly ties is twofold: the long-standing acceptance of Jews in Baku, and the secularism of the Azerbaijani regime and Baku society. It is precisely these factors that irritate the ayatollahs. Iran has accused Baku of providing a listening post for the Israelis and a staging ground for Mossad, its intelligence agency. Azerbaijani authorities occasionally have arrested Iranian citizens, whom they charge with planning attacks on Israeli diplomats.[31] But as Muslim consciousness increases in Azerbaijan, so does the discomfort with Baku–Tel Aviv relations, a concern that Ibrahimoglu has voiced.[32] Azerbaijan has maintained its close ties to Israel despite the Turkish-Israeli animosity since 2010.[33]

Iranian influence in Azerbaijan has been seriously dampened among some Azerbaijanis by Tehran's poor treatment of its own Azerbaijani minority, which is perhaps double or more the size of the population in the Azerbaijan Republic to the north. The issue is complex, since many Turkic speakers from Azerbaijan, or their offspring, are assimilated into Iranian culture and identify as Iranians with no particular attachment to Turkic language or culture. Many Islamic Republic leaders, including Supreme Leader Ayatollah Ali Khamenei, fall into this category. Many living in Iranian Azerbaijan, however, have demonstrated a strong cultural identity and anger at the pressure to adopt Persian language and culture.

As a political issue, the millions of Turkic speakers in Iranian Azerbaijan present a multilayered challenge to the unity of the Iranian state. Tehran was sensitive to Abulfez Elchibey's talk of Azerbaijani reunification, and for good reason: the Azerbaijanis in Iran are a large minority occupying a strategic border and coastal region. Heydar Aliyev did not play that card in the interests of improved relations with Tehran, and Ilham has followed suit. But Azerbaijani public opinion appears far stronger regarding Iranian Azerbaijanis than regarding relations with Israel. Azerbaijanis in Iran feel the pressure of Iranian cultural policies as well as ethnic prejudice. In 2006, Iranian authorities opened fire on a large demonstration of Iranian Azerbaijanis, mostly students, in Tabriz, the capital of East Azerbaijan Province. Between ten and twenty people reportedly were killed. Other demonstrations followed in several cities. The demonstration had been sparked by an anti-Azerbaijani cartoon in an Iranian newspaper that depicted cockroaches as Azerbaijani-speakers.[34] Azerbaijanis in the north remain sensitive to this problem.

Turkey: Turkish policy toward Azerbaijan, and the other Turkic post-Soviet states, was shaped by Ankara's foreign policy interests. Azerbaijanis, including their post-Soviet rulers, have preferred Turkish to Iranian influence, since the former comes from a secular state and is compatible with secular rule. The similarity of the two languages gave Turks easy access to Azerbaijan. Both Abulfez Elchibey and Heydar Aliyev supported a Turkish presence on the basis of historical ties, as a tool in nation-building, and as a bulwark against Iranian Shi'ism. In terms of religion, the overarching factor in the early post-Soviet period was Turkey's own secular history of Atatürkism. Turkish leader Turgut Özal saw an opportunity to implant moderate Islam, honed by diplomats and the Board of Spiritual Affairs (Diyanet İşleri Başkanlığı), in Azerbaijan as a bulwark against fundamentalist Islamism from Iran or Saudi Arabia. The board cooperated with Azerbaijan's State Committee on Work with Religious Organizations (SCWRO) in matters of school curriculum and mosque construction and governance.[35] Among several Turkish mosques in Azerbaijan, the most prominent is the one by Shahidler Khiyabani (Martyrs' Lane), the burial place of Karabagh war victims, in Baku.

A major vehicle for carrying out Turkey's policies was a nonstate religious movement under the inspiration and leadership of Fethullah Gulen (or Gülen). Gulen's followers, who are known as Gulenists or Fehtullaji, based their efforts on a tripod of education, media use, and trade.[36] The movement stresses "service" (*hizmet*), so that each individual not only practices but embodies his or her faith.[37] In Azerbaijan, Gulenist groups founded schools, a newspaper (*Zaman*; or *Time*), a magazine, and a television channel. The nationwide school network offered a secular Turkish-style curriculum. The Gulenist Qafqaz University was the best in Azerbaijan, with a curriculum of science, technology, and humanities. The clothing of the university's students and faculty suggested a wide range of religious observance and nonobservance, though a report on dormitories suggested that there was pressure on students to conform to Islamist norms of dress and behavior.[38] Striving to establish itself as friendly to both religious and state power, the university displayed portraits of Atatürk and Heydar Aliyev (proclaimed National Leader after his death in 2003) in the hallways, a practice that opened was it to criticism as being too accommodating to the Aliyev regime. The university was known for its high academic standards, research programs, and integrity. Even the Baku elite, discussing Qafqaz University, regularly remark, "Oh, they don't take bribes there."[39] The faculty members were usually members of the movement and they, like Gulenist journalists and businessmen, embody the Gulenist strategy for post-Soviet states: "to act on its religious discourse without mentioning explicitly," or "preaching by example."[40]

The 2013 split between Gulen (who lives in exile in the United States) and Turkish president Recep Tayyip Erdoğan led the latter to denounce Gulen and his network as subversives trying to unseat Erdoğan and his party, the AKP. Erdoğan purged suspected Gulenists from security forces and elsewhere in the state bureaucracy. The feud had seismic repercussions across the Turkic-speaking world.[41] In Azerbaijan, which was laced with Gulenist schools, the accusation of a secret Gulenist network in Turkey's state bureaucracy led to a parallel witch hunt in Azerbaijan, resulting in the removal of several officials and the head of the SCWRO.[42] Gulenist schools throughout Azerbaijan were threatened with closure, then placed under the unlikely umbrella of SOCAR, the state oil company. They were closed in July 2014, though Qafqaz University survived[43] until the coup attempt in Turkey in July 2016 unleashed an anti-Gulenist reaction in Azerbaijan as well as in Turkey.[44] Azerbaijani relations with Gulenists in the United States, especially lobbying and advocacy groups like the Turquoise Council of Americans and Eurasians in Houston, appear unchanged. (For more details on lobbying groups, see chapter 4.)

Saudi Arabia and the other Gulf states: Unlike Turkey and Iran, Saudi Arabia is not an immediate neighbor of Azerbaijan and has a more distant relationship with it. Saudi missionaries of Sunni Islam initially found little traction in Azerbaijan and invested more resources in the Caucasus Mountain peoples to the north. Yet the Saudis reacted against Iranian Shi'ism more strongly since 1979 and strove to take advantage of the independence of all post-Soviet states with Muslim populations.[45] Saudi and Kuwaiti charitable organizations provided funds for mosque construction in Azerbaijan, as they did among other Muslim populations. Most spectacularly, this funding helped construct the large Abu Bakr Mosque in Baku, which reportedly drew thousands of worshippers to Friday prayer. As Shi'ite Azerbaijanis studied in Iran, Sunnis studied in Sudan and Saudi Arabia.

Saudi- and Kuwaiti-funded Salafi fighters reportedly moved into northern Azerbaijan from Dagestan and Chechnya under Russian military pressure in the mid-1990s. "After the outbreak of the second Russo-Chechen war in August 1999, Chechen refugees who practiced Salafi Islam found refuge in Azerbaijan." Since the early 2000s, analyst Emmanuel Karagiannis has written, "most followers" are now from Azerbaijan, though Avars, Lezghins, and Russians have "a strong presence within the Salafi community." Estimates of the number of Salafis range from a few thousand to 30,000, but "more credible analysts" extrapolated from mosque attendance to suggest 8,000 Salafis countrywide in the mid-2000s.[46]

The numbers are uncertain, but the appeal is not. Local analysts said the draw of that mosque was the message of simplicity and piety, especially appealing because of the blatant corruption throughout Azerbaijani society. One self-identified Salafi described his own spiritual journey sparked by Muslim missionaries from Turkey, Iran, and the Gulf states. He described Salafism as a "purist," nonpolitical strain, and resisted conflating it with Wahhabism, as official Azerbaijani (and Russian) government rhetoric does. Scholars describe the Salafi "call" (*da'wa*) as nonpolitical. Salafis insist on following the Quran, the *hadith*, and the example of the first three generations of Muslims. They reject not only Shi'ism for its sole focus on the descendants of Muhammad's cousin and son-in-law Ali but they also reject the Sunni legal schools (*madhahib*) as authoritative sources of interpretation. Mainstream Salafis prefer to withdraw from sinful society into a pure Salafi community. However, as scholar Ahmad Moussalli has noted, a number of components within Salafism have drawn Salafis into political activism.[47] The activism of so-called neo-Salafis has been increasingly political and radical, and Salafis have been known to fight in the Syrian civil war.[48]

Institutional Islam within Azerbaijan

Post-Soviet Azerbaijani presidents take their oath of office on the Quran. The Azerbaijani state under both Aliyev presidents has continued the Spiritual Board of the Soviet era, although it exists under a new name, the Caucasus Muslim Board (CMB). The CMB asserts authority over both Shi'a and Sunni populations, and its chairman bears the Shi'ite title Sheikh-ul-Islam and the Sunni title of Grand Mufti. By an amendment of June 7, 1996, to the Freedom of Religion Act of 1992, all Muslim religious organizations were subordinated to the CMB.[49] As part of its duties, the CMB organizes hajj pilgrimage activities, appoints imams to new mosques, and occasionally monitors sermons. [It] also approves all Muslim organizations before they can register for official state recognition. Despite connections with the Azerbaijani government, CMB protests in 2010 were ineffective in preventing the closure and demolition of several mosques throughout Azerbaijan.[50]

The head of the board, Haji Allahsukur Pashazade, is the same man who had headed the Soviet-era Spiritual Board since 1980. The CMB's goal also appears to be the same as it was in Soviet days—to control Islam as a competing pole of attraction with an alternative narrative to that propounded by the state. At the same time, the decision to revamp the CMB reflected the government's understanding that the populace, whose reported level of faith and practice had been growing, was looking for religious leadership. The revival of Muslim identity and education by foreign missionaries apparently sharpened sectarian identity and thus increased the potential for clashes between Shi'ite and Sunni communities, especially the Salafis. But Pashazade is not respected as either a religious authority or an independent figure. As the old Soviet-era Sheikh-ul-Islam, he had been required to collaborate with the Soviet regime, a fact of Soviet life that the younger generation is less likely to understand or tolerate. Moreover, his training was entirely Soviet, and he is not regarded as a genuine Shi'ite *'alim* (scholar; the plural is *ulema*) with no chance to claim higher status in Shi'ism.[51] Despite his short-lived support for the Popular Front, he welcomed the return to power of Heydar Aliyev in 1993 and has been a staunch supporter of the regime and its decisions. His official pronouncements echo regime statements.

The other official organization for religious affairs is the State Committee on Work with Religious Organizations. It was established in June 2001 as a government agency with the dual purpose of regulating the activities of all religious organizations, not just the Muslim ones, and ensuring the constitutionally guaranteed (Article 48) freedom of religion. The committee's legal right to control religious activity stems from the requirement that religious organizations be registered before they can begin activity. In 2002, the SCWRO announced that all religious organizations would have to register, or re-register, though being granted a new registration was by no means assured. Another re-registration requirement was announced in 2010.[52] Moreover, SCWRO is charged with overseeing instructional curriculum and determining whether a group's activities conform to its charter. Its own statement of purpose is instructive and worth quoting at length:

Serious positive changes are observed in the religious life of the society in the years since freedom was attained . . . practical opportunities have been created to realize freedom of faith. . . . The state advocates for the freedom of conscience. . . . *Religion increases the human responsibilities for society and strengthens the feeling of patriotism. The state needs faithful, convinced citizens,* for morality is appreciated as national wealth by the state . . . .

On the other hand, the society of Azerbaijan is open to the world. The embassies of foreign states, the representatives of international organizations, different centers of culture, the organizations of humanitarian help and charity, as well as the businessmen of different faiths all conduct their activity in liberal Azerbaijan. Different religious convictions . . . [and] sects derived from non-traditional religious tendencies influence society, . . . consciousness, and the hearts of the people. The regulation of this contradicting process . . . made it urgent to establish the State Committee on Work with Religious Organizations.

The major responsibilities of the Committee are: to create conditions to implement the freedom of faith, the state registration of the religious organizations in accordance with the legislation of the Republic of Azerbaijan, to provide corresponding amendments and supplements to regulations (statutes) of these organizations . . . to help strengthen mutual understanding, tolerance and respect between the religious organizations of different religious convictions, to prevent confrontation and discrimination . . . on religious grounds.[53]

Although the SCWRO may seem to complement the CMB as a regulatory body, the SCWRO has a broader charge affecting all religious communities as a part of the state's security against radicalism. Thus, it and the CMB are to some extent in competition, as their leaders have been. The first head of the SCWRO, Rafik Aliyev, even insisted that the CMB register with it as a religious organization.[54]

Rafik Aliyev headed the SCWRO from its founding in 2001 until the summer of 2006. His successor was old communist leader Hidayat Orujov, who served until May 2012, when he was succeeded by the forty-year-old Elshad Iskenderov. Iskenderov, who had a US postgraduate education, served for two years and was removed from his post allegedly on suspicion of having ties to the Gulen movement, but possibly for displaying too much independence.[55] Mubariz Qurbanly, a longtime YAP member whose religious credentials are considered thin, was appointed on July 21, 2014.[56] His criticism of lavish funerals led to a clash with CMB Sheikh Pashazade, whose brother owns several funeral establishments.[57] Apart from the SCWRO, local officials appear to have considerable power over religious organizations, and this has been the source of numerous complaints.[58]

The mandates of state institutions tell only part of the story. First, the official purposes of the CMB and the SCWRO include both facilitating and controlling religious practices, but laws and individual cases suggest that control trumps facilitation. The SCWRO was founded in 2001, the same year that the radical (Sunni) Hizb ut-Tahrir founded a branch in northern Azerbaijan. In 2002, the SCWRO closed twenty-two Iranian madrassas and the (Sunni) Kuwaiti society that built the Abu Bakr mosque. Though the state might argue that those institutions constituted a threat, in other instances, the threat level was not so clear. The International Crisis Group's 2008 report described the arrests and closed trials of alleged radical Islamists. In one case, the accused members of a radical "cell" reportedly did not even know each other. The 2008 report noted that official secrecy prevented a clear assessment of the danger, but it suggested that the Azerbaijani government had exaggerated the threat to get "Western sympathy."[59] Some mosque leaders were almost surely arrested for criticism of the government and the president. (Their cases are described in greater detail later in this chapter.) The US Commission on International Religious Freedom monitors Azerbaijan's laws and individual prosecutions and protests. Its 2013 annual report noted that between 2009 and 2010, fines for violating religious laws in Azerbaijan were increased sixteen-fold.[60]

The 2011 amendment to the Law on Religion, adopted by the Milli Majlis on July 10, 2011 required that all Islamic organizations provide written reports on their activities to the CMB. The following December, President Aliyev signed into law amendments to both the criminal and administrative codes providing stricter punishments for the illegal production, distribution, and importation of religious literature, meaning literature that was not approved by the SCWRO. The new laws substantially raised the fines (from $6,000 to $8,000) and prison sentences (two years or more) for noncompliance. Moreover, the legal amendments declared that Islamic rituals and ceremonies "shall only be conducted by citizens who received their education in the country," or whose religious education abroad was approved by the government. If enforced, this provision would allow the state to ban religious leadership, Shi'ite and Sunni, by Azerbaijan's most prominent clerics. The chair of the Milli Majlis's Human Rights Committee,

Rabiyat Aslanova, insisted in a 2010 interview that the amendment did not come from the presidential administration, but another deputy said categorically that it had.[61] The Venice Commission issued a Joint Opinion in October 2012 that the 2011 amendments did not conform to European standards, and that they included vague wording that "may lead to arbitrary interpretation and implementation."[62] Ali Hasanov, speaking for the Aliyev government, claimed that the judgment was based on translation errors and that a new official translation had been sent. A Venice Commission spokesperson said that the commission had not received a new translation.[63]

A second obstacle to getting a clear picture of Islam in Azerbaijan is that reliable statistics are not always available. In the early post-Soviet era, scholars thought Azerbaijanis were 80 percent Shi'ite. Newer estimates place the number from 80 percent to as low as 65 percent with 35 percent Sunni, the figures given by the SCWRO.[64] But self-definition, sectarian awareness, and degree of religious practice have varied over time. "According to a survey conducted by the Baku-based Institute of Peace and Democracy in 2003, approximately 58 percent of respondents considered themselves simply 'Muslims,' as opposed to 30 percent who answered 'Shia Muslim' and 9 percent who identified as 'Sunni Muslim.'" However, notes one source, it seems that "65–75 percent of the population are Shia Muslims and 30–20 percent are Sunni."[65] Table 6.1 shows that more people identify as Muslim than as a person who believes in God until 2012, and regular practice remains low. How these figures might be extrapolated to political acts in the name of Islam remains to be investigated.

Table 6.1. The Increase in Believers in Post-Soviet Azerbaijan (percent)

	1998	2000	2004	2012
Identify as Muslim	89.5	94.0	96.8	97.0
Confirm (strong) belief in God	71.0	70.1	87.1	96.7
Confirm regular religious practice	11.5	19.1	19.9	20.1
Say religion very important daily	N/A	11.0	28.7*	36.0

*2007 figure.

Source: Bruno De Cordier, "Islamic Social Activism, Globalization and Social Change: A Case Study of Hajji İlgar İbragimoğlu and the Cüma Ehli in Baku, Azerbaijan," *Journal of Muslim Minority Affairs* 34, no. 2 (2014): 136. The table is compiled from eight sources listed by De Cordier.

Third, the Azerbaijani government conflates real threats to secular statehood with the lesser challenges of regime critics who use Islamic rhetoric, display posters of Khomeini, and/or have beards. Both faith and practice of Islam have grown. Though belief was nearly universal according to the 2012 figures, only about 20 percent of respondents said that they practice regularly. Yet the state's actions suggest that the only "nonthreatening" displays of piety or observance are those controlled by state institutions, an attitude that may reflect lingering Soviet-era intolerance of civil society and individual initiative. Prayer outside a mosque or wearing a hijab is considered, at a minimum, a threat to the secular way of life that dominates in most cities and defines the state itself. At worst, the hijab, the beard, and unregistered worship groups are regarded as signs of potential, if not actual, radicalism and subversion. Human rights groups in and outside Azerbaijan discuss actual threats versus protected behavior or speech. A ban on both the hijab and full-face veil have been argued in France and decided on the basis of principles such as the need to protect the secular republic and "reciprocity" of social interaction that is deemed necessary to democracy.[66] None of these arguments has been brought forth as a basis for the Azerbaijani regime's position, though its Constitution does proclaim protection of "secular life" (*hamının layiqli həyat səviyyəsini təmin etmək*).[67] Since about 2012, more and better research has been produced by Azerbaijanis and scholars with necessary language abilities and other training to delve deeper into the phenomena of Islamic communities, their goals, their methods, and their ideas.

Major Islamic Communities

Religious organizations need not be registered to be influential and to have institutional presence with offices (even without a mosque), bylaws, organized activities like classes, and publications. Many have a substantial Internet presence, as do smaller groups without developed organizations.

The best known Shi'ite leader in Azerbaijan is Haji Ilgar Ibrahimoglu, imam (leader) of the Juma (Friday) Mosque Congregation (Juma Ehli). The congregation took its name from the mosque in Baku's oldest section, the walled Icheri Sheher or Inner City. Under Bolshevik rule, the mosque's exterior inscriptions were partly obliterated (especially the name of God) and the building was used for various profane purposes, most recently since about 1968 as a carpet museum. In 1992, it was returned to its original purpose, and its congregation was revived by Azer Ramizoglu, whose goal was to show Islam as a vibrant faith that was more than merely a guide for funerals. In its early days, the mosque reportedly drew 3,000 people for Friday prayer.[68] The community's affiliated group, Islam-Ittihad (Islamic Union), was allowed to register as a religious community. Around 1998, it began to expand its activities to social concerns such as encouraging blood donation to replace the Shi'ite self-flagellation ritual of Ashura, and campaigning against drug and alcohol abuse. In 1999, Haji Ilgar Ibrahimoglu was elected the community's imam and these social outreach activities expanded, which some worshippers felt drew negative attention from authorities. Ibrahimoglu was one of several Azerbaijani Shi'ite students who studied in Iran at the University of Qazvin from 1992 to 1996.[69] He later spent several years in Poland, working on human rights issues with Solidarity, allowing him to present himself as a human rights activist who views religious freedom as the most important right.

Ibrahimoglu ran into legal trouble in the aftermath of the 2003 presidential election in which Ilham Aliyev became president. He was one of many protesters against the tainted elections which opposition supporters claimed had stolen the victory from Isa Gambar, head of the opposition Yeni Müsavat party. Ibrahimoglu and about a hundred others were arrested in the post-election demonstrations, some of which turned to violence (see chapter 3). Apparently, Ibrahimoglu's participation in the protests and criticism of the elections prompted the authorities to arrest him in December 2003. In April 2004, he was tried and convicted of arranging mass disorder, but was given a five-year suspended sentence. In January 2004, after the SCWRO denied the re-registration for the Juma congregation for a second time, the mosque building itself was declared a historic site that was being "illegally occupied" by the congregation. It was seized by police in June and its members were expelled. Appeals to Azerbaijani courts were decided in favor of the government. A later appeal to the European Court of Human Rights also found in favor of the state, mainly on technical grounds.[70]

Ibrahimoglu has continued to work through other organizations that are linked to the Juma congregation, the most prominent of which are DEVAMM (Dini Etiqad ve Vicdan Azadlıqlarının Müdafiye Merkezi; Center for the Defense of Freedom of Religious Faith and Conscience, founded in 2000) and the magazine *Deyerler* (*Values*), founded in 2005. These organizations have a substantial Web presence.[71] Haji Ilgar has been an active figure, working for openness in civil society and in support of the political opposition. He has spoken out against several cases of religiously motivated violence, such as the forced shaving of a bearded Sunni man in Sabirabad in July 2014. Two other Shi'ite leaders, Elshan Mustafaoglu and Shahin Hasanli, also spoke out against the attack.[72]

Since the closing of the Juma Mosque in Baku's Inner City in June 2004, the largest Shi'ite community appears to be Mashadi Dadash Mosque, led by Shahin Hasanli. Though this community was founded in the 1990s, it acquired a building in central Baku only in 2002 and was allowed to register in 2007. Hasanli identifies himself as "self-educated," though some reports suggest that he studied for a time in Qazvin, Iran. News reports often refer to him as a "theologian," and he is described as "charismatic." In 2008, the mosque was said to have attracted 800 people, often young professionals. The mosque's affiliated organization, the Association for Moral Purity, is identified as an NGO and has its own publication, *Salam*.[73] Hasanli has urged Shi'ites to give blood rather than practice self-flagellation at Ashura and has posted a video on his Facebook page showing himself giving blood.[74] Like most Muslim leaders, he opposes Azerbaijanis' going to fight in Syria. In March 2013, two men were arrested and charged with planning to set off a bomb in the Mashadi Dadash Mosque to "kill Shi'ites and sow panic."[75] In December 2014, Hasanli was appointed, surprisingly, to a post in the CMB as its representative to Baku's Nasimi district.[76]

Elshan Mustafaoglu is founder and head of an independent organization aimed at fostering Islamic morals. Until his arrest on reported charges of treason in December 2014, he was a spokesperson for the official CMB.[77] His arrest took place at the same time that Shahin Hasanli was appointed to the CMB post. The two cases seem related, but commentary on the two Shi'ite mullahs and CMB has been absent. Mustafaoglu's organization, the Menevi Safliqa Devet İctimai Birliyi ("The 'Call to Moral Purity' Social Union") was founded in 2001 in Baku.[78] It is nominally open to both Sunni and Shi'a Muslims, but Mustafaoglu himself, frequent speakers like Shahin Hasanli, and the organization's framework are clearly Shi'ite. Mustafaoglu is a hajji who first received an advanced education in Baku and then went to study theology and Islamic pedagogy at the University of Qazvin in Iran from 1993 to 1998, thus overlapping with the time that Haji Ilgar Ibrahimoglu studied there. Like DEVAMM, Menevi Safliqa has a substantial Web presence, showing the dangers of social immorality like drug addiction and alcoholism and decrying the corruption of officials.[79] The organization's education classes and discussion groups are aimed at creating a modest and moral lifestyle; the website and their magazine instruct readers on cleanliness in food preparation, attentive care for children, and religious topics including the basics of prayer, regulations for the hajj, and fasting at Ramadan. The fundamental values are applied to specific topics in the commentaries, such as guiding children in the use of the Internet. It has regular contributors and contributions by young writers.

The Rehime Khanim Mosque in Nardaran, a poor, heavily religious village northeast of Baku, is a huge Shi'ite mosque built in 1997 with Iranian money. It was led by Iran-trained "sheikh" Taleh Bagirzade (or Bagirov) until his arrest on March 31, 2013. (Bagirzade was released on July 31, 2015, after serving his two-year sentence, but was arrested again in the fall.) The mosque is built on the reputed burial place of Rehime Khanim, sister of Imam Reza. Imam Reza is recognized as the eighth imam in the Twelver Shi'ite tradition that is Iran's state religion and is followed by most Azerbaijanis. Reza was also the grandson of Jafar al-Sadiq, the sixth imam of Shi'ite tradition, and he is accepted as a legitimate leader by both Shi'a and Sunni Muslims. (The case of Nardaran will receive extended consideration later in the chapter.)

The main Sunni mosque in Baku is the Abu Bakr Mosque, led by Emir Qamet Suleymanov. The mosque itself was built in 1997 by a Kuwaiti religious group, the Revival of Islamic Heritage Society. It was the target of a bombing in 2008 by a radical Salafi group called the Forest Brothers that split from the congregation, allegedly because of Suleymanov's accommodating posture toward the authorities. The mosque was closed for a "full investigation," which has allowed the government, represented by the SCWRO, to keep it closed.[80] Suleymanov was born in Baku in the 1970s and, after serving in the Soviet army, went to Sudan in 1991 just as the Soviet Union was crumbling. He studied at the University of Khartoum for two years. From 1993 to 1998, he attended the Islamic University in Medina, considered "a leading center for the study and export of Salafism."[81] He was elected imam of the Abu Bakr Mosque in 1998; the mosque, though identified as Salafi, was successfully registered in 2002 but was not accepted by the CMB. Suleymanov articulates a nonpolitical posture, and various sources report his moderation and encouragement that believers support the state so long as the state respects believers. The mosque's congregation included educated Azerbaijanis and worshippers of other nationalities. As a result of his nonpolitical stance and avoidance of criticism against the Azerbaijani government, some members of his group split off and joined the more radical, anti-state, and violent Kharijite group. Members of this group reject paying taxes to the government because of its corruption and denounce the West for supporting such corruption. They regard Suleymanov as a traitor. Their numbers in 2008 were small, estimated to be about 100.[82]

In a Radio Liberty interview in April 2015, Suleymanov started by saying that the community did not advocate for young men going to fight with the Islamic State because they do not support extremism. He added that unemployment is not an adequate justification for joining the IS. When asked about applying shari'a (Islamic law) in Azerbaijan, he voiced his agreement. This view is commonly expressed in opinion polls in Muslim countries, but is often presented with the reasonable caveat that the meaning of "shari'a law" may not be clear to the respondents, given the decades without religious education and isolation from the rest of the Muslim world. In this case, the interviewer asked about specific applications of shari'a:

RL: What do you think about cutting off a hand or tongue as a punishment?

Suleymanov: It's a normal method. First, God said this; there is nothing unusual. Simply, we have grown distant from Islamic customs and now it seems strange to us. . . .

RL: Are you a proponent of radical measures?

Suleymanov: For the health and purity of society, sometimes radical measures must be taken.[83]

Suleymanov said that although he supports the application of shari'a in Azerbaijan, it is not possible in the foreseeable future.[84]

The themes and forms employed by Haji Ilgar Ibrahimoglu and Elshan Mustafaoglu highlight human rights and appeal to greater morality. Both men studied in Iran, in the same university at the same time, so it is unlikely that they did not know each other. They were there during the middle years of Azerbaijan's first decade of Soviet independence—1992–96 and 1993–98, respectively. They were not participants in the early Popular Front rise to power, the overthrow of Abulfez Elchibey and the return to power of Heydar Aliyev. By the time Ibrahimoglu returned to Baku, the Iranian-funded Islamic Party of Azerbaijan (IPA), based in Nardaran, had lost its registration (1995) and Iran clearly was pursuing other methods of influence. Ibrahimoglu and Mustafaoglu, like the less-trained Shahin Hasanli, cast religious practice in terms of human rights and healthy social practice, unlike the harsh official statements from Iran's religious leaders.

By comparison, the Salafi network presents itself as nonviolent, sometimes as nonpolitical. It is connected through, if not actually centered in, the Abu Bakr Mosque. Its emir, Suleymanov, has issued appeals for moderation and quietude, but in instances such as the RL interview he sounded frighteningly radical, ready to lop off hands and tongues as a "normal" punishment on the path of purifying society. From this perspective, the Iranian-trained Shi'ite leaders (and Shahin Hasanli might be included here if he did indeed spend time in Qazvin) look moderate and tolerant, and hence may be more appealing to society as a whole and certainly more tolerable to the regime. This more moderate approach is likely to be a tactic promoted by the Iranians who educated the religious leadership now in Azerbaijan. Consider the influence of German professors in the first Russian universities in the nineteenth century—they shaped the language, the curriculum, the academic methods, and the intellectual values of those institutions for generations. The same is happening in Azerbaijan. Studies have shown that Azerbaijanis who join religious groups may do so for emotional or social satisfaction, but values are inculcated with socialization in the groups.[85] How much are the Iran-trained Azerbaijanis conveying Islam as a faith and basis for moral life, and how much are they imparting an Iranian message? Certainly, these men sound different from Tehran's ayatollahs, who have denounced secular immorality, including the 2012 Eurovision song contest. And yet, since 2012, the meetings between Iranians and CMB head Haji Allahsukur Pashazade have increased and relations appear friendly. Questions remain: Is Iranian influence, possibly mitigated through the Azerbaijani *ulema*, a threat to Azerbaijan's statehood or to the long-established secularism in society? Or is the regime's intolerance of moderate democratic opposition groups creating a space for Islamist groups to gain followers?

The role and forms of Islam in Azerbaijan, as in most Muslim-majority societies, may be meaningfully conceived as a continuum rather than a dichotomy. At the religious endpoint is the town of Nardaran.

Nardaran

One of the most religious and restive villages in Azerbaijan, Nardaran is located about 15 kilometers northeast of Baku on the Apsheron Peninsula. It was an area of settlement in the nineteenth century for migrant labor from Iranian Azerbaijan coming to work in Baku oil fields. Nardaran has a population of about 8,000 and is one of the poorest and most overtly religious villages in this generally secular society.[86] As mentioned above, it is the home of the Iranian-funded Rehime Khanim Mosque, and the IPA was founded there in 1991. The main IPA office opened that year in Baku, but had virtually no impact on events there. The party was the staunch supporter of communist leader–turned–president Ayaz Mutalibov. The IPA was banned in 1995 when faith-based political parties were prohibited.[87] Its head, Alikram Aliyev, was arrested around the same time. The IPA currently functions as an unregistered, and therefore illegal, entity, and it is known for its anti-Western and anti-Semitic rhetoric. President Heydar Aliyev saw its existence, as he saw other foreign-supported efforts, as a direct threat to his own rule as well as to Azerbaijan's independence.[88] Referring to the party's website, Islamin Sesi (Voice of Islam), analyst Idrak Abbasov claimed in 2011 that it "still" has more members than any other party.[89]

The people of Nardaran have a reputation for public protest. Street protests occurred in late 2001 over chronic shortages of gas and electricity. In April and May 2002, villagers protested a ban on the hijab, first enforced in a local school (the ban was withdrawn) and then at higher educational institutions (officials said that the ban was merely a "recommendation"). In May 2002, about a thousand residents protested the appointment of Fezilet Mirzayev as head of the local executive committee at least partly because he was known to drink alcohol. In June 2002, however, riots in Nardaran brought the village to international attention. On June 3 and 4, riots led to at least one fatality and sixteen injuries. The actual number of injured villagers may have been as much as fifty, but the number is uncertain because many of those involved avoided hospitals. The government of Heydar Aliyev sent police to establish roadblocks and quell the rioting, and publicly stated that the unrest was fomented by "foreign agents"—implying Iranians—but sources outside government suggested that the cause was long-unresolved problems with public services:

An expert poll published June 9 [2002] by the Turan news agency revealed sentiment running strongly against President Heydar Aliyev's government. Almost 90 percent of those polled said "unresolved social problems" helped spark the clash, while 63 percent believed popular "dissatisfaction with official policy" was a major factor in the riot. Over 50 percent believed that the Nardaran incident would prompt a prolonged period of confrontation, with 30 percent saying that further bloodshed was probable.[90]

202

The dire prognosis was wrong. Rather, President Aliyev, though intolerant of protests, was responsive to the underlying complaints. On June 12, he sent an official delegation to meet in a closed-door session with Nardaran village representatives. A presidential aide said that the village elders had demanded the "release of those arrested following the riot, the lifting of a police cordon around the village and the dismissal of local officials." Aliyev himself reportedly agreed to "take steps to address villagers' economic and social complaints." Nonetheless, the roadblock continued for many months and Nardaran protesters remained in custody.[91]

A new phase of restiveness began a few years later. Movsum Samadov, head of the (still illegal) IPA since 2007, was arrested on January 7, 2011, allegedly for planning terrorist attacks and having weapons. His cousins and brother-in-law were arrested on January 11 for storing arms. Six months later, the same charges were brought against their associates, including journalist Ramin Bayramov, an editor of the Islamazeri.az website.[92] The real cause of Samadov's arrest was widely believed to have been his criticism of official corruption and the ban on wearing the hijab, and also his preaching of a sermon that insulted Ilham Aliyev by comparing him to the tyrannical early Muslim caliph Yazid ibn Muawiya, whose forces killed the grandsons of the prophet Muhammad. Even then, analysts were quoted as saying that Islamic groups were likely to grow with the crushing of moderate, mainstream democratic forces, especially after moderate opposition parties were excluded from the 2010 Milli Majlis elections—just before these arrests. Baku intellectual Zardusht Alizade, a journalist and a longtime supporter of the IPA, has called Samadov and his fellow detainees political prisoners, and said that the public does not believe they are radicals. Analyst Elkhan Shahinoglu, however, has argued that the IPA shares Iran's agenda and hopes to spread an Iranian type of religious system in Azerbaijan. He warned that "a strong Islamic opposition has formed in Azerbaijan, in opposition not just to the Aliyevs' rule, but to all Western values."[93]

Protests also erupted over the arrest of Taleh Bagirzade,[94] leader of the Rehime Khanim Mosque, on March 31, 2013. He was charged with alleged drug possession, but the real reason clearly was his radical sermons. Bagirzade's lawyer said that he was tortured and that the courts had delayed his hearings to allow him to heal.[95] Protests drawing 500 to 600 people began in Baku, and were echoed in Nardaran. Reports noted that protests were louder and longer in Nardaran, and that demonstrators conflated Bagirzade's arrest with poor local services, including irregular gas supply. Yevda Abramov, a YAP member of the Milli Majlis' Human Rights Commission, said that the protests were the result of Iranian influence, creating the "artificial impression" that some things are wrong.

Indeed, "some things" continued to be "wrong" in Nardaran. On November 26, 2015, government forces entered the village and opened fire on a home where people were gathered for prayer. Police detained fourteen members of the Muslim Unity Movement—including Taleh Bagirzade, who had served a two-year sentence after his previous arrest and had been released in July 2015. He had been detained for questioning in early November and beaten. He had returned to Nardaran and was staying in the home of the Bunyadov family, members of Muslim Unity, when police raided the house. A General Prosecutor's Office statement of November 26 charged that Muslim Unity was planning "a violent change to the constitutional system of government" to establish "a religious state governed by Sharia law." It asserted that the movement was an "armed criminal group" that had stockpiled ammunition and explosives. Five villagers and two police were reported killed. Authorities delayed returning the bodies for burial, in violation of Islamic custom.[96]

Police virtually blockaded Nardaran. Telephone communications were cut. Gas and electricity were cut off under the pretext that the entire village was delinquent in paying its bills. Police prevented most outsiders from entering Nardaran and villagers from leaving. Journalists could not learn about events; food deliveries were impeded. Residents could not always get to their jobs in Baku or elsewhere. Villagers said that they were religious, but not radical. Hundreds protested police violence, the deprivation of services, and their isolation from the outside. Protests and arrests continued into the middle of December. Reports from December 2015 and January 2016 detailed the escalation of events, and *Caucasian Knot* stated that seventy-one people were arrested during December, mostly for disobedience to the police. By the second half of December, according to village elder Natik Kerimov, gas had been restored and there were no more arrests. Kerimov himself was later arrested, charged with treason, then released.[97] Conditions were returning to the status quo ante just as the currency devaluation was announced, setting off country-wide protests. Perhaps the government actions in Nardaran had been timed to show how authorities would respond to public protests.

Islam's Growing Influence?

In the 2000s, analysts began to discuss Islam's growing influence in Azerbaijan as a whole and whether it took a political, even radical form. The increasing numbers of women wearing the hijab, and the growth in the numbers of religious shops, mosque attendance, and fasting during Ramadan, including among the younger generation, was noted by local and foreign observers. Most agreed that interest in Islam were, at least initially, a result of the lifting of Soviet atheism, the search for historical identity, and the impact of foreign proselytizing. More recently, Western diplomats and some domestic critics have suggested that it was also reinforced by the regime's own denigration of the prodemocracy secular opposition and the closing-off of avenues for political discourse. As fines and force increased against public demonstrations, attending a mosque became less risky than going to an opposition rally.[98] Once oil revenues began to surge in 2006 after completion of the BTC pipeline in 2005, corruption became more obvious and the appeal of religion as a basis for morality or distributive justice grew.[99] The difficulty of identifying political Islamism versus economic or political grievances that employed Islamic rhetoric remained. Meanwhile, the Aliyev regime played on Western fears of radical Islamism to disguise societal grievances against the regime. The disorders in Bananyar in the winter of 2009–10 illustrate the problem.

On December 28, 2009, people were arrested during the Shi'ite Ashura commemorations in the village of Bananyar in Nakhjivan, reportedly for ritual self-flagellation, a practice that had been criminalized. On the night of January 5, about a hundred people were "violently arrested" and questioned at the local office of the Ministry of Internal Affairs. Most were released within a week, but five remained in jail two weeks later, and two others were placed in a psychiatric hospital. US and Norwegian diplomats who headed to the village were "harassed" and turned back.[100] A Foreign Ministry spokesman publicly rebuked the diplomats for traveling to the area: "Activities of the Norwegian and US diplomats during this visit . . . ran counter to the ethics of diplomats in accrediting countries and the 1961 Vienna Convention on Diplomatic Relations. . . . The attempts of some countries to describe events in Azerbaijan as a violation of human rights and to politicize such cases are unacceptable."[101]

Although Azerbaijani officials said that the Bananyar events were instigated by Iran, local observers not only denied this alleged Iranian connection, but insisted that the issues were not even religious. Local NGOs and journalists specified that the incident was a result of petty commercial conflict and possibly involved targeting opposition party members. A few weeks later, Nakhjivan Supreme Assembly chairman Vasif Talibov denied accusations of police brutality at Bananyar, claimed that no charges had been filed and no one had been detained overnight, and stated that the investigation was now closed. On the issue of the US and Norwegian diplomats that were harassed in Bananyar village on January 13, he said that he regretted the incident.[102]

Individual incidents like those in Bananyar or Nardaran are difficult to place in the context of the entire country: are they representative of general sentiments, or are they outliers? The changing opinion polls shown in table 6.1 reflect an increase in belief, even though practice remains much lower. For instance, in 2012, 97 percent identified as Muslims but only 20 percent said that they practiced their faith regularly. But lack of faith in the authorities and the secular state and society are not limited to rural areas. A 2009 Bloomberg report, based on interviews conducted in Baku, documented a turn to Islam in the face of Azerbaijan's endemic corruption and quashing of legal opposition parties:

> Many Azerbaijanis have lost their belief in a better future. . . . They do not trust the government, perceiving its members as "parasites" who care only for their own interest. Some are obviously turning to Islam. "Only Islam can save Azerbaijan from the influence of the rotten West," said [one student]. . . . Many Azerbaijanis perceive the West as a cynical player that calls for democratization but values Azerbaijani oil more.[103]

Extremist Islamism capitalized on such disillusionment, and has succeeded in recruiting young people even in more tolerant societies. Investigate journalist Carlotta Gall documented the case of Kosovo in the spring of 2016, showing how Saudi- and Kuwaiti-funded mullahs and mosques preaching intolerance and jihadism gained followers in pluralist Kosovo.[104] In light of such cases, the Aliyev regime's argument that Islamism presents a genuine threat to Azerbaijan's secularism and even its political stability appears more reasonable.

Events in neighboring regions also influenced Islam in Azerbaijan. These events included the Second Chechen War (1999–2009), the beginning of US intervention in Iraq (2003), and the election of anti-Western firebrand Mahmoud Ahmadinejad as president of Iran (2005). Russian action in Chechnya not only pushed Salafis into Azerbaijan, but, like the US presence in Afghanistan and Iraq, enhanced a narrative of Islam under attack.

The subsequent successes of terrorist groups like al-Qaeda and its offshoots, especially IS, made the entire West appear powerless to stop them. Radical Islamism looked like an emerging power in the world—defiant, heroic, and willing to challenge corrupt imperial powers. Azerbaijan's moves against religious manifestations shifted from efforts to contain Iranian influence, most apparent in the 1990s, to targeting Salafis. Combined with high-level meetings between Azerbaijani and Iranian religious leaders, the Azerbaijani government was considered by many to have adopted a "pro-Shi'ite" posture, especially since 2012.[105] If this pattern is roughly accurate, it conforms to actual threats. Iran certainly was a greater threat to Azerbaijan in the immediate post-Soviet years, but the upsurge of Salafi fighters in Chechnya in the early 2000s entailed penetration into Azerbaijan and expanded recruitment efforts there. The greatest threat came with the Syrian civil war and the rise of the Islamic State (as discussed later in this chapter).

Religious critics in Azerbaijan have accused the Aliyev regime of "Islamophobia." But the prosecution of Muslims coincided with repression against critical journalists and civil society activists, and the latter more often caused Western criticism than did arrests of religious figures. Government spokespersons replied with their own anti-Western and anti-US rhetoric. By 2014, some Azerbaijani officials decried American or Western "Islamophobia," thereby positioning the Aliyev regime to pose as a defender of Islam (aided by the Aliyev family's mini-pilgrimage to Mecca in 2015) even as it threw religious leaders in jail, often on bogus arms and drug charges, as in the earlier cases of journalist Ramin Bayramov and cleric Taleh Bagirzade. Baku's "Islamophobia" accusations joined a chorus against Europe and the United States from other Muslims inside and outside Azerbaijan.

That said, Western actions do invite criticism. Despite repeated elections that international observers declared did not meet "free and fair" standards, Western leaders continued to meet with President Aliyev, and their all-smiles photos were shown repeatedly on state-controlled media. Human rights groups documented politically motivated arrests of rights defenders and journalists, but PACE and US legislators continued to come to Baku for conferences and "informational" junkets. They stayed in luxury hotels and skied in resorts built on land that had been appropriated with allegedly unfair compensation to the villagers who had owned that land (see chapter 4). Western diplomats stressed the tripod of engagement with Azerbaijan—security, energy, and human rights—but when the United States, the United Kingdom, and other European states continued to do business with Aliyev in the face of arrests and dirty elections, Azerbaijanis became convinced that energy and finances trump democracy and human rights.

The "Non-Banning" of the Hijab

The frequency of women wearing the hijab, including young urban women, is considered an example of Islamist influence. As one 2009 report noted, "As recently as a few years ago everyone would stare at a woman dressed in a hijab, whereas today there are so many that nobody seems to pay attention."[106] It is often true that Baku women often wear chic headscarves made of expensive silks, and that the women may be in full makeup and fashionable clothes. So it is hard to interpret the meaning of the hijab in all cases—what percentage are pious, what percentage are trendy? There is no sign of the full-face covering, such as the burqa, in Baku, and it appears rare elsewhere in the country. The Aliyev regime must have found the pattern unsettling, perhaps as a sign that the younger generation was abandoning long-established secularism. The authorities moved to restrict it.

In December 2010, the newly seated pro-YAP Milli Majlis established a school uniforms law, requiring all students to wear uniforms. Although head coverings were not specifically prohibited, the de facto result was a ban on the hijab. Education Minister Misir Mardanov verbally affirmed the hijab ban. In one incident caught on video and posted to YouTube, the door guard at the Oil and Gas Institute refused to allow about ten female students wearing the hijab to enter the building. One articulate young woman argued that Azerbaijan's Constitution guarantees the right to an education, so they cannot understand why they should be banned.[107] Haji Ilgar Ibrahimoglu repeated the same argument in a *Caucasian Knot* video. Protests ensued. The government argued that its decision was "just" a school uniform to aid pedagogy. Protests "could be staged by secret circles," said Majlis vice speaker Bahar Muradova.[108] In RL's coverage, the official line was recapped, while Azerbaijani analysts and human rights lawyer Intiqam Aliyev insisted that wearing the hijab is a personal right. One Baku television program argued against the ban. Some online programs included clips of people giving incorrect or imprecise information about Islamic norms.[109] Elsewhere, Muslim authorities argued that details of body covering are not mandated by Islam, only the need for covering; they said that Muslims still must obey the laws of their own society. Journalists on this story asked whether the clash had been artificially created

208

to distract from the corruption of ruling circles. The reporters claimed that the Aliyevs were wedded to the "Soviet-era culture of secularism," missing the nineteenth-century indigenous origins of Azerbaijani secularism, and that the family is out of touch with "Azerbaijan's growing religious ranks."[110]

In October 2012, over a hundred protesters against a hijab ban staged a demonstration in Baku outside the Education Ministry. Some demonstrators were armed with poles; they had placards that read "Freedom to Hijab" and "Stop Islamophobia." Clashes with police led to twenty-five police injuries—a video showed some minor bloody arms and one person who had received a significant blow to the head.[111] Sixty-five men were arrested. "The following April [several] were sentenced to 5–6 years for violation of Article 233 of the Criminal Code, Organizing actions that lead to violations of public order or active participation in them."[112]

The dispute around the hijab is not entirely about this article of clothing, or even about women's public appearance or religiosity, but rather is about efforts by the Aliyev regime to block radical Islamism, both Sunni and Shi'a. The demonstrations of December 2010 and January 2011 against the hijab ban quickly escalated to a call by IPA leader Movsum Samadov to "rise up and put an end to this despotic regime." Samadov was taken into custody on January 8, and in the following week thirty other Islamists were detained or arrested and formally charged.[113] Samadov and the other defendants were tried in October, and Samadov was sentenced to twelve years and his associates to ten and eleven years in prison.[114]

The implications of such clashes are serious. There is simmering anger in Azerbaijan, and it is not clear that it is all attributable to "radicalism," although radical activity does exist. With pockets of anger and demonstrations leading to violence, the threat may be more serious than the secular intellectual elite of Baku envision. Nonetheless, Azerbaijan is not Iran. Azerbaijan has no powerful clerical hierarchy, since most religious leaders emigrated or were brought under state control in the tsarist period. Nor does Azerbaijan have a history of religious authorities leading political protests in partnership with the commercial class as in nineteenth- and twentieth-century Iran.[115] On the contrary, the widespread ignorance of Islam in the Soviet period makes the post-Soviet situation potentially more dangerous, because undereducated people can be persuaded by unorthodox or extremist arguments precisely because their knowledge of Islam is simplistic or primitive.

Azerbaijani authorities did not elaborate substantial arguments against the hijab. The Minister of Education verbally affirmed a hijab ban as a by-product of the school uniform law, and others called it a "pedagogical tool." Although the pro-hijab arguments seemed to echo the US guarantee of freedom of religious expression, the regime did not appeal to such basic concepts as its own constitutional guarantee of secularism. Nor did Azerbaijani leaders employ concepts used in the French debate on the "headscarf," such as the secularism of the classroom as part of citizen formation or the defense of public order and the necessity of literal face-to-face interaction as essential to social (and therefore political) equality for a democracy.[116] Of course, these ideas are deeply rooted in French thinking, not in the thinking of Azerbaijan or other post-Soviet states that more often stress the forms, not the substance, of democracy. Azerbaijan faces different challenges than Western society does. In its post-Soviet life, Azerbaijan has yet to define for itself the substance of democracy, its underlying assumptions of the view of the individual and the source of sovereignty, the relationship of legislature and judiciary to Constitution and law, and related matters. The relative weight of the exercise of freedom versus public order—as well as how these terms are defined—has yet to be argued and decided. And without free public discourse, this or any public debate cannot occur. Thus, struggles around individual issues such as the hijab continue at a relatively surface level, as signs of radical Islamism and increasing sectarian violence threaten public order and the regime itself.

Some signs of recruitment to radicalism and even participation in the jihad of the Islamic State, or elsewhere, can be documented before and during the civil war in Syria.

Azerbaijan and the Syrian Civil War

The scholar Bayram Balci has argued that the Syrian civil war, a late manifestation of the 2011 Arab Spring uprisings, touches major cleavages in Azerbaijani society. Both states have an authoritarian president who inherited his post from his equally authoritarian (but more skillful) father, and a Shi'ite majority with a Sunni minority. In Azerbaijan's case, religion had not played a political role since the early twentieth century; by comparison, Syria's more recent secularization dates from the 1960s.[117] But the growing strength of sectarian identity in Azerbaijan increases the likelihood of sectarian conflict, if fueled by Syria. Previously, Azerbaijan did not have close relations with Syria, but for decades it has been been "under the direct influence of both Iran and Turkey," which are on opposite sides in the Syrian upheaval. President Ilham Aliyev does not want to see regime change in Syria, which might encourage his own opponents, secular or religious.[118]

Some Azerbaijanis, though few in number, are fighting jihad in Syria, Iraq, and elsewhere. Most Azerbaijani fighters in Syria are Sunni who are supporting the Islamic State, though a small number of Shi'a are fighting with Shi'ite groups. "The lack of democratic institutes is the reason that lies on the surface," said Azerbaijani analyst Hikmet Hajizadeh, president of the Center for Economic and Political Studies (Far Center). Hajizadeh identified other problems: "first is the low level of education, especially in the northern regions, where these radicals come from. And the second one is common poverty." People go to Syria to "fight for very little money."[119]

Individual stories support these contentions.[120] One young man who was killed in Syria in 2013 was described by his brother as having become "personally pious" during 2009, and soon disappeared. After some months, he contacted his family to say that he was working in Turkey. Then he was killed outside Aleppo. An Azerbaijani wrestler was similarly recruited, then killed in Syria in 2014.[121] Estimates on the number of Azerbaijanis fighting in Syria with the Islamic State suggest that there may be 200 to 400, with 100 to 120 dead as of early 2015.

Recruitment among Sunnis is apparently centered in major Sunni mosques, particularly the now-closed Abu Bakr Mosque in Baku and a popular Sunni mosque in the industrial town of Sumgayit to the northwest of Baku. According to a 2014 Eurasianet report, towns in northern Azerbaijan, near the border with Dagestan, are a frequent source of Syria-bound jihadists. But it is Sumgayit that appears to have become a center for Salafism. In late 2013, an armed clash there between alleged Salafis and a group of extremist Kharidjis led to injuries and sixteen arrests. Arif Yunus,[122] a specialist on Islam in Azerbaijan, said, "What makes Sumgayit stand out is its community of Kharidjis, who, contrary to other Azerbaijani Salafis, 'believe that they should not obey secular rules and must participate in jihad worldwide.'"[123] And Kharidjis recruit candidates in local mosques and teahouses.

Sumgayit is fertile ground for jihadist recruitment because of the shift in its population. The city was a steel and petrochemical center full of blue-collar workers, and was known for polluted air. In the late Soviet period, as the central government's investment levels dropped, the city became impoverished. With the armed clashes in Mountainous Karabagh, displaced people and Azerbaijani refugees from Armenia settled there, creating a large, poor, restless, and underemployed population. Reportedly, "women from Sumgayit are being encouraged to go to Syria, locals and media report. In April, anonymous leaflets appeared throughout the city urging females to conduct 'marriage jihad' (*jihad al nikah*)—provide sexual services to mujahidin—for entrance into heaven."[124]

The regime strives to block jihadist recruiting in the same way it approaches other societal problems—with carrots and sticks, though not always in that order. Police surveillance has been increased, and penalties for fighting as a mercenary have been raised. "In March [2014], prison terms for such activities were nearly doubled to [a range of] five to eleven years, while those who recruit or sponsor mercenaries face a nine to fifteen-year jail sentence." Of course, this policy drove the activities underground, making them harder to monitor or assess. The underlying causes of social and economic discontent are not being addressed.[125]

Using the SCWRO, the authorities carry out reeducation, or at least develop propaganda about it. As a SCWRO spokesperson explained, "We carry out administrative and educational work in several regions of Azerbaijan . . . mostly among young people, and our task is to decrease the effect of radical propaganda." The committee claimed that this work had been successful in reducing the number of young people joining radical groups and going to Syria in 2014.[126] Other regime methods are full of risk, namely manipulation of the religious communities. According to a 2015 report on OnIslam,[127] an Islamic website,

> for some time, Azerbaijani authorities were able to solve the problem of growing Sunni religious opposition groups through supporting the Shiite expansion into Sunni areas and pressing-out radical Sunnis into neighboring Dagestan, Russia. But today Sunni activists flow to Syria to join ISIL ranks, and Azerbaijani authorities do not actively resist this trend.[128]

The number of arrests that took place in 2014–15 suggest that this conclusion, if it was ever correct, is now outdated. Another source offers a somewhat more subtle picture. From about 2012, SCWRO meetings with local Shi'ite leaders and CMB meetings with Iranian religious figures increased a pattern to strengthen local Shi'ism as a bulwark against Salafism. In 2014–15, Salafi mosques in Qobustan and Baku were closed; their leaders were arrested.[129] As for Shi'ite fighters, analyst Zardusht Alizade has said that Hezbollah is expanding in Azerbaijan: "Members of Hezbollah penetrate Azerbaijan under the guise of scientists, entrepreneurs, students, doctors, merchants, believers; the field of their activity is very wide . . . using their positions in these spheres, they are trying to influence the minds of our citizens."[130]

Despite regime efforts, people do go to Syria or elsewhere to fight jihad, and some have returned to Azerbaijan. The returning fighters present a particular danger with their radicalized sectarian identity and routine use of violence. Commentators in and out of government have expressed concern about post-traumatic stress disorder, known in former Soviet spaces as "Afghan syndrome." Far more attention is paid to arrests and trials than to treatment. Reportedly, thirty-four returning fighters were arrested in 2014.[131] In January 2015, ten men, said to be returning from Syria, were arrested. Earlier returnees were sentenced to eighteen months in prison, shorter sentences than those given to journalists who cover oligarchs' corruption or human rights activists who incorrectly file the paperwork to register an NGO.[132] Alleged jihadists must sit in a cage during their trials, despite appeals by their lawyers.[133] Nor do officials express much sympathy for them or even presume their innocence: alleged former fighters have to "face the law, because *whatever they were doing was completely unlawful*," said Rabiyat Aslanova, chairperson of the Milli Majlis Committee on Human Rights.[134]

All sides, it seems, are trying to ward off internal violence. Both Ilgar Ibrahimoglu and Qamet Suleymanov spoke out against incidents of apparent sectarian violence within Azerbaijan. In July 2014, a group of people in a market in Sabirabad, a southern city in Shi'ite country, attacked and beat a bearded Sunni man they presumed to be a Salafi. Bystanders made a video of the incident and the subsequent events. At a local police station, the man was forcibly shaved. The video of the incident was widely shared on social media—suggesting that it was aimed at a young audience—and got favorable comment. Analysts quoted in a report from the Institute of War and Peace Reporting found this incident and its coverage chilling, as did Ibrahimoglu and Suleymanov. Arastun Orujlu, director of the East-West Research Center, continued to argue that both regime actions and missionary work of other Muslim states were responsible: "These countries, which have radicalized the people under their control, are now trying to sow discord among religious confessions in Azerbaijan. The first signs of this are already apparent," Orujlu told the Institute for War and Peace Reporting. "The [Azerbaijani] government deliberately destroyed civil society, the media and the political opposition, and radical religious movements are moving in to fill that space. In consequence, these groups could become very powerful."[135]

213

Arrests of Muslim activists continue, most often on drug or weapons charges, sometimes for importing illegal (unapproved) literature. Authorities say that all forms of Muslim activism—from hijab to jihadism—are threats to state security. Western criticism is not uncontroversial; human rights organizations continue to call on Azerbaijan to protect freedom of conscience, including peaceful expressions of religiosity, even as Western governments struggle with the same issues in an era of "Islamic" terrorism such as the 2013 Boston Marathon bombing and the 2015 attacks in Paris, first on the offices of the satirical magazine *Charlie Hebdo* (which the elders of Nardaran denounced)and a Jewish market in January, and on several Paris night spots in November.[136]

Muslim Azerbaijani activists, like their secular counterparts, sometimes appeal to the European Court of Human Rights. In 2013, the court ruled against the Juma Mosque appeal against closure, on technical grounds, as described above. On November 13, 2014, the court ruled in favor of its affiliate Islam-Ittihad Association in its case against Azerbaijan, stating that the association's dissolution by the state on the grounds of its conducting "religious activity" violated the right to freedom of association under Article 11 of the European Convention on Human Rights. In the November decision, the court stated that it was "struck by the fact that the domestic courts, instead of giving an interpretation of the term 'religious activity . . . , imposed the burden of proof on the Association, holding that it had failed to submit any reliable evidence proving that it had not engaged in any such activity.'"[137] This was a case which the state lost because it was careless in its language and definitions both in law and in court rulings. Yet the greater conflict between freedom and security remains unresolved. During the civil society repression of 2014, the SCWRO held a conference in the northern city of Quba on religion, national identity, and modernity.[138] Yet 1,500 workers building the Olympic Stadium for the 2015 Euro Games were fired for taking time to pray during the workday.[139]

Ilham Goes to Mecca

Baku news outlets provided a surprising series of photos in April 2015. President Ilham Aliyev had gone to Mecca. Photos showed the president in the required white robe, standing with his usually Chanel-clad wife and daughters in women's black pilgrim robes and veils. Indeed, the first family of Azerbaijan, with Sheikh-ul-Islam Allahsukur Pashazade in tow, made a "little pilgrimage" (*umrah*). The *umrah* does not entail all the complex ceremonies of the hajj itself, but the *umrah* nonetheless takes the pilgrim to Mecca and is normally an expression of religious devotion. But the secular president of the secular republic of Azerbaijan had not formerly showed such devotion, nor has anyone suggested that he had experienced an abrupt conversion. Aliyev was on a business trip to Jeddah, and seems to have used the visit as an opportunity to perform the *umrah*. But why? What was the meaning of this extensively photographed family pilgrimage?

At one level, the president might have been playing to the crowd. His father had made the hajj in 1994, and other Central Asian presidents had done so as well. Aside from the criminalization of expressions of religious extremism, displays of personal religiosity and desire for public morality have been growing throughout Azerbaijan. Ilham has been criticized for his secular ways, and the revealing clothes of the first lady have caused some distress. The *umrah* was not an overly inconvenient trip for the first family, and their participation in it could have been spun to suggest just enough piety to stave off the harshest criticism. Yet the much-photographed trip to Mecca was surely much more than that.

Azerbaijan, insists Aliyev, is stable and secular. But he knows that there are threats to stability, and the greatest of these threats may be Islamism, if only because so many leaders of the other challenges are in jail. With this "little hajj," Aliyev may have tried to get out in front and define an "Azerbaijani Islam," as he tried to do with democracy and fair elections. In this case, redefinition means a national and secularized way of being a Muslim in twenty-first-century Azerbaijan. Such a Muslim is not only no threat to the state, but she or he is an asset, a supporter of state interests as defined by the ruling elite. The goal has already been articulated in the founding statute for the the SCRWO, quoted above: "Religion increases the human responsibilities for society and strengthens the feeling of patriotism. The state needs faithful, convinced citizens, for morality is appreciated as national wealth by the state."

This approach is likely a response to the danger of radical Islamism as perceived by the ruling regime. Although the leaders may exaggerate the Islamist threat, the dangers to stability are real. Participants in religious rituals and demonstrations such as the "freedom for hijab" demonstrations are usually small, at most in the hundreds, not thousands. They are isolated and often spontaneous, so they can be quashed easily. Crowds at the Abu Bakr Mosque for Friday prayer were in the thousands, but it is now closed, and other mosques have been drawing smaller crowds. Islamist groups continue to be active, and send a small but steady stream of jihadis to Syria and Iraq and possibly to other hot spots. Extreme Islamist factions do not have to be large to be dangerous. Even without taking foreign funding and encouragement into consideration, three domestic factors could make such groups more dangerous. First, discontent born of poverty or injustice feeds radicalism. Despite the oil wealth and the striking modernization of Baku, continuing economic, social, and political inequality and rampant corruption have contributed to Azerbaijan's vulnerability to Islamist appeals. Second, the Aliyev regime has closed off independent avenues for open discussion or even mild dissent. Islamist groups in the world seem successful and dynamic, an image projected on social media, which reaches a young audience. Finally, the merging of religious communities with ethnic minorities, though an apparently slight danger, may be the most volatile threat to Azerbaijan and most likely to draw interference from abroad.

Aliyev's analysts surely have envisioned the permutations of religious and religious-ethnic threats. A Shi'ite threat to the Republic of Azerbaijan in the 1990s seemed the most likely threat, given Azerbaijani traditions and Iranian efforts to export its influence. The CMB under Allahsukur Pashazade aimed at controlling the Shi'a. By most accounts, leaving aside Nardaran and the IPA (which are outliers), the effort has been successful. If a Shi'ite-led uprising against the corrupt Aliyev regime were to occur, where might the needed coordination originate? Iran is the only candidate, possibly through Iran-trained clerics. Toward what end? Overthrowing the Aliyev regime would leave Azerbaijan with what rulers? No Azerbaijanis, including the imprisoned leaders of the IPA, are prepared to set up an Islamic regime without Iranian leadership or guidance. Nor would the secular majority, including the security services and armed forces, be likely to stand by while that happened. No Iranian leader could insinuate himself into the political mix without provoking intervention by Russia—which has not been the least bit subtle in its exercise of power, especially in former Soviet republics, under Vladimir Putin.

A Sunni threat at present, even with thousands at Friday prayer, can only be envisioned in connection with an outside group such as violent neo-Salafis or the Islamic State. By all accounts, most Salafis are seeking a simple, moral life. The Islamists of Sumgayit are focused on sending fighters abroad rather than organizing to oppose the Aliyev regime, but targets can change. Capability is the more important consideration. Returning fighters have achieved that capability; they are few, and most end up in jail. But leadership, arms, and more fighters would have to come from abroad. The successful Saudi- and Kuwaiti-funded jihadist propaganda efforts in Kosovo show that foreign Islamists nurture followers with patience and money, potentially to great effect. With surveillance and regular arrests, the Aliyev regime is preempting this threat—even as other policies make it more attractive—and the armed forces likely would be able to handle isolated incidents, as they have done in the past.

The greatest danger to Azerbaijan's stability would be sectarian fighting of Shi'ites against Sunnis, especially if that cleavage overlapped ethnic discontent. Survey data cited above suggest that the major ethnic groups, Talysh and Lezghi, have a high level of "civic nationalism" and do not feel particularly alienated or inclined to radicalism. Iranian Hezbollah reportedly is active in the south, so the danger there cannot be completely dismissed.[140] The Sunni Lezghis of the north straddle the border and are in touch with radicalized Muslims of the Caucasus Mountains. For instance, in March 2015, five Sunni Muslims from Baku's Lezghin Mosque were arrested, along with Shi'ite theologian Jeyhun Jafarov. All were held in Ministry of National Security facilities.[141]

Unrest along one or both borders, even if not aimed at toppling the regime, is the single greatest danger for several reasons. Both border areas could threaten to secede, as they did in the 1990s. Armenians certainly would use such weakness as an opportunity to press their demands on Karabagh and possibly break the cease-fire. The Aliyev regime could not reasonably fight on two or three fronts at once—it was a two-front fight in the north and in Karabagh that led to the fall of the first republic in 1920. Azerbaijan's destablization would invite intervention from Russia first of all, likely in response to a "request" from Ilham Aliyev or Ramiz Mehdiyev, the old communist chief of staff, or power ministers like Ramil Usubov of the Ministry of Internal Affairs. Even without an invitation in the case of open rebellion by Muslim groups, Russia reasonably could invoke the "responsibility to protect" the small Russian minority or Azerbaijan's secular society as potential victims of "Islamic fundamentalism." This is a worst-case scenario not only for Azerbaijan, which would revert to subservience to Moscow, with all that implies for lost chance to regain democracy or civil society; but also for Western interests, which would be frozen out of Azerbaijan's energy and security partnership.

These dangers do not appear imminent, because the religious groups seem isolated, poor, and perpetually at risk of government suppression. Moreover, if there is a leader capable of uniting factions, he is in the shadows. But the Aliyev regime's repressive policies that quash public discourse drive the politically conscious and the poor to more extreme positions. Worse, the ruling circles' extreme corruption and overtly lavish lifestyles provide grist for their critics' mills, perhaps first of all for the religious who long for morality in public life.

7

What's Next? The Choices Ahead

The fault, dear Brutus, lies not in our stars, but in ourselves.

—Shakespeare, *Julius Caesar* I.ii.140–41

Two Lists

A retired US government official was briefing a colleague who was new to the field of Azerbaijan. Imagine that there are two lists, said the retiree. First, there is the Azerbaijani government's list of its own strengths and value to the United States: Azerbaijan is a source of oil and gas with a pipeline to the Mediterranean and another under construction; it has been consistent in security cooperation, including assistance in the "war on terror," supplying access to bases and providing forces to Iraq and Afghanistan; it maintains good relations with Israel and sells it oil; and as a secular state with Westernized leaders, at risk to itself, it acts as a bulwark against Iranian influence and radical Islamism. The other list of traits comes from international oversight organizations and prodemocracy and human rights activists. This list shows that Azerbaijan is highly corrupt in governance and business; it has been ruled by the same family and its political party since 1993; state and personal finances of public officials are opaque despite its own laws; the country has not had a free and fair election since 1992; the regime violently represses dissent by political parties, civil society, and the media; journalists and human rights defenders are arrested, beaten, or thrown into jail; the courts are obedient to the executive. Azerbaijan has been ranked by watchdog groups as deeply nondemocratic with an unfree media. Both lists are true, said the retiree—and even though US policymakers may allow the considerations on the first list to trump those on the second one, at the very least they should not lie about the second one.

That summary captures the complexity of Azerbaijan. First, it dramatizes the stark difference between the profile that its government presents to the world and the problems on which prodemocracy activists, domestic and international, focus. That dichotomy reflects Azerbaijan's possibilities, the choices its rulers can make, and the range of aspirations of its population. Without security, independence is at risk, and development or democracy would be impossible. Without democratic institutions and processes, the country is an oil-rich fiefdom enriching the elite at the expense of the majority. Two questions arise. Can security be reconciled with democracy and human rights for a country in that location, with those neighbors, under current political circumstances? And, second, does the present regime want to find that balance? So far, the Aliyev regime has proclaimed its system to be democratic, but it has taken all steps to impede the elements of democracy, from open discourse to free elections and an independent judiciary. Nevertheless, conditions are changing.

US policymakers might be asked analogous questions. Are there steps that the United States can take to support Azerbaijan's security and stability while encouraging, even pressing toward, greater democracy, rule of law, and open civil society? Should the United States accept the idea of security *as opposed to* human rights, which the Aliyev regime has crafted? Do US policymakers want to get involved, and to what degree, in democracy promotion in postcommunist states? What are the implications of either choice for US leadership in its relations with Azerbaijan and, by extension, for former Soviet states and for democracy promotion throughout the world?

Attempting to forecast how Azerbaijan may look in five years or ten is perilous. This book has discussed several key elements of today's political, economic, and social configuration and their evolution over the past twenty-five years, and taken together they form a baseline. Looking forward, any examination of current issues must be contextualized by an awareness of that history. In 2016, the most likely drivers of change for Azerbaijan are the drop in oil prices, which began in 2014; the potential for renewed fighting in Mountainous Karabagh; and the shifting policies of major regional powers, especially an aggressive Russia, Iran's nuclear deal with the United States, and the ongoing crisis generated by the Syrian civil war and the power of the Islamic State.

The Oil Price Plunge: Azerbaijan's Game Changer

For Azerbaijan, as for other oil-exporting states, the collapse of oil prices has had a devastating impact. In twenty-five years of post-Soviet independence, oil revenues had grown into billions annually and transformed the economic, social, and political landscape. Azerbaijani authorities have been behind the curve on dropping oil prices. As with the 2008–9 recession, Ilham Aliyev and his leadership team denied that global changes would affect Azerbaijan. In November 2014, the YAP-dominated Milli Majlis built its 2015 budget on the assumption that oil would sell for $90 per barrel, a price that was already a dim memory when prices dropped through $50 a barrel as 2015 began. Regime spokespersons insisted that 2015 oil prices would *average* $90. One year later, the 2016 budget was built on the presumption of $50 oil (the same figure used by and perhaps borrowed from Russia), just weeks before global oil prices dipped below $30. Azerbaijani authorities insisted that because the production cost per barrel was only $15, they could manage revenue losses because of taxes from other areas.[1] But the country's economy was not diversified, despite Aliyev's claims at the World Economic Forum in Davos, Switzerland, in January 2016, and for more than a decade oil has accounted for over 80 percent of Azerbaijan's export revenues—a very large gap to bridge.[2]

Political leaders contended that the oil price would not affect Azerbaijan because the country had a multi-billion-dollar cushion of foreign currency, and even more billions in SOFAZ, where the state's share of oil revenues has been managed. Those billions were spent faster than envisioned, apparently, because a December 2015 report revealed that the SOFAZ cushion was down nearly 75 percent.[3] Moreover, from September 2014 to December 2015, the Central Bank of Azerbaijan had spent nearly $10 billion in foreign currency and gold, about two-thirds of its reserves, to support the manat.[4] President Aliyev had denied that the manat would be devalued, but in February 2015 it was devalued by changing the Central Bank's calculation of manat value from a dollar to a mixed dollar-euro basket. On December 21, the Central Bank announced the manat would "float," but actually set it at "a new exchange rate . . . that was 48 percent lower – now 1.55 AZN/$." One year earlier, the value had been 0.87 to the dollar, so the manat had lost just over half its value in the two devaluations of 2015.

The secrecy surrounding the currency devaluation led to panic.[5] Azerbaijani citizens scrambled to protect their assets by purchasing durable goods or converting their savings to foreign currencies. But dollars were scarce. In January 2016, the Central Bank of Azerbaijan limited foreign currency sales to banks, and excluded the small currency exchanges that most citizens used, especially in Baku. Even debtors who had only small loans fretted over the impact of the devaluation. Several explained that major banks granted loans in manat, but the loans themselves were denominated in dollars. With the devaluation, their manat loans worth $2,000 would now require far more manat to repay. Some people interviewed by local media said that they could not even guess how much money it would take to repay their loans.[6]

Demonstrations were triggered not by currency devaluation, an abstract concept for most consumers, but by the resulting rise in prices. Shop owners often raised prices, even on domestically produced goods, to offset their own increased costs. The increase in the food costs, reported as 15 to 35 percent before the December 2015 devaluation, was most painful. Eggs and rice became more expensive, and tomatoes and grapes far more so. Azersun, the food production and marketing company owned by the Aliyev family, raised prices on more than a dozen food brands for which it holds the trademarks, including the popular Pasha brand tea.[7] Flour is mostly imported, and price rises led to increases in bread prices. Remembering how bread riots had led to the fall of the tsar in 1917, the Soviet regime had always kept bread prices low. The increase seemingly was the trigger for the protests that began on January 13, 2016. The demonstrations in cities of five districts around Azerbaijan led to arrests (fifty-five just in the city of Siyazan) of protesters for "illegal" demonstrations, meaning actions that had not been authorized in advance. In most cities, local leaders of the major opposition parties, the Popular Front and Yeni Müsavat, were detained, even though they were apparently not involved in organizing the demonstrations.[8] Baku remained quiet because of a large and visible police presence in the streets and the long history of using violence to break up even peaceful demonstrations.

If arrests and police violence were the "sticks," promises of state relief and price reductions were the "carrots." The regime suspended the value-added tax on imported flour and rolled back the price of bread. Sellers who exceeded that price were to be prosecuted. No mention was made of packaged foods controlled by Azersun. The minister of labor and social welfare promised to raise welfare payments. Others suggested raising salaries of state employees. The Foreign Ministry looked for cost-cutting measures, including staff cuts, but it denied reports that it intended to close embassies.[9]

As for the future, neither nongovernment analysts nor "on the street" interviews reflected hope in the economy or confidence in the regime. Aliyev's official statement at Davos claimed that the Azerbaijani economy was diversified and thus was protected from the Dutch disease, suggesting that oil exports were more important to foreign buyers than to Azerbaijan's domestic economy.[10] A 2016 report by *US News* in conjunction with BAV Consulting and the University of Pennsylvania, however, confirmed earlier World Bank findings that diversification was lagging.[11] Azerbaijani analysts commented that Aliyev's performance at Davos lacked any sign that he was planning for reform, diversification, or greater social support in 2016. Locally based but nonstate media outlets interviewed people on the streets of Baku. Some refused to talk about economic troubles, while others openly said that it was impossible to believe the authorities when they had misrepresented the dangers of the loss of oil revenue and devaluation. Several commented on the need for more jobs.

In the midst of the oil price collapse and currency degradation, the regime apparently needed cash. In June 2015, on the eve of the European Games with oil prices around $50 a barrel, dozens of Azerbaijani millionaires who owed debts to major banks were arrested. Those who were later released told reporters that they had repaid at least some of the loans, but the sums paid were only portions of large balances that could not have solved the country's financial problems. The story of the "oligarch shakedown" soon disappeared from the press. None of the major families connected to the government was squeezed in this way. Because Azerbaijan's economic growth is dependent on spending effects (see chapter 4), the contraction of government spending leads to greater unemployment and inflation, threatening the social safety net as long as oil prices hover at present levels. Similar Russian economic woes have led to dramatic contraction of economic activity there and may lead to the return of Azerbaijanis from Russia, reducing important transfer payments and exacerbating Azerbaijan's income and unemployment problems. Despite year-end reports, assets and transactions involving SOFAZ and the central bank remain opaque, making it difficult to predict how long SOFAZ money might be available to support a state budget in the absence of high oil income. In Russia, with a larger economy facing financial sanctions after its invasion of

Ukraine, an August 2015 analysis concluded that Russia's oil fund could be expected to last only about a year.[12]

Aliyev's January 2016 appeal to the International Monetary Fund may have begun a transition, forcing the regime on a grudging path to financial reform that eventually might save both the system and the regime. Consultants from the IMF, the World Bank, and the European Bank for Reconstruction and Development headed to Baku in late January 2016 to determine needs for technical assistance and loans. Reacting apparently to press coverage of the visits, Finance Minister Samir Sharifov resumed the happy talk, claiming, "We aren't in an urgent need to borrow now."[13] When the IMF team left Baku, it announced its intention to continue cooperation on recommended reforms, which include economic diversification.[14] The upside of IMF involvement is that Azerbaijan could be forced to relinquish some of the long-established secrecy in the banking sector.[15] A spring 2016 IMF report noted with approval the currency devaluation, bank reforms, and reported aid to pensioners, while also urging transparency of privatization, expansion of private sector employment, and reforms to reduce corruption.[16] Whether the authorities will tolerate greater transparency and implement the reforms needed to stabilize the economy remains to be seen.

Potential for Resumption of War in Karabagh

Aside from the economic troubles, the other great risk is the possible renewal of fighting in Mountainous Karabagh. Azerbaijan's huge military budget and weapons purchases of the past several years have led increasingly to the expectation that Baku will restart the war. Indeed, the ground and air forces of Azerbaijan, like the population and energy supply, substantially outnumber those of Armenia. An upsurge in fighting and casualties along the line of contact was reported in international media throughout 2015, culminating in a dramatic and bloody renewal of fighting on April 2–5, 2016. Until the April battle, analysts had privately cast doubt on whether the Azerbaijan military was able to use all its sophisticated equipment. Purges in the army during 2013–14 were reportedly intended to support "increasing efficiency."[17] Naval exercises with the Russian and Kazakhstan navies in the summer of 2015 revealed poor performance by Azerbaijan.[18] Yet confidence in the armed forces remained high in both Azerbaijan and in Armenia and, as noted, both want to control Karabagh and adjacent territories. More than one diplomat has said privately that the widely shared "nightmare scenario" is the rogue action of a field commander that leads to another war.

The fighting of April 2016 altered many of these speculations. Azerbaijani forces pushed Armenian forces and artillery back from key long-held positions and retook land along the line of contact, including important high ground.[19] The short fighting was carefully controlled in a small area, and in the end, the new cease-fire affirmed Azerbaijan's gains. Regardless of who initiated the clash (and each side blamed the other), this was a test of Azerbaijan's abilities, and it was successful.

The argument that Ilham Aliyev, as a businessman, is unlikely to initiate fighting in Mountainous Karabagh still holds true but appears to require one caveat. He does not want a wider war, but might approve isolated action if he believes he can control the scale of fighting and the outcome. He and the oligarchs know that war would damage business, infrastructure, and tourism prospects. In the worst case, it could threaten the regime and the very existence of Azerbaijan as a country. Like his father and political leaders of Azerbaijan of all stripes, Aliyev has echoed the intense popular support for the reestablishment of Azerbaijani control over Karabagh. In his 2012 speech at the United Nations, in which he renewed Azerbaijan's support for US antiterrorism efforts, Aliyev associated Armenian actions with terrorism.[20] There as elsewhere, his rhetoric was carefully crafted to present Azerbaijan as a reliable ally and business partner of the West, while Armenia was identified as both aggressor and challenger to the principle of territorial integrity, a sensitive topic in Europe. This rhetoric is meant to isolate Armenia diplomatically.

The type of clash that took place in April 2016, though brief in this instance, presents the risk of escalation into a wider war. And a renewal of this war would be extremely costly by all measures. Russia might strive to act as negotiator to restore peace, but at what price to Baku? If Russia were to come to the defense of its ally Armenia, the Russian-dominated Collective Security Treaty Organization could be pulled into the conflict. Despite the differences in the situation, Russia would be likely to act as it did in the 2008 war against Georgia, possibly moving ground troops over Azerbaijan's northern border to support Armenia or the Lezghins in the north (should they choose that moment to proclaim autonomy) or to fend off a real or imagined move by Islamists. Turkey would be likely to urge a quick settlement rather than risk being pulled into the war. If Turkey did agree to support Azerbaijan militarily—a decision that is less likely in view of the purge of the Turkish military that followed the failed coup attempt of July 15, 2016—that action would create for Armenia a two-front war. Money and fighters from the Armenian diaspora would pour into the region. Implications for Turkey as a NATO member would be dangerous. Even limiting the action to these four powers, the potential for loss of life and destruction of industrial, cultural, and population centers is great. The risk of spilling over into a wider regional war involving the Islamic State and others would be grave. As in the case of the 2008 Russo-Georgian War, the United States (and the European Union) would avoid direct involvement. Even if the loss of oil income gives the Aliyev government the chance to reform, a new war could destroy the regime and the country before reforms could work.

Azerbaijan and Its Tough Neighborhood

Although the phrase has become an excuse for domestic repression, Azerbaijan is indeed in a tough neighborhood with enemies that would like its compliance, wealth, or land. The most important neighbor is Russia, as the imperial power that ruled Azerbaijan since the early 1800s and whose political culture still largely dominates Azerbaijan's post-Soviet government. Russia has loomed large in the Karabagh war and the negotiations surrounding it, energy policy, and other aspects of trade. Its invasions of Georgia in 2008 and Ukraine in 2014 sent a message to Baku that Moscow would be willing to use force in its national interests in its "near abroad." It has made overtures to get Azerbaijan to join the Russia-dominated Eurasian Economic Union, a move which Azerbaijan has so far avoided. Moscow has criticized Baku's inclination to the West for two decades, but thus far has used subtle means to keep Azerbaijan from shifting too far to the West. Azerbaijan's elites are products of Soviet education and career development. Those born in 1960, including the younger Azerbaijani leaders like Ilham Aliyev, spent their first thirty years of life in the Soviet system. Even the men and women born around 1980 spent their first ten years in it, and were schooled by teachers trained in Soviet methods and thinking.

Ilham Aliyev, with his father's advisers at his side, has followed Heydar's path, seeking to maintain a balance between the West and Russia. But Ilham's pattern of not merely tainted elections but increasing repressions against political opposition, civil society, journalists, and human rights defenders has drawn embarrassing Western criticism, making Russia a more attractive ally. After a barrage of anti-US, anti-EU, and pro-Russian rhetoric during the winter of 2014–15, Azerbaijan applied for observer status, a step toward full membership, to the Shanghai Cooperation Organisation in February 2015. The organization is dominated by Russia and China and includes several former Soviet republics in Central Asia. At the SCO's July 2015 meeting in the Russian city of Ufa, Azerbaijan, along with Armenia, Cambodia, and Nepal, was announced as a dialogue partner, a lower step than observer.[21] The lower level of cooperation moderates but does not erase Baku's signal that Azerbaijan is serious about potential realignment or perhaps merely rebalancing between West and East.

Russia, moreover, began ramping up its courtship toward Iran in the summer of 2016, using Azerbaijan as a necessary transit corridor. Both Russia and Iran suffer from Western, especially US-imposed, sanctions, and amid the summer's terror threats to Europe and the uncertainties of the US presidential election cycle (and the oddities of the 2016 campaign in particular), Vladimir Putin and Hassan Rouhani have partnered with Aliyev to discuss coordinated actions to bolster regional security and commerce. Discussions in Baku in August specifically addressed a projected transportation corridor, with railroads and highways, linking Iran and Russia via Azerbaijan. Putin has declared a free trade zone between the Eurasian Economic Union and Iran, and has mentioned facilitating closer ties between Tehran and the SCO, relations that might draw Azerbaijan closer to both Moscow and the SCO.[22]

Azerbaijan's developing relationship with the SCO touches on important considerations for Baku. Within the SCO, Azerbaijan would have another venue for the exercise of authoritarian rule without challenges to its human rights record, and for commercial agreements with states that want to acquire oil and gas. As a collective security organization, the SCO stresses themes that resonate in Azerbaijan with regard to Karabagh: territorial integrity and antiterrorism. Commercially, SCO membership facilitates the types of bilateral agreements with other members that Baku prefers. Azerbaijan would lose nothing financially if it sold oil to China and SCO states rather than to Europe. Indeed, after the Iranian-Western nuclear weapons limitation agreement of July 2015, Baku believes that Azerbaijan's oil is dwarfed by Iranian stocks and becomes much less important (except to Israel) as Iranian oil comes back to world markets. Azerbaijan's association with the SCO also strengthens Russia's hand within that organization—which is widely considered to be Chinese-dominated—thereby boosting Azerbaijani-Russian "friendship."

The greatest advantages of SCO membership for Azerbaijan are illuminated in the SCO's own documents. The statement from the September 2014

SCO meeting surely appealed to Baku in the midst of Western criticism that Azerbaijani authorities call interference. In contrast, the SCO commits to "principles of respect for national sovereignty and non-interference in the internal affairs of other countries." The SCO offers its pledge that all members "will cooperate in preventing the use of information and communications technologies which intend to undermine the political, economic and public safety and stability of the Member States." The SCO document stresses "the universal moral foundations of social life," but not individual human rights or rule of law. Finally it provides the assurance that "Member States advocate equal rights of all countries in Internet governance and the sovereign right of states to govern the Internet in their respective national segments."[23] This 2014 statement is a concisely worded defense of antidemocratic authoritarian rule. Azerbaijan's desire to affiliate itself with the SCO dovetails with its domestic policies.

Has Azerbaijan shaken the Western dust off its sandals and turned toward Russia? Not entirely. Most Azerbaijani elites badly want and need to keep options open. Few in Azerbaijan's ruling circles want to forsake the West and all it has to offer. The newest oil pipeline runs through Turkey to Europe, and a major gas export pipeline is being built alongside it. The energy deals are politically significant and lucrative, and the idea of an east-west transportation corridor through Azerbaijan has not been dropped. Despite the pro-Russian rhetoric and inclination of some people or factions within Azerbaijani ruling elites, those close to the regime have huge investments in the West, ranging from oil contracts and soccer teams to homes in London and lobbyists in Washington. The Aliyev family and the oligarchs in his inner circle prefer the alignment with the West because they both see and present themselves as Westerners, especially as Europeans. Indeed, as a nearer neighbor, Europe is the more likely partner for Azerbaijan than is the United States. When Martin Schulz, president of the European Parliament, criticized the August 2015 sentences of activists Leyla and Arif Yunus as "scraping the bottom when it comes to developing a modern, pluralist state," the regime responded, as in the past, as if betrayed with angry rejection.[24] Domestic analysts have insisted that the leaders care about European opinion. The SCO has been dubbed the "club for authoritarians," and Aliyev does not see himself as an authoritarian ruler.[25] On the contrary, he has repeated on recent European visits that he is elected by his people and is popular with over 90 percent of them. The regime has supported a number of other efforts to attract Westerners and Western money. After the European Games in June 2015, Baku hosted the third annual Eurovillage

2015, an event designed to acquaint Europeans with Azerbaijani culture, with experiences that included museum tours, music, and face painting.[26] Baku played host to the Formula One race in the summer of 2016 by paving old cobblestone streets with asphalt, in spite of the protests of local residents. The total cost for the race preparations is estimated at $12 million, money spent as bread prices rose.[27]

Anger on the Home Front

Pocketbook issues, especially housing troubles and higher prices, have propelled ordinary people into the streets time after time and unleashed their fury. Given Azerbaijan's high birth rate, a "youth bulge" has developed and is growing, creating a pool of potentially discontent youth demanding vast expansion of jobs. Spontaneous public demonstrations on these issues have arisen and been quashed, as when people were evicted from their homes to make way for Eurovision venues and other new construction projects. Abrupt price increases in early 2016 produced the same pattern throughout Azerbaijan. Other problems with political implications can be exacerbated by the economic downturn, including perceptions of regime corruption and repression of civil society. Such pressures suggest the need for immediate change, but the ruling elites and the system they have created resist change, except in their rhetoric.

Thanks to investigative reporting, the Azerbaijani public has become more aware of the private wealth of oligarchs. People can observe the proliferation of expensive foreign cars and exclusive shops in central Baku, but it is reporting by journalists like Khadija Ismayilova that has linked the Aliyev-Pashayev family to banks, hotels, cell phone companies, and gold mines that potentially lays the foundation for more profound public anger toward the elites. Recently, Azerbaijanis have been willing to talk more openly with local and foreign print and Internet journalists. Although immediate problems may spark protests, anger continues to simmer over the regime's lavish spending for international "vanity" events like Eurovision, the European Games, the Formula One race, and the rumored bid for a future Olympics. Without leadership, however, angry crowds that form over some isolated incident—a car crash, a building fire, or a tainted election—can be easily suppressed. Leaders or potential leaders are needed to explain to the public the diverting of oil funds from genuine public works projects to those that enrich elite families. But those leaders, because their ideas and words threaten the oligarchs, have been the target of both Aliyev regimes, becoming worse since 2005, and have been the victims of force, intimidation, draconian laws, and a compliant judiciary. For these reasons, Khadija Ismayilova, Ilgar Mammadov, Rasul Jafarov, Intiqam Aliyev, the Yunuses, and dozens of other spent months or years in prison, in solitary confinement, and were subjected to psychological pressure and torture.[28] Young political activists and journalists are set up on fake drug charges and sentenced to years in prison.

Longing for the return of Mountainous Karabagh and surrounding territories, though powerful, rarely generates demonstrations anymore. Polls show that all Azerbaijanis want these areas to be restored to Azerbaijan's control so the refugees can go home. But people are not clamoring for war. They wait for their leaders or for international mediators to get the land back. The government is not preparing them for compromise, and if that becomes necessary as the price of peace, the result will be popular disillusionment and perhaps rage.

Outside Criticism

Western criticism is not new. The Organization for Security and Cooperation in Europe's Office for Democratic Institutions and Human Rights has revealed the violations in every election since 1995. The Parliamentary Assembly of the Council of Europe; the Venice Commission; and antitorture, media freedom, and human rights commissions have issued reports that exposed Azerbaijan's failures to comply with agreements the government had signed. Often, there were contrary voices about Azerbaijan's strategic and energy importance, its "new democracy," or its "tough neighborhood." Since 2013, however, when Ilham Aliyev's third term of office began and repressions increased, Western criticism intensified as well.

In June 2015, just a week after the closing of the Baku OSCE office, PACE passed a resolution on the functioning of democratic institutions in Azerbaijan.[29] This resolution (2062) was comprehensive in describing Azerbaijan's international position and domestic political system. It enumerated the areas in which Azerbaijan had failed to respond to previous recommendations to improve the electoral process and other democratic indicators, including the composition of the Central Election Commission, impartiality of the judiciary, and corruption. Regime spokespersons rejected the report as interference.

230

In the United States, after months of congressional hearings, members of Congress finally began to realize the breadth and significance of human rights violations in Azerbaijan, and began to react. Leading the efforts was the US Helsinki Commission (Commission for Security and Cooperation in Europe), the US government agency that monitors and encourages compliance with the OSCE. Its chair, Representative Chris Smith (R-NJ), had held hearings on media repressions in the fall of 2014, leaving an empty chair for Khadija Ismayilova, who had been barred from foreign travel just a month before her arrest. At the end of 2015, Smith initiated the Azerbaijan Democracy Act, condemning Azerbaijan's human rights record and calling for the denial of visas to senior Azerbaijani officials. Baku reacted to the pressure with charges the bill was "anti-Azerbaijani" and a result of Armenian influence damaging the US-Azerbaijan relations. Members of the Milli Majlis proposed a retaliatory bill to deny visas to US officials.[30]

Ruling Circles

Azerbaijan appears stable, and its leadership has hardly changed since the 1990s, when Heydar Aliyev returned to power and appointed his cabinet of old communists from the so-called clan of the Nakhjivan region. He and his support system were formed in the 1970s and 1980s, and have deep roots in central and regional administrative structures. Since 1991, Azerbaijan has joined the UN, the OSCE, and Council of Europe. Heydar Aliyev articulated the official aim of drawing closer to the West, and since 2003 his son Ilham has maintained the memberships, the rhetoric, and the forms. His government says that it is building democracy, though it continues to commit violations of all the agreements, both in letter and in spirit.

Conditions in 2013–14 changed for several reasons. First, Ilham stood for election to a third term in the fall of 2013, as a result of a constitutional change led by the YAP-controlled Milli Majlis. This change was unusual for the post-Soviet states—even Vladimir Putin had stepped down for one term in line with Russia's Constitution, which also has two-term limits on its presidency. Ilham and his supporters seemed to think that he was above even the appearance of legality. During the 2013 election, the handpicked foreign election monitors did not have the credibility of those from the ODIHR. At the same time, the EuroMaidan uprising began in Kyiv, raising the specter that had dogged Ilham since 2003 of a color revolution led by opposition parties and youth activists after a tainted election monitored by OSCE/ODIHR. After the 2013 elections, the Aliyev regime jailed critics, especially those under forty years of age. The Baku office of the OSCE was downgraded to a projects office. Top figures in Aliyev's government attacked European observers and the United States, dismissing their criticism of official actions as anti-Azerbaijani—thus conflating the regime with the state.

Throughout 2014, many more human rights activists and journalists, including some of the most prominent ones, were jailed. From December 2014 through early 2015, on the heels of a conversation with US State Department representatives, including Secretary John Kerry, the Aliyev government arrested Radio Liberty contributor Khadija Ismayilova and shut down the Radio Liberty offices in Baku, and extended the detention of major human rights defenders. Regime politicians, including Ramiz Mehdiyev and Ali Hasanov, claimed that the West was trying to overthrow the Aliyev government in another color revolution. At the same time, commercial deals and cultural exchanges continued, ambassadors in Western capitals continued their normal routines, and Baku played host to high-profile European events. The president and oligarchs trumpeted Azerbaijan's good business climate while they kept second homes in the United Kingdom and the United States and sent their children to Western universities.

What is going on in Baku? Put crudely, there are two possibilities—the president is either in control, or he is not. In the first case, Ilham Aliyev is in control, orchestrating the entire show, giving here and taking there. He agrees to working commissions, declarations of intent, and draft laws, but honors none of them and continues the corrupt practices and human rights crackdowns, unleashing security services against critics and their families. He has embraced the many advisers inherited from his father, and they subordinate themselves to him. In this scenario, Aliyev is the master deceiver, a ruthless mafia boss (as a January 2015 *New York Times* editorial put it) with good English and expensive suits who is at ease in the West. Having weathered previous threats of Western disfavor, he ignores them because he believes that he can continue to get away with the dual image in exchange for his oil, his country's strategic location, and his anti–Islamic State policies. This is the profile of a man who craves the power of his office.[31] The wealth, notoriety, and perquisites of office are welcome by-products but are not the objects of desire.

The other possibility is that Ilham Aliyev does not control all the actions of his appointees and may not even have complete knowledge about them. State power and wealth are divided among oligarchs, the most important ministers and their families. Aliyev is the "keystone," as one Azerbaijani official called him, binding the system together and offsetting pressures of various factions because all agree to support him as president, as head of his own powerful "clan," as Azerbaijan's now familiar face to the world, and as son of the National Leader. But each minister is a boss in his own right with a budget, a hierarchy of retainers, and in some cases an armed force. Aliyev and his inner circle agree to certain levels of cooperation and some repressions, especially those that protect the wealth and privilege of the first family or the oligarchs. The power brokers may fight among themselves, using their clients like pawns. Individual repressions, the harsh anti-American rhetoric, and even the turn toward Russia may have been initiatives of Aliyev or of power ministers or others in the inner circle. In this scenario Ilham may be more interested in the wealth, privilege, and comfort of himself and his family; political power is the means for him to achieve and protect these gains. If this is the case, he is, in part, a tool also for the real politicos, the old Soviet-era "crocodiles" whose influence has led not only to the regime's copying of Vladimir Putin's repression of civil society and its critics, but also of Azerbaijan's parroting the Kremlin's criticism of the United States and turning toward Russia. They dominate the system, which has changed very little since Soviet times, and although Ramiz Mehdiyev and Ali Hasanov may take turns in the public eye, in reality, nothing changes.

There is ample evidence, though most of it is anecdotal, that Azerbaijan's government operates on some variation of the latter model, allowing that Aliyev has grown stronger with experience. Analysts have noted that Ilham made no changes to the initial array of top ministers and advisers left by his father in 2003. The few changes he made in 2005 did not affect the power ministries, except for the creation of the National Security Ministry, which had to coexist with the Ministry of Internal Affairs until the dissolution of the former in late 2015. In a 2009 report, one journalist reported remarks by Azerbaijani analysts: "Ilham is an indecisive man who fears contacts with journalists, avoids speaking in public, and has a weakness for risk; . . . [he] cannot equal his father as far as political games are concerned." Moreover, "Many commentators on the Azerbaijani political scene claim that it is the [old guard], especially the chief of the president's administration, Ramiz Mehdiyev, and Interior [Internal Affairs] Minister Ramil Usubov, not the president, who rule from behind the scenes."[32] An added complication is the need to manage challenges from the so-called clans, the two most powerful being the patron-client networks from Nakhjivan, home of the Aliyev family, and the "YerAz," those whose families came from territory now in Armenia. One Azerbaijani analyst suggested in 2009 that the groups were competing for oil money and creating internal disruption.[33] Foreign diplomats have reported in private that Mehdiyev kept them in meetings so they were late for an appointment with the president, who reportedly shrugged it off by saying that "he does that all the time."

This leadership is not likely to leave the scene in five years or even ten, barring ill health or unforeseen events such as removal from office or assassination. In Azerbaijan, there are presently no incentives for an elite change of cadres or of heart. Although Mehdiyev is almost eighty and Usubov is nearly seventy, others are in their fifties or early sixties and surely are anticipating that they will be staying in their posts for the next five to ten years: Minister of Emergency Situations Kemaleddin Heydarov, Presidential Advisor Ali Hasanov, Transportation Minister Ziya Mammedov, and Ilham Aliyev himself. None will be a source of change unless they all to agree to relinquish some power and wealth, an unlikely eventuality even under current economic pressures.

What does all this mean for Aliyev, and for Azerbaijan? This regime's primary source of stability is the interdependent oligarchy, not the president as an individual and certainly not the system defined by the Constitution, which describes division of power among branches of government and the rule of law that exists only as a formality. Even if Aliyev wanted to make changes, like curtailing the outrageous use of violence by the police, he would run up against the rest of the system. The rise to power of a proreform faction, possibly in some sort of "palace coup," appears unlikely. The structure suggests that change will only come with the proverbial gun to the head—and all concerned should hope that the gun is only proverbial.

The Gun to the Head

One source of change could be violence either from war or revolution, the literal "gun to the head" of the regime. In the case of war, Aliyev and the oligarchs could rally the populace against an external enemy—polls on attitudes toward Mountainous Karabagh and Azerbaijan's neighbors show that the majority distrusts outsiders more than its own rulers. The result would be catastrophic, with millions displaced or killed. These are reasons that renewed war in Karabagh must be avoided.

A color revolution, Aliyev's fear since his accession to power, would generate a different scenario. In such a revolution, Aliyev's character and relation to
power could be a predictor of his response. On one hand, he might choose to
fight for power and plunge the country into chaos, using all the force available
to him against his opponents. His most likely source of help would be Russia,
which would gladly assist for its own interest more than for any notion of supporting Aliyev or Azerbaijan. On the other hand, he and his family could be
on the first plane to their foreign condos and never look back, but doing so
would not save the country.

The bloodshed would be ordered by the crocodiles, not only the old generation but also those they have nurtured in their image and likeness, who
would not hesitate to open fire on their countrymen to preserve their status quo. Whether one faction called for Russian assistance, or whether civil
war broke out and led Putin to provide "fraternal assistance" in the interests
of stability against "fascists" (or Islamists), the danger of a blood bath and
the partitioning of Azerbaijan among its neighbors would increase. Russia
would certainly take the north and Baku, thus gaining control of the oil, gas,
and pipelines. Calm might be restored over streets choked with corpses. Or
Russian intervention could open the door for extremists, including Islamist
radicals from the Caucasus Mountains, Syria, Iraq, or elsewhere. Iran, with its
mostly defensive military doctrine, would be likely to focus on guarding its
border against Sunni radicals rather than striving to take a piece of Azerbaijani
territory in the south. But Iranians would certainly favor transportation and
energy deals with Russia and might aid their sometime ally Armenia, and
Armenian forces in Karabagh could use the unrest to advance. Revolution
would thereby become an existential threat to Azerbaijan, not merely to the
regime. Since Azerbaijan is a small country, about the size of Maine,[34] sudden
occupation and partition would make it difficult for outside powers to mount
a defense, even if they wanted to do so. Ironically, corrupt and brutal as the
current government is, its overthrow could be disastrous.

But there are many variations short of violent revolution. First, revolutions
do not happen abruptly, or merely "happen" at all. Revolutions are made, as
historians will attest. The causes develop over months and years. They require
leaders who can articulate grievances and a vision for the future and who can
then mobilize people for action. An attentive regime can see signs of popular discontent, weaknesses of its own system, the emergence of an alternate
scenario, and, often, rival leaders. Prudent rulers can respond. Rulers who
do not see the potential for revolution, who underestimate it, or who believe

that it can be quashed with violence alone, may appear strong but are more vulnerable. Such was the case with the French, Russian, and Iranian revolutions of the past two hundred and fifty years, and with the post-Soviet color revolutions of the past twenty-five. The present regime in Baku is vigilant and tends to overestimate rather than underestimate potential threats. Azerbaijanis have complaints, and these have grown, but opinion polls, at least until the economic convulsions of 2015, suggest that the majority still expects a better future. The real question in this case is not whether the regime would notice trouble brewing—because anger is apparent now—but whether it would handle it with some combination of concessions, persuasion, and punishment, or only with brute force. Thus far, force has been the preferred method, using police, security forces, jails, and compliant courts.

How long force could be used without producing backlash is an open question. The last time that ordinary Azerbaijanis fought back against armed force was at the end of the Soviet period, when their own party-state system was divided and the accumulated anger and frustration of Soviet rule and the Karabagh conflict had become intolerable. Leadership came from respected intellectuals who formed the Popular Front under the nose of the communist party. In mid-2016, Azerbaijan was not at such a point, and it is hard to tell whether the economic disruptions of 2016 could push the public to that stage. The most provocative issues in recent years have been economic, and with oil prices hovering between $30 and $40 a barrel in the winter of 2015–16,[35] currency devaluation and inflation have already produced public protests. Concessions by the regime would mean getting a handle on inflation, creating jobs, and bolstering other social and economic supports such as state salaries and pensions. If effective support does not come soon, popular anger and desperation could peak in the coming years. Aliyev talked soothingly about currency reevaluation; in his Davos speech in January 2016, he claimed that the manat value was 1.3 to the dollar (it was 1.55), which was "normal," and that Azerbaijan's economy was diversified and not overly dependent on oil revenue. Not only were these claims untrue, but they did not address the daily needs of the people of Azerbaijan.

Given the accumulated wealth of a small minority, taxing that wealth to return money to state coffers would seem essential. What would the oligarchs do, in that case—pay up or abandon their country and president? If Aliyev and the regime cannot or will not make the decisions that ensure that money goes into the state budget and reaches the populace, they become yet more vulnerable to opposition criticism and radical appeals. It is hard to know how much public trust the regime or the Milli Majlis enjoy, given that past elections were too manipulated to gauge anyone's actual popularity. The major opposition, mainly in the Milli Shura (formed from the Popular Front and Yeni Müsavat), is prepared to lead popular sentiment and has already articulated the problems of poverty and corruption. But that older generation is quickly being supplanted by younger activists whose leaders (Ilgar Mammadov and, until the spring of 2016, Rasul Jafarov) are in jail. The more radical faction on the horizon is the extremist faction of Salafis and their link to the Islamic State. At present, the radicals are too few to threaten the regime or to lead the secular society (as described in chapter 6), but if the regime fails to solve economic problems in two or three years and the secular opposition remains marginalized, the Islamists might have a better chance to gain followers.

If the Aliyev regime can restore the economy with a combination of lower prices, jobs, and reduced public spending, it will have secured its position, because improved economic conditions have been more powerful than improved political conditions. Well-designed economic policies implemented in the next year or two could allow Azerbaijan to continue much like has in the past, supporting or raising the standards of living for the bulk of the population while isolating the minority that demands free speech and competitive elections.

In the longer term, change comes from the rise to power of a new generation, which is inevitable, and that this generation will have a new vision of the future, which is not inevitable. The elites in and out of government have worked hard within the established structures to shape the next generation. A generational change in some ministries would not affect aims or methods, nor is there any guarantee that younger men or women would be interested in greater distribution of wealth or power. Some perhaps believe their own propaganda, that Azerbaijan is already democratic and tolerant as well as stable and prosperous and therefore is in no need of reform.

Over time, the number of Western-educated women and men will increase. Many of them are already returning from abroad and work in the government. Their views will slowly change Azerbaijani society, just as creeping modernization changed the Soviet Union. A Western educational experience will have allowed young Azerbaijanis to see models of public life that are different from and possibly preferable to those that Azerbaijan inherited from the Soviet Union. Students in the United Kingdom, France, or Germany would see police that can enforce order without violence or caprice. They would see that demonstrations and public debate are not inherently destabilizing, and that leaders can tolerate direct criticism, even ridicule, without resort to criminal prosecution of satirists and comics. The opposite view, the claim that debate means chaos and a rigid sense of "respect" for authority is required, feeds the Azerbaijani backlash against critics of the present rulers. A new generation might see that it is in their own interest to base society's stability on a more equitable distribution of resources and political opportunity, rather than force. This is a vision for the long term. Its victory depends on the ability of Western-educated women and men to present its benefits and nuances persuasively, and in contrast to a competing vision brought by youth trained in Iran, Saudi Arabia, or Russia.[36] It is a vision that can win if Azerbaijan avoids violent upheaval or war in the coming decade.

Azerbaijan and the United States: Struggle of Image, Influence, and Values

Since the opening of the US Embassy in Baku in March 1992, the US government has been able to receive high-quality information about Azerbaijani government, society, economy, ruling elites, opposition politics, media, and more. The State Department, the intelligence community, US-based nongovernmental organizations, academic institutions, serious media organizations, and research groups have many knowledgeable experts who have been producing excellent assessments of Azerbaijan. International organizations such as Freedom House, Amnesty International, OSCE/ODIHR, and others report regularly on conditions in Azerbaijan. In short, good information is available. Not everyone makes use of it.

At the policy level, many factors come into play. Policymakers may be unsure how to assess contradictory information of varying quality from experts who disagree. The best informed still face the competing priorities and political sensitivities of allies or constituents. Azerbaijan has lavished resources on lobbying, which has become ubiquitous and has helped to muddy the waters. Lobbyists target critics and anticipate criticism. Experts paid by lobbyists or SOCAR present Azerbaijan's case from a seemingly neutral position, using regime verbiage and stressing energy and military cooperation while ignoring or even excusing the regime's antidemocratic practices. Legislators are invited on trips to Baku paid for by funds that are funneled through so-called cultural organizations to disguise the actual sources of funds in Azerbaijan government entities. On highly choreographed trips, they see what the ruling elites want them to see and hear again the same message about the "tough neighborhood" and strategic partnership. Watchdog groups and investigative journalists have revealed the patterns, the money involved, and the people who not only support Azerbaijan's government but misrepresent its record on democracy and human rights. Yet the lobbying in all forms continues to have successes, and it is not likely to stop as long as Azerbaijani representatives have the money to sustain their effort.

For more than a decade, the annual Freedom House Nations in Transit reports detailed the successes and failures of Azerbaijan (and other postcommunist states) according to seven indicators: central governance, local governance, electoral process, judiciary, civil society, media, and corruption. The 2016 Freedom House report gave Azerbaijan the lowest scores yet, and affirmed that it was a "consolidated authoritarian regime."[37] With approximately a hundred political prisoners, trumped-up criminal charges against regime critics, long prison sentences for opposition figures, the beatings, arrests and murder of journalists, and ignoring findings of OSCE/ODIHR election monitors, recommendations of the Venice Commission, and rulings of the European Court on Human Rights, Azerbaijan has earned its bad reputation. Since 2011, Berlin-based European Stability Initiative reports *Caviar Diplomacy* and *Disgraced* revealed how Azerbaijani lobbying and gifts won over representatives of democratic states in the CoE, leading them to assert that Azerbaijan was democratic. Print and online coverage of news and opinion on Azerbaijan in the *Washington Post*, *New York Times*, and *Foreign Policy* have raised the profile of both human rights abuses in Azerbaijan and Baku's Western "friends" in the United States. International reporting on Azerbaijan's human rights violations and tainted elections seems to have collided during 2014–16, with the steady expansion of persuasion and lobbying efforts from Baku and public revelations about them.

In May 2015, the *Washington Post* reported the findings of an Office of Congressional Ethics investigation that ten members of Congress (some accompanied by spouses), thirty-two staff members, and three former White House staff took an all-expenses-paid trip to Azerbaijan in 2013 and received expensive gifts. The money was paid through two Houston-based nonprofit corporations, the Turquoise Council of Americans and Eurasians and the Assembly of the Friends of Azerbaijan (AFAZ).[38] But the funds came from SOCAR, Azerbaijan's state oil company, which had founded AFAZ just before the invitations to the conference were issued. The members told the investigators that they had obtained approval for the trip from the congressional ethics committee and were not aware of the source of funding at the time.[39] Analytical articles by journalists—from Michael Weiss's "Corleones of the Caspian,"[40] to Till Bruckner's "How to Build Yourself a Stealth Lobbyist"[41]— soon followed, furnishing detail to a wider audience on the corruption of the Aliyev regime and the "willing blinders" which legislators, some think tanks, and even a few academic institutions have donned in allowing the regime's apologists to function without scrutiny or challenge.

Is the lobbying successful? Many current and former members of Congress are members of AFAZ, the Congressional Azerbaijan Caucus, or the Azerbaijan-America Alliance, the last of which was (until early 2016) run by the millionaire son of Azerbaijan's transportation minister. These "friends of Azerbaijan" blur the lines between the Aliyev regime and the people of Azerbaijan. They present themselves as vocal supporters of "Azerbaijan," but really advocate for the Aliyev regime and its business opportunities, not the well-being or rights of the people of Azerbaijan. Some claim that Azerbaijan is not merely a valuable strategic or energy partner, but a democratic state that "shares US values," in the words of former US congressman Dan Burton, then-president of the AAA.[42] Past and current members of Congress and various state representatives remain members of AAA and AFAZ, despite repeated revelations about fixed elections, political prisoners, and influence peddling. Some try to moderate their language while preserving the essential message. In a March 2015 post on the *Roll Call* website, former Texas congressman Silvestre Reyes repeated the official Aliyev regime arguments about Azerbaijan as a strategic partner for the United States and as a tolerant, moderate Muslim-majority state that enfranchised women and sells oil to Israel. Reyes clarified that the regime's tolerance was toward the Jewish community (rather than dissenting Azerbaijanis) and he avoided calling Azerbaijan a democracy, although he was one of the 2013 election monitors who affirmed the quality of the election that ODIHR would denounce. Reyes revealed, in this post, at least one reason why these deals will continue—they bring money into US businesses and states that partner with Azerbaijan.[43]

One Washington reporter posed the question about the impact of US congressional representatives "parroting Baku mantras about democracy" to exiled dissident Emin Milli during his visit to Washington in the spring of 2015. The reporter wrote:

> When I asked him what difference it made if US members of Congress praised the regime, he could barely contain his fury: "The effect

is devastating," he said, "because you have democratically elected representatives confirming the legitimacy of a mafia. The legitimacy of thugs. The legitimacy of a group of people who kill, torture, and put people in jail just for expressing their opinion."[44]

A political actor might argue that the United States cannot prioritize individual rights when considering international crises on a vast scale, or even that the United States should stay out of the troubles of the world. According to Freedom House, democracy is on a global downswing. Transparency International rates two-thirds of the countries in the world as "very corrupt." Does Azerbaijan's pattern simply represent a global phenomenon, one of those periodic swings of the pendulum, against which the prodemocracy forces cannot win? Might that pattern be a reason to excuse Azerbaijan as being no worse than many other places? And in the present high-risk international environment, how important are fair elections and a free press, even a hundred political prisoners, if Azerbaijan serves as a bulwark against Islamist radicalism? There is a case to be made on both sides of this dichotomy, as the example of US-Iranian relations in the twentieth century illustrates.

For complex geopolitical reasons, including Cold War–era anticommunism, the United States supported the shah of Iran, taking over Britain's place of primacy in that country after World War II. The US gained an ally along the southern border of the Soviet Union, a source of good intelligence, and enhanced energy security. To defend Mohammad Reza Shah, the young but increasingly repressive monarch, the United States orchestrated in 1953 the overthrow of elected Prime Minister Mohammad Mossadeq. As the shah became more corrupt and brutal, successive US administrations turned a blind eye, used the Central Intelligence Agency to create and train his security apparatus SAVAK, and sold billions of dollars of weapons to him despite the growing poverty of the populace and rising number of political prisoners. Most Americans were unaware of Iran's grievances against the United States, particularly the overthrow of Mossadeq, until the Islamic Revolution of 1979, when the victorious Islamist forces used them to portray the United States as the Great Satan.[45]

Although Azerbaijan is quite different from Iran, as discussed in chapter 6, there are lessons to be learned from the events of 1979. Despite his claims, the shah's repressions were not essential to "stability" in Iran's "tough neighborhood." On the contrary, the regime's brutality and corruption caused the instability that led to his fall. US support for the shah's regime turned his opponents into America's enemies. The work of American advisers and sales of weapons enabled the shah's manipulation of the political and economic systems; repression of intellectuals; and the arrest, torture, and murder of hundreds of thousands of Iranians. The damage to US soft power and reputation throughout the nonaligned and developing world was great, even when the shah remained on his throne. When the shah's opponents came to power, the United States paid for its choices—a political and economic price as well as a loss of face, of its image as a uniquely moral power grounded in values of liberty, equality, and rule of law, as articulated in its founding documents.

Azerbaijan, like Iran, is energy rich and strategically located. It is similarly a society ruled by a highly centralized, personalized regime. Western criticism regarding its human rights violations and tainted elections indeed earns the wrath of the Aliyev regime. In a private conversation in 2015, one proregime Western analyst insisted that such pressure "only succeeds in driving a wedge" between Baku and Washington or Brussels. But when Azerbaijan's government joins Western organizations whose aims include building democracy and rule of law, and then does not uphold those values, who is driving the wedge? Western critics are holding up a mirror to authorities in Baku. Ruling circles may not like the image, but the solution to the problem is not covering the mirror; it is changing the reality the mirror reflects. The quashing of free speech, assembly, and investigative reporting, and the fixing of elections and jailing monitors who uncover fraud, are not tools to build a stable society, and US and European observers should not accept the claim that they are. Criticism of dirty elections, bogus arrests, torture, and the manipulation of laws and courts to serve an autocratic regime is appropriate, even a duty, for those who embrace Western values. Truthtelling about Azerbaijan's political climate would show that Americans are committed, or renewing a commitment, to their own stated values and are giving principled support to the democratic opposition that struggles in Azerbaijan. Vocal and policy support for democratic open society from Washington would, moreover, rob extremists (as well as authoritarians in Baku or Moscow) of the argument that the United States is more interested in oil and landing rights than in the fate of human rights defenders and human rights themselves. If that opposition later comes to power, the United States reaps the benefit of having supported it and its values when it was weak. Under the current regime, the United States (and the EU) can maintain military and commercial relations with the government on a commercial "as needed" (transactional) basis, but not pretend the regime is democratic or that it shares US values.[46]

In the present international climate, the United States and other Western actors need to do more than reveal and criticize abuses of human beings and principles of democracy. The West faces a global war of ideas in which its political and intellectual leaders must make the case for democracy and human rights in order to counteract the blurring of lines between democracy and authoritarianism. As Gerald Knaus has eloquently and passionately argued (see chapter 5), authoritarians argue for a "special type of democracy" and strive to confuse legitimate elections with rigged elections and actual criminals with political prisoners. Documents like those of the SCO further develop the antidemocratic offensive, using Western terminology like "universal moral foundations of social life" to describe social norms that are defined by and support an authoritarian regime against the rights and the dignity of the individual in society. Authoritarian regimes have cleverly used Western rhetoric and electronic technology to make their case to the world audience, not by arguing for repression but by arguing for stability and "public safety," as if to imply that public discourse and dissent are a threat to both. The West has relaxed in the idea that its vision is clear and its ideals "sell themselves" because they are noble and advantageous for societies and individuals. Western thinkers do not always see that public debate can be construed as chaos. The influence of authoritarian ideas from the SCO and Russia's news outlet RT to right-wing parties in Western states, notably in the comforting appeal of the concept that *Die Zeit* political editor Jochen Bittner has called "orderism," has shown itself to be persuasive around the world—including, Bittner notes, in Europe and the United States.[47] The success of authoritarian ideas relies in part on the deceptive use of words and information, but also on widespread ignorance of the real meaning of democracy and human rights. The antiauthoritarian response must entail clarity of ideas and their foundations.

Democracy and human rights in the Western view are grounded in respect for the individual based on the idea of human worth, that all are "created equal" and endowed with "inalienable rights." Indeed, the documents that enshrine these concepts are Western and come from the Judeo-Christian tradition. As a result, they are not "universal" in origin but are believed to be universal in applicability. This is a case that Westerners must make. Human rights and the democratic system that protects them are not incompatible with stability or social peace. On the contrary, respect for and protection of the individual, rather than a system that privileges a single class or a governing "order," are the best guarantee of social harmony and stability. Making an argument for the "social contract," for defining the rights and responsibilities of citizenship, and for protecting the individual or the minority in a system of majority rule may seem like debate points from an old-fashioned civics class. But this is not a return to eighteenth-century documents. Rather, the ideas at the core of Western democracy must be renewed and restated in light of the lessons from the challenges of totalitarianism and the present authoritarianism. They must be made new in the globalism of the twenty-first century and presented to a global audience as an answer to the claims of authoritarian states.

What does Washington risk in the case of Azerbaijan by telling the truth and arguing for democratic principles? Aliyev regime spokespersons have shown their rejection of criticism with their repeated vitriolic attacks on the United States, accusations of subversion, and the claim of Western "double standards" because the Western democracies have problems of their own which, Azerbaijanis ignore, are repeatedly the subject of publicly conducted domestic clashes within the United States and Europe. Realistically, what are Baku's alternatives to dealing with the West on a transactional basis? Will the West lose influence in Baku by "showing less love"? Judging by the interactions of the past two years, neither the United States nor Europe has much influence left to lose. Will the Aliyev regime turn fully to Russia? Certainly, plans for a north–south trade corridor connecting Iran and Russia through Azerbaijan have accelerated during 2015–16, and public talk of coordinating antiterrorism activity among the three powers has increased.[48] Nonetheless, for the reasons noted, Aliyev and the oligarchs want to keep their Western profile, their condos, and their shell companies, even as Baku's representatives alternately lobby and insult Western leaders. Will Azerbaijan deprive Turkey and Europe of oil and gas and sell them instead to Russia and China? It is not likely to narrow its own options by forsaking the Baku–Tbilisi–Ceyhan pipeline or the planned TANAP and TAP gas pipelines. Finally, the gap between the regime and the state must be stressed. Despite the presentations of the Aliyev regime, what is good for the regime is not necessarily good for the state or the people of Azerbaijan.

For the United States, the concern for democracy and human rights is both a practical and an ideological matter. As former US ambassador to Azerbaijan Richard D. Kauzlarich argued in congressional testimony in February 2015,

> Human rights are a major US security concern. We support, as we have for two decades, the independence and territorial integrity of Azerbaijan. We are limited in what we can do, however, when the regime in Baku suppresses liberal democratic institutions, arrests those who peacefully

oppose the lack of democracy and human rights in Azerbaijan, and creates political and social space for other forces that are more dangerous to real stability in Azerbaijan. Make no mistake: radical Islamists are quickly filling the void. They not only burn American and Israeli flags but also send recruits to fight in Syria. When these fighters return to Azerbaijan they represent not only a threat to Azerbaijan but to US security interests as well. That is why human rights are not a minor issue.[49]

In 2016, with a global oil glut depressing prices and financial turmoil in the world and in Azerbaijan, the Aliyev regime faces a new environment. The leaders have choices. Official rhetoric adjusts, but actual change is so far incremental. Economic reform, limited in scope, is beginning; political reform is remote. Cheap oil makes Azerbaijan more vulnerable to pressure for prodemocratic change from within and without. Aliyev has long feared a color revolution, but has pursued precisely the repressive policies that caused those revolutions. His turn to Russia and Iran for partnerships in trade may be transactional, but both suffer the same losses with lower oil prices. The partnership against terrorism, a term all three countries have used to repress regime critics, bodes ill for human rights.

The United States, too, has choices in dealing with Azerbaijan in a new political environment with aggressive Russia, a new framework for Iran, and the vitality of the Islamic State. The US government can continue its nominally "tripod" approach to Azerbaijani relations, one that appears to privilege energy and strategic cooperation over democratization. Alternately, it can elevate the importance of democracy and human rights as both a component of security in the region and an investment in American influence ("soft power") for the long run. Washington cannot compel Baku to democratize, but it can decide what American power stands for in the twenty-first century—with or against the forces that seek to muzzle open discourse and mobilize regime violence against those who stand, peacefully, against repression, corruption, theft of public wealth, and free speech. Washington's choice, if it is upheld, is pressure on the Aliyev regime to support domestic rights and open society for Azerbaijan. The next choice will be up to Baku.

Notes

Chapter 1

1. Voltaire, "Reflections on Modern Historians and the Uncertainty of History," *The London Magazine*, 38 (July 1769): 375.

2. See, e.g., a series of edited volumes by Bruce Parrott and Karen Dawisha, including *Conflict, Cleavage and Change in Central Asia and the Caucasus* (Cambridge: Cambridge University Press, 1997); and Freedom House's Nations in Transit program and reports at https://freedomhouse.org/report-types/nations-transit.

3. See a useful critical review of this body of literature in Bohdan Harasymiw, "In Search of Post-Communism: Stalking Russia's Political Trajectory," *Canadian Slavonic Papers* 53, no. 2/4 (2011): 401–20; on 2010, see 410.

4. Crimean and Volga Tatars had the same experience, but never had SSR status in the Soviet Union.

5. Audrey L. Altstadt, *The Azerbaijani Turks: Power and Identity under Russian Rule* (Stanford, CA: Hoover Institution Press, 1992), chaps. 3–4; also Audrey L. Altstadt, "The Azerbaijani Bourgeoisie and the Cultural-Enlightenment Movement in Baku: First Steps toward Nationalism," in *Transcaucasia, Nationalism, and Social Change: Essays in the History of Armenia, Azerbaijan, and Georgia*, ed. Ronald Grigor Suny (Ann Arbor: University of Michigan Press, 1983), 197–207; and Tadeusz Swietochowski, *Russian Azerbaijan, 1905–1920: The Shaping of National Identity in a Muslim Community* (Cambridge: Cambridge University Press, 1985). On the politics of the independence period, see Richard Pipes, *The Formation of the Soviet Union: Communism and Nationalism, 1917–1923* (Cambridge, MA: Harvard University Press, 1955), chaps. 1, 2, and 6.

6. The term used was *Turk dili*, translated as either "Turkic" or "Turkish." The language was called "Azerbaijani" starting in 1937.

7. I am arguing against applying to Azerbaijan the popular "national building" thesis advanced by post-Soviet scholars about this early Soviet period. For full development of

this argument and details of the interwar period, see Audrey L. Altstadt, *The Politics of Culture in Soviet Azerbaijan, 1920–1940* (Abingdon, UK: Routledge: 2016).

8. For a detailed discussion of these topics, see Altstadt's *Azerbaijani Turks* and *Politics of Culture.*

9. I have written in detail about this and the Soviet-era Popular Front in *Azerbaijani Turks*, chaps. 12–13. Svante E. Cornell, *Azerbaijan since Independence* (Armonk, NY: M. E. Sharpe, 2011), 50–54, adds some details. Thomas de Waal, *Black Garden: Armenia and Azerbaijan through Peace and War*, rev. ed. (New York: New York University Press, 2013), 83–88, provides important nuances on the leadership.

10. These events were covered in the central and Azerbaijani newspapers. Among the more detailed were R. Lynev and A. Stepanova, "Razgovor na ploshchadi," *Izvestiia*, November 28, 1988; and in the Russian-language Azerbaijani daily *Bakinskii Rabochii* (*Baku Worker*, *BR*): E. Abaskulieva and R. Mustafa, "Trevozhnye dni i nochi," *BR*, November 23, 1988.

11. An English-language translation appeared in the *Caucasus and Central Asian Chronicle* (London) 8, no. 4 (August 1989); it is discussed by Audrey L. Altstadt, "Azerbaijan's Struggle toward Democracy," in Dawisha and Parrott, *Conflict, Cleavage, and Change*, 121.

12. Bill Keller, "Nationalists in Azerbaijan Win Big Concessions from Party Chief," *New York Times*, October 13, 1989, http://www.nytimes.com/1989/10/13/world/nationalists-in-azerbaijan-win-big-concessions-from-party-chief.html.

13. Incident reported by Z. Dzhapparov, "Trevozhnyi ianvar' v Lenkorane," *BR*, January 17, 1989. Etibar Mamedov confirmed in a private conversation in May 1991 that the Baku Popular Front had opposed the actions in Lenkoran.

14. Etibar Mamedov, private conversation with author, May 1991. See also Altstadt, *Azerbaijani Turks*, 195–99.

15. De Waal, *Black Garden*, 90–95, describes the events, and notes that rights activist Arzu Abdullayeva was also told that forces were ordered not to intervene to protect Armenian civilians.

16. Primakov was concurrently chairman of the Soviet of the Union, one of the two chambers of the Supreme Soviet of the Soviet Union. He had a background in intelligence, and had spent time in the Middle East as a *Pravda* reporter (his cover) and was a graduate of the Moscow Institute for Oriental Studies.

17. Radio Liberty (RL) Daily Report, report of Radio Free Europe/Radio Liberty (RFE/RL) Research Branch, quoting an "unnamed source," January 16, 1990.

18. RL continued to report from Moscow, where Soviet authorities said that "militants" were threatening Soviet power in Azerbaijan but that Soviet troops were "calming" them; Altstadt, *Azerbaijani Turks*, 300n152.

19. "Zaiavlenie chlena pravleniia NFA Etibara Mamedova na press konferentsii v Moskve," *Akhin*, no. 3 (March 1990). *Akhin* was a publication of the Popular Front. For details on Mamedov's remarks and on the events of Black January, see Altstadt, *Azerbaijani Turks*, 213–20.

20. "Ianvar' v Baku," *Moskovskie novosti*, August 12, 1990; and in *BR*, August 17, 1990. Thomas de Waal quoted Politburo member Andrei Girenko's suggestion that those on barricades were armed and that Elchibey had control over them, but neither Russian

nor local journalists who covered events, nor nonaligned observers, suggest that either of Girenko's assertions was true; see de Waal, *Black Garden*, 93.

21. Sheikh-ul-Islam Pashazade, private conversation with author, October 1992.

22. RL Daily Report, February 20, 1990, citing article in *Moskovskie novosti*, No. 7.

23. *Parliamentary Elections in Azerbaijan: 30 September 1990*, Commission for Security and Cooperation in Europe Report on Parliamentary Elections in Azerbaijan (Washington, DC: CSCE, 1990); for a detailed discussion, see Altstadt, "Azerbaijan's Struggle toward Democracy."

24. Altstadt, "Azerbaijan's Struggle toward Democracy," 125; and Cornell, *Azerbaijan since Independence*, 57–58.

25. "Birlesdiriji Xett: Milli-azadliq xett olmalidir," *Aydinliq*, August 2, 1991; English translation in H. B. Paksoy, ed., *Central Asia Reader: The Rediscovery of History* (Armonk, NY: M. E. Sharpe, 1994), 191–200.

26. Crimean and Volga Tatars were also involved in this movement, but the Volga Tatars were farther away and the purging and deportation of Crimean Tatars removed them from the post–World War II equation.

27. The Arabic script did not use all vowels (and varied in the use of consonants), which were often the source of differences in pronunciation between Anatolia and the eastern Caucasus.

28. Cornell, *Azerbaijan since Independence*, 318, provides summaries of several estimates. Some observers call these people "Azeri," but they call themselves and their language "Turk" or "Turki."

29. In the mid-1920s, Reza Shah (formerly Khan) rooted his legitimacy in the pre-Islamic ancient Persian cultural and historic identity. The regime's historian, Ahmed Kasravi, produced an official historical interpretation that mirrored the lingering nineteenth-century views of race and nationality, just as the Nazi and Soviet regimes would do in the 1930s and after.

30. Cornell, *Azerbaijan since Independence*, 320.

31. Thomas Goltz, *Azerbaijan Diary: A Rogue Reporter's Adventures in an Oil-Rich, War-Torn, Post-Soviet Republic* (Armonk, NY: M. E. Sharpe, 1998), 107–9.

32. I observed this during my first trip to Baku in 1980–81, when a reportedly French company was using three US and three British technical experts to assist its own employees.

33. For dispassionate yet personal coverage and analysis of the war, see de Waal, *Black Garden*.

34. Observed on my May–June 1992 trip to Baku.

35. Detailed accounts, but from different angles, are found in Altstadt, "Azerbaijan's Struggle toward Democracy," 125–27; Audrey L. Altstadt, "*O Patria Mia*: National Conflict in Mountainous Karabagh," in *Ethnic Nationalism and Regional Conflict: The Former Soviet Union and Yugoslavia*, ed. W. Raymond Duncan and G. Paul Holman Jr. (Boulder, CO: Westview Press, 1994), 101–36; Cornell, *Azerbaijan since Independence*, 62–66; Thomas Goltz, *Requiem for a Would-Be Republic: The Rise and Demise of the Former Soviet Republic of Azerbaijan: A Personal Account of the Years 1991–1993* (Ankara: Isis Press, 1994), chaps. 8 and 10, later reissued as his *Azerbaijan Diary*.

36. Cornell, *Azerbaijan since Independence*, 65.

37. Thomas Goltz, *Georgia Diary: A Chronicle of War and Political Chaos in the Post-Soviet Caucasus* (Armonk, NY: M. E. Sharpe, 2006), gives an eyewitness account on

Abkhazia. On the Russian-Georgia war over South Ossetia, see Charles King, "The Five-Day War: Managing Moscow After the Georgia Crisis," *Foreign Affairs* 87, no. 6 (November/ December 2008), https://www.foreignaffairs.com/articles/russia-fsu/2008-11-01/five-day -war. Ajaria was deprived of its high level of autonomy under President Mikheil Saakashvili in 2004.

38. See NATO secretary-general Anders Fogh Rasmussen's press conference with Ilham Aliyev at "NATO Secretary-General with President of Azerbaijan: Joint Press Point, 15 January 2014," YouTube video, 16:41, posted by "NATO," January 15, 2014, https://www .youtube.com/watch?v=5MlneMakw80.

39. See Ramiz Mehdiyev, "İkili standartların dünya nizamı ve müasir Azərbaycan," Milli. az, December 3, 2014, http://news.milli.az/politics/312011.html; or the Russian version at http://news.day.az/politics/539699.html. It was criticized in opposition publications, e.g., "Ramiz Mehdiyev Rauf Arifoğlunu tek qoymadı," *Azadlıq*, December 4, 2014, http://www.azadliq.info/56717.html.

40. At the time of writing, the amendments have not yet been ratified but are expected to be in September 2016. See Liz Fuller, "Azerbaijani President Unveils Proposed Constitutional Amendments," RFE/RL, July 19, 2016, http://www.rferl.org/content /azerbaijan-aliyev-proposed-constitutional-amendments-caucasus-report/27867826.html.

41. Dominika Bychawska-Siniarska, "An Alarming Situation in Azerbaijan," *New Eastern Europe*, August 7, 2014, http://www.neweasterneurope.eu/interviews/1288-an -alarming-situation-in-azerbaijan.

42. Azerbaijan Republic State Migration Service, accessed June 9, 2016, http://www .migration.gov.az/index.php?section=009&subsection=043&lang=en&pageid=4681

43. Audrey L. Altstadt, "Poverty Among the Cell Phones," *Caspian Crossroads*, Fall 2000, 18–26.

44. Margarita Antidze, "IMF Warns Azerbaijan on Oil Dependence, Business Climate," Reuters, November 21, 2014, http://reut.rs/1uhLGyg.

45. RL reporter Khadija Ismayilova was harassed repeatedly for reporting on secretly owned real estate and other assets of the ruling family. In December 2014, she was arrested, and in September 2015 she was sentenced to seven and a half years in prison on charges of tax evasion and embezzlement. She was released on probation in May 2016.

46. See "Corruption Perceptions Index 2014: Results," Transparency International, 2014, http://www.transparency.org/cpi2014/results; its score had improved slightly since 2012, and it remains better than Russia and most post-Soviet Central Asian states.

47. This is Goltz's vivid and apt term.

48. In the fall of 2014, the Extractive Industries Transparency Initiative (EITI), an international organization that maintains transparency standards for countries' oil, gas, and mineral resources, suggested that it might initiate an early review of Azerbaijan's compliance with its norms, in view of its crackdown on civil society. In retaliation, Azerbaijan announced that it was considering leaving EITI because that organization was interfering in Azerbaijan's internal affairs and beginning to act "like an NGO."

49. Mehdiyev, "İkili standartların dünya nizamı ve müasir Azərbaycan."

50. Azerbaijan is under European Command (EUCOM) rather than Central Command (CENTCOM). CENTCOM covers all the countries immediately to the south and east of Azerbaijan.

51. Israel buys substantial amounts of Azerbaijani oil, but precise data are elusive. A 2014 Bloomberg article quotes Brenda Shaffer, who has advised both the Israeli Ministry of Energy and Water Resources and Azerbaijan's SOCAR, as saying that the amount is 40 percent: see Zulfugar Agayev, "Israel's Top Oil Supplier Endures Gaza as Azeri Ties Grow," *Bloomberg*, September 28, 2014, http://bloom.bg/1LxuFc8; the figure was repeated on the website of the Azerbaijan Embassy in the United States, in "Israel Buys 40% of Its Oil from Azerbaijan," Embassy of the Republic of Azerbaijan to the United States of America, accessed December 28, 2015, http://www.azembassy.us/755-israel-buys-40-of -its-oil-from-azerbaijan.html. Maayan Jaffe-Hoffmann says that Israel's annual trade with Azerbaijan is $5 billion, an amount greater than Israel's trade with France; see Maayan Jaffe-Hoffmann, "Azerbaijan and Israel: A Covert but Strategic Relationship," *Jewish Press*, September 17, 2015, http://www.jewishpress.com/indepth/analysis/azerbaijan-israel -a-covert-but-strategic-relationship/2015/09/17/. But see also the argument by David Sheppard, John Reed, and Anjli Raval, "Israel Turns to Kurds for Three-Quarters of Its Oil Supplies," *Financial Times,* August 23, 2015, https://next.ft.com/content/150f00cc-472c -11e5-af2f-4d6e0e5eda22.

52. Wayne Merry, "Karabakh: 'Frozen' Conflict Nears Melting Point," *Open Democracy Review*, May 14, 2012, https://www.opendemocracy.net/od-russia/wayne-merry/karabakh -frozen-conflict-nears-melting-point.

53. "Russia, Azerbaijan, Iran Leaders Adopt Joint Declaration Following Baku Summit," *Sputnik News*, August 8, 2016, http://sputniknews.com/politics/20160808/1044065059 /summit-declaration-joint.html.

54. During Ilham Aliyev's visit to NATO in May 2014, an Azerbaijani journalist asked NATO secretary-general Anders Fogh Rasmussen about a possible double standard, and he replied that we criticize each other all the time; there's no double standard. See "NATO Secretary-General with President of Azerbaijan."

55. Rovshan Ibrahimov, *US-Azerbaijan Relations: A View from Baku*, Rethink Paper 17 (Washington, DC: Rethink Institute, 2014).

56. "İlham Aliyev: 'Bizim üçün Rusiya bazarı perspektilidir,'" Azadlıq Radiosu, December 2, 2014, http://www.azadliq.org/a/26720446.html.

57. The argument against "frozen" conflicts in favor of the image of "simmering" conflicts is from Dr. Rajan Menon, City College of New York.

58. Sibusiso Tshabalala, "The World's Super-Rich Are Seeking Second Citizenship in These Eight Countries," *Quartz*, July 10, 2015, http://qz.com/449621/the-worlds-super -rich-are-seeking-second-citizenship-in-these-eight-countries/.

Chapter 2

1. Suleiman Aliyarov (Aliyarli) and Bahtiyar Vahabzade, "Redaktorun Pochtundan," *Azerbaijan*, February 1988; English translation by the author with the title "Azerbaijan and the Nagorno-Karabagh Issue," *Journal of the Institute of Muslim Minority Affairs* 9, no. 2 (1988): 429–34. At an academic conference at Khazar University (Baku) in 2000, Professor Aliyarli told the inside story of this incident and the difficulties

of getting the "Open Letter" published in the Azerbaijani-language journal of the Writers Union.

2. Audrey L. Altstadt, "NagornoKarabagh: 'Apple of Discord'" in the Azerbaijan SSR," *Central Asian Survey* 7, no. 4 (1988): 63–78; Altstadt, "*O Patria Mia*"; and "Ethnic Conflict in Nagorno-Karabagh," in *Ethnic Conflict in the Post-Soviet World: Case Studies and Analysis*, ed. Leokadia Drobizheva, Rose Gottemoeller, Catherine McArdle Kelleher, and Lee Walker (Armonk, NY: M. E. Sharpe, 1996), 227–53.

3. De Waal, *Black Garden*. See also Svante E. Cornell, *Small Nations and Great Powers: A Study of Ethnopolitical Conflict in the Caucasus* (Richmond, UK: Curzon, 2001).

4. Similarly, the common spelling "Karabakh" is a transliteration from Russian. Both Azerbaijani and Armenian use a spelling that can be transliterated as "Garabagh," though the Armenian name is Artsakh. DeWaal correctly notes that when the phrase stands alone, it should be written as "Nagornyi" Karabagh.

5. Altstadt, "*O Patria Mia*." The Census of the Russian Empire of 1897, in its breakdowns by province and region *(uezd)*, shows an Armenian population through the area, but the dislocations of World War I led to population movement, and the subsequent NKAR boundaries did not coincide with old *uezd* boundaries.

6. The treaties of Moscow (March 16, 1921) and Kars (October 13, 1921), between the Bolsheviks and the Kemalist movement in Turkey, agreed to this status of Nakhjivan as part of Azerbaijan as well as other territorial matters.

7. I first made the argument about the distribution of the three territories in 1988 in "NagornoKarabagh: 'Apple of Discord.'" The information on the national composition of the communist party apparat comes from Michael Rywkin's presentation at the Third International Conference on Central Asia (University of Wisconsin, Madison), Fall 1988.

8. Cornell, *Azerbaijan since Independence*, 48, noted the topic had been "dormant." But de Waal, *Black Garden*, 156–57 and 164–71, explores several arguments and scholars who made them, noting that they had been made since the 1960s.

9. Felicity Barringer with Bill Keller, "A Test of Change Explodes in Soviet," *New York Times*, March 11, 1988, http://nyti.ms/1XLtMsq.

10. Cornell, *Azerbaijan since Independence*, 48–49.

11. See *L'Humanité*, November 18, 1987.

12. One of the earliest visitors to confirm this was a cameraman for journalist Hedrick Smith during their trip through Russia and the Caucasus in the early 1990s. We discussed his observations in 1992.

13. Refugees are defined as people who crossed an international border; IDPs are displaced within their own state.

14. Shusha IDP group interview with author, summer of 1992.

15. "Ekonomika Nagorno-Karabakhskoi Avtonomnoi Oblasti Azerbaidzhanskoi SSR: Problemy i perspektivyi," *Azarbayjan khalg tasarrufati / Narodnoe khoziaistvo Azerbaidzhana* 7 (1988): 8–16. See also Thomas de Waal, "The Nagorny Karabakh Conflict: Origins, Dynamics and Misperceptions," in *The Limits of Leadership: Elites and Societies in the Nagorny Karabagh Peace Process*, ed. Laurence Broers, *Accord* Issue 17 (London: Conciliation Resources, 2005), 12–16, http://www.c-r.org/downloads/17_Nagorny_Karabakh.pdf.

16. Hadjibeyli also wrote the national anthem of the independent republic of Azerbaijan, which was banned in the Soviet period.

17. Haykuhi Barseghyan and Shahla Sultanova, "History Lessons in Armenia and Azerbaijan," *CRS* Issue 631, Institute for War and Peace Reporting, March 2, 2012, https://iwpr.net/global-voices/history-lessons-armenia-and-azerbaijan.

18. For details of the cases, see Altstadt, *Azerbaijani Turks*, 200–201.

19. Cornell, *Azerbaijan since Independence*, 47–49, discusses the impact of rumors in 1988.

20. De Waal, *Black Garden*, 85, cites Soviet physicist and human rights activist Andrei Sakharov's memoirs that the planned building was a guest house for workers, not an aluminum plant, and the story was distorted in Baku. "Topkhana obretaet pervozdannyi vid," *Izvestiia*, November 28, 1988, reported on heavy equipment.

21. Azar Panahli, "When a Tree Isn't a Tree: The Topkhana Demonstrations of 1988," *Azerbaijan International* 2, no. 3 (1994): 56, http://www.azer.com/aiweb/categories/magazine/23_folder/23_articles/23_demonstrations.html. (Covers the following two block quotations.)

22. Nadia M. Diuk, *The Next Generation in Russia, Ukraine, and Azerbaijan: Youth, Politics, Identity, and Change* (Lanham, MD: Rowman & Littlefield, 2012), 70–71.

23. For the text of the Bishkek Protocol, see "Bishkek Protocol," United Nations Peacemaker, UN Department of Political Affairs, May 5, 1994, http://peacemaker.un.org/armeniaazerbaijan-bishkekprotocol94.

24. De Waal, *Black Garden*, 327–28.

25. Ibid., 96-98.

26. The most detailed account of Khojaly was published by an American reporter who lived in Azerbaijan during 1992 and 1993 and had just been to the town before the massacre: see Goltz, *Azerbaijan Diary*, 117–30. Thomas de Waal (*Black Garden*, 355n25) records the different numbers reported, and uses the total 477; I have followed his lead.

27. Noa Shori-Eyal, Eran Halperin, and Daniel Bar-Tal, "Three Layers of Collective Victimhood: Effects of Multileveled Victimhood in Intergroup Conflicts in the Israeli-Arab Context," *Journal of Applied Social Psychology* 44, no. 12 (2014): 778–94. Thanks to Ella McElroy, my research assistant at the Wilson Center, for bringing this article to my attention.

28. Russians constituted a plurality in Baku from the 1897 census to the 1959 census; Azerbaijanis were second largest group. For population data, see chapter 6 of this volume.

29. Cornell, *Azerbaijan since Independence*, 130–32; Section 907 has been suspended since 2001 but never rescinded.

30. Shori-Eyal, Halperin, and Bar-Tal, "Three Layers of Collective Victimhood."

31. This amendment was passed on October 24, 1992; before that time, US aid did come to Azerbaijan. An outstanding and frank description of the formulation, passage, and impact of Section 907 can be found in Thomas Goltz , "A Montana Perspective on International Aid and Ethnic Politics in Azerbaijan," Virtual Azerbaijan, 1996, http://www.zerbaijan.com/azeri/goltz1.htm. The article is more about politics in Washington concerning Azerbaijan.

32. Documents and other information on the Minsk Group are available at Minsk Group, "Who We Are," Organization for Security and Cooperation in Europe (OSCE), accessed June 9, 2016, http://www.osce.org/mg/108306.

33. The 1996 Lisbon Document outlines the principles, and includes a statement from Armenia that the inclusion of Karabagh within Azerbaijan predetermined its status, and

therefore was unacceptable. See *Lisbon Document 1996* (Lisbon: OSCE, 1996), 15–16, http://www.osce.org/mc/39539?download=true.

34. The Azerbaijan Ministry of Foreign Affairs website's chronology of negotiations on Karabagh does not include Key West among the 2001 meetings. See "Negotiations Chronology between Azerbaijan and Armenia," Republic of Azerbaijan Ministry of Foreign Affairs, accessed August 20, 2016, http://www.mfa.gov.az/en/content/856.

35. "Statement by the OSCE Minsk Group Co-Chair Countries," OSCE, July 10, 2009, http://www.osce.org/mg/51152. In April 2008, Serzh Sargsyan had succeeded Kocharyan as president of Armenia.

36. Esmira Jafarova, "OSCE Mediation of Nagorno-Karabagh Conflict," *Washington Review of Turkish and Eurasian Affairs*, March 2014, http://www.thewashingtonreview.org /osce-nagorno-karabakh/, citing *Nagorno-Karabakh: Risking War*, International Crisis Group Europe Report No. 187 (Tblisi/Brussels: International Crisis Group, November 14, 2007), 2.

37. One example of a concise, dispassionate report is Isak Svensson, *The Nagorno Karabakh Conflict: Lessons from the Mediation Efforts* (Brussels: Initiative for Peacebuilding/ Crisis Management Initiative, 2009).

38. Merry, "Karabakh."

39. Laurence Broers, *The Nagorny Karabakh Conflict: Defaulting to War* (London: Chatham House, 2016), 6.

40. "Caucasus Barometer 2013 Azerbaijan: Codebook," Caucasus Research Resource Centers, December 2013, http://caucasusbarometer.org/en/cb2013az/codebook/.

41. "Speech by Heydar Aliyev at the 55th session of the UN General Assembly, 07.09.2000," YouTube video, 10:04, posted by "undp_azerbaijan," November 7, 2015, https://www.youtube.com/watch?v=9KVTNDI3_Uw.

42. Shaun Walker, "Nagorno-Karabakh: Azeri-Armenian Ceasefire Agreed in Disputed Region," *Guardian* (London), April 5, 2016, https://www.theguardian.com/world/2016 /apr/05/nagorno-karabakh-azeri-armenian-ceasefire-agreed.

43. US diplomat, private conversation, 2015.

44. Elmar Chakhtakhtinskii, "Karabagh and Democracy: Putting Carriage Before Horse," *Azeri Report*, July 8, 2013, http://azerireport.com/index.php?option=com_conte nt&task=view&id=4055&Itemid=48.

45. Olga Kuzmina, "CGI Around Town: A Critical Look at Russia's Mediation in Nagorno-Karabakh," Center on Global Interests, July 1 2013, http://globalinterests .org/2013/07/01/cgi-around-town-a-critical-look-at-russias-mediation-in-nagorno -karabakh/. This is a report on Thomas de Waal's comments at the launch of the tenth anniversary edition of his book *Black Garden* at the Carnegie Endowment for International Peace on June 20, 2013, but he acknowledged that it was a reasonable summary.

46. The presenters were Ambassador Carey Cavanaugh, OSCE Minsk Group cochair Hamlet Isaxanli of Khazar University, Baku, and University of Chicago professor Ronald Suny; Brenda Shaffer, research director of the Belfer Center's Caspian Studies Program, was chair. "Negotiations on Nagorno-Karabagh: Where Do We Go From Here? (Event Summary)," Caspian Studies Program, Belfer Center, Harvard University, n.d. [2001], http://live.belfercenter.org/publication/12774/negotiations_on_nagornokarabagh.html.

47. These comments were denounced as antinationalist in an Armenian diaspora newspaper: Appo Jabarian, "Bardakjian and Suny Undermine Interests of Armenia and

Diaspora," *Armenian Life*, July 6, 2011, http://www.armenianlife.com/2011/07/06 /bardakjian-and-suny-undermine-interests-of-armenia-and-diaspora/.

48. See "The Karabagh Contact Group," Conciliation Resources, 2016, http://www.c-r .org/where-we-work/caucasus/karabakh-contact-group-0. Among written products were brochures "Individual Rights, Societal Choices" (November 2011) and "Beyond Exclusion" (February 2012). In December 2014, a KCG discussion with past and current Minsk Group members was held at the Carnegie Endowment for International Peace in Washington.

49. Among stories of this scandal, see Chakhtakhtinskii, "Karabagh and Democracy"; Damien McGuinness, "Azeri Writer Akram Aylisli Hounded for 'Pro-Armenian' Book," BBC, February 15, 2013, http://www.bbc.com/news/world-europe-21459091; and Daisy Sindelar, "In Azerbaijan, Anger at an Author, but Not Necessarily at His Argument," RFE/RL, February 8, 2013, http://www.rferl.org/content/azerbaijan-author-akram -aylisli/24897008.html.

50. "Caucasus Barometer 2013 Azerbaijan: Codebook."

Chapter 3

1. Quoted by Goltz, *Azerbaijan Diary*, xviii and 146.

2. The Milli Majlis restored Uzeyir Hadjibeyli's *National March*, with the original lyrics by Ahmad Javad, on May 27, 1992. I thank Isa Gambar for providing the link to the document from the Ministry of Foreign Affairs of Azerbaijan: http://www.mfa.gov.az/files /file/12.pdf.

3. Keller, "Nationalists in Azerbaijan."

4. I was part of a group of Western scholars and journalists acting as "informal observers" who met with US Embassy and CSCE personnel during election day. Our observations from polling places near Baku and from a few other places in the country noted similar patterns.

5. Goltz, *Azerbaijan Diary*, 223, describes the announcing of results.

6. On the details of the spring of 1992, including the changes of president, see Altstadt, "Azerbaijan's Struggle toward Democracy." For a dramatic eyewitness account, see Goltz, *Azerbaijan Diary*, chap. 8, esp. 114, 145–46, 186–205, 215–23.

7. "The Constitutional Act on the State Independence of the Republic of Azerbaijan (18 October, 1991)" [English translation], Presidential Library, Administrative Department of the President of the Republic of Azerbaijan, http://files.preslib.az/projects/republic /en/azr4_2.pdf; also "The Constitution of the Azerbaijan Republic," Constitution Finder, University of Richmond, accessed August 17, 2016, http://confinder.richmond.edu /admin/docs/local_azerbaijan.pdf.

8. Goltz, *Azerbaijan Diary*, 132–39.

9. Ibid., 135–39.

10. The Declaration of Restoration of State Independence of the Republic of Azerbaijan, adopted on August 31, 1991; the Constitutional Act on the State Independence of the Republic of Azerbaijan, adopted on October 18, 1991; and several laws governing

presidential succession were incorporated into the old Soviet-era Constitution of 1977. A new Constitution would be adopted in 1995.

11. Goltz, *Azerbaijan Diary*, 143–48.

12. This phrase is from ibid., 187; Goltz recounts this incident, at which he was present, on 185–90.

13. Ibid., 185–205.

14. Cornell, *Azerbaijan since Independence*, 65, uses this term, echoing the later Aliyev tone with regard to the Popular Front. However, he incorrectly says that the parliament building was "undefended."

15. The individuals were Iskendar Hamidov (internal affairs), Tofiq Gasimov (foreign affairs), Rahim Gaziyev (defense), and Sabit Bagirov (SOCAR).

16. Gambar and his advisers were fearful of a reversal during his weeks as acting president. When I first met him in June 1992, it seemed as if his entire staff virtually lived in their offices, nervously watching television for news in the presidential administration.

17. Altstadt, "*O Patria Mia.*"

18. De Waal, *Black Garden*, 210–17.

19. Goltz describes the "Mule" in *Azerbaijan Diary*, 149–53.

20. Goltz notes these and other examples of large-scale illegality in ibid., 267–82.

21. Azerbaijan adopted the Latin alphabet in June 1924; Turkey adopted it several years later. Each alphabet has some letters that the other does not, mostly reflecting differences in pronunciation.

22. Sharon Werning Rivera provides a useful summary of this literature; see Sharon Werning Rivera, "Elites in Post-communist Russia: A Changing of the Guard?" *Europe-Asia Studies* 52, no. 3 (2000): 413–32.

23. See the discussion in Goltz, *Azerbaijan Diary*, 289 and 477; the text of section 907 is available at "S.2532: FREEDOM Support Act (Enrolled Bill (Sent to President))," Federation of American Scientists, November 18, 2001, http://fas.org/terrorism/at/docs/s2532-102-sec907.htm. A waiver was adopted by President George W. Bush in response to Azerbaijan's aid for the US antiterrorism campaign following September 11, 2001.

24. Cornell, *Azerbaijan since Independence*, 72–73; and de Waal, *Black Garden*, 222–28.

25. Goltz went to Ganje before the other reporters and described the unfolding scene; see *Azerbaijan Diary*, 356–65.

26. During and after the events, I was in contact with Azerbaijani government advisers who were participants in the process and detailed these exchanges.

27. Heydar Aliyev was promoted to the Soviet Politburo under Yuri Andropov in November 1982 and purged by Mikhail Gorbachev in the summer of 1987. Aliyev's purge, I argue, allowed the Karabagh crisis to unfold. During his time in Nakhjivan, Aliyev became speaker of that autonomous republic's Supreme Soviet. See Altstadt, *Azerbaijani Turks*, chap. 11; and Goltz, *Azerbaijan Diary*, 64–73 and 177–82.

28. Goltz notes this (*Azerbaijan Diary*, 385–86), but is unclear on the dates. Since the inauguration was June 16, Elchibey must have departed on June 15, when he left the National Council, although his departure was not publicly known at the time. Cornell (*Azerbaijan since Independence*, 78) says that Elchibey's departure took place on June 18.

29. Altstadt, *Azerbaijani Turks*, chap. 11. His repatriation of the remains of purged poet Husein Javid from a numbered grave site in Siberia was the most dramatic gesture, but Javid—like Aliyev—was from Nakhjivan.

30. Goltz uses the term "arm-twisting" by the Turks to get Elchibey's agreement; see *Azerbaijan Diary*, 366–70.

31. Ibid., 385.

32. Ibid., 408–9, describes the claim made in the Milli Shura. Neither Goltz nor others at the time gave it any credence. The issue has been revisited by a younger generation of Azerbaijanis; Emin Milli, conversation with the author, May 2015. The twenty- and thirty-somethings of 2015 consider the newspaper coverage of the time to be persuasive. Robert Finn said that he was aware of the claim and considered it part of the smear campaign against Elchibey.

33. "Yer-Az" is said to mean "Yerevan-Azerbaijan."

34. Goltz, *Azerbaijan Diary*, 388–89.

35. "17 İYUN 1993, MİLLİ MƏCLİS," YouTube video, posted by "Etibar 1978," June 13, 2008, https://www.youtube.com/watch?v=lrEmkSEb0z0 (link discontinued); the final report, as adopted by the Milli Majlis on July 16, is found at the Milli Majlis website at http://www.meclis.gov.az/?/az/topcontent/46.

36. In addition to efforts of the US Embassy, the US Helsinki Commission (Commission for Security and Cooperation in Europe) circulated to members of Congress a letter addressed to Heydar Aliyev, urging Gambar's release and suggesting that the use of televised questioning was reminiscent of Stalin's show trials. Gambar and others credit this letter with securing his release.

37. Goltz, *Azerbaijan Diary*, 392.

38. Ibid., 415–21. Goltz noted few international observers, and recorded his personal observations and interviews. Although official figures were inflated, in Goltz's opinion they were not in essence wrong.

39. Mehmet Ali Bayar looms large in Goltz's *Azerbaijan Diary*. Bayar went on to serve at the UN and the Turkish Embassy in Washington. Goltz also describes conversations with Finn and Remler throughout 1992 and 1993.

40. Robert Finn, interview with author, May 2015.

41. Ibid. Finn said that people told him that they cried when he spoke. Several Azerbaijanis interviewed for this book said that they wept at hearing Finn speak Turkish.

42. Richard Miles later became US ambassador to Bulgaria and Georgia; Robert Finn became ambassador to Tajikistan and Afghanstan; and Philip Remler became OSCE ambassador in Moldova.

43. The brief episode of the Talysh-Mugan rebellion is described by Cornell, *Azerbaijan since Independence*, 75 and 84; and Goltz, *Azerbaijan Diary*, 412–14.

44. Goltz, *Azerbaijan Diary*, 414 and 448.

45. Ibid., 447–48.

46. The name was changed in 1994. On inclusion of Azerbaijan and related dates, see the timeline at "Our History," OSCE, accessed June 20, 2016, http://www.osce.org/whatistheosce.

47. This section, except where otherwise noted, is based on OSCE/ODIHR, *OSCE/UN Report of the OSCE/UN Joint Electoral Observation Mission in Azerbaijan*

on *Azerbaijan's 12 November 1995 Parliamentary Election and Constitutional Referendum* (Warsaw: OSCE/ODIHR, 1996), http://www.osce.org/odihr/elections /azerbaijan/14291?download=true.

48. See Goltz, *Azerbaijan Diary*, 459; on 410–11, Goltz describes Tofiq's "trial by television."

49. Each OSCE report noted the challenges of enfranchising displaced persons from Karabagh. The mobility of IDPs and incomplete voter lists for them provided thousands of people who might be used for multiple voting.

50. OSCE/ODIHR, *OSCE/UN Report for 1993*, 13–14.

51. OSCS/ODIHR *OSCE/UN Joint Electoral Observation Mission in Azerbaijan, 12 November 1995*.

52. OSCE/ODIHR, *Presidential Election in the Republic of Azerbaijan* (Warsaw: OSCE/ ODIHR, 1998), http://www.osce.org/odihr/elections/azerbaijan/14329?download=true.

53. Numbers noted by Cornell, *Azerbaijan since Independence*, 96.

54. Cornell's view; ibid.

55. OSCE/ODIHR, *Republic of Azerbaijan: Parliamentary Elections, 5 November 2000 & 7 January 2001—Final Report* (Warsaw: OSCE/ODIHR, 2001), http://www.osce.org/odihr/elections/azerbaijan/14265?download=true.

56. Phillip Remler, *Chained to the Caucasus: Peacemaking in Karabakh, 1987–2012* (New York: International Peace Institute, 2016), https://www.ipinst.org/2016/05 /peacemaking-in-karabakh.

57. Cornell, *Azerbaijan since Independence*, 98.

58. OSCE/ODIHR, *Armenian Presidential Election, September 24, 1996: Final Report* (Warsaw: OSCE/ODIHR, 1996), http://www.osce.org/odihr/elections/armenia /14149?download=true.

59. See Cornell, *Azerbaijan since Independence*, 99–103, for a sympathetic view of both Aliyevs.

60. The Turkish press announced his death seven months later, on July 31. Though officially denied, the rumor persisted that he had died long before the fall election. See editor's note to Audrey L. Altstadt, "Azerbaijan and Aliyev; A Long History and An Uncertain Future," *Problems of Post-Communism* 50, no. 5 (2003): 3–13.

61. OSCE/ODIHR, *Republic of Azerbaijan; Presidential Election 15 October 2003, OSCE/ODIHR Election Observation Mission Report* (Warsaw: OSCE/ODIHR, 2003), http://www.osce.org/odihr/elections/azerbaijan/13467?download=true.

62. Ibid., 10–11.

63. In 2000, there were 17 long-term and 200 short-term observers.

64. OSCE/ODIHR, *Republic of Azerbaijan; Presidential Election 15 October 2003,* 8.

65. Ibid., 26–29.

66. Jahan Aliyeva, "Georgia Pushes Friendship, Not Revolution with Azerbaijan," Azerbaijan Elections 2005, Eurasianet, October 31, 2005, http://www.eurasianet.org /azerbaijan/news/friendship_20051031.html.

67. Valerie J. Bunce and Sharon L. Wolchik, "Azerbaijan: Losing the Transitional Moment," in *Transitions to Democracy: A Comparative Perspective*, ed. Sharon Stoner and Michael McFaul (Baltimore: Johns Hopkins University Press, 2013), 411–12.

68. "Azerbaijan: Elections 2005, Party Profiles," Eurasianet, 2005, http://www
.eurasianet.org/azerbaijan/parties/index.html. Among pro-YAP parties were the Alliance
for Azerbaijan, Motherland (Ana Vatan) and Muasir (Modern) Müsavat.

69. Ibid.

70. Private conversation in Baku, 2005.

71. OSCE/ODIHR, *Republic of Azerbaijan: Parliamentary Elections, 6 November
2005—Final Report* (Warsaw: OSCE/ODIHR, 2006), http://www.osce.org/odihr
/elections/azerbaijan/17946?download=true. Separate was the final report for repeat
elections in May 2006 at OSCE/ODIHR, *Republic of Azerbaijan: Partial Repeat
Parliamentary Elections, 13 May 2006—Annex to the Final Report on the 6 November 2005
Parliamentary Elections* (Warsaw: OSCE/ODIHR, June 23, 2006), http://www.osce.org
/odihr/elections/azerbaijan/19596?download=true.

72. I witnessed this reaction in a conference in New York around this time.

73. Warren Mitofsky and Joe Lenski, "Adventure in Baku: Exit Polling in Azerbaijan,"
National Council on Public Polls, [n.d., circa 2006], http://ncpp.org/?q=node/77.

74. Christine Quirk lists the individuals and their districts: see Christine Quirk,
"Managed Democracy: Azerbaijan's Presidential Election," Quirk Global Strategies,
February 29, 2008, http://quirkglobalstrategies.com/blog/42-azerbaijan/63-managed
-democracy-azerbaijans-presidential-election.html. On 2005, see also Stoner and McFaul,
Transitions to Democracy, especially Valeria Bunce and Sharon Wolchik's article.

75. Noted by Andreas Herkel, PACE rapporteur in Azerbaijan, cited in *Caviar
Diplomacy*, 13, 14.

76. European Stability Initiative, *Caviar Diplomacy: How Azerbaijan Silenced
the Council of Europe* (Berlin: ESI, 2012), 11–14, http://www.esiweb.org/index.php
?lang=en&id=156&document_ID=131; on the United States, see page 10, citing the US
Embassy press release of December 2, 2005.

77. The range of views is described in ESI analytical papers, including *Caviar Diplomacy*
and *Disgraced: Azerbaijan and the End of Election Monitoring as We Know It* (Berlin: ESI, 2013),
http://www.esiweb.org/index.php?lang=en&id=156&document_ID=145.

78. "PACE Monitoring Committee Concerned with Deterioration of Human Rights
Situation in Azerbaijan," *Azeri Report*, May 28, 2008, http://azerireport.com/index2
.php?option=com_content&do_pdf=1&id=173.

79. Giorgi Gogia, *Tightening the Screws: Azerbaijan's Crackdown on Civil Society and
Dissent* (New York: Human Rights Watch, 2013), 4.

80. Private interview, 2015.

81. OSCE/ODIHR, *Republic of Azerbaijan: Presidential Election, 15 October 2008—
Final Report* (Warsaw: OSCE/ODIHR, 2008), http://www.osce.org/odihr/elections
/azerbaijan/35625?download=true.

82. "PACE Monitoring Committee Concerned With Deterioration of Human Rights
Situation in Azerbaijan."

83. See the European Commission for Democracy through Law (hereafter, Venice
Commission) 2008 activities at Venice Commission, "Activities by Year: 2008," Council of
Europe, 2014, http://www.venice.coe.int/webforms/events/?v=2008.

84. European Parliament, *Presidential Elections in Azerbaijan: Election Observation
Delegation, 13–16 October 2008* (Brussels: European Parliament, 2008), http://www

.europarl.europa.eu/document/activities/cont/200908/20090807ATT59480/20090807A TT59480EN.pdf.

85. In May 2008, US ambassador Anne Derse called on Azerbaijan's Ministry of Justice to reverse its decision to deregister the Election Monitoring Center. See "US Ambassador Urged Azerbaijani Authorities to Restore Registration of Election Monitoring Center," Azerireport.com, May 17, 2008, http://azerireport.com/index2.php?option=com _content&do_pdf=1&id=143.

86. The European Platform for Democratic Elections website gives the organization's official founding as December 1, 2008; see http://www.epde.org/en/emdsc-azerbaijan. html. See also "Azerbaijan: Prominent Election Monitor Arrested," Human Rights Watch, December 18, 2013, https://www.hrw.org/news/2013/12/18/azerbaijan-prominent -election-monitor-arrested.

87. One reason for closing voter registration thirty or more days before an election, as is the case in many US states, is precisely to stop multiple registration that allowed for multiple voting on election day.

88. ESI, *Caviar Diplomacy*, 18–19.

89. "Azerbaijani Parliament Approves Referendum on Presidential Term Limit," RFE/ RL, December 26, 2008, http://www.rferl.org/content/Azerbaijani_Parliament_Approves _Referendum_On_Presidential_Term_Limit/1364057.html.

90. Venice Commission, *Opinion on the Draft Amendments to the Constitution of the Republic of Azerbaijan* (Opinion 518/2008), Council of Europe, March 16, 2009, 5, para. 16, http://www.venice.coe.int/webforms/documents/?pdf=CDL-AD%282009%29010-e. These constitutional amendments also contained a problematic provision that the Milli Majlis and presidential elections could be postponed during a "state of war" and "military action."

91. Diuk, *Next Generation in Russia, Ukraine, and Azerbaijan*, 79–80, suggests that the continuity of leadership provided no path to power for younger members.

92. OSCE/ODIHR, *Republic of Azerbaijan, Parliamentary Elections, 7 November 2010: OSCE/ODIHR Election Observation Mission Final Report* (Warsaw: OSCE/ODIHR, 2011), http://www.osce.org/odihr/75073?download=true.

93. See the Venice Commission's 2010 activities at Venice Commission, "Activities by Year: 2010," Council of Europe, 2014, http://www.venice.coe.int/webforms /events/?v=2010.

94. The proregime members of international monitoring groups insisted that Azerbaijan's democracy was developing and that remaining flaws were minor. See ESI, *Caviar Diplomacy*, 19–23.

95. OSCE/ODIHR, *Republic of Azerbaijan, Presidential Election, 9 November 2013: OSCE/ODIHR Election Observation Mission, Final Report* (Warsaw: OSCE/ODIHR, December 24, 2013), esp. 6n8, http://www.osce.org/institutions/110015?download=true.

96. Cited by Venice Commission, *Opinion on the Legislation Pertaining to the Protection against Defamation of the Republic of Azerbaijan* (Opinion No. 692/2012), Council of Europe, October 14, 2013, 4n5, http://www.venice.coe.int/webforms /documents/?pdf=CDL-AD%282013%29024-e.

97. Kenan Aliyev and Robert Coalson, "Baku Leans on NGOs as Presidential Election Nears," RFE/RL, March 21, 2013, http://www.rferl.org/content/azerbaijan-presidential -election-/24934952.html.

98. "Democracy and the Presidential Elections in Azerbaijan in 2013" survey, conducted by independent sociological service ADAM, as part of the League of Democratic Journalists project with financial support from Black Sea Trust–Regional Cooperation, BST, German Marshall Fund; report of Turan News Agency, August 19, 2013.

99. OSCE/ODIHR, *Republic of Azerbaijan, Presidential Election, 9 November 2013.*

100. RFE/RL Azerbaijani Service, "Televised Azerbaijani Presidential Debate Descends into Chaos," RFE/RL, September 19, 2013, http://www.rferl.org/content/azerbaijan -election-debate-attack-television-president-hasanli/25111775.html.

101. OSCE/ODIHR, *Republic of Azerbaijan, Presidential Election, 9 November 2013.*

102. Venice Commission, *Opinion on the Legislation Pertaining to the Protection against Defamation of the Republic of Azerbaijan.*

103. "Ali Hasanov: A 'Crusade' against Azerbaijan," Contact.az, December 29, 2015, http://contact.az/docs/2015/Politics/122900142006en.htm.

104. ESI, *Disgraced.*

105. Azerbaijan: Prominent Election Monitor Arrested," Human Rights Watch, December 18, 2013, https://www.hrw.org/news/2013/12/18/azerbaijan-prominent -election-monitor-arrested.

106. Shahtakhtinski had arrived in the spring of 2014. "Mandate of OSCE Azerbaijan Project Coordinator Suspended," WorldNews Network, June 6, 2015, http://article.wn.com /view/2015/06/02/Mandate_of_OSCE_Azerbaijan_Project_Coordinator_suspended/.

107. OSCE/ODIHR, *Republic of Azerbaijan, Parliamentary Elections, 1 November 2015: OSCE/ODIHR Needs Assessment Mission Report, 12–14 August 2015* (Warsaw: OSCE/ ODIHR, 2015), http://www.osce.org/odihr/elections/azerbaijan/179216?donload=true; and "ODIHR Refuses to Monitor Azerbaijani Poll after Government Tries to Restrict the Size of the Mission," Caucasus Elections Watch, September 12, 2015, http://elections watch.org/2015/09/12/odihr-refuses-to-monitor-azerbaijani-poll-after-government-tries -to-restrict-the-size-of-the-mission/.

108. Hasanli told this story in his acceptance speech for the Ion Ratiu Democracy Award, which he received at the Woodrow Wilson International Center for Scholars in Washington on December 8, 2015. See "Political Challenges of Contemporary Azerbaijan-2," YouTube video, 1:39:32, posted by "Woodrow Wilson Center," December 8, 2005, https://www .youtube.com/watch?v=y7IaBOUC_tc. The published transcript, with corrected English translation, is forthcoming.

Chapter 4

1. For an overview of Azerbaijan's post-Soviet oil industry, see Cornell, *Azerbaijan since Independence*, chap. 9; Jan H. Kalicki and David L. Goldwyn, ed., *Energy and Security: Strategies for a World in Transition*, rev. ed. (Washington, DC: Woodrow Wilson Center Press; Baltimore: Johns Hopkins University Press, 2013); and Steve Levine, *The Oil and the Glory: The Pursuit of Empire and Fortune on the Caspian Sea* (New York: Random House, 2007).

2. Ilya Zemstov, *Partiia ili mafia?* (Paris: Les Editeurs Réunis, 1976) detailed cases in the Heydar Aliyev era when this became common.

3. Personal observations from 1980s Baku.

4. ESI, *"Caviar Diplomacy"*; see also *Washington Post* and OCCRP reports on US politicians who received trips and gifts from Azerbaijanis, discussed in this chapter.

5. Transparency International measures *perceptions*, using at least seven separate sources, which cannot be as precise as measuring quantities of oil produced or dollars earned. It is useful nonetheless. Transparency International's scope has expanded, and its methods have become more refined, since 2012; it now uses a 100-point scale. See the organization's overview assessment of Azerbaijan's corruption at http://www.transparency.org/country#AZE.

6. *Nations in Transit 2015*, Freedom House, 2015, https://freedomhouse.org/report /nations-transit/nations-transit-2015.

7. See Thomas L. Friedman, discussing the work of Michael L. Ross, in "The First Law of Petropolitics," *Foreign Policy*, October 16, 2009, http://foreignpolicy.com/2009/10/16 /the-first-law-of-petropolitics/. See also Sarah Chayes, *Thieves of State; Why Corruption Threatens Global Security* (New York: W. W. Norton, 2015).

8. Altstadt, *Azerbaijani Turks*, chaps. 2–4; and Sh. S. Fatullaev, *Gradostroitel'stvo Baku: XIX-nachale XX vekov* (Leningrad: Stroizdat, 1978).

9. Several books discuss Baku's oil history. Daniel Yergin, *The Prize: The Epic Question for Oil, Money, and Power* (New York: Simon & Schuster, 1990) is detailed, engaging, and puts Baku oil in global context. Levine, *Oil and the Glory*, focuses on Baku oil during the nineteenth and twentieth centuries as well as in the post-Soviet period.

10. Observed in Baku, 1980.

11. Mahmud Ismayil(ov), "Azerbaijan's Colonial Economy," *Caucasus and Central Asia Chronicle* 8, no. 3 (July 1989).

12. Azer Allahveranov and Emin Huseynov, *Costs and Benefits of Labor Mobility between the EU and the Eastern Partnership Partner Countries. Country Report: Azerbaijan*, CASE Network Studies and Analysis No. 460/2013 (Warsaw: CASE–Center for Social and Economic Research, 2013), 9, http://www.case-research.eu/sites/default/files/publications /CNSA_2013_460.pdf.

13. The State Oil Company of Azerbaijan (SOCAR) was formed in 1992 from Soviet-era oil agencies.

14. Kalicki and Goldwyn, *Energy and Security*, 203n14.

15. Shannon O'Lear, "Azerbaijan's Resource Wealth: Political Legitimacy and Public Opinion," *Geographical Journal* 173, no. 3 (2007): 210.

16. The foundation for the 1995 project was a 1993 Energy Sector Report, according to the World Bank project report; see *Implementation Completion Report on a Credit in the Amount of SDR 14.3 Million (US$20.8 Million Equivalent) to the Azerbaijan Republic for a Petroleum Technical Assistance Project*, Report No. 22113 (Washington, DC: World Bank, 2001), 2, http://www-wds.worldbank.org/external/default/WDS ContentServer/WDSP/IB/2001/07/06/000094946_01062604045124/Rendered/PDF /multi0page.pdf.

17. This holiday was initiated in 2000. See "Azerbaijan's 'Flower Day': Americans Duped into Celebrating Communist Dictator's Birthday," *Azeri Report*, May 5, 2013, http://azerireport.com/index.php?option=com_content&task=view&id=3969.

18. Energy industry analyst, private conversation with the author, 2002.

19. In 2007, Azerbaijan's oil output was 2.2 quadrillion BTU, and in the peak year of 2010 it was just over 2.8 quadrillion BTU. See "Total Primary Energy Production: Azerbaijan," International Energy Statistics, US Energy Information Administration, US Department of Energy, accessed July 11, 2016, http://www.eia.gov/beta/international /data/browser/#?iso=AZE&c=001&ct=0&cy=2012&start=1980&end=2012&ord=SA& vs=INTL.44-1-AZE-QBTU.A&v=C&vo=0&so=0&io=0&pa=004000001&f=A&ug=g &tl_type=p&tl_id=44-A.

20. Fakhri Hasanov, "Dutch Disease and the Azerbaijan Economy," *Communist and Post-Communist Studies* 46, no. 4 (2013): 467. Figures are in the new manat (AZN) that was issued in 2006, at 0.78 to the USD.

21. Personal observations. See also Altstadt, "Poverty Among the Cell Phones."

22. Cornell, *Azerbaijan since Independence*, 245.

23. Ibid., 246–47.

24. O'Lear, "Azerbaijan's Resource Wealth," 210–11. Budget figures include investments.

25. Cornell, *Azerbaijan since Independence*, 247–49.

26. Allahveranov and Huseynov, *Costs and Benefits of Labor Mobility*, 16.

27. World Bank, *Azerbaijan Partnership Program Snapshot* (Washington, DC: World Bank, 2015), 5, http://www.worldbank.org/content/dam/Worldbank/document /Azerbaijan-Snapshot.pdf.

28. O'Lear, "Azerbaijan's Resource Wealth," 217.

29. Hasanov, "Dutch Disease," 467 and 470 (based on Azerbaijan State Statistical Committee figures). For income from hydrocarbon exports and related fees and taxes, see EITI, *Report 2012: Azerbaijan* (Oslo: EITI, 2012) https://eiti.org/files/Azerbaijan-2012 -EITI-Report.pdf.

30. Palash Ghosh, "Azerbaijan: A Repressive, Corrupt Country That the West Loves— There Must Be Oil," *International Business Times*, June 23, 2013, http://www.ibtimes.com /azerbaijan-repressive-corrupt-country-west-loves-there-must-be-oil-704066.

31. Hasanov, "Dutch Disease." This article stops before the 2008–9 global recession.

32. Aitor Ciarreta and Shahriyar Nasirov, "Analysis of Azerbaijan Oil and Gas Sector," presentation at the 30th USAEE/IAEE North American Conference, Washington, October 11, 2011, https://www.usaee.org/usaee2011/submissions/OnlineProceedings /Ciarreta_Nasirov-Article1.pdf.

33. Hasanov, "Dutch Disease," 470–71.

34. Respondents ranged in age from 18 up, with the largest group, ages 18–35, making up just under half the pool, ages 36–55 just under 40 percent, and the rest age 56 and over. This conforms to the population's profile. Just over 40 percent lived in rural locations, around 25 percent lived in Baku, and a further 25 percent lived in other cities.

35. See the Caucasus Research Resource Centers, "Time-Series Dataset Azerbaijan," http://caucasusbarometer.org/en/cb-az/ICITGOV/.

36. Currency reform was decided in 2005 and reissuance took place during 2006, when 5,000 old manat (AZM) were exchanged for 1 new manat (AZN). See "National Currency Reform: Manat as One of the Valuable Currency [*sic*] of the World," Azerbaijans.com, accessed July 15, 2016, http://www.azerbaijans.com/content_1791 _en.html. Exchange nominally ended on January 1, 2007, but was still allowed without a final deadline. The Azerbaijani government said that there was no disruption during

this period, and foreign diplomats then serving in the country did not recall that there was disruption.

37. For some reason, 2011 was an outlier, with only 14 percent of respondents saying that they needed this highest amount.

38. Nigar Orujova, "Netherlands Invests $800 Million in Non-Oil Sector in Azerbaijan," *AzerNews*, April 24, 2015, http://www.azernews.az/business/81000.html.

39. Nigar Orujova, "Italy Views Azerbaijan as Alternative Market," *AzerNews*, April 15, 2015, http://www.azernews.az/business/80497.html.

40. Vladimir Iontsev and Irinia Ivakhnyuk, *The Role of International Labour Migration in Russian Economic Development* (Florence: European University Institute, 2012), 1, estimate that 80 percent of migrants working in Russia do not sign work contracts.

41. Anna Bara, Anna di Bartolomeo, Zuzanna Brunarska, Shushanik Makaryan, Sergo Mananashvili, and Agnieszka Weinar, *Regional Migration Report: South Caucasus* (Florence: European University Institute, 2013), 133; Russia attempted to regularize reporting in 2006.

42. Iontsev and Ivakhnyuk, *Role of International Labour Migration*, 22.

43. Building Migration Partnerships, *Azerbaijan: Extended Migration Profile*, 2010. This is much higher than the estimate by Iontsev and Ivakhnyuk, *Role of International Labour Migration*.

44. Sixty-five percent of $1.5 billion is $653 million.

45. See Caucasus Research Resource Centers, "Time-Series Dataset Azerbaijan: Paid Bribe? (%)"; the number dipped to 20 percent in 2012 but rose to 24 percent in 2013.

46. Transparency International, "Global Corruption Barometer, 2010/11," accessed July 15, 2016, http://www.transparency.org/gcb201011/results.

47. Marie Chêne, "Overview of Corruption and Anti-Corruption in Azerbaijan," Anti-Corruption Helpdesk (Berlin: Transparency International, 2013), http://www.transparency.org/files/content/corruptionqas/Overview_of_corruption_in_Azerbaijan_2.pdf.

48. European Commission, High Representative of the European Union for Foreign Affairs and Security Policy, *Implementation of the European Neighborhood Policy in Azerbaijan: Progress in 2013 and Recommendations for Action* (Brussels: European Commission, 2014), http://eeas.europa.eu/enp/pdf/2014/country-reports/azerbaijan_en.pdf.

49. Aynur Jafarova, "Official: Transparency International Report Confirms Azerbaijan's Advances in Anti-Graft Fight," *AzerNews*, July 10, 2013, http://www.azernews.az/azerbaijan/56581.html.

50. This was reported by citizens involved in the events, 2010.

51. L. Askerov, "Robbery in the Name of Our State (Our Investigation)," *Azeri Daily*, February 22, 2015, http://azeridaily.com/society/5295 (link discontinued), but originally from Haqqin.az. Local housing monitors told a similar story, but it seemed to have taken place in Bayil not in the Baku center. The thugs who rousted the residents from their homes worked for Azimport.

52. "Azerbaijan: Out of Tune?" Transparency International, May 21, 2012, http://www.transparency.org/news/feature/azerbaijan_out_of_tune.

53. "Honouring of Obligations and Commitments by Azerbaijan," PACE Resolution 1545 (April 16, 2007), http://assembly.coe.int/nw/xml/XRef/X2H-Xref-ViewPDF.asp?FileID=17527&lang=en.

54. "Rumblings of Instability in Azerbaijan," *Bloomberg*, November 24, 2009, http://www.bloomberg.com/news/articles/2009-11-24/rumblings-of-instability-in-azerbaijan.

55. Ibid.

56. Hikmet Hajizade, director of the FAR Center for Political and Economic Research, Baku, quoted in ibid.

57. Ibid.

58. Azerbaijan also joined the UN in 1992 and several European bodies. The government has not always completed the process, as with WTO, or ratified signed agreements. Some deal with human rights, other with commercial relations and transparency. Lists of agreements—one signed and approved, the other signed but not approved—are available at "Search on States and International Organisations: Statistics on Signatures and Ratifications—Azerbaijan," Council of Europe, accessed July 15, 2016, http://conventions .coe.int/Treaty/Commun/ListeStats.asp?PO=AZE&MA=999&CM=17&CL=ENG.

59. Government Accountability Project, *Privatization and Corruption: The World Bank and Azerbaijan* (Washington, DC: Government Accountability Project, 2008), 8, http:// whistleblower.org/sites/default/files/Privatization_and_Corruption.pdf.

60. Cited in ibid.

61. "Accession Status: Azerbaijan," WTO, 2016, https://www.wto.org/english /thewto_e/acc_e/a1_azerbaidjan_e.htm.

62. See the organization's website at https://eiti.org.

63. The sales statistics reports can be found on the websites of BP (www.bp.com /caspian) and SOCAR (www.socar.az).

64. The anticorruption law was adopted on January 13, 2004. See "Law of The Republic of Azerbaijan on Combating Corruption," Azerbaijan Republic Commission on Combating Corruption, April 28, 2009, http://commission-anticorruption.gov.az/view .php?lang=en&menu=19&id=32.

65. "Azerbaijan: Out of Tune?"

66. See "Azerbaijan: NRGI Limited Engagement Country—Eurasia," Natural Resource Governance Institute, accessed August 18, 2016, http://www.resourcegovernance.org/our -work/country/azerbaijan.

67. The phrase "tough neighborhood" has been used repeatedly by Azerbaijani and Western analysts and officials, but a scan of both Google results (a Google search of "Azerbaijan 'Tough Neighborhood'" turned up 14,800 hits) and the *Congressional Record* search on Azerbaijan reveals that most of these references began after 2011. Members of Congress formerly used more specific phrases about the country being "wedged between Russia and Iran" or being in a "geopolitically complex" region. Samples of "tough neighborhood" comments are given in the cited works in note 131 below.

68. "Rumblings of Instability in Azerbaijan."

69. Ghosh, "Azerbaijan."

70. Khadija Ismayilova, "Azerbaijani President's Family Benefits from Eurovision Hall Construction," RFE/RL, May 9, 2012, http://www.rferl.org/content/azerbaijan _first_family_build_eurovision_arena/24575761.html; Nushabe Fatullayeva and Khadija Ismayilova, "Azerbaijani Government Awarded Gold-Field Rights to President's Family," RFE/RL, May 3, 2012, http://www.rferl.org/content/azerbaijan_gold-field_contract _awarded_to_presidents_family/24569192.html; and Khadija Ismayilova, "Azerbaijani

President's Daughters Tied to Fast-Rising Telecoms Firm," RFE/RL, June 27, 2011, http://www.rferl.org/content/azerbaijan_president_aliyev_daughters_tied_to_telecoms _firm/24248340.html.

71. Robert Coalson, "Azerbaijani President Aliyev Named Corruption's 'Person of the Year,'" RFE/RL, January 3, 2013, http://www.rferl.org/content/azerbaijan-ilham-aliyev -corruption-person-of-the-year/24814209.html.

72. "Oil and Gas," Transparency International, accessed July 20, 2016, http://www .transparency.org/topic/detail/oil_and_gas.

73. This description is drawn from Ciarreta and Nasirov, "Analysis of Azerbaijan Oil and Gas Sector," 7–8; and Global Witness, *Azerbaijan Anonymous: Azerbaijan's State Oil Company and Why the Extractive Industries Transparency Initiative Needs to Go Further* (London: Global Witness, 2013), 10, https://www.globalwitness.org/sites /default/files/library/azerbaijan_anonymous_lr.pdf. The basis for this report was Khadija Ismayilova, "Anar aliyev kimdir va hardadır?," Azadlıq Radiosu, December 12, 2013, http://www.azadliq.org/a/25195029.html.

74. Freedom House's 2003 Nations in Transit report suggested that SOFAZ's money flow was relatively transparent. See "Nations in Transit 2003: Azerbaijan," *Nations in Transit*, Freedom House, August 4, 2003, https://freedomhouse.org/report/nations -transit/2003/azerbaijan#.VXc7iUY7ci0.

75. That is revenues, after cost recovery; from a diagram of money flow in Ciarreta and Nasirov, "Analysis of Azerbaijan Oil and Gas Sector," 18.

76. Ibid., 7, based on SOFAZ data.

77. Ghosh, "Azerbaijan."

78. In late 2015, Trend News Agency reported the SOFAZ assets as of October 1, 2015, at $34.7 billion, down from $37.1 billion in early 2015; see "Azerbaijani President Approves Country's State Oil Fund's Budget for 2016," Trend News Agency, December 29, 2015, http://en.trend.az/azerbaijan/business/2475581.html. These are government figures without an independent audit. The independent website Contact.az reported the 91 percent figure: "SOFAZ Expenses Mainly in Transfers to State Budget," Contact.az, December 31, 2015, https://contact.az/docs/2015/Economics&Finance/123000142050en.htm.

79. "Is State Budget of Azerbaijan Transparent?" Social Watch, October 23, 2013, http://www.socialwatch.org/node/16253.

80. "Qubad İbadoğlu: 'Başqan olmaq iddiam var,'" Yeni Müsavat, February 19, 2014, http://musavat.com/news/siyas%C9%99t/Qubad-%C4%B0bado%C4%9Flu:-Ba%C5% 9Fqan-olmaq-iddiam-var_183658.html.

81. Ciaretta and Nasirov, "Analysis of Azerbaijan Oil and Gas Sector," 7.

82. Gubad Bairamov, "Privatization in Azerbaijan: Results and Prospects," *Central Asia and the Caucasus* 4, no. 10 (2001), http://www.ca-c.org/journal/eng-04-2001/10 .baiprimen.shtml.

83. "Implementation Completion Report (PPFB-P1920; IDA-27080) on a Credit in the Amount of SDR 14.3 Million (US$20.8 Million Equivalent) to the Azerbaijan Republic for a Petroleum Technical Assistance Project," Report No. 22113, World Bank, May 31, 2001, http://www-wds.worldbank.org/external/default/WDSContentServer /WDSP/IB/2001/07/06/000094946_01062604045124/Rendered/PDF/multi0page.pdf.

84. Government Accountability Project, *Privatization and Corruption*, 16.

85. Ibid., 26.

86. See the organization's mission statement at "About Us," Global Witness, accessed July 20, 2016, https://www.globalwitness.org/about-us/.

87. Global Witness, *Azerbaijan Anonymous*, esp. 13–27.

88. In December 2013, Anar Aliyev granted an interview to Baku-based online magazine *Business Time* about his history as a businessman. Although originally available in *Business Time*, the links to the story failed, but it was also printed in the British eNewsWire publication as "Anar Alizade (Aliyev) Speaks to Business Time about Global Witness Report," eNewsWire UK, December 28, 2013, http://www.enewswire.co.uk/2013/12/28/anar-alizade-aliyev-speaks-to-business-time-about-global-witness-report/.

89. Global Witness, *Azerbaijan Anonymous*, 13; this amount (see page 22 of the report) included profits on sales and the resale of shares to SOCAR in 2012.

90. The first company seems to have been UGE-Lancer, discussed in Global Witness, *Azerbaijan Anonymous*, 26–27.

91. See the overview of this problem given by Sheila S. Coronel, "The Secret World of Private Companies," WatchDog Watcher, October 9, 2012, http://watchdog-watcher.com/2012/10/09/company-information/.

92. Global Witness, *Azerbaijan Anonymous*, 18–19.

93. Ibid., 23 and 22.

94. Summarized in ibid., 33.

95. Fidan Bagirova, "Radio Liberty Program Discusses EITI New Standards and Azerbaijan," National Resource Governance Institute, October 1, 2013, http://www.resourcegovernance.org/news/blog/radio-liberty-program-discusses-eiti-new-standards-and-azerbaijan.

96. Global Witness, *Azerbaijan Anonymous*, 7.

97. "Azerbaijan Downgraded to Candidate Country," EITI, April 14, 2015, https://eiti.org/news/azerbaijan-downgraded-candidate-country.

98. The Azerbaijani versions were often longer and more detailed; in some cases, there was no English version.

99. Khadija Ismayilova, "Prezidentin qızı banka necə sahib oldu?," Azadlıq Radiosu, August 11, 2010, http://www.azadliq.org/a/2123076.html; for a shorter English-language version, see Ulviyye Azadzade and Khadija Ismayilova, "Aliyev's Azerbaijani Empire Grows, as Daughter Joins the Game," RFE/RL, August 13, 2010, http://www.rferl.org/content/Aliyevs_Azerbaijani_Empire_Grows_As_Daughter_Joins_The_Game/2127137.html.

100. Ismayilova, "Azerbaijani President's Daughters Tied to Fast-Rising Telecoms Firm."

101. As vice president of SOCAR since mid-1994, Ilham Aliyev in 1998 has purchased a multi-million-dollar London mansion; the home next door to it was worth $26 million. In 2010, the title of this house was transferred to his daughter Leyla. See the OCCRP report, mentioned at "The Mansion on the Heath: Photo Gallery of Ilham Aliyev's Mansion in London," *Azeri Report*, June 15, 2015, http://azerireport.com/index.php?option=com_content&task=view&id=4593&Itemid=43.

102. Azadzade and Ismayilova, "Aliyev's Azerbaijani Empire Grows, as Daughter Joins the Game."

103. See "Azerbaijan Airports," Azerbaijan Airlines, accessed August 20, 2016, https://

www.azal.az/about/azerbaijan-airports; and "History," Azerbaijan Airlines, accessed August 20, 2016, https://www.azal.az/en/about/history.

104. Ismayilova, "Azerbaijani President's Daughters Tied to Fast-Rising Telecoms Firm."

105. Khadija Ismayilova, "TeliaSonera's Behind-the-Scenes Connection to Azerbaijani President's Daughters," RFE/RL, July 15, 2014, http://www.rferl.org/content/teliasonera -azerbaijan-aliyev-corruption-investigation-occrp/25457907.html.

106. Leyla Mustafayeva, "Sadness as Media Rights Group Closes in Azerbaijan," Institute for War and Peace Reporting, September 12, 2014, https://iwpr.net/global -voices/sadness-media-rights-group-closes-azerbaijan.

107. Fatullaeva and Ismayilova, "Azerbaijan Government Awarded Gold-Field Rights to President's Family."

108. Khadija Ismayilova, "Azerbaijani President's Family Benefits from Eurovision Hall Construction," RFE/RL, May 9, 2012, http://www.rferl.org/content/azerbaijan_first _family_build_eurovision_arena/24575761.html.

109. Afgan Muhtarlı, "Bidding Secrets of the Armed Forces Part 1: Purchases without Tenders," Meydan TV, October 16, 2014, http://www.meydan.tv/en/site/politics/3402 /Bidding-Secrets-of-the-Armed-Forces-Part-1-Purchases-without-tenders.htm. Azenco dominates military construction, and the Aliyevs' family–owned Azersun Holding is the main food supplier for the military.

110. "Nazir Ziya Məmmədov, oğlu Anar Məmmədov və ZQAN Holdinq," Azadlıq Radiosu, December 6, 2009, http://www.azadliq.org/a/1896083.html.

111. Ibid. This covers the quotations in the following two sentences.

112. Nushabe Fatullaeva, "Mixing Government and Business in Azerbaijan," RFE/RL, April 4, 2013, http://www.rferl.org/content/azerbaijan-transport-minister -corruption/24947711.html.

113. "K.Heydərovun oğulları böyük biznesdə," Azadlıq Radiosu, February 17, 2010, http://www.azadliq.org/a/1960290.html.

114. Author's interviews in Baku, 2008 and 2012.

115. See the Gilan Holding website at http://www.gilanholding.com/. The site also has English and Russian versions.

116. "Inspection Development Monitoring," Gilan Holding, accessed June 11, 2015, http://gilanholding.com/construction/Inspection+Development+Monitoring+ IDM+71.

117. Khadija Ismayilova, "Paşa Holdinq haqda bilmədikləriniz," Azadlıq Radiosu, May 7, 2014, http://www.azadliq.org/a/pa%C5%9Fa-holdinq--%C9%99liyevl%C9%99rin -hollandiyadan-ba%C5%9Flayan-ail%C9%99-biznesi/25376221.html.

118. "Arif Pashayev Gave Control of Commercial Companies to Granddaughters," Contact.az, May 2, 2014, http://www.contact.az/docs/2014/Economics&Finance/05020 0077384en.htm. Their brother, Heydar (born August 2, 1997), is not yet twenty-one, but millions of dollars of property have been registered in his name in Dubai.

119. Historic buildings elsewhere were razed for modern construction, and one historical preservation specialist blamed the lack of a general city plan: Khanim Javadov, "A Tale of Two Bakus," Transitions Online, August 31, 2010, http://www.tol.org/client /article/21756-a-tale-of-two-bakus.html.

120. "'Paşa Holdinq' Şahdağda biznesini necə qurdu [Video]," Azadlıq Radiosu, January 13, 2014, http://www.azadliq.org/a/25228353.html. The rest of this paragraph is based on this source.

121. The Austria-based Kohl & Partner, a "hotel and tourism consulting" business, notes this project on its website and says that it prepared the development plan. See "Tourism Development Plan for the Mountain Resort Shahdag Azerbaijan," Kohn & Partner, accessed July 20, 2016, http://www.kohl-int.com/en/projects-references/tourism -development-plan-for-the-mountain-resort-shahdag-azerbaijan/81-1038.html.

122. Khadija Ismayilova, "əli Həsənovun siyasiləşmiş biznes şəbəkəsi," Azadlıq Radiosu, December 9, 2014, http://www.azadliq.org/a/%C9%99li-h%C9%99s%C9%99novun -siyasil%C9%99%C5%9Fmi%C5%9F-biznes-%C5%9F%C9%99b%C9%99k%C9 %99si/25432624.html. A slightly shorter version was published earlier on the OCCRP website; see Khadija Ismayilova, "Azerbaijan: Media and Regulators a Family Affair," OCCRP, June 24, 2014, https://www.occrp.org/en/investigations/2494-azerbaijan-media -and-regulators-a-family-affair.

123. "Ilham Aliyev Appoints Ali Hasanov as Aide for Social, Political Issues," Trend News Agency, February 23, 2015, http://en.trend.az/azerbaijan/politics/2367285.html.

124. Ismayilova, "əli Həsənovun siyasiləşmiş biznes şəbəkəsi."

125. The ECHR website does not seem to have a record of this case as of early 2016; it may have been one of the many cases dismissed by the Court each year.

126. Ismayilova, "əli Həsənovun siyasiləşmiş biznes şəbəkəsi"; Ismayilova, "Azerbaijan: Media and Regulators a Family Affair."

127. See, e.g., Matthew Moore, "WikiLeaks: William, Harry and the Abramovich of Azerbaijan," *Telegraph* (London), February 11, 2011, http://www.telegraph.co.uk /news/worldnews/wikileaks/8299344/WikiLeaks-William-Harry-and-the-Abramovich -of-Azerbaijan.html; Scott Cohn, "Crude of All Evil? How Oil Is Fueling Some Tough Choices," CNBC, February 22, 2012, http://www.cnbc.com/id/46430231; and GAN Integrity Solutions, "Business Corruption in Azerbaijan," Business Anticorruption Portal, October 2014, http://www.business-anti-corruption.com/country-profiles/europe-central -asia/azerbaijan/show-all.aspx.

128. World Bank Group–Doing Business, *Ease of Doing Business in Azerbaijan* (Washington, DC: World Bank, 2014), http://www.doingbusiness.org/data/exploreeconomies/azerbaijan; and World Bank Group–Doing Business, *Doing Business 2016: Economy Profile 2016— Azerbaijan* (Washington, DC: World Bank, 2016) http://www.doingbusiness.org/~/media /giawb/doing%20business/documents/profiles/country/AZE.pdf. For comparative rankings of all 189 countries as of June 2015, see the World Bank's Doing Business rankings at http:// www.doingbusiness.org/rankings. The site describes new methodologies and adjustments that are reflected in rankings that are not quite the same as those from the previous year; for instance, ten factors are now measured, compared with the five factors measured in the old system.

129. "Azerbaijan: Transparency Group Should Suspend Membership," Human Rights Watch, August 14, 2014, http://www.hrw.org/news/2014/08/14/azerbaijan-transparency -group-should-suspend-membership.

130. GAN Integrity Solutions, "Business Corruption in Azerbaijan," Business Anti-Corruption Portal, October 2014, http://www.business-anti-corruption.com/country -profiles/europe-central-asia/azerbaijan/snapshot.aspx.

131. Thomas Goltz, "Bad Blood in Baku,'" *Foreign Policy*, June 11, 2010, http://foreignpolicy.com/2010/06/11/bad-blood-in-baku/; and Michael Weiss, "The Corleones of the Caspian,'" *Foreign Policy*, June 10, 2014, http://foreignpolicy.com/2014/06/10/the-corleones-of-the-caspian/.

132. See, e.g., former rep. Michael E. McMahon (D-NY), "It's Unfair to Hold Azerbaijan to a Higher Standard than Russia," *Roll Call*, April 16, 2013, http://www.rollcall.com/news/mcmahon_its_unfair_to_hold_azerbaijan_to_a_higher_standard_than_russia-224068-1.html; "Sixteen US Lawmakers Join Azerbaijanis to Remember Khojaly Tragedy in DC," Azerbaijan-Lithuania Intergovernmental Commission, February 27, 2015, http://azlit.info/en/news/67/2322; and Scott Perry (R-PA), "Floor Speech: Azerbaijan," *Congressional Record* 162, no. 75 (May 12, 2016), E690, https://www.congress.gov/congressional-record/2016/05/12/extensions-of-remarks-section/article/E690-5.

133. Bill Shuster (R-PA), "Honoring the Republic of Azerbaijan on the 20th Anniversary of the Restoration of Azerbaijan's Independence," *Congressional Record* 157, no. 156 (October 18, 2011), E1893, https://www.congress.gov/congressional-record/2011/10/18/extensions-of-remarks-section/article/E1893-2.

134. Kevin Bogardus, "Azerbaijan Plants Flag in DC Lobbying Scene," *The Hill*, December 7, 2011, http://thehill.com/business-a-lobbying/197681-azerbaijan-plants-flag-in-dc-lobbying-scene-.

135. Azerbaijan America Alliance, "About the Azerbaijan America Alliance," accessed March 20, 2016, http://azerbaijanamericaalliance.org/mission (link discontinued). The organization's Facebook page (https://www.facebook.com/Azerbaijan-America-Alliance-296931403654112/) was last updated in November 2015.

136. Azerbaijan America Alliance, "The Azerbaijan America Alliance Announces Former Congressman Dan Burton as Chairman of the Board," PR Newswire, February 12, 2013, http://prn.to/235HxBm.

137. Ibid.

138. Rosie Gray, "Inside Azerbaijan's Bizarre US Lobbying Push," *BuzzFeed News*, June 2, 2014, http://www.buzzfeed.com/rosiegray/inside-azerbaijans-bizarre-us-lobbying-push.

139. See Hannah Hess, "Ethics Office Release Report Detailing Lawmaker Travel to Azerbaijan," *Roll Call*, October 7, 2015, http://www.rollcall.com/news/home/ethics-office-releases-report-detailing-lawmaker-travel-to-azerbaijan.

140. Larry Luxner, "Azerbaijan Rolls Out Red Carpet for Visiting US Lawmakers," *Washington Diplomat*, June 26, 2013, http://www.washdiplomat.com/index.php?option=com_content&id=9391:azerbaijan-rolls-out-red-carpet-for-visiting-us-lawmakers&Itemid=428.

141. Ibid.

142. Dan Burton, "Why Azerbaijan Is Important to America and the Free World," *Washington Times*, January 28, 2015, http://www.washingtontimes.com/news/2015/jan/28/dan-burton-why-azerbaijan-is-important-to-america-/; Burton attended a Europe, Eurasia, and Emerging Threats Subcommittee meeting of the House Committee on Foreign Affairs on February 12, 2015, at which two of three expert witnesses—including this author—testified that Azerbaijan was not upholding democratic norms.

143. Nicholas Confessore, "Meet the Press: How James Glassman Reinvented Journalism—As Lobbying," *Washington Monthly*, December 2003, http://www

.washingtonmonthly.com/features/2003/0312.confessore.html; and Til Bruckner, "How Azerbaijan Manipulates Public Opinion in the US," OCCRP, June 19, 2015, https://www .occrp.org/freekhadijaismayilova/stories/how-azerbaijan-manipulates-public-opinion-in -the-US.php.

144. The young woman's expensive attire cast doubt on her graduate student persona— as did her attendance at a meeting that was not advertised to the public. Ilya Lozovsky, "How Azerbaijan and Its Lobbyists Spin Congress," *Foreign Policy*, June 11, 2015, http:// foreignpolicy.com/2015/06/11/how-azerbaijan-and-its-lobbyists-spin-congress/.

145. Daisy Sindelar, "Deadly Blaze Reveals Ugly Truth Behind Baku Beautification," RFE/RL, May 20, 2015, http://www.rferl.org/content/azerbaijan-public-anger-over -deadly-fire/27027429.html.

146. Khadija Ismayilova, "185 milyon manat Beynəlxalq Bankdan necə çıxıb?," Azadlıq Radiosu, July 12, 2011, http://www.azadliq.org/a/24263362.html.

147. "Pro-Government TV Red-Faced after Fake-Fan Fail," RFE/RL, June 18, 2015, http://www.rferl.org/content/azerbaijan-tv-interview-baku-games-foreigners/27079263 .html; and Tony Wesolowsky, "Aliyev's Azerbaijan in Spotlight as European Games Begin," RFE/RL, June 11, 2015, http://www.rferl.org/content/azerbaijan-aliyev-european-games -spotlight-human-rights/27067182.html.

148. "A. Rahimov: The European Games Cost One Billion Manat," Contact.az, June 11, 2015, http://www.contact.az/docs/2015/European%20games%202015/0611 00119025en.htm.

149. "Azerbaijani President Reviews Several Baku Roads after Reconstruction," Trend News Agency, December 29, 2015, http://en.trend.az/azerbaijan/society/2475415. html; and "Azerbaijani President Approves Country's State Oil Fund's Budget for 2016," Trend News Agency, December 29, 2015, http://en.trend.az/azerbaijan /business/2475581.html.

150. "International Bank of Azerbaijan First Victim of Devaluation," Contact.az, March 19, 2015, http://www.contact.az/docs/2015/Analytics/031900110324en.htm.

151. "Hakimiyyətin 'oliqarx ovu' davam edir," Azadlıq Radiosu, May 14, 2015, http:// www.azadliq.org/a/27015273.html; and "The Government Failed to Prevent Holland Disease (End)," Contact.az, June 17, 2015, http://www.contact.az/docs/2015/Economic s&Finance/061600119735en.htm.

152. Keçmiş deputat, "Globus Plaza"nın sahibi Dünyamin Xəlilov, 'Avesta Concern' Holdinqin rəhbəri Hacı İbrahim Nehrəmli, Azərinşaat"; MMC-nin rəhbəri Mehdi əliyev, Şəkinin sabiq icra başçısı, "BakFen" MMC sahibi Murad Cabbarlı—all listed in "Saxlanan işadamları 'dollar/manat maxinasiyası'nda ittiham oluna bilər," Azadlıq Radiosu, May 13, 2015, http://www.azadliq.org/a/27014260.html.

153. "Saxlanan işadamları 'dollar/manat maxinasiyası'nda ittiham oluna bilər"; and "Hakimiyyətin 'oliqarx ovu' davam edir."

154. "Nizami Piriyev: 'Borcumun bir hissəsini qaytardım,'" *Azadlıq*, May 29, 2015, http://www.azadliq.info/67645.html.

155. "Dövlət Bayrağı Meydanı Kompleksi İdarəsinin keçmiş rəisi də həbs olundu" Azadlıq Radiosu, May 14, 2015, http://www.azadliq.org/a/27016137.html.

156. See the Azimport website at http://azimport.az/; this site was accessed on May 14, 2015, the day after Mammedov was taken into custody.

157. L. Askerov, "Robbery in the Name of Our State (Our Investigation)."

158. "Azerbaijan's National Security Minister Fired Without Explanation," RFE/RL, October 17, 2015, http://www.rferl.org/content/azerbaijan-security-minister-fired-without-explanation/27311878.html; quotation from Aydin Mammadov, "Azerbaijan Conducts Sweeping Arrests in Ministry of National Security," Silk Road Reporters, November 6, 2015, http://www.silkroadreporters.com/2015/11/06/azerbaijan-conducts-sweeping-arrests-in-ministry-of-national-security/.

159. "Moody's: Outlook Changes to Negative for Azerbaijan's Banking System," Moody's Investors Service, June 29, 2015, https://www.moodys.com/research/Moodys-Outlook-changes-to-negative-for-Azerbaijans-banking-system--PR_329088.

160. "Azerbaijan: Important Economic Events of 2015," Contact.az, December 31, 2015, https://contact.az/docs/2015/Analytics/123100142144en.htm.

161. "International Bank of Azerbaijan First Victim of Devaluation."

162. "'Shortage' of Azerbaijani Customs in Imports from Three Countries Amounts to 1.6 Billion USD," Contact.az, February 20, 2016, http://www.contact.az/docs/2016/Economics&Finance/022000147513en.htm.

163. "Azerbaijanis Paying Price for Aliyev's 2015 European Games," RFE/RL, June 11, 2015, http://www.rferl.org/content/azerbaijan-european-games-paying-the-price/27067100.html.

164. "Lavish Price Tag Fans More Flames over Baku's European Games," RFE/RL, June 11, 2015, http://www.rferl.org/content/european-games-cost-azerbaijan-ceremony/27070753.html.

Chapter 5

1. "Commissioner Muižnieks Intervenes in Cases Concerning Azerbaijan before the European Court of Human Rights," Azadlıq Radiosu, February 24, 2015, http://www.azadliq.org/content/article/26865884.html.

2. "Eşşekle (Esel Heinz) müsahibe: QHT qanunu haqqında şok açıqlamalar," YouTube video, 5:15, posted by "OL! Azerbaijan Youth Movement," June 28, 2009, https://www.youtube.com/watch?v=Aaecvg7xCIk. Adnan is the son of political analyst Hikmet Hadjzade (see chapter 4), and Emin's surname is Abdullaev. "Milli" is a pseudonym meaning "national."

3. See "FILM: Amazing Azerbaijan," Azerbaijan Free Expression Platform, 2016, http://azerbaijanfreeexpression.org/film-amazing-azerbaijan/. This is the original critical video, first made in 2013. Since this video was first posted in 2013, it has been "swamped" on the Internet by another film, probably made by the authorities, also called "Amazing Azerbaijan." The newer video paints a regime-friendly picture of the wealth and beauty of Azerbaijan.

4. In his 2012 book *The Color Revolutions,* Lincoln A. Mitchell has argued that youth organizations got more attention from analysts because they were more accessible, even though they were not as influential as groups such as Georgia's International Society

for Fair Elections and Democracy, which was full of middle-aged activists who did not speak English. See Lincoln A. Mitchell, *The Color Revolutions* (Philadelphia: University of Pennsylvania Press, 2012), 12–14.

5. Another such hunger strike under similar conditions was reported in early 2006. There seem to be no reports of the summer 2005 hunger strike, but I visited the hunger strikers then, and shortly thereafter met Bashirli and his associate Seymur Hazi who would come to prominence later. The 2006 hunger strike story in Eurasia Net was reported on RefWorld; see Rufat Abbasov and Mina Muradova, "Azerbaijani Hunger Strikers: Opposition of the Future?," RefWorld, January 30, 2006, http://www.refworld.org/docid/46f2588fc.html.

6. Diuk, *Next Generation of Youth in Russia, Ukraine and Azerbaijan*, 84–85.

7. Findings of Rey (Opinion) Monitoring Center (Baku), reported in Assa-Irada, August 30, 2005.

8. "Azerbaijan: Opposition Youth Activists on Trial," Human Rights Watch, March 30, 2006, http://www.hrw.org/news/2006/03/30/azerbaijan-opposition-youth-activists-trial.

9. "Azerbaijan: New Information on Mr. Ruslan Bashirli and Mr. Ramin Tagiyev," OMCT, April 7, 2006, http://www.omct.org/urgent-campaigns/urgent-interventions /azerbaijan/2006/04/d17962/; and "Azerbaijan: Ruslan Bashirli (m)], Said Nuri (m)] Members of Yeni Fikir Youth Movement, Ramin Tagiyev (m)]," EUR 55/004/2006, Amnesty International, August 4, 2006, http://www2.amnesty.se/uaonnet.nsf/dfab8d7f5 8eec102c1257011006466e1/c153f611ca657ad5c12571c30036bbe8.

10. "Azerbaijan: Verdict Against Youth Activists Raises International Concern," Eurasianet, July 16, 2006, http://www.eurasianet.org/departments/civilsociety/articles /eav071706.shtml.

11. Karl Rahder, "The Secret Trial of Baku Youth Activists," ISN Security Watch, April 24, 2006, http://www.css.ethz.ch/content/specialinterest/gess/cis/center-for-securities -studies/en/services/digital-library/articles/article.html/108363.

12. "Azerbaijan: Ruslan Bashirli (m)], Said Nuri (m)] Members of Yeni Fikir Youth Movement, Ramin Tagiyev (m)]." Nuri was not incarcerated and left Azerbaijan in 2006; he would return and again make the news in the fall of 2014. Taghiyev's sentence was reduced to three years in 2006, and he was released in the spring of 2008; Bashirli was released in March 2012.

13. Ibid.

14. Nick Paton Walsh, "Azerbaijan Ministers Accused of Coup Plot," *Guardian* (London), October 20, 2005, http://www.theguardian.com/world/2005/oct/21/nickpaton walsh.mainsection1; Walsh quotes Eynulla Fatullayev.

15. Minister of Education Misir Mardanov was sacked, then reinstated, allegedly because he presented Ilham Aliyev with evidence that he (Mardanov) knew more about the workings of government than the president did. Perhaps he possessed *kompramat* (compromising material) on the president.

16. IPGA Campaign for Free Expression in Azerbaijan, "Impunity for Violence Against Journalists," http://azerbaijanfreexpression.org/campaigns/impunity/murdered-elmar-hu seynov/ (link discontinued). For details of the comprehensive coverage discussed in this paragraph, see Nina Ognianova, "Azerbaijan Special Report: Finding Elmar's Killers," Committee to Protect Journalists, September 16, 2008, https://cpj.org/reports/2008/09 /azerbaijan-elmar.php.

17. "Honouring of Obligations and Commitments by Azerbaijan," PACE Resolution 1545 (2007), on events of 2006, http://assembly.coe.int/nw/xml/XRef/X2H-Xref -ViewPDF.asp?FileID=17527&lang=en (emphasis added).

18. Ibid.

19. "In the Future, I Do Not Think of Politics, Ruslan Bashirli," APA News, March 16, 2012, http://en.apa.az/azerbaijan-politics/domestic-news/in-the-future-i-do-not-think-of -politics-ruslan-bashirli-updated.html.

20. "Honouring of Obligations and Commitments by Azerbaijan."

21. Ibid.

22. Ibid.

23. The vote was 99-1-4, with one member of the Azerbaijani delegation abstaining. See "Resolution: Honouring of Obligations and Commitments by Azerbaijan, RES 1545," PACE, April 16, 2007, http://assembly.coe.int/nw/xml/XRef /Xref-DocDetails-EN.asp?fileid=17527&lang=EN&search=QXplcmJhaWphbnxj YXRlZ29yeV9zdHJhfZW46IkFkb3B0ZWQgdGV4dCI=.

24. "Ambassador's Introductory Call on Presidential Chief of Staff Ramiz Mehdiyev," WikiLeaks, July 11, 2006, https://wikileaks.org/cable/2006/07/06BAKU993.html; see also "Ambassador's Introductory Call on Foreign Minister Mammadyarov," July 6, 2006, https://wikileaks.org/cable/2006/07/06BAKU980.html.

25. Rovshan Ismayilov, "Broadcaster Shut-Down, Office Evictions Stir Free-Speech Concerns in Azerbaijan," EurasiaNet, November 27, 2006, http://www.refworld.org /docid/46f258c7c.html.

26. Mina Muradova and Khazri Bakinsky, "Azerbaijan: Another Opposition Paper, Party under Pressure for 'Back Rent,'" EurasiaNet, December 10, 2006, http://www .refworld.org/docid/46f258c723.html.

27. "Azerbaijan: Court Defies European Court Instruction to Free Journalist," Human Rights Watch, November 13, 2010, http://www.hrw.org/news/2010/11/13/azerbaijan -court-defies-european-court-instruction-free-journalist.

28. "The Functioning of Democratic Institutions in Azerbaijan," Resolution 1614 (2008), PACE, June 24, 2008, http://assembly.coe.int/nw/xml/XRef/Xref -XML2HTML-en.asp?fileid=17654&lang=en (emphasis added).

29. ESI, *Caviar Diplomacy*, 15–16.

30. "PACE Monitoring Committee Concerned with Deterioration of Human Rights Situation in Azerbaijan," *Azeri Report*, May 28, 2008, http://azerireport.com/index2 .php?option=com_content&do_pdf=1&id=173.

31. "DRL A/S Kramer Urges President Aliyev to Improve Azerbaijans [*sic*] Human Rights Performance," WikiLeaks, July 8, 2008, https://wikileaks.org/cable/2008 /07/08BAKU652.html.

32. ESI, *Caviar Diplomacy*, 15–16, citing "Council of Europe Head Anticipates Improved Vote in Azerbaijan," RFE/RL, July 15, 2008, http://www.rferl.org/content /Council_Of_Europe_Azerbaijan_Election/1183802.html.

33. OSCE/ODIHR, Republic of Azerbaijan, Presidential Election, 9 October 2013.

34. Novruzali Mammedov, an activist for Talysh rights, was sentenced to ten years in prison. He later died in custody.

35. See "BBC Panorama: Eurovision's Dirty Secret—Azerbaijan" YouTube video, 28:56, posted by "Chaîne de AzerbaijanRevolution," May 22, 2012, https://www.youtube.com/watch?v=Oea2XGsIbvI.

36. "Azerbaijani Authorities Interrogate Music Fan over Eurovision Vote for Armenia," RFE/RL, August 14, 2009, http://www.rferl.org/content/feature/1800013.html.

37. ESI, *Caviar Diplomacy*, 18.

38. *Azerbaijan's Presidential Poll Marked Considerable Progress, but Did Not Meet All Election Commitments*, OSCE/ODIHR, October 16, 2008, http://www.osce.org/odihr/elections/75250.

39. ESI, *Caviar Diplomacy*, 27–28.

40. Diuk, *Next Generation of Youth in Russia, Ukraine and Azerbaijan*, 85; see also page 80 on "patriarchalism" in the opposition parties.

41. ESI, *Caviar Diplomacy*, 1–2.

42. Contrast the example of President George H. W. Bush asking comedian Dana Carvey to do his impression of the president in the White House; see Aaron Blake, "H. W. Bush Imitates Dana Carvey," *Washington Post*, August 29, 2012, http://www.washingtonpost.com/blogs/post-politics/wp/2012/08/29/h-w-bush-imitates-dana-carvey/.

43. "Azerbaijan: Changes to Media Law Constrict Journalists, Activities," WikiLeaks, February 25, 2010, https://wikileaks.org/cable/2010/02/10BAKU132.html.

44. "Case of Fatullayev v. Azerbaijan (Application no. 40984/07)," ECHR, April 22, 2010, http://hudoc.echr.coe.int/eng?i=001-98401. Citation covers remainder of paragraph, including five block quotations.

45. "Azerbaijan: Court Defies European Court Instruction to Free Journalist," Human Rights Watch, November 13, 2010, http://www.hrw.org/news/2010/11/13/azerbaijan-court-defies-european-court-instruction-free-journalist.

46. "Sevil Aliyeva Congratulated Haqqin.az Group," Azeri Daily, July 23, [2015], http://azeridaily.com/news/9118.

47. Andrew Higgins, "Pricey Real Estate Deals in Dubai Raise Questions about Azerbaijan's President," *Washington Post*, March 5, 2010, http://www.washingtonpost.com/wp-dyn/content/article/2010/03/04/AR2010030405390.html.

48. See an overview of her coverage in an online story by Drew Sullivan, "An Exceptionally Brave Journalist," International Consortium of Investigative Journalists, May 14, 2012, http://www.icij.org/blog/2012/05/exceptionally-brave-journalist.

49. Ulviyye Asadzade and Khadija Ismayilova, "Aliyev's Azerbaijani Empire Grows, as Daughter Joins the Game," RFE/RL, August 13, 2010, http://www.rferl.org/content/Aliyevs_Azerbaijani_Empire_Grows_As_Daughter_Joins_The_Game/2127137.html.

50. The official claim that both were pardoned for "humanitarian reasons" is not credible, especially since Milli's father died while his son was in prison. Milli's father-in-law lost his job, and his wife divorced him. See Ellen Barry, "A Dissident Is Free from Jail, but His Punishment Is Not Over," *New York Times*, June 24, 2011, http://www.nytimes.com/2011/06/25/world/europe/25azerbaijan.html.

51. The word *nida* means "exclamation mark." See the organization's official website at http://www.nidavh.org/.

52.   "Right to Freedom of Association in Azerbaijan: Call for an Opinion from the Venice Commission," Human Rights House Foundation, April 8, 2011, http://humanrightshouse.org/Articles/16237.html.

53.   "Venice Commission Critical to Azerbaijani NGO Law," Human Rights House Foundation, November 23, 2011, http://humanrightshouse.org/Articles/17215.html.

54.   Ibid.

55.   Khadija Ismayilova, "Azerbaijani President's Family Benefits from Eurovision Hall Construction," RFE/RL, May 9, 2012, http://www.rferl.org/content/azerbaijan_first_family_build_eurovision_arena/24575761.html.

56.   "Sing for Democracy: Azerbaijan," Rafto Foundation for Human Rights, May 21, 2012, http://archive.rafto.no/article/835/Sing_for_democracy_Azerbaijan.

57.   A UN-produced film from 2011 provides more details on evictions and women's rights. See "Azerbaijan: Not Safe in Her Own Home," YouTube video, 4:52, posted by "United Nations," November 18, 2011, https://www.youtube.com/watch?v=1JBi4kAu67E.

58.   Milana Knezevic, "Azerbaijan: Six-Year Jail Sentence for Human Rights Activist," Index on Censorship, April 16, 2015, https://www.indexoncensorship.org/2015/04/azerbaijan-six-year-jail-sentence-for-human-rights-activist/.

59.   "Azerbaijan Eurovision 2012: Sing For Democracy Human Rights Campaign," YouTube video, 3:00, posted by "Geysar Gurbanov," May 14, 2012, https://www.youtube.com/watch?v=R5pMrPaJ1Bs.

60.   Hugh Williamson, "The Azerbaijanis Who Aren't Feeling the Eurovision Glow," Human Rights Watch, May 17, 2012, http://www.hrw.org/news/2012/05/17/azerbaijanis-who-arent-feeling-eurovision-glow. This article was also published in the *Guardian* on May 17, 2012.

61.   Steve Rosenberg, "Eurovision: Singing in Baku for Prizes and Freedom," *BBC Magazine*, May 26, 2012, http://www.bbc.com/news/magazine-18204154.

62.   "Azerbaijani President Amnesties 66 Inmates, Including Political Prisoners," RFE/RL, June 22, 2012, http://www.rferl.org/content/azerbaijan-president-pardons-66-inmates-including-9-political-prisoners/24623273.html.

63.   Knezevic, "Azerbaijan."

64.   The scenes are included in the original "Amazing Azerbaijan" video.

65.   "RFE/RL Correspondent in Azerbaijan Targeted in Blackmail Campaign," RFE/RL, March 7, 2012, http://www.rferl.org/content/press_release_azerbaijan_journalist_ismailova_blackmail/24508606.html.

66.   Valerie Hopkins, "Azerbaijan Fails to Investigate Harassment of OCCRP Reporter," Organized Crime and Corruption Reporting Project (OCCRP), April 5, 2012, https://occrp.org/occrp/index.php/en/ccwatch/cc-watch-indepth/1474-azerbaijan-fails-to-investigate-harassment-of-occrp-reporter.

67.   OSCE, "Regular Report to the Permanent Council," March 29, 2012, available on the US Department of State website at http://photos.state.gov/libraries/osce/242783/misc_pdfs/MAr_2012_RFOM_Report.pdf.

68.   Khadija Ismayilova and Nushabe Fatullayeva, "Azerbaijan's President Awarded Family Stake in Gold Fields," OCCRP, May 3, 2012, https://occrp.org/occrp/index.php/en/ccwatch/cc-watch-indepth/1495-azerbaijans-president-awarded-family-stake-in-gold-fields. For more details, see chapter 4.

69. "Amnesty International Calls on Azerbaijan to Free Youth Activist," Amnesty International, October 1, 2012, http://www.amnestyusa.org/news/press-releases/amnesty -international-calls-on-azerbaijan-to-free-youth-activist.

70. "Harassment of Yagublu Family," Azerbaijan TL;DR, August 14, 2012 (updated March 15, 2013), http://azerbaijantldr.com/harassment-of-yagublu-family/.

71. "Nigar Yagublu Is Sentenced to 2.5 Years," Contact.az, December 19, 2012, http://www.contact.az/docs/2012/Politics/121900022098en.htm#.VO98SuE7daw.

72. "Nigar Yaqublu azadlıqda," YouTube video, 4:09, posted by "Kanal13AZ," March 2, 2013, https://www.youtube.com/watch?v=AM5LVOXy2vM.

73. Claire Bigg, "Vote on Political Prisoners Highlights Azerbaijan's Attempts to 'Silence' PACE," RFE/RL, October 5, 2012, http://www.rferl.org/content/pace-azerbaijan -political-prisoners-lobbying/24730257.html.

74. See, e.g., an open letter to PACE from ESI; "Open Letter to 125 Current and Former Members of the Parliamentary Assembly of the Council of Europe (PACE)," ESI, April 23, 2014, http://www.esiweb.org/index.php?lang=en&id=556.

75. "Relations with Azerbaijan," NATO, April 7, 2016, http://www.nato.int/cps/en /natohq/topics_49111.htm.

76. See RL summary at "Azerbaijani Police Break Up Protests in Ismayilli," RFE/RL, January 24, 2013, http://www.rferl.org/content/azerbaijan-unrest-ismayilli/24882059.html.

77. Shahla Sultanova, "Two Opposition Leaders Arrested in Azerbaijan," Institute for War and Peace Reporting, February 5, 2013, https://iwpr.net/global-voices/two-opposition -leaders-arrested-azerbaijan.

78. REAL was founded in 2008 but became active in 2009. See Faik Medzhid, "In Azerbaijan, Public Movement 'ReAL' Founds Political Party," *Caucasian Knot*, May 29, 2014, http://eng.kavkaz-uzel.ru/articles/28276/.

79. Committee to Protect Journalists, "2014 Prison Census: Azerbaijan—Tofiq Yaqublu," RefWorld, December 17, 2014, http://www.refworld.org/docid/5498052215 .html.

80. "Ilgar Mammedov Put in Punishment Cell," Contact.az, August 14, 2015, http:// contact.az/docs/2015/Social/081400126241en.htm.

81. "Ilgar Mammadov Severely Beaten in Prison," Human Rights Freedoms, October 19, 2015, http://hrf.report/ilgar-mammadov-severely-beaten-in-prison/.

82. "Azerbaijani Protesters Fined Under New Mass-Gatherings Law," RFE/RL, January 14, 2013, http://www.rferl.org/content/azerbaijan-protests/24823470.html.

83. The amendments were passed by the Milli Majlis on February 15, 2013; see "Azerbaijani Parliament Ignores Call from Civil Society on New NGO Law," Eastern Partnership Civil Society Forum, February 15, 2013, http://eap-csf.eu/en/news-events /news/azerbaijani-parliament-ignores-call-from-civil-society-on-new-ngo-law/.

84. Discussion in *Nations in Transit 2014: Azerbaijan*, Freedom House, 2014, https://freedomhouse.org/report/nations-transit/2014/azerbaijan; and Human Rights Watch, *Tightening the Screws: Azerbaijan's Crackdown on Civil Society and Dissent* (Washington, DC: Human Rights Watch, 2013), http://www.hrw.org/reports/2013/09 /02/tightening-screws-0.

85. "NGOs in Azerbaijan Receive Grants below 50 Million Manats over 2013," Trend News Agency, December 3, 2013, http://en.trend.az/news/society/2218003.html.

86. Center for Legal Initiatives Public Union, Situation with the Right to Association in Azerbaijan (Warsaw: Center for Legal Initiatives Public Union, 2012), http://www.osce.org/odihr/94545.

87. "Stop Further Restrictions to the Right to Freedom of Association in Azerbaijan," Human Rights House Foundation, March 5, 2013, http://humanrightshouse.org/Articles/19106.html.

88. See the original "Amazing Azerbaijan" video. A full version aired on Belgian television, with original interviews in English or Azerbaijani and Flemish subtitles; see "PANORAMA 24/05: BAKU BACKSTAGE (UITZENDING)," YouTube, 50:16, posted by "munheb's channel," May 26, 2012, https://www.youtube.com/watch?v=Aes_56N92Nc.

89. "Presidential Election in Azerbaijan: Joint Statement by PACE and EP delegations," PACE, October 10, 2013, http://www.assembly.coe.int/nw/xml/News/News-View-EN.asp?newsid=4699&lang=2&cat=31.

90. OSCE/ODIHR, Republic of Azerbaijan, Presidential Election, October 9, 2013.

91. For a report on the dispute between Azerbaijan and the OSCE in Vienna that led to this downgrade, see "Stand-Off in Vienna as Azerbaijan Tries to Change the Mandate of the OSCE Office in Baku," Caucasus Elections Watch, May 20, 2013, http://electionswatch.org/2013/05/20/stand-off-in-vienna-as-azerbaijan-tries-to-change-the-mandate-of-the-osce-office-in-baku/; the language of the new mandate can be found at "OSCE Office in Baku Downgraded to Project Coordinator," Azerbaijan News Network, January 3, 2014, http://ann.az/en/osce-office-in-baku-downgraded-to-project-co-ordinator/.

92. OSCE/ODIHR, Republic of Azerbaijan, Presidential Election, October 9, 2013.

93. "Mysterious Explosions and Discretionary Arrests: A Day in the Life of Azerbaijan's Opposition," Amnesty International, March 5, 2014, https://www.amnesty.org/en/latest/news/2014/03/mysterious-explosions-and-discretionary-arrests-day-life-azerbaijan-s-opposition/.

94. On their arrest and torture in 2013, see "Azerbaijan: Authorities Targeting Youth Activists," Human Rights Watch, April 2, 2013, http://www.hrw.org/news/2013/04/02/azerbaijan-authorities-targeting-youth-activists. On the sentences they received, see the Meydan TV report, "NIDA Activists Sentenced (UPDATED)," Meydan TV, May 6, 2014, http://www.meydan.tv/en/site/news/1581/NIDA-Activists-Sentenced-%28UPDATED%29.htm.

95. "World Report; Azerbaijan," Human Rights Watch, 2014, http://www.hrw.org/world-report/2014/country-chapters/azerbaijan. On the hunger strike, see "Open Letter to 125 Current and Former Members of the Parliamentary Assembly of the Council of Europe (PACE)."

96. Vugar Gojayev, "Azerbaijan: Rights Activists on the Brink," Eurasianet.org, November 14, 2014, http://www.eurasianet.org/node/70936.

97. "PACE Awards Annual Havel Prize to Azerbaijani Activist," RFE/RL, September 29, 2014, http://www.rferl.org/content/havel-rights-prize-azerbaijan-mammadli/26611598.html.

98. See the ruling at "Case of Ilgar Mammedov v. Azerbaijan (Application no. 15172/13)," ECHR, May 22, 2014, http://hudoc.echr.coe.int/eng?i=001-144124. The decision was affirmed in October.

99. See Medzhid, "In Azerbaijan, Public Movement 'ReAL' Founds Political Party," and "Azerbaijan: Political Activists Held on Fabricated Charges Must Be Released," Amnesty

International, March 14, 2014, http://www.amnesty.org/en/news/azerbaijan-political -activists-held-fabricated-charges-must-be-released-2014-03-14. The French government issued a statement that France "deplores" the sentencing of Ilgar Mammadov; see "Azerbaijan: Sentencing of Ilgar Mammadov (March 17, 2014)," French Ministry of Foreign Affairs and International Development, March 17, 2014, http://www.diplomatie.gouv.fr/en/country-files /azerbaijan/events-7746/article/azerbaijan-sentencing-of-ilgar.

100. The following section is slightly modified from the Azerbaijan country report in the Freedom House NIT volume for 2015, of which I am the author. I thank Freedom House for guidance in making use of this passage.

101. See the "Joint Staff Working Document: Implementation of the European Neighbourhood Policy in Azerbaijan—Progress in 2013 and Recommendations for Action," High Representative of the European Union for Foreign Affairs and Security Policy, European Commission, March 27, 2014, http://eeas.europa.eu/enp/pdf/2014 /country-reports/azerbaijan_en.pdf.

102. "NGO Law Monitor: Azerbaijan," International Center for Not-for-Profit Law, updated March 23, 2016, http://www.icnl.org/research/monitor/azerbaijan.html.

103. Venice Commission, "Opinion on the Law on Non-Governmental Organizations (Public Associations and Funds) as Amended of the Republic of Azerbaijan," CoE, December 15, 2014, http://www.venice.coe.int/webforms/documents/default.aspx?pdffile=CDL -AD%282014%29043-e.

104. "Prezident İlham Əliyev QHT-lər haqqında qanunvericiliyə mürtəce düzəlişləri imzalayıb," Contact.az, November 19, 2014, http://contact.az/docs/2014 /Politics/111900097069az.htm.

105. "QHT-lərlə bağlı qanunvericiliyə dəyişikliklər kimin xeyrinədir?" Contact.az, November 19, 2014, http://contact.az/docs/2014/Social/111900097093az.htm.

106. Sara Rajabova, "Azerbaijan Possesses Sufficient Funds for NGO Financing," *AzerNews*, November 20, 2014, http://www.azernews.az/azerbaijan/73524.html.

107. "Azerbaijani Officials Raid US-Based NGO," RFE/RL, September 5, 2014, http://www.rferl.org/content/azerbaijan-raids-us-ngo-irex/26569077.html; and "IREX Azerbaijan Office Searched, Equipment Seized," IREX, September 8, 2014, http://www .irex.org/news/irex-azerbaijan-office-searched-equipment-seized (link discontinued).

108. "Surviving a Crisis: Q&A with Azerbaijan's Gubad Ibadoglu," Natural Resources Governance Institute, accessed August 20, 2016, http://archive.resourcegovernance.org /node/70210.

109. "Azerbaijan: Transparency Group Should Suspend Membership," Human Rights Watch, August 14, 2014, http://www.hrw.org/news/2014/08/14/azerbaijan-transparency -group-should-suspend-membership.

110. "Transparency International Under Pressure in Azerbaijan," RFE/RL, August 27, 2014, http://www.rferl.org/content/azerbaijan-corruption-transparency-international -baku/26553162.html.

111. Tahmina Tagizade, "Six Years' Jail for Leading Azeri NGO Head," Institute for War and Peace Reporting, July 21, 2014, https://iwpr.net/global-voices/six-years-jail -leading-azeri-ngo-head.

112. "Opposition Journalist in Azerbaijan Detained on Hooliganism Charges," RFE/ RL, August 29, 2014, http://www.rferl.org/content/azerbaijan-free-press-arrest/26556989

.html; see a summary of reports on his case on the Human Rights Freedoms site at "Seymur Hazi: HRF Report," accessed July 20, 2016, http://hrf.report/tag/seymur-hazi/page/2/.

113. "Prosecutor Requests 7 Years Imprisonment for Journalist Rauf Mirkadirov," Trend News Agency, December 16, 2015, http://en.trend.az/azerbaijan/society/2470165 .html; "Prominent Azerbaijani Journalist Jailed for Six Years," RFE/RL, December 28, 2015, http://www.rferl.org/content/prominent-azeri-journalist-jailed-for-six-years/27453794 .html; and "Azerbaijani Court Rules to Release Journalist Rauf Mirkadirov," Trend News Agency, March 17, 2016, http://en.trend.az/azerbaijan/society/2508281.html.

114. Ilham Aliyev purged the followers of Fatullah Gülen, a former ally-turned-enemy of Erdoğan, soon after this.

115. Shahin Abbasov, "Will Journalist's Arrest End Azerbaijani-Armenian Citizen Diplomacy?" Eurasianet.org, April 22, 2014, http://www.eurasianet.org/node/68297; and "Leyla Yunus: Subject of 'People's Diplomacy' Is Just an Excuse for Repression," Federal Lezghi: National and Cultural Autonomy, May 5, 2014, http://flnka.ru/digest/6310-leyla -yunus-subject-of-peoples-diplomacy-is-just-an-excuse-for-repression.html.

116. "Azerbaijan: Leading Rights Defender Arrested," Human Rights Watch, August 5, 2014 http://www.hrw.org/news/2014/08/05/azerbaijan-leading-rights-defender-arrested-0.

117. For details on these and more than ninety-five other cases, see *The List: Political Prisoners in Azerbaijan*, ESI, August 10, 2014, http://www.esiweb.org/pdf/THE%20 LIST%20-%2098%20political%20prisoners%20in%20Azerbaijan%20-%20August%20 2014.pdf. On Yunus' lawyers, see "Azerbaijani Rights Activist 'Deprived of Lawyer,'" RFE/RL, October 30, 2014, http://www.rferl.org/content/yunus-leyla-azerbaijan-lawyer -cavadov-rights-armenia/26665992.html.

118. "The List of Political Prisoners in Azerbaijan," Eastern Partnership Civil Society Forum, August 10, 2014, http://eap-csf.eu/assets/files/List_of_Political_Prisoners _AZ-%282%29-%281%29.pdf. Rasul Jafarov's Human Rights Club had issued a list of 143 prisoners in October 2013.

119. On the court decision of August 19, 2014, to arrest him, see "Azerbaijani Foreign Ministry: Emin Huseynov Went into Hiding at Swiss Embassy to Avoid Investigation," Apa.az, February 12, 2015, http://en.apa.az/xeber_azerbaijani_foreign_ministry__emin _husey_223014.html; see also "Emin Huseynov Forced into Hiding in Azerbaijan," Human Rights House Foundation, February 11, 2015, http://humanrightshouse.org /Articles/20730.html.

120. See *The List: Political Prisoners in Azerbaijan*.

121. "Səid Nuri Azərbaycandan çıxarılıb," Azadlıq Radiosu, September 11, 2014, http://www.azadliq.org/a/26565995.html.

122. "Milli Şura sədri DİN rəsmisinin cavabını verdi FOTO," Azadliq.info, October 3, 2014, http://www.azadliq.info/xeberler/358-xeber/53422-milli-ura-sdrindn-dn-rsmisin -cavab.html.

123. "Transparency International Under Pressure in Azerbaijan," RFE/RL, August 27, 2014, http://www.rferl.org/content/azerbaijan-corruption-transparency-international -baku/26553162.html.

124. "Azerbaijan: Government Repression Tarnishes Chairmanship," Human Rights Watch, September 29, 2014, http://www.hrw.org/news/2014/09/29/azerbaijan -government-repression-tarnishes-chairmanship.

125. Thorbjørn Jagland, "Azerbaijan's Human Rights Are on a Knife Edge," *Guardian* (London), November 4, 2014, http://www.theguardian.com/commentisfree/2014 /nov/03/azerbaijan-human-rights-uk-tory-echr.

126. "Council of Europe Commissioner Slams Baku for Human Rights Violations," RFE/RL, September 8, 2014, http://www.rferl.org/content/muiznieks-council-of-europe -human-rights-commissioner-azerbaijan/26572064.html.

127. "Prevention of Torture: UN Human Rights Body Suspends Azerbaijan Visit Citing Official Obstruction," United Nations Human Rights Office of the High Commissioner, September 17, 2014, http://www.ohchr.org/EN/NewsEvents/Pages/DisplayNews .aspx?NewsID=15047&LangID=E.

128. See the testimony of Deputy Assistant Secretary of State Thomas O. Melia to the Helsinki Commission, "US-Azerbaijan Relations: The Democracy and Human Rights Dimension," Bureau of Democracy, Human Rights, and Labor, US Department of State, June 11, 2014, http://www.state.gov/j/drl/rls/rm/2014/227450.htm; and the State Department official statement, "Welcoming the Release of Civil Society Activists in Azerbaijan (Marie Harf)," Bureau of Public Affairs: Office of Press Relations, US Department of State, October 22, 2014, http://www.state.gov/r/pa/prs/ps/2014/10/233268.htm.

129. See the note by Chargé d'Affaires Gary Robbins to the Special Permanent Council, Vienna, "Ongoing Detentions and Arrests of Peaceful Activists in Azerbaijan," US Department of State, August 14, 2014, http://photos.state.gov/libraries/azerbaijan/749085 /highlights/osce_Azerbaijan_Ongoing_Detentions.pdf. Since September 10, 2013, Daniel Baer has been US ambassador to the OSCE.

130. Nils Muižnieks, "Nils Muižnieks: Azerbaijan's Reprisals against Brave Activists and Journalists Must Stop Now," Index on Censorship, November 24, 2014, http:// www.indexoncensorship.org/2014/11/nils-muiznieks-azerbaijans-reprisals-brave-activists -journalists-must-stop-now/.

131. The sudden disbarment of Khalid Bagirov, one of Khadija Ismayilova's attorneys, is a case in point; see Giorgi Lomsadze, "Azerbaijan: Next They'll Come for the Lawyers?," Eurasianet.org, December 11, 2014, http://www.eurasianet.org/node/71301.

132. "Daily Press Briefing (Jan Psaki)," Bureau of Public Affairs: Office of Press Relations, US Department of State, December 1, 2014, http://www.state.gov/r/pa/prs /dpb/2014/12/234568.htm#AZERBAIJAN; and "US Criticizes Azerbaijan Crackdown," *Covcas Bulletin*, December 2, 2014, http://www.covcasbulletin.info/?p=1059.

133. Khadija Ismayilova, "TeliaSonera's Behind-the-Scenes Connection to Azerbaijani President's Daughters," RFE/RL, July 15, 2014, http://www.rferl.org/content/teliasonera -azerbaijan-aliyev-corruption-investigation-occrp/25457907.html.

134. Till Bruchner, "Ten Days in the Life of Ilham Aliyev, President of Absurdistan," *Huffington Post*, January 4, 2015, http://www.huffingtonpost.com/till-bruckner/state -department-barely-c_b_6390974.html.

135. Andrei Korybko, "Azerbaijan Should Be Very Afraid of Nuland," *Oriental Review*, March 1, 2015, http://orientalreview.org/2015/03/01/azerbaijan-should-be-very-afraid -of-nuland/. This piece was reprinted in several other venues.

136. Quoted by Michael Weiss, "Trapped in Baku," *Foreign Policy*, February 11, 2015, https://foreignpolicy.com/2015/02/11/trapped-in-baku-azerbaijan-emil-huseynov-swiss -embassy.

137. "New Amendments to the Criminal Code Are Aimed against Investigative Journalism?," Human Rights Freedoms, March 6, 2015, http://hrf.report/tougher -responsibility-for-disclosure-of-state-secrets/ (emphasis added).

138. "Vəkillərdən biri Xədicə İsmayılın müdafiəsindən kənarlaşdılıb," Azadlıq Radiosu, March 13, 2015, http://www.azadliq.org/a/26899798.html.

139. "Zhurnalist Mustafaev zaiavil o davlenii sledstviia posle vystupleniia v zashchitu Ismailovoi," *Kavkazskii uzel,* May 5, 2015, http://www.kavkaz-uzel.ru/articles/261788/.

140. "2015 PEN / Barbara Goldsmith Freedom to Write Award: Khadija Ismayilova," PEN America, 2015, http://www.pen.org/2015-pen-goldsmith-freedom-write-award.

141. See a list of the main figures at "Leyla Yunus: 'They're Planning to Wipe Us Out,'" Index on Censorship, August 7, 2015, https://www.indexoncensorship.org/2015/08/leyla -yunus-theyre-planning-to-wipe-us-out/.

142. "Azerbaijan: Ailing Rights Defenders Convicted in Political Trial," Human Rights Watch, August 13, 2015, https://www.hrw.org/news/2015/08/13/azerbaijan-ailing-rights -defenders-convicted-political-trial.

143. An initial hearing was held on July 24, in which Ismayilova rejected the legitimacy of the charges. The trial continued on August 7. "Hearing on Khadija Ismayilova's Case Proceeded," Apa.az, August 14, 2015, http://en.apa.az/xeber_hearing_on_khadija _ismayilova___s_case_pro_230806.html.

144. "In Blow to Independent Media, Azerbaijan Sentences Ismayilova to 7½ Years," Broadcasting Board of Governors, September 1, 2015, http://www.bbg.gov /blog/2015/09/01/in-blow-to-independent-media-azerbaijan-sentences-ismayilova-to -7-12-years/; see also Committee to Protect Journalists, "2015 Prison Census – Khadija Ismayilova," RefWorld, December 14, 2015, http://www.refworld.org/docid/56701fbf15 .html.

145. Shaun Walker, "Azerbaijani Journalist Dies after Criticizing Footballer on Facebook," *Guardian* (London), August 11, 2015, http://www.theguardian.com /world/2015/aug/10/azerbaijani-journalist-rasim-aliyev-javid-huseynov.

146. "KZGO Requires Public Control into Investigation over Murder of Journalist," Contact.az, August 14, 2015, http://contact.az/docs/2015/Social/081400126273en.htm.

147. Emin Milli, "Death Threats, Prison and Eurovision: Exiled Journalist Answers Your Questions about Azerbaijan," *Guardian* (London), December 7, 2015, http://www .theguardian.com/world/live/2015/dec/05/azerbaijan-press-freedom-emin-milli-bloggers.

148. "PACE President Welcomes Release of Azerbaijani Civil Society Activist Arif Yunus," PACE, November 13, 2015, http://assembly.coe.int/nw/xml/News/News -View-EN.asp?newsid=5873&cat=15.

149. "The Functioning of Democratic Institutions in Azerbaijan," Resolution 2062 (2015), PACE, June 23, 2015, http://assembly.coe.int/nw/xml/XRef/Xref -XML2HTML-en.asp?fileid=21953&lang=en.

150. "Rights Activist Leyla Yunis Freed from Jail in Azerbaijan," RFE/RL, December 9, 2015, http://www.rferl.org/content/leyla-yunus-released-azerbaijan/27416597.html.

151. Private communication with Ramis Yunus, Arif's brother.

152. "Azerbaijan: Leyla and Arif Yunus Finally Out of the Country to Receive Urgent Medical Treatment," OMCT, April 19, 2016, http://www.omct.org/human-rights -defenders/urgent-interventions/azerbaijan/2016/04/d23722/.

153. Azerbaijan Democracy Act of 2015, H. R. 4264, 114 Cong. (December 16, 2015), https://www.congress.gov/bill/114th-congress/house-bill/4264/text.

154. "İlham əliyev 210 məhbusu əvf edib, aralarında bir nəfər belə siyasi məhbus yoxdur (YENİLƏNİB)," Contact.az, December 28, 2015, https://contact.az/docs/2015/Politics/122800141869az.htm.

155. "Rauf Mirqədirov 6 il müddətinə azadlıqdan məhrum edilib (YENİLƏNİB-Foto)", Contact.az, December 28, 2015, https://contact.az/docs/2015/Social/122800141831az.htm.

156. It was issued simultaneously in Russian (most likely the language in which it was written) and in Azerbaijani. Ramiz Mehdiyev, "Ikili standartlarin dunya nizami ve muasir Azərbaycan," Yeni Müsavat, December 3, 2014, http://musavat.com/news/siyaset/ramiz-mehdiyev-ikili-standartlar-siyaseti-ve-beshinci-kolon_231451.html.

157. Robert Coalson, "Azerbaijan Tightens Screws on Civil Society, Independent Media," Eurasianet.org, September 10, 2014, http://www.eurasianet.org/node/69931.

158. A brief description is available in English at "Mehdiyev Accuses US of 'Color Revolution,'" Contact.az, December 4, 2014, http://www.contact.az/docs/2014/Politics/120400098728en.htm.

159. Institute for Reporters' Freedom and Safety, "Civil Society Harassed as Azerbaijan Assumes Council of Europe Chairmanship," IFEX, May 14, 2014, https://www.ifex.org/azerbaijan/2014/05/14/council_chairmanship/.

160. Posted on the @presidentaz Twitter account on November 22, 2014, at https://twitter.com/presidentaz?original_referer=http%3A%2F%2Fwww.rferl.org%2Fcontent%2Fhavel-rights-prize-azerbaijan-mammadli%2F26611598.html&tw_i=536168564445949952&tw_p=embeddedtimeline&tw_w=346592683231424513. A similar message was posted one year later, on November 27, 2015, after tainted parliamentary elections.

161. "Triumph of Caviar Diplomacy?" YouTube video, 15:26, posted by "MeydanTV," January 23, 2014, https://www.youtube.com/watch?v=BiWO22cDRHo.

162. Ibid.

163. "Client Profile: Azerbaijan American Alliance," Open Secrets, 2015, http://www.opensecrets.org/lobby/clientsum.php?id=D000064546.

164. Burton, "Why Azerbaijan is Important to America and the Free World" (emphasis added).

Chapter 6

1. In this case, I am focusing mainly on freedom of speech, assembly, association, and worship. I am leaving aside a body of "revisionist" literature on human rights that considers the entire concept problematic.

2. Altay Goyushov, "Islam in Azerbaijan (Historical Background)," *Caucasus Analytical Digest* 44 (November 20, 2012), 3, http://e-collection.library.ethz.ch/eserv/eth:7148/eth-7148-01.pdf. Goyushov says that Nader considered Shi'ism a "Jafari" fifth legal school (*madhhab*), thus suggesting that it could fit into a Sunni framework.

3. Anar Valiyev, "Azerbaijan: Islam in a Post-Soviet Republic," *Middle East Review of International Affairs* 9, no. 4 (2005): 1–13.

4. There was a larger modernist movement in the nineteenth-century Muslim world associated with leaders like the Islamic political reformer Jamal al-Din al-Afghani.

5. Altstadt, *Azerbaijani Turks*, chaps. 3–4; and Swietochowski, *Russian Azerbaijan, 1905–1920*. On the movements and consciousness of this cohort of Muslim reformers, see James H. Meyer, *Turks across Empires: Marketing Muslim Identity in the Russian-Ottoman Borderlands, 1856–1914* (New York: Oxford University Press, 2014).

6. The groups advocated for different approaches to cultural autonomy. The Tatar approach was territorial-based, and the Azerbaijani approach was nonterritorial. This was not a sectarian matter. See A. Arsharuni and Kh. Gabdullin, *Ocherki pan-Islamizma i pan-Tiurkizma v Rossii* (Moscow: Bezbozhnik, 1931). According to Alexandre Bennigsen, Russia's Muslims regarded Shi'ism as a fifth *madhhab*, the Jafari, as in note 2 to this chapter.

7. The novel *Ali and Nino*, by the pseudonymous writer Kurban Said, captures the emotional dilemmas of the early twentieth century.

8. Edith Ybert, "Islam, Nationalism and Socialism in the Parties and Political Organizations of Azerbaijani Muslims in the Early Twentieth Century," *Caucasus Survey* 1, no. 1 (2013): 43–58. Ybert updates earlier work on this topic, including my own work and that of Bennigsen, Swietochowski, and others, by her use of newly opened archives.

9. Altstadt, *Politics of Culture in Soviet Azerbaijan*, chap. 1.

10. In 1913, the population of Baku reached 214,672, according to the city census. Azerbaijanis were nearly 46,000, or 21 percent of the population, but Iranian citizens, mostly Azerbaijanis (Turkic speakers), were another 25,000 or 12 percent. Since 1903, however, the ethnic Russians outnumbered the locally born Azerbaijanis. Jews numbered only 9,690, but this figure would more than double by the 1926 census; that census shows 57,000 Jews in Azerbaijan, of which 7,500 were Tats or Mountain Jews.

11. Dzheikhun Khadzhibeili [Jeyhun Hadjibeyli], *Anti-islamskaia propaganda i ee metody v Azerbaidzhane* (Munich: Institute for the Study of the USSR, 1957).

12. Alexandre Bennigsen, in his graduate seminar "Soviet Islam" at the University of Chicago in the 1970s, contrasted Soviet treatment of the Russian and Armenian Orthodox churches to the more aggressive prosecution of Roman Catholicism, Judaism, Islam, and Buddhism, arguing that religions with centers abroad presented a competing pole of political loyalty as well as beliefs.

13. Author's conversation with Azerbaijani students at the Mir-i Arab Madrassa in 1984.

14. See Alexandre Bennigsen and Marie Broxup, *The Islamic Threat to the Soviet State* (New York, St. Martin's Press, 1983); and Michael Rywkin, *Moscow's Muslim Challenge: Soviet Central Asia* (Armonk, NY: M. E. Sharpe, 1983). The magazine *Muslims of the Soviet East* was a main propaganda arm for foreign distribution, and it was published in English, Arabic, and other languages; however, it was not available inside the Soviet Union itself.

15. Much of this analysis is based on my own observations and diaries from my first trip to Baku in 1980–81, the year after Khomeini came to power. A fine work on US involvement in Iran is James Bill, *The Eagle and the Lion: The Tragedy of American-Iranian Relations* (New Haven, CT: Yale University Press, 1988).

16. One sign of this Russian arrogance was the refusal of longtime residents, even second- or third-generation Russian residents in Baku, to speak Azerbaijani, even though some knew the language.

17. Demographer Murray Feshbach and others have analyzed the impact of continued relative growth of Central Asian peoples to Russians, extrapolating to such issues as the composition of the Soviet military in the year 2000. See, e.g., Murray Feshbach, "Between the Lines of the 1979 Soviet Census," *Population and Development Review* 8, no. 2 (1982): 347–61.

18. I witnessed many such practices during my travels in Azerbaijan in 1980–81 and 1984–85.

19. Michael Rywkin, "National Symbiosis: Vitality, Religion, Identity, Allegiance," in *The USSR and the Muslim World*, ed. Yaacov Ro'i (London: Allen Unwin, 1984), 3–15.

20. During more than a year of work in Baku in the 1980s, I had many such conversations with people in their twenties.

21. David S. Siroky and Ceyhun Mahmudlu, "E Pluribus Unum? Ethnicity, Islam and the Construction of Identity in Azerbaijan," *Problems of Post-Communism* 63, no. 2 (2016): 94–107.

22. A note of caution on work of foreign analysts who visit for short periods, or use only Russian: they face special challenges when describing Islam. They sometimes extrapolate their individual observations for a general truth.

23. Cornell, *Azerbaijan since Independence*, 333–34.

24. I was sitting in Panakh Huseinov's office when he dealt with such an incident in the summer of 1992.

25. Valiyev, "Azerbaijan," 8.

26. In 2006, Müsavat Party chairman Isa Gambar noted that his party workers saw this pattern. See also Thomas A. Liles, "Commanding Right and Forbidding Wrong: The Rise of Sectarian Contention and Politics in Independent Azerbaijan" (master's thesis, Harvard University, March 2015).

27. Bayram Balci, "Le chiisme en Azerbaïdjan post-soviétique: Entre influences iraniennes et dynamiques internes," in *Les mondes chiites et l'Iran*, ed. Sabrina Mervin (Paris: Karthala, 2007), 163–88, cited by International Crisis Group, *Azerbaijan: Independent Islam and the State*, Europe Report No. 91 (Baku: International Crisis Group, 2008), 7n74, http://www.crisisgroup.org/-/media/Files/europe/191_azerbaijan_independent_islam _and_the_state.pdf.

28. Valiyev, "Azerbaijan," 6.

29. James Reynolds, "Why Azerbaijan Is Closer to Israel than Iran," BBC News, August 12, 2012, http://www.bbc.com/news/world-europe-19063885. See also Jaffe-Hoffmann "Azerbaijan and Israel: A Covert but Strategic Relationship."

30. Figures on Israeli oil imports vary. The 40 percent figure comes from Brenda Shaffer, who is quoted by Agayev, "Israel's Top Oil Supplier Endures Gaza as Azeri Ties Grow." Shaffer is identified as former adviser to Israeli's Ministry of Energy and Water Resources. She also has been an adviser to SOCAR and, since 2013, a visiting researcher at Georgetown University. Her advocacy in the US Congress for the Aliyev regime became controversial in 2014 when she failed to disclose her SOCAR links.

31. Reynolds, "Why Azerbaijan Is Closer to Israel than Iran"; and Afet Mehdiyeva, "Iranian Denies Plan to Attack Israeli Embassy in Azerbaijan," Reuters, November 21,

2013, http://www.reuters.com/article/2013/11/21/us-azerbaijan-iran-arrest-idUSBRE9A K11E20131121.

32. Quoted by Reynolds, "Why Azerbaijan Is Closer to Israel than Iran."

33. The clash over Turkey's upsurge of support for Palestinians starting in 2010 ruined relations, but a thaw seemed to be starting in early 2016.

34. "Reactions to the Insulting Article Published in Iran Newspaper about Azerbaijanis," *South Azerbaijan* (blog), June 1, 2006, http://southazerbayjan.blogspot.com/2006/06 /reactions-to-insulting-article.html.

35. Cornell, *Azerbaijan since Independence*, 282–83.

36. The Gulen movement is an offshoot of the Nurcu, founded by Said Nursi. According to Bayram Balci, classical Nurcu place more emphasis on religion than education; they are also active in Azerbaijan, as are the Naqshibandi group of Osman Nuri Topbash. Much of this section is based on Bayram Balci, "Between Secular Education and Islamic Philosophy: The Approach and Achievement of Fethullah Gülen's Followers in Azerbaijan," *Caucasus Survey* 1, no. 1 (2013): 107–16.

37. Fuad Aliyev, "The Gülen Movement in Azerbaijan," *Current Trends in Islamist Ideology*, vol. 14 (Hudson Institute Series, December 2012), 90–103, http://www.hudson .org/content/researchattachments/attachment/1160/20130124_ct14aliev.pdf.

38. Eldar Mammedov, "Azerbaijan: Evaluating Baku's Attitude toward the Gulen Movement," Eurasianet.org, February 16, 2012, http://www.eurasianet.org/node/65013.

39. Author's personal observation during a 2008 trip to Baku.

40. Balci, "Between Secular Education and Islamic Philosophy," 108 and 112.

41. Bayram Balci, *The AKP/Gülen Crisis in Turkey: Consequences for Central Asia and the Caucasus*, Central Asia Policy Brief No. 16 (Washington, DC: Elliott School of International Affairs, George Washington University, 2014); and Shahla Sultanova, "Azerbaijan: Wary of Breaking Ties with Gülen in US?," Contact.az, October 3, 2014, www.contact.az /docs/2014/Analytics/100300092367en.htm#.VVIPVZPPpyE.

42. Shahla Sultanova, "Azerbaijan Backing Turkey's Crackdown on Gülen Movement," Eurasianet.org, April 15, 2014, http://www.eurasianet.org/node/68274.

43. Lamiya Adilgizi, "Azerbaijan Closes Gülen Schools," Institute for War and Peace Reporting, July 4, 2014, https://iwpr.net/global-voices/azerbaijan-closes-g%C3%BClen-schools.

44. "Azerbaijan: University, Paper Closed as Anti-Gülen Cleanup Continues," Eurasianet, July 20, 2016, http://www.eurasianet.org/node/79781.

45. Guido Steinberg, "Jihadi Salafism and the Shi'is: Remarks about the Intellectual Roots of Anti-Shi'ism," in *Global Salafism: Islam's New Religious Movement*, ed. Roel Meijer (London: Hurst, 2009), 107–25.

46. Emmanuel Karagiannis and Emil Souleimanov and Maya Ehrmann present the same picture; see Emmanuel Karagiannis, "Political Islam in the Former Soviet Union: Uzbekistan and Azerbaijan Compared," *Dynamics of Asymmetric Conflict* 3, no. 1 (2010): 53–54; and Emil Souleimanov and Maya Ehrmann, "The Rise of Militant Salafism in Azerbaijan and Its Regional Implications," *Middle East Policy* 20, no. 3 (2013): 111–20; both draw on Valiyev, "Azerbaijan."

47. Ahmad Moussalli describes complex considerations leading Salafis to jihadi extremism in *Wahhabism, Salafism and Islamism: Who Is the Enemy?* Conflicts Forum Monograph (Beirut/London: Conflicts Forum, 2009), 19–22. I thank Mohammad Ataie for bringing this excellent analysis to my attention.

48. On Gulf State funds, see Liles, "Commanding Right and Forbidding Wrong," 25–26. On Salafism, see also Altay Goyushov, "Islamic Revival in Azerbaijan," in *Current Trends in Islamist Ideology*, vol. 7, ed. Hillel Fradkin, Husain Haqqani, Eric Brown, and Hassan Mneimneh (Washington, DC: Hudson Institute, 2008), 66–81; and International Crisis Group, *Azerbaijan*, 7.

49. "Decision [on] Application no. 15405/04; Juma Mosque Congregation and others Against Azerbaijan," ECHR, January 8, 2013, 2.

50. See Georgetown University's Berkeley Center for Religion, Peace, and World Affairs at http://berkleycenter.georgetown.edu/organizations/caucasus-muslim-board (site requires login to access).

51. He cannot aspire to "*marja-i taqlid*" (authoritative interpreter status). Even this concept is not widely understood in Azerbaijan. Bayram Balci, private communication with author.

52. *Joint Opinion on the Law on Freedom of Religious Belief of Azerbaijan*, Opinion 681/2012 (Warsaw: Venice Commission, 2012), http://www.venice.coe.int /webforms/documents/default.aspx?pdffile=CDL-AD%282012%29022-e.

53. See the English-language version of the SCWRO website, modified for style, at "The State Committee of Azerbaijan Republic for the Work with Religious Associations," Azerbaijan.az, accessed July 20, 2016, http://www.azerbaijan.az/_StatePower/_Committee Concern/committeeConcern_02_e.html (emphasis added).

54. On personal animosities and the SCWRO demand for CMB registration, see Liles, "Commanding Right and Forbidding Wrong," 45–47.

55. Sultanova, "Azerbaijan Backing Turkey's Crackdown on Gülen Movement."

56. See the presidential decree at the official "President of Azerbaijan" website, http:// az.president.az (Azerbaijani) or http://en.president.az/ (English):, http://president.az /articles/12420.

57. See Liles, "Commanding Right and Forbidding Wrong," 48 and 63, citing Goyushov.

58. "International Religious Freedom Report for 2011: Azerbaijan," Bureau of Democracy, Human Rights and Labor, US Department of State, July 30, 2012, http:// www.state.gov/documents/organization/192997.pdf.

59. International Crisis Group, *Azerbaijan*, 3–6; and Liles, "Commanding Right and Forbidding Wrong," 50.

60. "USCIRF Annual Report for 2013: Azerbaijan," US Commission on International Religious Freedom, accessed July 20, 2016, http://www.uscirf.gov/sites/default/files /resources/Azerbaijan%202%20Pager%202013%20final%281%29.pdf.

61. Felix Corley, "Azerbaijan: The Latest Devious Move to Control Religious Communities," Forum 18 Report, June 6, 2011, http://www.refworld.org /pdfid/4df067572.pdf.

62. Joint Opinion on the Law on Freedom of Religious Belief of Azerbaijan," Opinion 681/2012.

63. Felix Corley, "Government Blames 'Errors' for Negative Venice Commission/ OSCE Opinion," Forum 18 Report, October 23, 2012, http://www.refworld.org /docid/5087cb1d2.html.

64. "International Religious Freedom Report for 2011: Azerbaijan."

65. Karagiannis, "Political Islam in the Former Soviet Union," 47, citing Arif Yunusov and the US State Department's Bureau of Democracy, Human Rights, and Labor.

66. Peter Baehr and Daniel Gordon, "From the Headscarf to the Burqa: The Role of Social Theorists in Shaping Laws against the Veil," *Economy and Society* 42, no. 2 (2013): 249–80.

67. See Azerbaijan's 1995 Constitution, with amendments, at http://www.azerbaijan.az /portal/General/Constitution/doc/constitution_a.pdf.

68. See the interview with Ramizoglu in International Crisis Group, *Azerbaijan*, 16.

69. Bruno De Cordier, "Elşan Mustafaoğlu and Mənəvi Safliğa Dəvət: A Portrait of Islamic Social Activism in Baku, Azerbaijan," Research and Analysis Paper No. 28 (Ghent University, June 2013), 137–39, religion.info/pdf/2013_06_azerbaijan.pdf; and International Crisis Group, *Azerbaijan*, 16.

70. Jean-Christophe Peuch, "Azerbaijan: Authorities in Baku Target Shi'a Mosque, Say It Is Being Illegally Occupied," RFE/RL. March 3, 2004, http://www.rferl.org/content /article/1051756.html; and "Azerbaijani Mosque Loses Eight-Year Struggle for Religious Freedom," Becket Fund, February 11, 2013, http://www.becketfund.org/azerbaijan -mosque-loses-eight-year-struggle-for-religious-freedom/.

71. See, e.g., the news articles on Ibrahimoglu on the Deyerler news website, http:// deyerler.org/user/Hac%C4%B1+%C4%B0lqar+%C4%B0brahimo%C4%9Flu/news/.

72. Farid Mirzayev, "Azeris Shocked by Sectarian Attack," Institute for War and Peace Reporting, July 22, 2014, https://iwpr.net/global-voices/azeris-shocked-sectarian-attack.

73. International Crisis Group, *Azerbaijan*, 16; see also Liles, "Commanding Right and Forbidding Wrong," 61.

74. Hacı Şahin Həsənli's Facebook page, accessed August 20, 2016, https://az-az .facebook.com/HaciShahinHasanli.

75. "Azerbaijani Security Services Neutralize Group Planning to Bomb Mosque," Islam. ru, November 25, 2013, http://islam.ru/en/content/news/azerbaijani-security-services -neutralize-group-planning-bomb-mosque.

76. "Hacı Şahin Həsənli Qafqaz Müsəlmanları İdarəsində vəzifə təyinatı alıb," Report. az, December 3, 2014, http://report.az/din/haci-sahin-hesenli0312/.

77. Mustafaoglu was put in pretrial detention for four months, but was not released when the time expired. He had been spokesperson for the official CMB, which as of April 2015 had not commented on the case.

78. De Cordier, "Elşan Mustafaoğlu and Mənəvi Safliğa Dəvət."

79. The Social Union home page (http://www.manevisafliq.com/index.php) was no longer available in August 2016. Elshan Mustafaoglu's Facebook page (https://www .facebook.com/elshan.mustafaoglu) was last updated at the end of 2014.

80. Shahla Sultanova, "Worshiping in the Crosshairs," Transitions Online, August 7, 2012; http://www.tol.org/client/article/23292-worshiping-in-the-cross-hairs.html.

81. Anar Valiyev, "The Two Faces of Salafism in Azerbaijan," Jamestown Foundation, December 7, 2007, http://www.jamestown.org/single/?no_cache=1&tx_ttnews%5Btt _news%5D=4587.

82. International Crisis Group, *Azerbaijan*, 13–15 (after interviews with Suleymanov); and Valiyev, "Azerbaijan."

83. "Qamət Süleymanov: 'İŞİD-ə qoşulanların sayı ona görə artır ki . . . ,'" Azadlıq Radiosu, April 15, 2015, http://www.azadliq.org/a/26957555.html.

84. Arif Yunus refered to him as a moderate; see Sultanova, "Worshiping in the Crosshairs."

85. Cited by Liles, "Commanding Right and Forbidding Wrong," 33, 40–41.

86. The population was close to 8,300 in 2014.

87. The IPA maintains a website twenty years later; see http://www.islaminsesi.org/.

88. See Aliyev's speech at the Institute of Near East Policy in Washington on November 18, 1998, at Ilham Aliyev, "Where We Stand Now," *Azerbaijan International* 6, no. 4 (1998): 80–81, http://azer.com/aiweb/categories/magazine/64_folder/64 _articles/64_socar_ilham.html.

89. Idrak Abbasov, "Crackdown on Islamists in Azerbaijan," Institute for War and Peace Reporting, January 15, 2011, https://iwpr.net/global-voices/crackdown-islamists -azerbaijan; and "Azeri Islamic Party Leaders Sentenced to 12 Years in Jail," *AzerNews*, October 8, 2011, http://www.azernews.az/azerbaijan/37201.html.

90. Konul Khalilova, "Government Struggles to Defuse Discontent in Baku Suburb," Eurasianet.org, June 12, 2002, http://www.eurasianet.org/departments/insight/articles /eav061302.shtml.

91. Hooman Peimani, "Nardaran's Unrest Reflects Unresolved Woes in Azerbaijan," Eurasianet.org, March 3, 2003, http://www.eurasianet.org/departments/rights/articles /eav030403.shtml.

92. Bayramov was arrested in July 2011, and in March 2012 he was sentenced for possession of firearms and illegal drugs.

93. Abbasov, "Crackdown on Islamists in Azerbaijan"; and "Azeri Islamic Party Leaders Sentenced to 12 Years in Jail."

94. Idrak Abbasov, "Azeri Muslims Protest Theologian's Arrest," Institute for War and Peace Reporting, April 9, 2013, https://iwpr.net/global-voices/azeri-muslims-protest-theologians-arrest.

95. "Judges Are Waiting Recovery of Tale Bagirzade," International Organization for Legal Researches, April 11, 2013, http://www.iolr.org/?p=7244&lang=en.

96. Felix Corley, "Azerbaijan: Police Killings, Shooting and Mass Arrests as Muslims Pray," Forum 18 News Service, December 1, 2015, http://www.forum18.org /archive.php?article_id=2127. Corley's report noted that the police beating of Bagirzade occurred the week before a review by the UN Committee Against Torture.

97. *Kavkazskii uzel* (*Caucasian Knot*) has covered the Nardaran story in detail; see, e.g., "Advocate of Talekh Bagirzade Claims His Client Being Tortured," *Caucasian Knot*, January 8, 2016, http://eng.kavkaz-uzel.ru/articles/34215/; and on Natiq Kerimov, "Osvobozhden iz-pod strazhi sta+reishina Nardarana Natig Kerimov," *Kavkazskii uzel*, January 19, 2016, http://www.kavkaz-uzel.ru/articles/276205/. See also "Nardaran in Blockade," November 26–December 1, 2015, Human Rights Freedoms, http://hrf.report/during-clashes-with -police-there-are-killed-and-wounded/.

98. Liz Fuller and Babek Bakir, "Azerbaijan: Why Is 'Alternative Islam' Gaining Strength?," Eurasianet.org, August 14, 2007, http://www.eurasianet.org/departments /insight/articles/pp081507.shtml.

99. Bloomberg reported that Azerbaijan's gross domestic product grew over 30 percent in 2005 and over 20 percent in 2007. See "Rumblings of Instability in Azerbaijan."

100. Bhavani Raveendran, "Devout Muslim Azerbaijani Villagers Arrested after Religious Ceremony," Human Rights Brief, February 11, 2010, http://hrbrief.org/2010/02/sca-17-3/.

101. "Foreign Ministry Protests to US, Norwegian Envoys over Nakhichivan Trip," News.az, January 16, 2010, http://news.az/articles/politics/6713.

102. Ibid.

103. "Rumblings of Instability in Azerbaijan."

104. Carlotta Gall, "How Kosovo Was Turned into Fertile Ground for ISIS," *New York Times,* May 21, 2016, http://nyti.ms/1XHNdRh.

105. Liles, "Commanding Right and Forbidding Wrong," 42-43 and 67–70.

106. "Rumblings of Instability in Azerbaijan."

107. "Bakıda hicablı tələbələr dərsə buraxılmadı," YouTube video, 3:41, posted by "Kanal13AZ," April 2, 2013, https://www.youtube.com/watch?v=Sm1UhNoySDo.

108. "Veil Ban Protests 'Could Be Staged from Secret Circles,'" *AzerNews,* December 16, 2010, http://www.azernews.az/azerbaijan/27882.html.

109. "'El içində' biabırçı biçimdə (hicab qadağası haqqında)," YouTube video, 29:39, posted by "Islam azeri," December 29, 2010, https://www.youtube.com/watch?v=hsZetKM7t8Y.

110. Arifa Kazimova and Nushabe Fatullayeva, "In Azerbaijan, Hijab Debate a Mounting Challenge for Government," RFE/RL, December 23, 2010, http://www.rferl.org/content/azerbaijan_hijab_debate/2257429.html.

111. "Police, Armed Pro-Hijab Activists Clash in Baku," RFE/RL, October 5, 2012, http://www.rferl.org/content/police-azerbaijan-baku-forcibly-disperse-pro-hijab-activists/24729975.html.

112. "Azerbaijan Condemned Protestors of 'Freedom to Hijab!'" Islam.ru, April 23, 2013, http://islam.ru/en/content/news/azerbaijan-condemned-protesters-freedom-hijab.

113. "Assessing the Jihadist Threat to Azerbaijan," RFE/RL, January 14, 2011, http://www.rferl.org/content/azerbaijan_jihadist_threat/2275892.html.

114. "Islamic Party of Azerbaijan Head Jailed for 12 Years," RFE/RL, October 7, 2011, http://www.rferl.org/content/islamic_party_of_azerbaijan_head_jailed_for_12_years/24352745.html.

115. Examples are the tobacco boycott of the 1890s and revolutionary movements in the early twentieth century and, more recently, the Islamic Revolution that unseated the shah and brought Ayatollah Khomeini to power. On the former, see Nikki R. Keddie, "Iranian Revolutions in Comparative Perspective" *American Historical Review* 88, no. 3 (1983): 579–98.

116. Baehr and Gordon, "Headscarf to Burqa." I thank Dan Gordon for providing this article.

117. This important distinction is misunderstood by Eldar Mamedov; see "Iraq's Unravelling and Azerbaijan," Eurasianet.org, September 10, 2014, http://www.eurasianet.org/node/69921.

118. Bayram Balci, "The Syrian Crisis: A View from Azerbaijan," *Foreign Policy Journal,* March 18, 2013, http://carnegieendowment.org/2013/03/18/syrian-crisis-view-from-azerbaijan/h6rp; see also Kenan Rovshanoglu and Bayram Balci, "Syria: Azerbaijan, and the Sunni-Shi'a Divide," *The Globalist,* September 6, 2013, http://www.theglobalist.com/syria-azerbaijan-sunni-shia-divide/.

119. Aydin Mammadov, "Azeri Radical Islamists Flee Repressions at Home, Join Syrian Conflict," Silk Road Reporters, January 15, 2015, http://www.silkroadreporters.com/2015/01/15/azeri-radical-islamists-flee-repressions-home-join-syrian-conflict/.

120. Aaron Y. Zelin, a Washington-based analyst, has compiled extensive data on fighters from Azerbaijan for his blog; see his "Azerbaijan" posts at Jihadology, http://jihadology.net/category/countries/azerbaijan/.

121. Joanne Paraszczuk, "Why Did an Azerbaijani Wrestling Champion Join (and Die for) IS?" RFE/RL, October 17, 2014, http://www.rferl.org/content/islamic-state-azerbaijan-killed-syria/26642573.html.

122. He was jailed in connection with human rights activity from August 2014 to November 2015.

123. Quoted by Shahin Abbasov, "Azerbaijan: Sumgayit Becomes Font of Syria-bound Jihadists," Eurasianet.org, May 5, 2014, http://www.eurasianet.org/node/68341.

124. Ibid.

125. Ibid.

126. Mammadov, "Azeri Radical Islamists."

127. OnIslam was a website launched in 2010 under the umbrella of Mada Media Development Associates, a nonprofit in Egypt, according to Islamopedia: http://islamopediaonline.org/websites-institutions/onislamnet. As of August 2016, the site no longer exists.

128. Ruslan Kurbanov, "Azerbaijan-Iran Relations: Secularism vs. Shiism?" OnIslam. net, March 31, 2015, http://www.onislam.net/english/politics/europe/484347-azerbaijan-iran-tensions-secular-shiite-conflict.html (link discontinued). The article reviews basics of revival after 1991, saying that the Azerbaijani regime's restrictions on hijab are a sign of its Islamophobia. He quotes Zafar Guliyev saying that the intensity of Islamic protests will escalate.

129. Liles, "Commanding Right and Forbidding Wrong," 61–67 and 70–73.

130. Kurbanov, "Azerbaijan-Iran Relations."

131. Mammadov, "Azeri Radical Islamists."

132. Joanna Paraszczuk, "Azerbaijan Arrests 10 Citizens Suspected of Fighting in Syria," RFE/RL, January 7, 2015, http://www.rferl.org/content/azerbaijan-syria-connection-islamic-state-isis/26781551.html.

133. "Azerbaijanis Accused of Militancy Shouldn't Be Placed in Iron Cages, Lawyers Say," RFE/RL, March 31, 2015, http://www.rferl.org/content/azerbaijan-trial-cages-human-rights/26930311.html.

134. Mammadov, "Azeri Radical Islamists" (emphasis added).

135. Mirzayev, "Azeris Shocked by Sectarian Attack."

136. Elders of Nardaran denounced the killings: "Elder of Nardaran: True Muslim Does Not Accept Terrorism," Contact.az, January 10, 2015, http://www.contact.az/docs/2015/Social/011000102568en.htm.

137. "NGO Law Monitor: Azerbaijan," ECHR Case No. 5548/05, The International Center for Not-for-Profit Law, updated March 23, 2016, http://www.icnl.org/research/monitor/azerbaijan.html.

138. "Conference for Religious Communities Opened in Azerbaijan," islam.ru, September 17, 2014, http://islam.ru/en/content/news/conference-religious-communities-opened-azerbaijan.

139. "Employees Fired for Prayer in Azerbaijan," islam.ru, March 24, 2014, http://islam.ru/en/content/news/employees-fired-prayer-azerbaijan.

140. Julie Wilhelmsen, "Islamism in Azerbaijan: How Potent?" *Studies in Conflict & Terrorism* 32, no. 8 (2009): 726–42.

141. Felix Corley, "Azerbaijan: Six New Freedom of Religion or Belief Prisoners of Conscience," Forum 18 News Service, March 16, 2015, http://www.forum18.org/archive .php?article_id=2048.

Chapter 7

1. "Azerbaijan Puts Brave Face on Slumping Oil Price," Reuters, January 16, 2015, http://reut.rs/1G7r1sN.

2. Ilham Aliyev, "The Future of Azerbaijan's Economy," World Economic Forum, January 20, 2016, http://www.weforum.org/agenda/2016/01/azerbaijan.

3. "Dövlət Neft Fondu: 'Vəsaitlərin 73 faizi xərclənib,'" *Azadlıq*, December 17, 2015, http://www.azadliq.org/content/neft-fondu-pul-milyard-bohran/27433456.html.

4. "16 ayda AMB $10,2 mlrd itirib," Contact.az, December 28, 2015, https://contact. az/docs/2015/Economics&Finance/122800141770az.htm; and "Azerbaijan Spent Two-thirds of Its Gold and Currency Reserves in 2015," *Vestnik Kavkaza*, January 22, 2016, http://vestnikkavkaza.net/news/Azerbaijan-spent-two-thirds-of-its-gold-and-currency -reserves-in-2015.html. The Central Bank of Azerbaijan's reserves went from about $15 billion to $5 billion.

5. Aydin Mammadov, "Azerbaijan's Currency Lost Half Its Value in a Day," Silk Road Reporters, December 22, 2015, http://www.silkroadreporters.com/2015/12/22 /azerbaijans-currency-lost-half-its-value-in-a-day/.

6. Arzu Geybullayeva and Tony Wesolowsky, "Azerbaijan Suffers from Currency, Low Oil Prices," RFE/RL, January 10, 2016, http://www.rferl.org/content/azerbaijan-suffers -currency-crash-oil-prices/27479606.html.

7. See "In Azerbaijan, Foodstuff Prices Went Up by a Third," *Azeri Daily*, August 19, 2015, http://www.azeridaily.com/economy/10018.

8. "Protests Erupt in Azerbaijan over Jobs, Economic Woes," RFE/RL, January 13, 2016, http://www.rferl.org/content/azerbaijan-protests-unemployment-price-hikes/27485740.html.

9. Geybullayeva and Wesolowsky, "Azerbaijan Suffers."

10. Aliyev, "The Future of Azerbaijan's Economy."

11. "Best Countries: Azerbaijan," *US News*, 2016, http://www.usnews.com/news /best-countries/azerbaijan.

12. Sergei Guriev, economist at Sciences Po (Paris), quoted by Sabrina Tavernise, "Inflation Robs Russians of Buying Power," *New York Times*, August 18, 2015, http://nyti .ms/1E0zzBR.

13. Zulfugar Agayev, "Azerbaijan Turns to IMF, World Bank, after Collapse in Crude," Bloomberg, January 28, 2016, http://bloom.bg/1KGK1Mh.

14. The February 3 press release discussed categories rather than many specific measures: "IMF Staff Team Concludes Visit to Azerbaijan," IMF, February 3, 2016, https://www.imf .org/external/np/sec/pr/2016/pr1640.htm.

15. Agayev, "Azerbaijan Turns to IMF, World Bank."

16. Martin Sommer et al., *Learning to Live with Cheaper Oil: Policy Adjustment in Oil-Exporting Countries of the Middle East and Central Asia* (Washington, DC: IMF, 2016).

17. Joshua Kucera, "What's Behind the Purges in Azerbaijan's Military?" Eurasianet.org, March 18, 2014, http://www.eurasianet.org/node/68163.

18. Joshua Kucera, "Recriminations Follow Azerbaijan's Poor Showing in Caspian Naval Games," Eurasianet.org, August 11, 2015, http://www.eurasianet.org/node/74626.

19. "A Frozen Conflict Explodes," *Economist*, April 9, 2016, http://www.economist.com/news/europe/21696563-after-facing-decades-armenia-and-azerbaijan-start-shooting-frozen-conflict-explodes; see also Almaz Rza, "Cease-Fire Restored after Intense Fighting around Nagorno-Karabakh," Central Asia Caucasus Analyst, April 12, 2016, http://www.cacianalyst.org/publications/field-reports/item/13350-case-fire-restored-after-intense-fighting-around-nagorno-karabakh.html. For a discussion of Azerbaijan's change in strategy and tactics as well as a detailed (but not dispassionate) description of the conflict, see Masis Ingilizian, "Azerbaijan's Incremental Increase on the Nagorno-Karabakh Frontline," Bellingcat blog, April 12, 2016, https://www.bellingcat.com/news/rest-of-world/2016/04/12/detailing-azerbaijans-incremental-increase-in-nagorno-karabaghs-frontline/; for an analysis of the deeper reasons for the continued status on the ground, see Audrey L. Altstadt and Rajan Menon, "Unfrozen Conflict in Nagorno-Karabakh: Why Violence Persists," *Foreign Affairs*, April 12, 2016, https://www.foreignaffairs.com/articles/armenia/2016-04-12/unfrozen-conflict-nagorno-karabakh.

20. See the presidential address of Ilham Aliyev at the 6,765th meeting of the UN Security Council on May 4, 2012; "Security Council, Highlighting Changing Nature, Character of Scourge of Terrorism, Says Can Be Defeated Only by Sustained, Global Approach, in Presidential Statement," UN Security Council, May 4, 2012, http://www.un.org/press/en/2012/sc10636.doc.htm.

21. "After BRICS, Putin Hosts Shanghai Cooperation Organization Summit in Ufa," RFE/RL, July 10, 2015, http://www.rferl.org/content/russia-putin-shanghai-cooperation-organization-summit-brics-ufa/27120442.html.

22. "Putin: Free Trade Zone between EEU and Iran to Give Impetus to Its Relations with Russia," *Vestinik Kavkaza*, August 5, 2016, http://vestnikkavkaza.net/news/Putin-free-trade-zone-between-EEU-and-Iran-to-give-impetus-to-its-relations-with-Russia.html.

23. NATO Cooperative Cyber Defence Centre of Excellence (Tallinn), "Information Security Discussed at the Dushanbe Summit of the Shanghai Cooperation Organisation," *Incyder News*, October 27, 2014, http://ccdcoe.org/information-security-discussed-dushanbe-summit-shanghai-cooperation-organisation.html.

24. "Martin Schulz on the Verdict Handed Down to Leyla Yunus and Arif Yunus," President of the European Parliament, August 15, 2015, http://www.europarl.europa.eu/the-president/en/press/press_release_speeches/press_release/press_release-2015/press_release-2015-august/html/martin-schulz-on-the-verditct-handed-down-to-leyla-yunus-and-arif-yunus.

25. See, e.g., Swagata Saha, "The Future of the Shanghai Cooperation Organisation," East Asia Forum, October 17, 2014, http://www.eastasiaforum.org/2014/10/17/the-future-of-the-shanghai-cooperation-organisation/.

26. "Eurovillage-2015" to be held in Baku," *Azeri Daily*, August 17, 2015, http://azeridaily.com/society/9937.

27. "Preparations For Formula 1 Transform Historic Baku," RFE/RL, March 4, 2016, http://www.rferl.org/media/video/azerbaijan-baku-formula-one-race/27589226.html.

28. On the increase in uses of torture from the winter of 2014 to the fall of 2015, see "Ilgar Mammadov Severely Beaten in Prison," Human Rights Freedoms, October 19, 2015, http://hrf.report/ilgar-mammadov-severely-beaten-in-prison/.

29. "The Functioning of Democratic Institutions in Azerbaijan," Resolution 2062 (2015).

30. "Fury in Baku over Azerbaijan Democracy Act," Institute for Reporters' Freedom and Safety, December 17, 2015, https://www.irfs.org/news-feed/fury-in-baku-over -azerbaijan-democracy-act/.

31. In a January 2015 editorial, the *New York Times* contemplated the "two faces" of Ilham Aliyev, concluding that he is in fact the "mafia boss." Nevertheless, the analysis did not account for his political context and competition among oligarchs. See "The Two Faces of Azerbaijan's Mr. Aliyev," *New York Times*, January 11, 2015, http://www.nytimes .com/2015/01/12/opinion/the-two-faces-of-azerbaijans-mr-aliyev.html.

32. "Rumblings of Instability in Azerbaijan."

33. Ibid.

34. Azerbaijan is 86,600 square kilometers. According to the *CIA World Factbook* (accessed August 3, 2016), this makes it slightly smaller than Maine; see https://www.cia .gov/library/publications/the-world-factbook/geos/aj.html.

35. See the crude oil commodity pricing data over time on the NASDAQ website at "Commodities: Crude Oil," accessed August 19, 2016, http://www.nasdaq.com/markets /crude-oil.aspx?timeframe=6m.

36. According to Vladimir Putin, about 15,000 Azerbaijani students are studying in Russia; see "Relations between Russia and Azerbaijan Are Those of Strategic Partnership," News.az, August 5, 2016, http://news.az/articles/interviews/111275.

37. "Nations in Transit 2016: Azerbaijan," *Nations in Transit*, Freedom House, https:// freedomhouse.org/report/nations-transit/2016/azerbaijan.

38. See the organizations' websites at http://www.tcae.org/ and http://www.afaz.org/.

39. Scott Higham, Steven Rich, and Alice Crites, "10 Members of Congress Took Trip Secretly Funded by Foreign Government," *Washington Post*, May 13, 2015, http://www .washingtonpost.com/investigations/10-members-of-congress-took-trip-secretly-funded -by-foreign-government/2015/05/13/76b55332-f720-11e4-9030-b4732caefe81_story.html.

40. Weiss, "Corleones of the Caspian."

41. Bruckner's reports were a three-part series for OCCRP; see Till Bruckner, "How to Build Yourself a Stealth Lobbyist, Azerbaijani Style," OCCRP, June 22, 2015, https://www .occrp.org/freekhadijaismayilova/stories/profile-of-an-undercover-lobbyist-for-azerbaijan .php. They appeared in a short form at Till Bruckner, "Foreign Lobbyist Gets Free Platform at Georgetown University, Atlantic Council," *Huffington Post*, June 25, 2015, http://www .huffingtonpost.com/till-bruckner/brenda-shaffer-oil-gas_b_7654646.html.

42. Carl Schreck, "Ex-US Congressman Quits Azerbaijani Lobby Group, Citing Nonpayment," RFE/RL, March 2, 2016, http://www.rferl.org/content/former-us -congressman-dan-burton-quits-azerbaijan-lobby-group-nonpayment/27585777.html. Schreck reported that AAA had spent over $12 million on lobbying efforts in the United States since 2011. Even after Burton's resignation, the AAA website continued to list him

as its president. For more information, see "Lobbying Spending Database: Azerbaijan American Alliance," OpenSecrets.org, Center for Responsive Politics, accessed August 19, 2016, http://www.opensecrets.org/lobby/clientsum.php?id=D000064546.

43. See Silvestre Reyes, "Azerbaijan Must Remain a Strong Ally of the United States," *Roll Call*, March 18, 2015, http://www.rollcall.com/news/home/azerbaijan-must-remain -a-strong-ally-of-the-united-states.

44. Luxner, "Azerbaijan Rolls Out Red Carpet for Visiting US Lawmakers."

45. These events have been much studied since 1979. Two revealing studies from the US side are James Bill, *The Eagle and the Lion*, who noted that the shah disliked John F. Kennedy because of Kennedy's concerns about human rights in Iran; and Stephen Kinzer, *The Brothers: John Foster Dulles, Allen Dulles, and Their Secret World War* (New York: Times Books, 2013).

46. Ambassador (ret.) Richard D. Kauzlarich, who served as US ambassador to Azerbaijan from 1994 to 1997, argued for transactional basis of commerce and against "soft regionalism" in a Brookings blog post: Richard D. Kauzlarich, "The Human Costs of 'Strategic Partnerships' with South Caucasian States," Brookings: Order from Chaos blog, August 12, 2015, http://www.brookings.edu/blogs/order-from-chaos/posts/2015/08/12 -human-costs-south-caucasus-kauzlarich.

47. Jochen Bittner, "The New Ideology of the New Cold War," *New York Times*, August 1, 2016, http://nyti.ms/2ac8YbC.

48. "Russia, Azerbaijan, Iran Leaders Adopt Joint Declaration Following Baku Summit," *Sputnik International*, August 8, 2016, http://sputniknews.com /politics/20160808/1044065059/summit-declaration-joint.html.

49. Richard D. Kauzlarich, "Azerbaijan's New Direction: Human Rights Challenges and the Situation in Nagorno-Karabakh" (testimony before the House Foreign Affairs Committee, Subcommittee on Europe, Eurasia and Emerging Threats), Brookings, February 12, 2015, http://www.brookings.edu/research/testimony/2015/02/12-azerbaijan-human -rights-abuses-kauzlarich.

Selected Bibliography of Major Sources

Abbasov, Idrak. "Crackdown on Islamists in Azerbaijan." Institute for War and Peace Reporting, January 15, 2011. https://iwpr.net/global-voices/crackdown-islamists -azerbaijan.

Abbasov, Shahin. "Will Journalist's Arrest End Azerbaijani-Armenian Citizen Diplomacy?" Eurasianet, April 22, 2014. http://www.eurasianet.org/node/68297.

Aliyarov (Aliyarli), Suleiman, and Bahtiyar Vahabzade. "Redaktorun Pochtundan." *Azerbaijan*, February 1988. Translated by Audrey L. Altstadt. "Azerbaijan and the Nagorno-Karabakh Issue." *Journal of the Institute of Muslim Minority Affairs* 9, no. 2 (1988): 429–34.

Aliyev, Fuad. "The Gülen Movement in Azerbaijan." *Current Trends in Islamist Ideology* 14, Hudson Institute Series (December 2012): 90–103.

Allahveranov, Azer, and Emin Huseynov. *Costs and Benefits of Labor Mobility between the EU and the Eastern Partnership Partner Countries: Country Report—Azerbaijan.* CASE Network Studies and Analysis No. 460/2013. Warsaw: CASE–Center for Social and Economic Research, 2013. http://www.case-research.eu/sites/default/files/publications /CNSA_2013_460.pdf.

Altstadt, Audrey L. "Azerbaijan and Aliyev: A Long History and an Uncertain Future." *Problems of Post-Communism* 50, no. 5 (2003): 3–13.

———. "Azerbaijan's Struggle toward Democracy." In *Conflict, Cleavage, and Change in Central Asia and the Caucasus*, edited by Karen Dawisha and Bruce Parrott, 110–55. Cambridge: Cambridge University Press, 1997.

———. "The Azerbaijani Bourgeoisie and the Cultural-Enlightenment Movement in Baku: First Steps toward Nationalism." In *Transcaucasia, Nationalism, and Social Change: Essays in the History of Armenia, Azerbaijan, and Georgia*, edited by Ronald Grigor Suny, 197–207. Ann Arbor: University of Michigan Press, 1983.

———. *The Azerbaijani Turks: Power and Identity under Russian Rule.* Hoover Institution Series on Nationalities. Stanford, CA: Stanford University Press, 1992.

———. "Ethnic Conflict in Nagorno-Karabagh." In *Ethnic Conflict in the Post-Soviet World: Case Studies and Analysis*, edited by Leokadia Drobizheva, Rose Gottemoeller, Catherine

McArdle Kelleher, and Lee Walker, 227–53. Armonk, NY: M. E. Sharpe, 1996.

———. "*O Patria Mia*: National Conflict in Mountainous Karabagh." In *Ethnic Nationalism and Regional Conflict in the Former Soviet Union and Yugoslavia*, edited by Ray Duncan and G. Paul Holman Jr., 101–36. Boulder, CO: Westview Press, 1993.

———. *The Politics of Culture in Soviet Azerbaijan, 1920–1940.* No. 27 in the Routledge Series on the History of Russia and Eastern Europe. Abingdon, UK: Routledge, 2016.

"Assessing the Jihadist Threat to Azerbaijan." Radio Free Europe/Radio Liberty, January 14, 2011. http://www.rferl.org/content/azerbaijan_jihadist_threat/2275892 .html.

"Azerbaijan: Ailing Rights Defenders Convicted in Political Trial." Human Rights Watch, August 13, 2015. https://www.hrw.org/news/2015/08/13/azerbaijan-ailing-rights -defenders-convicted-political-trial.

"Azerbaijan: Authorities Targeting Youth Activists." Human Rights Watch, April 2, 2013. http://www.hrw.org/news/2013/04/02/azerbaijan-authorities-targeting-youth-activists.

"Azerbaijan: Court Defies European Court Instruction to Free Journalist." Human Rights Watch, November 13, 2010. http://www.hrw.org/news/2010/11/13/azerbaijan-court -defies-european-court-instruction-free-journalist.

"Azerbaijan: Government Repression Tarnishes Chairmanship." Human Rights Watch, September 29, 2014. http://www.hrw.org/news/2014/09/29/azerbaijan-government -repression-tarnishes-chairmanship.

"Azerbaijan: Opposition Youth Activists on Trial." Human Rights Watch, March 30, 2006. http://www.hrw.org/news/2006/03/30/azerbaijan-opposition-youth-activists-trial.

"Azerbaijani Parliament Ignores Call from Civil Society on New NGO Law." Eastern Partnership Civil Society Forum, February 15, 2013. http://eap-csf.eu/en/news-events /news/azerbaijani-parliament-ignores-call-from-civil-society-on-new-ngo-law/.

Baehr, Peter, and Daniel Gordon. "From the Headscarf to the Burqa: The Role of Social Theorists in Shaping Laws against the Veil." *Economy and Society* 42, no. 2 (2013): 249–80.

Bagirova, Fidan. "Radio Liberty Program Discusses EITI New Standards and Azerbaijan." National Resource Governance Institute, October 1, 2013. http://www.resourcegov ernance.org/news/blog/radio-liberty-program-discusses-eiti-new-standards-and-azerbaijan.

Bairamov, Gubad. "Privatization in Azerbaijan: Results and Prospects." *Central Asia & Caucasus Journal*, 2001. http://www.ca-c.org/journal/eng-04-2001/10.baiprimen.shtml.

Balci, Bayram. *The AKP/Gülen Crisis in Turkey: Consequences for Central Asia and the Caucasus*, Central Asia Policy Brief No. 16. Washington, DC: Elliott School of International Affairs, George Washington University, 2014.

———. "Between Secular Education and Islamic Philosophy: The Approach and Achievement of Fethullah Gülen's Followers in Azerbaijan." *Caucasus Survey* 1, no. 1 (2013): 107–16.

———. "Le chiisme en Azerbaïdjan post-soviétique: Entre influences iraniennes et dynamiques internes." In *Les mondes chiites et l'Iran*, edited by Sabrina Mervin, 163–88. Paris: Karthala, 2007.

———. "The Syrian Crisis: A View from Azerbaijan." *Foreign Policy Journal*, March 18, 2013. http://carnegieendowment.org/2013/03/18/syrian-crisis-view-from-azerbaijan /h6rp.

Bara, Anna, Anna di Bartolomeo, Zuzanna Brunarska, Shushanik Makaryan, Sergo Mananashvili, and Agnieszka Weinar. *Regional Migration Report: South Caucasus.* Florence: European University Institute, 2013.

Barseghyan, Haykuhi and Shahla Sultanova, "History Lessons in Armenia and Azerbaijan," *CRS* Issue 631. Institute for War and Peace Reporting, March 2, 2012. https://iwpr.net /global-voices/history-lessons-armenia-and-azerbaijan.

Bennigsen, Alexandre, and Marie Broxup. *The Islamic Threat to the Soviet State.* New York: St. Martin's Press, 1983.

Bogardus, Kevin. "Azerbaijan Plants Flag in DC Lobbying Scene." *The Hill*, December 7, 2011. http://thehill.com/business-a-lobbying/197681-azerbaijan-plants-flag-in-dc -lobbying-scene-.

Broers, Laurence. *The Nagorny Karabakh Conflict: Defaulting to War.* London: Chatham House, 2016.

Bruckner, Til. "How Azerbaijan Manipulates Public Opinion in the US." Organized Crime and Corruption Reporting Project, June 19, 2015. https://www.occrp.org/freekhadija ismayilova/stories/how-azerbaijan-manipulates-public-opinion-in-the-US.php.

Bunce, Valerie J., and Sharon L. Wolchik. "Azerbaijan: Losing the Transitional Moment." In *Transitions to Democracy: A Comparative Perspective*, edited by Sharon Stoner and Michael McFaul, 400–28. Baltimore: Johns Hopkins University Press, 2013.

Caucasian Knot. "Advocate of Talekh Bagirzade Claims His Client Being Tortured." *Caucasian Knot*, January 8, 2016. http://eng.kavkaz-uzel.ru/articles/34215/.

Caucasus Research Resource Centers. "Caucasus Barometer 2013 Azerbaijan: Codebook." Caucasus Research Resource Centers, December 2013. http://caucasusbarometer.org /en/cb2013az/codebook/.

———. "Time-Series Dataset Azerbaijan." http://caucasusbarometer.org/en/cb-az /ICITGOV/.

Chêne, Marie. "Overview of Corruption and Anti-Corruption in Azerbaijan." Anti-Corruption Helpdesk Berlin, Transparency International, July 2013. http://www.transparency.org /files/content/corruptionqas/Overview_of_corruption_in_Azerbaijan_2.pdf.

Ciarreta, Aitor and Shahriyar Nasirov. "Analysis of Azerbaijan Oil and Gas Sector." Presentation at the 30th USAEE/IAEE North American Conference, Washington, October 11, 2011. https://www.usaee.org/usaee2011/submissions/OnlineProceedings /Ciarreta_Nasirov-Article1.pdf.

Commission for Security and Cooperation in Europe (Helsinki Commission, Washington). "Parliamentary Elections in Azerbaijan: 30 September 1990." Washington, DC: Helsinki Commission, 1990.

Commission on Combating Corruption. "Law of the Republic of Azerbaijan on Combating Corruption." Republic of Azerbaijan, April 28, 2009. http://commission -anticorruption.gov.az/view.php?lang=en&menu=19&id=32.

Corley, Felix. "Azerbaijan: Six New Freedom of Religion or Belief Prisoners of Conscience." Forum 18 News Service, March 16, 2015. http://www.forum18.org/archive .php?article_id=2048.

———. "Government Blames 'Errors' for Negative Venice Commission/OSCE Opinion." Forum 18 Report, October 23, 2012. http://www.refworld.org/docid/5087cb1d2.html.

Cornell, Svante E. *Azerbaijan since Independence.* Armonk, NY: M. E. Sharpe, 2011.

Coronel, Sheila S. "The Secret World of Private Companies." WatchDog Watcher, October 9, 2012. http://watchdog-watcher.com/2012/10/09/company-information/.

de Cordier, Bruno. "Elşan Mustafaoğlu and Mənəvi Safliğa Dəvət: A Portrait of Islamic Social Activism in Baku, Azerbaijan." Research and Analysis Paper No. 28, Ghent University, June 2013. http://religion.info/pdf/2013_06_azerbaijan.pdf.

de Waal, Thomas. *Black Garden: Armenia and Azerbaijan through Peace and War*, rev. ed. New York: New York University Press, 2013.

Diuk, Nadia M. *The Next Generation in Russia, Ukraine, and Azerbaijan: Youth, Politics, Identity, and Change*. Lanham, MD: Rowman & Littlefield, 2012.

"Emin Huseynov Forced into Hiding in Azerbaijan." Human Rights House Foundation, February 11, 2015. http://humanrightshouse.org/Articles/20730.html.

European Commission for Democracy through Law (Venice Commission). "Joint Opinion on the Law on Freedom of Religious Belief of Azerbaijan," Opinion 681/2012. Warsaw: Venice Commission, October 15, 2012. http://www.venice.coe.int/webforms /documents/default.aspx?pdffile=CDL-AD%282012%29022-e.

————. *Opinion on the Draft Amendments to the Constitution of the Republic of Azerbaijan* (Opinion 518/2008). Warsaw: Venice Commission, March 16, 2009. http://www .venice.coe.int/webforms/documents/?pdf=CDL-AD%282009%29010-e

————. "Opinion on the Law on Non-Governmental Organizations (Public Associations and Funds) as Amended of the Republic of Azerbaijan." Warsaw: Venice Commission, December 15, 2014. http://www.venice.coe.int/webforms/documents/default .aspx?pdffile=CDL-AD%282014%29043-e.

————. *Opinion on the Legislation Pertaining to the Protection against Defamation of the Republic of Azerbaijan* (Opinion No. 692/2012). Warsaw: Venice Commission, October 14, 2013. http://www.venice.coe.int/webforms/documents/?pdf=CDL -AD%282013%29024-e.

European Commission, High Representative of the European Union for Foreign Affairs and Security Policy. *Implementation of the European Neighborhood Policy in Azerbaijan: Progress in 2013 and Recommendations for Action*. Brussels: European Commission, 2014. http:// eeas.europa.eu/enp/pdf/2014/country-reports/azerbaijan_en.pdf.

————. "Joint Staff Working Document: Implementation of the European Neighbourhood Policy in Azerbaijan: Progress in 2013 and Recommendations for Action." Brussels: European Commission, March 27, 2014. http://eeas.europa.eu/enp/pdf/2014/country -reports/azerbaijan_en.pdf.

European Court of Human Rights. "Case of Fatullayev v. Azerbaijan (Application no. 40984/07)." Strasbourg: European Court of Human Rights, April 22, 2010. http:// hudoc.echr.coe.int/eng?i=001-98401.

————. "Case of Ilgar Mammdov v. Azerbaijan (Application no. 15172/13)." Strasbourg: European Court of Human Rights, May 22, 2014. http://hudoc.echr.coe.int /eng?i=001-144124.

————. "Decision [on] Application no. 15405/04; Juma Mosque Congregation and others Against Azerbaijan." Strasbourg: European Court of Human Rights, January 8, 2013.

European Parliament. *Presidential Elections in Azerbaijan: Election Observation Delegation, 13–16 October 2008*. Brussels: European Parliament, 2008. http://www.europarl.europa .eu/document/activities/cont/200908/20090807ATT59480/20090807ATT59480EN.pdf.

European Stability Initiative. *Caviar Diplomacy: How Azerbaijan Silenced the Council of Europe*. Berlin: European Stability Initiative, 2012. http://www.esiweb.org/index .php?lang=en&id=156&document_ID=131.

————. *Disgraced: Azerbaijan and the End of Election Monitoring as We Know It*. Berlin: European Stability Initiative, 2013. http://www.esiweb.org/index.php?lang =en&id=156&document_ID=145.

————. "Open Letter to 125 Current and Former Members of the Parliamentary Assembly of the Council of Europe (PACE)." Berlin: European Stability Initiative, April 23, 2014. http://www.esiweb.org/index.php?lang=en&id=556.

————. *The List: Political Prisoners in Azerbaijan*. Berlin: European Stability Initiative, 2014. http://www.esiweb.org/pdf/THE%20LIST%20-%2098%20political%2prison ers%20in%20Azerbaijan%20-%20August%202014.pdf.

Fatullayeva, Nushabe. "Mixing Government and Business in Azerbaijan." Radio Free Europe / Radio Liberty, April 4, 2013. http://www.rferl.org/content/azerbaijan-transport-minister -corruption/24947711.html.

Fatullayeva, Nushabe, and Khadija Ismayilova. "Azerbaijani Government Awarded Gold-Field Rights to President's Family." Radio Free Europe / Radio Liberty, May 3, 2012. http://www.rferl.org/content/azerbaijan_gold-field_contract_awarded_to_presidents _family/24569192.html.

"FILM: Amazing Azerbaijan" (2012 video). Free Expression Platform, 2016. http:// azerbaijanfreexpression.org/film-amazing-azerbaijan/

Freedom House. *Nations in Transit 2015*. Washington, DC: Freedom House, 2015. https:// freedomhouse.org/report/nations-transit/nations-transit-2015.

Fuller, Liz. "Azerbaijani President Unveils Proposed Constitutional Amendments." Radio Free Europe / Radio Liberty, July 19, 2016. http://www.rferl.org/content/azerbaijan -aliyev-proposed-constitutional-amendments-caucasus-report/27867826.html.

GAN Integrity Solutions. "Business Corruption in Azerbaijan," Business Anticorruption Portal, October 2014. http://www.business-anti-corruption.com/country-profiles /europe-central-asia/azerbaijan/show-all.aspx.

Global Witness. *Azerbaijan Anonymous: Azerbaijan's State Oil Company and Why the Extractive Industries Transparency Initiative Needs to Go Further*. London: Global Witness, 2013. https://www.globalwitness.org/sites/default/files/library/azerbaijan _anonymous_lr.pdf.

Gogia, Giorgi. *Tightening the Screws: Azerbaijan's Crackdown on Civil Society and Dissent*. New York: Human Rights Watch, 2013. http://www.hrw.org/reports/2013/09/02 /tightening-screws-0.

Goltz, Thomas C. *Azerbaijan Diary: A Rogue Reporter's Adventures in an Oil-Rich, War-Torn Post-Soviet Republic*. Armonk, NY: M. E. Sharpe, 1998.

————. "A Montana Perspective on International Aid and Ethnic Politics in Azerbaijan," Virtual Azerbaijan, 1996. http://www.zerbaijan.com/azeri/goltz1.htm.

Goyushov, Altay. "Islam in Azerbaijan (Historical Background)." *Caucasus Analytical Digest* 44 (November 20, 2012): 2–4. http://e-collection.library.ethz.ch/eserv/eth:7148/eth -7148-01.pdf.

Hadjibeyli, Jeyhun. *See* Khadzhibeili, Dzheikhun.

Hajizade, Adnan, and Emin Milli, producers. "Eşşekle (Esel Heinz) müsahibe: QHT qanunu haqqında şok açıqlamalar." From "OL! Azerbaijan Youth Movement." YouTube video, 5:15, June 28, 2009. https://www.youtube.com/watch?v=Aaecvg7xCIk.

Harasymiw, Bohdan. "In Search of Post-Communism: Stalking Russia's Political Trajectory." *Canadian Slavonic Papers* 53, no. 2/4 (2011): 401–20.

Hasanov, Fakhri. "Dutch Disease and the Azerbaijan Economy." *Communist and Post-Communist Studies* 46, no. 4 (2013): 463–80.

Ibrahimov, Rovshan. *US-Azerbaijan Relations: A View from Baku.* Rethink Paper 17. Washington, DC: Rethink Institute, 2014.

International Crisis Group. *Azerbaijan: Independent Islam and the State.* Europe Report No. 91. Baku: International Crisis Group, 2008. http://www.crisisgroup.org/~/media/Files /europe/191_azerbaijan_independent_islam_and_the_state.pdf.

———. *Nagorno-Karabakh: Risking War.* International Crisis Group Europe Report No. 187. Tblisi/Brussels: International Crisis Group, 2007.

Iontsev, Vladimir, and Irinia Ivakhnyuk. *The Role of International Labour Migration in Russian Economic Development.* Florence: European University Institute, 2012.

Ismayilova, Khadija. "Azerbaijani President's Family Benefits from Eurovision Hall Construction." Radio Free Europe / Radio Liberty, May 9, 2012. http://www.rferl.org /content/azerbaijan_first_family_build_eurovision_arena/24575761.html.

———. "Paşa Holdinq haqda bilmədikləriniz," Azadlıq Radiosu, May 7, 2014. http:// www.azadliq.org/a/pa%C5%9Fa-holdinq--%C9%99liyevl%C9%99rin-hollandiyadan -ba%C5%9Flayan-ail%C9%99-biznesi/25376221.html.

———. "Prezidentin qızı banka necə sahib oldu?" Azadlıq Radiosu, August 11, 2010. http://www.azadliq.org/a/2123076.html.

———. "TeliaSonera's Behind-the-Scenes Connection to Azerbaijani President's Daughters." Radio Free Europe / Radio Liberty, July 15, 2014. http://www.rferl.org /content/teliasonera-azerbaijan-aliyev-corruption-investigation-occrp/25457907.html.

Jafarova, Esmira. "OSCE Mediation of Nagorno-Karabagh Conflict." *Washington Review of Turkish and Eurasian Affairs,* March 2014. http://www.thewashingtonreview.org/osce -nagorno-karabakh.

Jagland, Thorbjørn. "Azerbaijan's Human Rights Are on a Knife Edge." *Guardian* (London), November 4, 2014. http://www.theguardian.com/commentisfree/2014 /nov/03/azerbaijan-human-rights-uk-tory-echr.

"Judges Are Waiting Recovery of Tale Bagirzade." International Organization for Legal Researches, April 11, 2013. http://www.iolr.org/?p=7244&lang=en.

Kalicki, Jan H., and David L. Goldwyn, ed. *Energy and Security: Strategies for a World in Transition,* rev. ed. Washington, DC: Woodrow Wilson Center Press; Baltimore: Johns Hopkins University Press, 2013.

Karagiannis, Emmanuel. "Political Islam in the Former Soviet Union: Uzbekistan and Azerbaijan Compared." *Dynamics of Asymmetric Conflict* 3, no. 1 (2010): 46–61.

Khadzhibeili, Dzheikhun [Jeyhun Hadjibeyli]. *Anti-islamskaia propaganda i ee metody v Azerbaidzhane.* Munich: Institute for the Study of the USSR, 1957.

Khalilova, Konul. "Government Struggles to Defuse Discontent in Baku Suburb." Eurasianet, June 12, 2002. http://www.eurasianet.org/departments/insight/articles /eav061302.shtml.

Levine, Steve. *The Oil and the Glory: The Pursuit of Empire and Fortune on the Caspian Sea.*

New York: Random House, 2007.

Liles, Thomas A. "Commanding Right and Forbidding Wrong: The Rise of Sectarian Contention and Politics in Independent Azerbaijan." Master's thesis, Harvard University, March 2015.

Lomsadze, Giorgi. "Azerbaijan: Next They'll Come for the Lawyers?" Eurasianet.org, December 11, 2014. http://www.eurasianet.org/node/71301.

Luxner, Larry. "Azerbaijan Rolls Out Red Carpet for Visiting US Lawmakers." *Washington Diplomat*, June 26, 2013. http://www.washdiplomat.com/index.php?option=com_content &id=9391:azerbaijan-rolls-out-red-carpet-for-visiting-us-lawmakers&Itemid=428.

Mammadov, Aydin. "Azerbaijan Conducts Sweeping Arrests in Ministry of National Security." Silk Road Reporters, November 6, 2015. http://www.silkroadreporters.com/2015/11/06 /azerbaijan-conducts-sweeping-arrests-in-ministry-of-national-security/.

Mehdiyev, Ramiz. "İkili standartların dünya nizamı ve müasir Azərbaycan." http://news.milli. az/politics/312011.html; Russian version at http://news.day.az/politics/539699.html.

Merry, Wayne. "Karabakh: 'Frozen' Conflict Nears Melting Point." *Open Democracy Review*, May 14, 2012. https://www.opendemocracy.net/od-russia/wayne-merry/karabakh -frozen-conflict-nears-melting-point.

Meyer, James H. *Turks across Empires; Marketing Muslim Identity in the Russian-Ottoman Borderlands, 1856–1914*. Oxford: Oxford University Press, 2014.

Mitofsky, Warren, and Joe Lenski. "Adventure in Baku: Exit Polling in Azerbaijan." National Council on Public Polls, [n.d., circa 2006]. http://ncpp.org/?q=node/77.

Moussalli, Ahmad. *Wahhabism, Salafism and Islamism: Who Is the Enemy?* Conflicts Forum Monograph. Beirut/London: Conflicts Forum, 2009.

Muižnieks, Nils. "Azerbaijan's Reprisals against Brave Activists and Journalists Must Stop Now." Index on Censorship, November 24, 2014. http://www.indexoncensorship.org/2014/11 /nils-muiznieks-azerbaijans-reprisals-brave-activists-journalists-must-stop-now/.

"Nardaran in Blockade." Human Rights Freedoms, November 26–December 1, 2015. http://hrf.report/during-clashes-with-police-there-are-killed-and-wounded/.

"Nazir Ziya Məmmədov, oğlu Anar Məmmədov və ZQAN Holdinq" [unsigned article], Azadlıq Radiosu, December 6, 2009. http://www.azadliq.org/a/1896083.html.

North Atlantic Treaty Organization. "Relations with Azerbaijan." April 7, 2016, http:// www.nato.int/cps/en/natohq/topics_49111.htm.

"ODIHR Refuses to Monitor Azerbaijani Poll after Government Tries to Restrict the Size of the Mission," Caucasus Elections Watch, September 12, 2015. http://electionswatch .org/2015/09/12/odihr-refuses-to-monitor-azerbaijani-poll-after-government-tries-to -restrict-the-size-of-the-mission/.

O'Lear, Shannon. "Azerbaijan's Resource Wealth: Political Legitimacy and Public Opinion." *Geographical Journal* 173, no. 3 (2007): 207–23.

Organization for Security and Cooperation in Europe (OSCE), Office of Democratic Institutions and Human Rights (ODIHR). *Armenian Presidential Election, September 24, 1996: Final Report*. Warsaw: OSCE/ODIHR, 1996. http://www.osce.org/odihr /elections/armenia/14149?download=true.

———. *Azerbaijan's Presidential Poll Marked Considerable Progress, but Did Not Meet All Election Commitments*. Warsaw: OSCE/ODIHR, 2008. http://www.osce.org /odihr/elections/75250.

———. *Presidential Election in the Republic of Azerbaijan.* Warsaw: OSCE/ODIHR, 1998. http://www.osce.org/odihr/elections/azerbaijan/14329?download=true.

———. *Republic of Azerbaijan: Parliamentary Elections, 5 November 2000 & 7 January 2001—Final Report.* Warsaw: OSCE/ODIHR, 2001. http://www.osce.org /odihr/elections/azerbaijan/14265?download=true.

———. *Republic of Azerbaijan, Parliamentary Elections, 1 November 2015: OSCE/ODIHR Needs Assessment Mission Report, 12–14 August 2015.* Warsaw: OSCE/ODIHR, 2015. http://www.osce.org/odihr/elections/azerbaijan/179216?download=true.

———. *Republic of Azerbaijan, Parliamentary Elections, 7 November 2010: OSCE/ODIHR Election Observation Mission Final Report.* Warsaw: OSCE/ODIHR, 2011. http:// www.osce.org/odihr/75073?download=true.

———. *Republic of Azerbaijan: Parliamentary Elections, 6 November 2005—Final Report.* Warsaw: OSCE/ODIHR, 2006. http://www.osce.org/odihr/elections/azerbaijan /17946?download=true.

———. *Republic of Azerbaijan: Partial Repeat Parliamentary Elections, 13 May 2006—Annex to the Final Report on the 6 November 2005 Parliamentary Elections* (Warsaw: OSCE/ ODIHR, 2006), http://www.osce.org/odihr/elections/azerbaijan/19596?download=true.

———. *Republic of Azerbaijan; Presidential Election 15 October 2003, OSCE/ODIHR Election Observation Mission Report.* Warsaw: OSCE/ODIHR, 2003. http://www.osce .org/odihr/elections/azerbaijan/13467?download=true.

———. *Republic of Azerbaijan: Presidential Election, 15 October 2008—Final Report.* Warsaw: OSCE/ODIHR, 2008. http://www.osce.org/odihr/elections/azerbaijan /35625?download=true.

———. *Republic of Azerbaijan, Presidential Election, 9 November 2013: OSCE/ODIHR Election Observation Mission, Final Report.* Warsaw: OSCE/ODIHR, 2013. http:// www.osce.org/institutions/110015?download=true.

OSCE/ODIHR Center for Legal Initiatives Public Union. *Situation with the Right to Association in Azerbaijan.* Warsaw: Center for Legal Initiatives Public Union, 2012. http://www.osce.org/odihr/94545.

———. *OSCE/UN Report of the OSCE/UN Joint Electoral Observation Mission in Azerbaijan on Azerbaijan's 12 November 1995 Parliamentary Election and Constitutional Referendum* Warsaw: OSCE/ODIHR, 1996. http://www.osce.org/odihr /elections/azerbaijan/14291?download=true.

Parliamentary Assembly of the Council of Europe (PACE). "The Functioning of Democratic Institutions in Azerbaijan." Resolution 1614 (2008), June 24, 2008. http://assembly .coe.int/nw/xml/XRef/Xref-XML2HTML-en.asp?fileid=17654&lang=en.

———. "Resolution: Honouring of Obligations and Commitments by Azerbaijan, RES 1545." April 16, 2007, http://assembly.coe.int/nw/xml/XRef/Xref-DocDetails -EN.asp?fileid=17527&lang=EN&search=QXplcmJhaWphbnxjYXRlZ29 yeV9zdHJfZW46IkFkb3B0ZWQgdGV4dCI=.

Pipes, Richard. *The Formation of the Soviet Union: Communism and Nationalism, 1917–1923.* Cambridge, MA: Harvard University Press, 1955.

Remler, Phillip. *Chained to the Caucasus: Peacemaking in Karabakh, 1987–2012.* New York: International Peace Institute, 2016. https://www.ipinst.org/2016/05/peacemaking-in -karabakh.

Rivera, Sharon Werning. "Elites in Post-Communist Russia: A Changing of the Guard?" *Europe-Asia Studies* 52, no. 3 (2000): 413–32.

Ro'i, Yaacov, ed. *The USSR and the Muslim World*. London: Allen & Unwin, 1984.

Rosenberg, Steve. "Eurovision: Singing in Baku for Prizes and Freedom." *BBC Magazine*, May 26, 2012. http://www.bbc.com/news/magazine-18204154.

Rywkin, Michael. *Moscow's Muslim Challenge: Soviet Central Asia*. Armonk, NY: M. E. Sharpe, 1983.

Shori-Eyal, Noa, Eran Halperin, and Daniel Bar-Tal. "Three Layers of Collective Victimhood: Effects of Multileveled Victimhood in Intergroup Conflicts in the Israeli-Arab Context." *Journal of Applied Social Psychology* 44, no. 12 (2014): 778–94.

"Sing for Democracy: Azerbaijan." Rafto Foundation for Human Rights, May 21, 2012. http://archive.rafto.no/article/835/Sing_for_democracy_Azerbaijan.

Siroky, David S., and Ceyhun Mahmudlu. "E Pluribus Unum? Ethnicity, Islam and the Construction of Identity in Azerbaijan." *Problems of Post-Communism* 63, no. 2 (2016): 94–107.

State Committee on Work with Religious Organizations. "The State Committee of Azerbaijan Republic for the Work with Religious Associations" [Statement of Purpose]. Republic of Azerbaijan, 2016. http://www.azerbaijan.az/_StatePower/_CommitteeConcern/committeeConcern_02_e.html.

Steinberg, Guido. "Jihadi Salafism and the Shi'is: Remarks about the Intellectual Roots of Anti-Shi'ism." In *Global Salafism: Islam's New Religious Movement*, edited by Roel Meijer, 107–25. London: Hurst, 2009.

Souleimanov, Emil, and Maya Ehrmann. "The Rise of Militant Salafism in Azerbaijan and Its Regional Implications." *Middle East Policy* 20, no. 3 (2013): 111–20.

Sultanova, Shahla. "Azerbaijan Backing Turkey's Crackdown on Gülen Movement." Eurasianet.org, April 15, 2014, http://www.eurasianet.org/node/68274.

———. "Worshiping in the Crosshairs." Transitions Online, August 7, 2012. http://www.tol.org/client/article/23292-worshiping-in-the-cross-hairs.html.

Svensson, Isak. *The Nagorno Karabakh Conflict: Lessons from the Mediation Efforts*. Brussels: Initiative for Peacebuilding/Crisis Management Initiative, 2009.

Swietochowski, Tadeusz. *Russian Azerbaijan, 1905–1920: The Shaping of National Identity in a Muslim Community*. Cambridge: Cambridge University Press, 1985.

Transparency International. "Corruption Perceptions Index 2014: Results." 2015. http://www.transparency.org/cpi2014/results.

United Nations. "Prevention of Torture: UN Human Rights Body Suspends Azerbaijan Visit Citing Official Obstruction." United Nations High Commission for Human Rights, September 17, 2014. http://www.ohchr.org/EN/NewsEvents/Pages/DisplayNews.aspx?NewsID=15047&LangID=E.

———. "Bishkek Protocol." United Nations Department of Political Affairs, May 5, 1994. http://peacemaker.un.org/armeniaazerbaijan-bishkekprotocol94.

United States Commission on International Religious Freedom. *USCIRF Annual Report for 2013: Azerbaijan*. http://www.uscirf.gov/sites/default/files/resources/Azerbaijan%202%20Pager%202013%20final%281%29.pdf.

United States Government Accountability Project. *Privatization and Corruption: The World Bank and Azerbaijan*. Washington, DC: Government Accountability Project, 2008.

http://whistleblower.org/sites/default/files/Privatization_and_Corruption.pdf.

"US-Azerbaijan Relations: The Democracy and Human Rights Dimension." Testimony of Deputy Assistant Secretary of State Thomas O. Melia, Bureau of Democracy, Human Rights, and Labor, US Department of State, June 11, 2014. http://www.state.gov/j/drl /rls/rm/2014/227450.htm.

US House of Representatives. "Azerbaijan Democracy Act of 2015, H. R. 4264, 114 Cong." December 16, 2015. https://www.congress.gov/bill/114th-congress/house -bill/4264/text.

Valiyev, Anar. "Azerbaijan: Islam in a Post-Soviet Republic." *Middle East Review of International Affairs* 9, no. 4 (2005): 1–13.

———. "The Two Faces of Salafism in Azerbaijan." Jamestown Foundation, December 7, 2007. http://www.jamestown.org/single/?no_cache=1&tx_ttnews%5Btt_news%5D =4587.

Weiss, Michael. "The Corleones of the Caspian: How Azerbaijan's Dictator Woos the United States and Europe." *Foreign Policy*, June 10, 2014. http://foreignpolicy .com/2014/06/10/the-corleones-of-the-caspian/.

Wilhelmsen, Julie. "Islamism in Azerbaijan: How Potent?" *Studies in Conflict & Terrorism* 32, no. 8 (2009): 726–42.

"Who We Are." Organization for Security and Cooperation in Europe, Minsk Group, 2016. http://www.osce.org/mg/108306.

World Bank. *Azerbaijan Partnership Program Snapshot.* Washington, DC: World Bank, 2015. http://www.worldbank.org/content/dam/Worldbank/document/Azerbaijan-Snap shot.pdf.

———. *Ease of Doing Business; Economy Profile 2016 Azerbaijan.* Washington, DC: World Bank, 2016. http://www.doingbusiness.org/~/media/giawb/doing%20business /documents/profiles/country/AZE.pdf Azerbaijan.

———. *Implementation Completion Report on a Credit in the Amount of SDR 14.3 Million (US$20.8 Million Equivalent) to the Azerbaijan Republic for a Petroleum Technical Assistance Project*, Report No. 22113. Washington, DC: World Bank, 2001. http:// www-wds.worldbank.org/external/default/WDSContentServer/WDSP/IB/2001/07/0 6/000094946_01062604045124/Rendered/PDF/multi0page.pdf.

Ybert, Edith. "Islam, Nationalism and Socialism in the Parties and Political Organizations of Azerbaijani Muslims in the Early Twentieth Century." *Caucasus Survey* 1, no. 1 (2013): 43–58.

Yergin, Daniel. *The Prize: The Epic Question for Oil, Money, and Power.* New York: Simon & Schuster, 1990.

Index

Milošević, Slobodan, 41–42, 141
mining industry, 121
Mir-i Arab Madrassa, 183–84
Mirqadirov, Rauf, 167–68, 172, 176
Mirzayev, Fezilet, 202
Modern Musavat Party, 94
Mollazade, Asim, 81
Mossadeq, Mohammad, 241
Mountainous Karabagh region (NKAR),
 31–47, 252n4; 1992 election and,
 51–52; Armenian presence in, 39,
 252n5; arrest of journalists and, 146,
 168; attempts to resolve conflict
 in, 21–22, 39, 42–47; Azerbaijan-
 Armenia conflict over, 2, 10–11,
 19–20, 27, 38, 44, 55, 66, 224–225,
 253n33; Azerbaijan "victimhood" and,
 39–42; contemporary conflict in, 21;
 de-facto separation from Azerbaijan,
 21; environmental destruction
 in, 36–37; independence of, 39;
 internal Azerbaijan politics and, 45;
 Khojaly massacre in, 19, 39–40, 50,
 146; Organization for Security and
 Cooperation in Europe (OSCE) and,
 21, 42–43; Popular Front and, 36–39,
 59; potential for resumption of war
 in, 224–26, 234; roots of Armenia-
 Azerbaijan conflict in, 32–36, 40;
 Soviet-Azerbaijan conflict and, 14–15,
 31–32; during Soviet era, 32–33;
 United States–Azerbaijan relations
 and, 27
Moussalli, Ahmad, 191
Muižnieks, Nils, 91, 139, 170–71
Müsavat ("Equality") Party, 8, 76; election
 of 2013 and, 93; elections of 1995
 and, 69; elections of 1998 and, 71–72;
 elections of 2000 and, 73–74; elections
 of 2005 and, 83; elections of 2010
 and, 88–89; Islam and, 182; as part of
 Azadlıq ("Freedom") bloc, 79; youth
 movements and, 80, 159
Mustafaoglu, Elshan, 198, 200
Mustafayev, Tural, 173

Mutalibov, Ayaz, 15–16; 1992 attempted
 coup of, 50–54; elections of 2005 and,
 82; Islam and, 187, 202; Karabagh
 conflict and, 55; resignation of, 19–20,
 51–52

Nakhjivan, 32, 252n6
Namazov, Eldar, 81
Nardaran, 201–4, 206
Nasirli, Rovshan, 149
Natavan, 35
National Democratic Institute (NDI),
 142, 166
Natural Resource Governance Institute,
 111–12
Netherlands, 107
New Azerbaijan Party (Yeni Azerbaijan
 Partiyası, YAP), 23, 25; elections of
 1995 and, 68–70; elections of 1998
 and, 71; elections of 2000 and, 73–74;
 elections of 2003 and, 77; elections of
 2005 and, 82–83; elections of 2008
 and, 85; elections of 2010 and, 88–89;
 elections of 2013 and, 95; transfer of
 power within, 76
NIDA (youth organization), 156, 159,
 164, 175, 275n51
1984 (Orwell, 1948), 178
Nuland, Victoria, 171–72
Nurcu movement, 286n36
Nuriyev, Said, 142, 169, 273n12

Obama, Barack, 177
oil industry, 1, 2–3, 8, 23–24, 99–102,
 263n19; anticorruption measures
 and, 111–13, 118; antidemocratic
 tendencies of, 84–85, 112; Azerbaijani
 economy and, 106–7; Baku–Tbilisi–
 Ceyhan (BTC) pipeline, 24, 80, 84,
 98–99, 101–5, 114, 130, 142, 150,
 244; benefits of, 219; collapse of
 oil prices, 221–24, 245; corruption
 and, 98–99, 108–10, 113–18, 130,